IN TIME WITH GOD

IN TIME WITH GOD

Daily Devotional Bible Readings
In Accordance With
The Biblical Hebrew Calendar

R K Bamber

IN TIME WITH GOD PUBLICATIONS

First published in Great Britain 2012
by
IN TIME WITH GOD PUBLICATIONS
PO Box 2316 Salisbury, Wiltshire
SP4 5AN UK

www.intimewithgod.com

Illustrations by Ann Starkey
S. Adler – cover paintings, of wheat, barley, grapes, figs,
pomegranates, olives and dates

ISBN 978-0-9572871-0-5

Printed in Great Britain by
Imprint Digital, Exeter

Contents

Acknowledgements   7

Introduction   9

Month 1   'Nisan' also called 'Abib' – falls in March/April   29

Month 2   'Iyar' also called 'Ziv' – falls in April/May   59

Month 3   'Sivan' – falls in May/June   88

Month 4   'Tamuz' – falls in June/July   118

Month 5   'Av' – falls in July/August   147

Month 6   'Elul' – falls in August/September   177

Month 7   'Tishrei' also called 'Ethanim' – September/October   207

Month 8   'Heshvan' also called 'Bul' – falls in October/November   237

Month 9   'Kislev' – falls in November/December   267

Month 10 'Tevet' – falls in December/January   297

Month 11 'Shvat' – falls in January/February   326

Month 12 'Adar I' in a Leap Year   356

Month 12 'Adar' in a normal year   385
'13th Month' 'Adar II' in a Leap Year

ACKNOWLEDGEMENTS

I want to say a massive 'thank you' to everyone who supported me over the years that I spent working on this book. I am grateful to all my friends who gave me the finances, accommodation, encouragement, and the prayer that I needed. Without your support I would not have been able to dedicate my time and energy to this task. Thank you, too, to my proof readers for their meticulous attention to detail, and thanks to Ann Starkey for her lovely illustrations and S. Adler for her beautiful artwork used in the cover design.

The most special thanks goes to my parents, for their amazing support, patience and faith, which enabled me to bring this book to completion.

INTRODUCTION

The aim of this book is to give you scriptures and 'daily devotionals', which are related, as much as possible, to the actual day on which you are reading, so you can recognise when you are in a time that is 'significant' in the Bible, and apply the biblical truth it reveals to your own life. To do this, you need to use the calendar the Bible uses, the Lunar Calendar, where each month begins when the new moon appears in the night sky, and each 'day' begins at nightfall. (Genesis 1:5) The months of January to December are not mentioned in the Bible because they are based on the position of the sun in the sky. God 'appointed the moon for seasons', (Psalm 104:19) so all the biblical feasts are set on dates of the Lunar Calendar.

To make this study, I created a chart for each month of the Lunar Calendar, then using Strong's Bible Concordance, I looked up as many Bible references as I could which mention the date. I noted these scriptures on the charts and studied them. As I did so, I found themes and topics emerged. I discovered that some days had several notable events happen on them, and at other times, whole weeks had no mention in Scripture. But the most interesting correlation was to see how perfectly the New Testament connected with the Old Testament. It is abundantly clear that the Biblical Calendar, and the Biblical Feasts in particular, are still significant to God, since 'Yeshua' (Hebrew for 'Jesus') died on the Old Testament 'Feast of Passover', was raised from the dead on the Old Testament 'Feast of First Fruits', and the Holy Spirit was poured out on the Old Testament 'Feast of Weeks' (Pentecost), fifty days later. He fulfilled the prophetic meaning of these feasts on the actual days that they occurred.

The Biblical Feasts, as given to Moses in Exodus 12, Leviticus 23, Numbers 28, 29 and Deuteronomy 16, are called in Hebrew 'moedim' which means 'appointed times'. They were times appointed by God to give a specific revelation to mankind, and for something to happen. God gave the Jewish people particular commandments concerning what to do on these 'appointed times', so that He could reveal truth about Himself and His plan to redeem and bring people into His kingdom, not only from the Jewish nation, but to save people from every 'tribe and tongue'. The seven main 'appointed times' of Scripture form two main clusters – the first three 'feasts', as they are often called, occur in the spring, the fourth in early summer, then the final three occur in the autumn in the seventh month.

At His first coming, Yeshua fulfilled the symbolism of the feasts that come in the spring, on the exact days they occurred on the Lunar Calendar of the Old Testament. But the symbolism of the autumn 'moedim' has yet to be fulfilled in its entirety. John's Gospel records the words Yeshua taught during the autumn 'Feast of Tabernacles' (John 7:37–39) about the living water of the Holy Spirit, which we can now receive. The reference to 'living water' also hints at Zechariah 14:8, where it speaks of the second coming of the Messiah and the water which will flow from Jerusalem when He has returned. Zechariah 14 connects the 'Feast of Tabernacles' with the future rule and reign of Messiah on earth. So the 'moedim' of Scripture in the Biblical Calendar represent a 'time-line of history'. Furthermore, this time-line also connects to the natural seasons and harvests in the physical Land of Israel.

The beginning of the 'time-line' concerns God's plan to redeem and save our souls – through the perfect sacrifice of Yeshua who takes away our sins, and redeems us back to God. After this, through spring and early summer, as the barley and wheat harvests are gathered in Israel, we have the growth of the 'redeemed congregation', the Church. The hot months of summer represent for us the time of the predominantly Gentile Church. In the seventh month we come to the autumn feasts and our focus turns to the ending of the 'time of the Gentiles' (Luke 21:24) God's activity among the Jews, and His second coming.

Aside from the seven months containing the spring and autumn 'moedim', which God gave to Moses, we have many other days mentioned in Scripture. We have a series of fast days, which are connected with God's dealings with Jerusalem and the Jewish people as a consequence of breaking His commandments. We also have the 'Feast of Dedication' (Hanukah) and the 'Feast of Purim' (from the book of Esther). In between the specific dates mentioned in Scripture are many days about which nothing is written. I have filled the gaps with readings on different topics and themes, which I felt 'fitted' the overall structure that emerged from my study of the dates. Key themes are: God's plan of redemption, the kingdom of God and God's plan for the Jews and Gentiles, the preparation of Yeshua's 'Bride' from among the nations and

God's progressive restoration of Israel, in fulfilment of biblical prophecy. (My definition of a Jew is someone who has genetic ancestry that traces back to Abraham, Isaac and Jacob, and my definition of a Gentile is a person who does not have any genetic ancestry back to Abraham, Isaac and Jacob.)

The year begins with 'Yeshua', the 'Lamb of God' who fulfils the symbolism of the lamb at the spring 'Feast of Passover'. After the feasts of the first month we move into a study of the formation of Israel. A cluster of modern 'memorial days' happen in Israel at this time and I have included them when they occur in the first and second months, since they fit with the first formation of Israel in the wilderness, and Yeshua's command to the disciples to 'wait in Jerusalem' until the promise of the Holy Spirit has been fulfilled. (Acts 1:8)

The 'Feast of Weeks', follows in the third month. This is the feast of the ingathering of the first fruits of the harvest, which leads into a study of the book of Ruth, and the imagery of the 'Bride'. The fourth month concerns fruitfulness through the Holy Spirit, then in the fifth month we focus on the repeated desolations of Jerusalem and God's plan for the 'end times', since it contains the 'Fast of the Fifth Month' – when recurring calamities have fallen upon the Jewish people throughout history. In the sixth month we turn to God's wake-up call to the Church, before the culmination of the seven month 'feast cycle' and the arrival of the autumn feasts in the seventh month. After that, I have turned to a study of the ancient portions of Scripture – the Jewish Torah portions – still read by Jews in Synagogues each Sabbath, just as Yeshua would have done. Then we have the 'Feast of Dedication' (of the temple) in the ninth month when the focus is on God helping us to purge away any elements of paganism, false religion and sin from the practice of our faith. In the tenth month we focus on God's preparation of His people under His rule and reign for His soon return, and for the eleventh month I have chosen to focus on the kingdom of God in the teachings and miracles of Yeshua. The 12th month, for use in leap years only, (which occur seven times every nineteen years), is a study of what Yeshua has accomplished for us through His sacrifice upon the cross for the cleansing and healing of every part of our lives. The 12th month in normal years, (which is the thirteenth month in leap years), contains Purim. This contains a study of the book of Esther and what the Bible says about anti-Semitism in the end times, God's final dealings with Israel and the nations before He returns, and the year ends where we began, with Yeshua, the holy 'Lamb of God'.

If you would like to read the readings on the actual days of the Biblical

Lunar Calendar, you can purchase a calendar from Christian Friends of Israel, or you can look on the internet for today's date, on www. jewfaq.org/calendar.htm You can also look at and purchase resources at the 'intimewithgod.com' website. The readings I have written are not meant to be a substitute for reading Scripture, but an introduction to prepare you to study the Bible passages and to think about the practical application given at the base of the page. Some of the Scripture passages are quite long, so you can ask the Lord to guide you to what He wants you to read, in the time that you have available. Our goal is not just to increase understanding in our 'heads', but to grow in our relationship with God in our hearts, through the Holy Spirit, resulting in a changed life, and a 'harvest' for God's glory.

The 'moedim' of Exodus 12, Leviticus 23, Numbers 28, 29 and Deuteronomy 16.

God's Appointed Time	Date on the Lunar Calendar	Hebrew Name
Passover	14th Day of the 1st Month (Nisan)	Pesach
Unleavened Bread	15th Day of the 1st Month (Nisan) Until 21st Day of the 1st Month	Hag HaMatzot
The First Sheaf/ First Fruits	*16th Day of the 1st Month (Nisan)	HaBikkorim
Weeks/First Fruits	6th Day of the 3rd Month (Sivan)	Shavuot/Hag HaBikkorim
Blowing Trumpets	1st Day of the 7th Month (Tishrei)	Yom HaTruah
Atonement	10th Day of the 7th Month (Tishrei)	Yom Kippur
Tabernacles	15th – 21st Day of the 7th Month (Tishrei)	Succot

INTRODUCTION

For a current copy of the Lunar Calendar go to www.jewfaq.org/calendar. htm and look for 'current calendar' or go to 'intimewithgod.com'. There you can find today's date on the Jewish Lunar Calendar.

1st Month –	'Nisan' also called 'Abib' (Meaning 'Green ears of corn') – falls in March/April
2nd Month –	'Iyar' also called 'Ziv' (Meaning 'Blossom') – falls in April/May
3rd Month –	'Sivan' – falls in May/June
4th Month –	'Tamuz' – falls in June/July
5th Month –	'Av' – falls in July/August
6th Month –	'Elul' – falls in August/September
7th Month –	'Tishrei' also called 'Ethanim' (Meaning 'The Permanent Brooks') – September/October
8th Month –	'Heshvan' also called 'Bul' (Meaning 'Rain') – falls in October/November
9th Month –	'Kislev' – falls in November/December
10th Month –	'Tevet' – falls in December/January
11th Month –	'Shvat' – falls in January/February
12th Month in a Leap Year –	
	'Adar 1' – used 7 times in every 19 years – falls in February/March
12th Month or 13th Month in a Leap Year –	
	'Adar' or 'Adar 2' – falls in February/March/April.

Note: Months have either 29 or 30 days, and not always consistently, so check your calendar.

*According to Leviticus 23:15, First Fruits is on the 'day after Shabbat' in the week of unleavened bread: the modern custom is to hold it on 16th Nisan.

Day	Main Title	Sub-Title	Text
1	**Biblical New Year**	The Lamb of God	Exodus 12:2
2	"	The Flood Dried Up	Genesis 8:13
3	"	Moses set up the Tabernacle	Exodus 40:17
4	"	The Glory filled the Tabernacle	Exodus 40:34
5	"	Hezekiah re-dedicated the Temple	2 Chronicles 29:17
6	"	Ezra left Babylon	Ezra 7:9
7	"	The Future Sanctuary is Cleansed	Ezekiel 45:18
8	The Covenant-Keeping God	The Blood Covenant	Luke 2:21
9	Preparation for Passover	Mary anointed Yeshua	John 12:3
10	"	Yeshua entered Jerusalem	John 12:12
11	"	Yeshua taught about His death	John 12:24
12	"	Those who didn't believe	John 12:37, 38
13	"	The New Covenant	Luke 22:19, 20
14	**Passover – Pesach**	The Sacrifice of Yeshua	John 19:16-18
15	**The Feast of Unleavened Bread –**	Yeshua in the Grave	John 19:41, 42
16	**The Sheaf of the First Fruits – HaBikkorim**	The Resurrection of Yeshua	Luke 24:6
17	Resurrection Appearances	Yeshua appeared to Mary Magdalene	John 20:14
18	"	The Men on the Road to Emmaus	Luke 24:13-15
19	"	Yeshua appears to His disciples	John 20:19, 20
20	"	Yeshua and the Great Catch of Fish	John 21:1
21	**The Final Day of Unleavened Bread**	Coming up from Egypt	Exodus 13:6-8
22	Times and Seasons	Winter is Past, Spring has Come	Song of Songs 2:10-12
23	"	God's Kingdom Plan	John 18:36
24	"	God's Kingdom Order	Romans 1:16
25	"	God's Plan for Israel	Romans 11:5
26	"	Gentiles 'grafted in'	Romans 11:17, 18
27	Holocaust Memorial Eve	The Persecution of Israel	Romans 11:23
28	Holocaust Memorial Day	Israel's Travail	Jeremiah 4:31
29	Israel and the Nations	Israel's Re-birth	Isaiah 66:9
30	"	God's Call to Return	Jeremiah 31:7b-9

Day	Main Title	Sub-Title	Text
1	Israel and the Nations	The Numbering of Israel	Numbers 1:19
2	"	Israel, a blessing to the Nations	2 Chronicles 3:1,2
3	"	Nations Judged on Account of Israel	Joel 3:1, 2
4	Remembrance Day	The Day of the Vengeance of God	Joshua 5:13, 14
5	Independence Day	Back in the Land	Hosea 1:10b
6	Israel and the Nations	The Apple of God's Eye	Zechariah 2:8
7	"	Not Reckoned among the Nations	Numbers 23:9
8	"	Ishmael and Isaac	Genesis 17:19
9	"	Law and Grace	Galatians 2:21
10	"	Circumcised Heart	Galatians 5:6
11	"	All One in Yeshua	Galatians 3:28
12	"	God's Appointed Times	Leviticus 23:1, 2
13	"	Sons of Zion, Sons of Greece	Zechariah 9:13
14	The Second Passover	A Second Chance	Numbers 9:9-11
15	Testing in the Wilderness	Israel entered the Wilderness	Exodus 16:1
16	"	God Calls Us into the Wilderness	Song of Songs 8:5
17	"	He Humbles and Tests Us	Deuteronomy 8:2
18	"	He Provides for Us	Deuteronomy 8:4
19	"	He Speaks to Us	Exodus 33:11
20	"	He Leads Us	Numbers 10:11,12
21	"	He Heals Us	Exodus 15:26
22	"	He Prepares Us	Deuteronomy 4:1
23	"	He Tests our Faith	Numbers 14:24
24	"	He Reveals Himself	Song of Songs 5:9
25	40th Sheaf Gathered In	Yeshua is 'taken up' to Heaven	Acts 1:3
26	10 Days Waiting in Jerusalem	Wait for Baptism in the Holy Spirit	Acts 1:4, 5
27	"	Prayer in One Accord	Acts 1:14
28	Jerusalem Day	Unified Jerusalem	Psalm 122:6
29	Jerusalem	Melchizedek, King of Salem	Genesis 14:18

Day	Main Title	Sub-Title	Text
1	Jerusalem	The City of David	2 Chronicles 6:6
2	"	His Dwelling Place	Psalm 132:13, 14
3	"	The Messiah's Kingdom	Isaiah 2:2
4	"	A Cup of Trembling	Zechariah 12:2
5	"	A City Not Forsaken	Isaiah 62:12
6	**The Feast of Weeks – Shavuot**	Firstfruits of the Wheat Harvest	Leviticus 23:16, 17
7	The Congregation of Believers	The Holy Spirit	Acts 2:16
8	"	The Redeemed Congregation	Acts 2:42
9	"	The Rock of the Church	Matthew 16:16-18
10	Ruth	The House of Bread	Ruth 1:6
11	"	The Friend	Ruth 1:16
12	"	Gleaning	Ruth 2:15, 16
13	"	The Redeeming Relative	Ruth 2:20
14	"	The Threshing Floor	Ruth 3:2
15	"	Marriage and Covering	Ruth 3:9
16	"	The Marriage of Ruth	Ruth 4:11
17	The Ancient Jewish Wedding	The Chosen Bride	John 15:16
18	"	The Bride Price	1 Corinthians 6:19-20
19	"	The Betrothal	2 Corinthians 11:2
20	"	The Cup	Luke 22:17, 18
21	"	Gifts for the Bride	Genesis 24:53
22	"	The Bridal Baptism	Mark 16:16
23	"	The Bridegroom Prepares a Place	John 14:2
24	"	The Waiting Bride	John 14:26, 27a
25	"	The Return of the Bridegroom	Matthew 25:13
26	"	The Bridal Chamber	1 John 3:2
27	"	The Marriage Supper	Revelation 19:7-9
28	Israel the Wife	The Lord her Husband	Hosea 2:7
29	"	Comfort	Isaiah 40:1, 2
30	"	The Vineyard	Isaiah 5:7

Day	Main Title	Sub-Title	Text
1	The Fruit of the Holy Spirit	Love	Genesis 22:2
2	"	Joy	John 15:10, 11
3	"	Peace	John 14:27
4	"	Long-Suffering	Acts 14:22
5	"	Kindness	Titus 3:4, 5
6	"	Goodness	Romans 2:4
7	"	Faithfulness	Lamentations 3:22, 23
8	"	Gentleness	2 Samuel 22:36, 37
9	"	Self-Control	1 Timothy 1:7
10	The Seven Species of Israel	A Harvest from God	Deuteronomy 11:13, 14
11	"	Wheat and Barley	Deuteronomy 8:7, 8
12	"	Grapevines	John 15:1
13	"	Fig Trees	Hosea 9:10
14	"	Pomegranates	Song of Songs 6:7
15	"	Olives	Acts 10:38
16	"	Honey	John 12:12, 13
17	Redeemed from the Curse	The Fast of the Fourth Month	Lamentations 1:3
18	"	Broken Walls	Jeremiah 52:14
19	"	Rebuilding the Walls	Nehemiah 2:17
20	God's Laws Written on Our Hearts	Who God is	Exodus 20:2
21	"	Not having Idols	Exodus 20:3, 4
22	"	Reverencing God's Name	Exodus 20:7
23	"	Keeping Sabbath	Exodus 20:8
24	"	Honour your Parents	Exodus 20:12
25	"	Do Not Murder	Exodus 20:13
26	"	Do Not Commit Adultery	Exodus 20:14
27	"	Do Not Steal	Exodus 20:15
28	"	Do Not Lie	Exodus 20:16
29	"	Do Not Covet	Exodus 20:17

Day	Main Title	Sub-Title	Text
1	The New Month	Death of Aaron the High Priest	Numbers 33:38
2	Israel Enters the Promised Land	Joshua	Joshua 1:2
3	"	The Walls of Jericho	Joshua 6:20
4	Israel's failure to keep the Law	The Judges	Judges 2:13, 14
5	"	The Kings	1 Chronicles 17:14
6	"	The Prophets	Jeremiah 1:16
7	"	Nebuzaradan Arrived	2 Kings 25:8
8	"	The City Burned	2 Kings 25:9
9	The Fast of the 5th Month	Fasts Will Become Feasts	Zechariah 8:19
10	Israel in Exile	Hope in the Midst of Judgement	Ezekiel 20:1
11	"	The Remnant	Isaiah 37:31, 32
12	"	Do Not Go to Egypt	Jeremiah 42:19
13	"	Babylon	Psalm 137:1, 2
14	"	Babylon is Judged	Jeremiah 50:29
15	The Increase in Dew	A Celebration of Love	Judges 21:19a, 20
16	"	Understanding The Times	1 Chronicles 13:32
17	Prophecies of Daniel for the Latter Days	Changing Times	Daniel 2:20, 21
18	"	The Final Persecuting World Powers	Daniel 7:23
19	"	The Seventy Weeks	Daniel 9:24
20	"	A Covenant with Many	Daniel 9:26b, 27a
21	"	The Abomination of Desolation	Daniel 9:27b
22	"	The Time of Trouble and Deliverance for the Jews	Daniel 12:1
23	"	Travel and Knowledge Increase	Daniel 12:4
24	Gospel Prophecies for the Latter Days	The Temple Destroyed	Matthew 24:1, 2
25	"	False Messiahs and False Prophets	Matthew 24:4, 5
26	"	Betrayals, Persecutions and Martyrdoms	Luke 21:17, 18
27	"	Wars, Pestilence and Famine	Matthew 24:7, 8
28	"	Jewish Jerusalem	Luke 21:24
29	"	The Return of the Lord	Matthew 24:32
30	"	An Unexpected Hour	Matthew 25:13

Day	Main Title	Sub-Title	Text
1	Awaken the Believers	Building the House of God	Haggai 1:1
2	The Church of Ephesus	Apostolic Church	Revelation 2:2
3	"	Recover our First Love	Revelation 2:4, 5
4	"	The Nicolaitans	Revelation 2:6
5	The Church of Smyrna	The Martyred Church	Revelation 2:8
6	"	Tribulation and Poverty	Revelation 2:9
7	"	Do not Fear Suffering	Revelation 2:10
8	"	Not hurt by the Second Death	Revelation 2:11
9	The Church of Pergamos	The Paganised Church	Revelation 2:12
10	"	Satan's Throne Defeated	Revelation 2:13
11	"	The Doctrine of Balaam	Revelation 2:14
12	"	Hidden Manna	Revelation 2:17
13	The Church of Thyatira	The Compromised Church	Revelation 2:18
14	"	Jezebel	Revelation 2:20
15	"	The Call to Repent	Revelation 2:21
16	"	Power over Nations	Revelation 2:26
17	The Church of Sardis	The Lifeless Church	Revelation 3:1
18	"	Be Watchful	Revelation 3:2
19	"	White Garments	Revelation 3:4
20	"	Overcomers	Revelation 3:5
21	The Church of Philadelphia	The Loving Church	Revelation 3:7
22	"	The Open Door	Revelation 3:8
23	"	Persevere	Revelation 3:10, 11
24	"	Pillars in the Temple	Revelation 3:12
25	The Church of Laodicea	The Apostate Church	Revelation 3:14
26	"	Lukewarm	Revelation 3:15
27	"	Buy Gold Refined in the Fire	Revelation 3:17, 18
28	"	The Knock at the Door	Revelation 3:20
29	The Trumpet Call	Wake-up Call	Joel 2:15
30	Eve of Blowing Trumpets	A Memorial	Leviticus 23:23, 24

Day	Main Title	Sub-Title	Text
1	**The Feast of Blowing Trumpets – Yom HaTruah**	A Holy Convocation	Leviticus 23:24, 25
2	The Seven Trumpets of Revelation	God's Judgements Released	Revelation 8:2
3	The Fast of Gedaliah	A Broken Nation	Jeremiah 41:2
4	Atonement	The Cloud and the Mercy Seat	Leviticus 16:2
5	"	The Blood of the Bull and the Ram	Leviticus 16:3
6	"	The Priest and the Holy Place	Leviticus 16:4
7	"	The Two Goats	Leviticus 16:8
8	"	Sweet Incense	Leviticus 16:13
9	Eve of the Day of Atonement	Afflict Yourselves	Leviticus 23:32
10	**The Day of Atonement – Yom Kippur**	The Jubilee Trumpet	Leviticus 25:9
11	Joseph and His Brothers	The Ingathering	Genesis 37:5-7
12	"	Joseph among the Gentiles	Genesis 37:28
13	"	Joseph reunited with His Brothers	Genesis 42:1, 2
14	Eve of the Feast of Tabernacles – Succot	Sabbath Rest	Leviticus 23:33-35
15	**The Feast of Tabernacles – Succot Day1**	Waving Palms, Leaves and Fruit	Leviticus 23:40
16	**" Day 2**	Sacrifice and Offerings	Leviticus 23:36
17	**" Day 3**	Dwell in Tabernacles	Leviticus 23:42, 43
18	**" Day 4**	Yeshua Dwelt Among Us	John 1:14
19	**" Day 5**	Rejoice at the Sacred Feast	Deuteronomy 16:15
20	**" Day 6**	The Nations come up to Jerusalem	Zechariah 14:16
21	**" Day 7**	The Desire of All Nations	Haggai 2:6, 7
22	**The Eighth Day of Assembly**	Final Sabbath Rest	John 7:37, 38
23	God's Word	Yeshua Teaches in the Temple	John 8:2
24	"	Returning to the Scriptures	Nehemiah 9:1
25	"	Understanding the Word	Nehemiah 8:8
26	"	Yeshua, the Word of God	John 1:1-3
27	"	The Fruitfulness of the Word	Isaiah 55:10, 11
28	"	A Lamp	Psalm 119:105
29	"	Preach the Gospel	Rom 10:14, 15
30	In the Beginning	A Saviour Promised	Genesis 3:15

8th Month Heshvan, sometimes called Bul in the Bible
– usually falls in October/November

Day	Main Title	Sub-Title	Text
1	In the Beginning	God's Covenant with Noah	Genesis 9:11
2	The Patriarchs	God's Covenant with Abraham	Genesis 15:5, 6
3	"	The Seed of Abraham	Genesis 22:18
4	"	God gives Isaac a Wife	Genesis 24:67
5	"	Jacob and Esau	Genesis 25:23
6	"	God's Covenant with Jacob	Genesis 28:13, 14
7	"	Jacob is named Israel	Genesis 32:28
8	"	God Breaking Through	Genesis 38:29
9	"	Joseph in Egypt	Genesis 41:39, 40
10	"	Jacob in Egypt	Genesis 45:25, 26
11	"	The Twelve Tribes of Israel	Genesis 48:14
12	The Formation of Israel	The Burning Bush	Exodus 3:14
13	"	God's Promise of Redemption	Exodus 6:6, 7
14	"	Redemption of the Firstborn	Exodus 13:13
15	"	Israel Crossed the Red Sea	Exodus 15:1
16	"	Israel Pledged to Keep the Law	Exodus 18:18
17	"	The Blood of the Covenant	Exodus 24:8
18	The Tabernacle	God's Instructions for the Tabernacle	Exodus 25:8
19	"	The Priesthood	Exodus 27:20, 21
20	"	God is a Jealous God	Exodus 34:14
21	"	The Work and Construction	Exodus 35:10
22	"	The Coverings	Exodus 40:19
23	Israel, Set-Apart and Holy	The Blood Sacrifices	Leviticus 1:2
24	"	The Sin, Trespass and Peace Offerings	Leviticus 6:25
25	"	Holiness	Leviticus 10:9, 10
26	"	Diagnosis of Leprosy	Leviticus 13:45
27	"	Cleansing from Leprosy	Leviticus 14:18
28	"	The Power of the Blood	Leviticus 17:10,11
29	"	A Holy Nation	Leviticus 20:26
30	"	A Holy Calendar	Leviticus 22:32

Day	Main Title	Sub-Title	Text
1	Israel, Set Apart and Holy	The Jubilee Redemption	Leviticus 25:23,24
2	"	Dwell in the Land	Leviticus 26:44
3	Israel in the Wilderness	The Levites	Numbers 3:12, 13
4	"	The Nazirites	Numbers 6:2
5	"	The Cloud	Numbers 9:17, 18
6	"	The Fruit of the Land	Numbers 13:23
7	"	The Rebellion of Korah	Numbers 16:6
8	"	The Ashes of the Red Heifer	Numbers 19:2
9	"	The Four Oracles of Balaam	Numbers 24:17
10	"	A Man to Shepherd Israel	Numbers 27:16, 17
11	"	Pressing On	Numbers 32:6, 7
12	"	An Inheritance	Numbers 34:1, 2
13	Enter the Land	Defeat the Giants	Deuteronomy 2:36
14	"	Love the LORD your God	Deuteronomy 6:4, 5
15	"	Know your Frailty	Deuteronomy 8:3
16	"	The Place that God Chooses	Deuteronomy 12:5
17	"	A Prophet Like Moses	Deuteronomy 18:15
18	"	Hung on a Tree	Deuteronomy 21:22, 23
19	"	The Stones of the Law	Deuteronomy 27:2, 3
20	"	Choose Life	Deuteronomy 30:19
21	"	Be Strong and of Good Courage	Deuteronomy 31:8
22	"	The Song of Moses	Deuteronomy 32:43
23	"	Blessings on the Children of Israel	Deuteronomy 33:12
24	Eve of the Feast of Dedication	The Prophecy of Haggai	Haggai 2:18, 19
25	The Feast of Dedication – Hanukah Day 1	The Dedication of the Altar	Numbers 7:10, 11
26	" Day 2	Yeshua walked in the Temple	John 10:22, 23
27	" Day 3	Yeshua, the Door of the Sheep	John 10:7
28	" Day 4	Told Plainly	John 10:24
29	" Day 5	Yeshua beyond the Jordan	John 10:40
30	" Day 6	Dedicated for a Purpose	John 11:51, 52

Day	Main Title	Sub-Title	Text
1	The Feast of Dedication – Hanukah Day 7	Cast out Paganism	Ezra 10:16
2	" Day 8	An Undefiled Temple	Ezekiel 43:7
3	A Prepared Bride	Grace and Favour	Esther 2:16, 17
4	"	Loves Much	Luke 7:47
5	"	Responds to the Lord	Song of Songs 7:10
6	"	Faith in the Covenant	John 3:16
7	"	A Worship Warrior	Psalm 149:6
8	"	Clothed in Fine Linen	Revelation 19:7, 8
9	"	Loves His Appearing	2 Timothy 4:8
10	The Fast of the 10th Month	The Siege of Jerusalem	2 Kings 25:1, 2
11	Laying Siege	Live by the Spirit	Ezekiel 24:16
12	"	God's Kingdom Siege	Ezekiel 4:1, 2
13	"	A Way of Escape	Luke 21:20, 21
14	"	A Kingdom Which Cannot Be Shaken	Hebrews 12:28
15	Prepare the Way	John the Baptiser	Luke 7:27
16	"	A Virgin Conceives	Luke 1:30, 31
17	"	Signs of the Messiah	Luke 2:34
18	"	Yeshua aged Twelve	Luke 2:40
19	"	The Baptism of Yeshua	John 1:32
20	"	The Temptations of Yeshua	Matthew 4:1
21	"	The Disciples Follow Yeshua	John 1:35-37
22	The Beatitudes	Blessed Are the Poor in Spirit	Matthew 5:3
23	"	Blessed Are Those Who Mourn	Matthew 5:4
24	"	Blessed Are the Meek	Matthew 5:5
25	"	Blessed Are Those Who Hunger and Thirst	Matthew 5:6
26	"	Blessed Are the Merciful	Matthew 5:7
27	"	Blessed Are the Pure in Heart	Matthew 5:8
28	"	Blessed Are the Peacemakers	Matthew 5:9
29	"	Blessed Are Those who are Persecuted	Matthew 5:10, 11

Day	Main Title	Sub-Title	Text
1	Receive the Kingdom of God	The Eleventh Hour	Deuteronomy 1:3
2	"	Yeshua Calls for Disciples	Luke 10:2
3	Learn to Pray	Our Father in Heaven	Matthew 6:8, 9
4	"	Hallowed Be Thy Name	Matthew 6:9
5	"	Thy Kingdom Come	Matthew 6:10
6	"	Give Us This Day Our Daily Bread	Matthew 6:11
7	"	And Forgive Us Our Debts	Matthew 6:12
8	"	And Do Not Lead Us Into Temptation	Matthew 6:13
9	"	For Yours Is the Kingdom	Matthew 6:13
10	Build the Kingdom	The Branch	Isaiah 11:1
11	"	The Spirit of the Lord	Isaiah 11:2
12	"	Gifts of Grace	Romans 12:4, 5
13	"	Spiritual Gifts	1 Corinthians 12:7
14	"	The Body of Messiah	1 Corinthians 12:27, 28
15	"	Spiritual Gifts in Church Meetings	1 Corinthians 14:12
16	"	Come to Maturity	Ephesians 4:11-13
17	Parables of the Kingdom	The Parable of the Sower and the Seed	Matthew 13:1-3
18	"	The Wheat and the Tares	Matthew 13:30
19	"	The Mustard Seed	Matthew 13:31
20	"	The Leaven	Matthew 13:33
21	"	Treasure Hidden in a Field	Matthew 13:44
22	"	The Pearl of Great Price	Matthew 13:45, 46
23	"	The Dragnet	Matthew 13:47, 48
24	Signs of the Kingdom	Turning Water into Wine	John 2:30, 31
25	"	The Healing of the Nobleman's Son	John 4:46
26	"	Healing at the Pool of Bethesda	John 5:5, 6
27	"	The Feeding of the Five Thousand	John 6:14
28	"	Walking on the Water	John 6:19
29	"	The Healing of the Man Born Blind	John 9:39
30	"	The Raising of Lazarus	John 11:25, 26

12th Month in the Leap Year only, Adar 1
– usually falls in February/March

Day	Main Title	Sub-Title	Text
1	The Leap Month	Going Deeper	Hebrews 5:12
2	Psalm 22	Forsaken by God	Psalm 22:1
3	"	Despised and Ridiculed	Psalm 22:7, 8
4	"	His Mother	Psalm 22:9
5	"	Trusting God	Psalm 22:10, 11
6	"	Father Forgive Them	Psalm 22:12, 13
7	"	Thirsty	Psalm 22:14, 15
8	"	Pierced	Psalm 22:16-18
9	"	God's Answer	Psalm 22:21
10	"	His Brethren	Psalm 22:22
11	"	With Him in Paradise	Psalm 22:29
12	"	It is Finished	Psalm 22:30, 31
13	Isaiah 53	God's Servant	Isaiah 52:13
14	"	No Beauty to Desire	Isaiah 53:2
15	"	A Man of Sorrows	Isaiah 53:3
16	"	Our Griefs and Sorrows	Isaiah 53:4
17	"	Misunderstood	Isaiah 53:4
18	"	Wounded	Isaiah 53:5
19	"	Bruised	Isaiah 53:5
20	"	Chastised	Isaiah 53:5
21	"	His Stripes	Isaiah 53:5
22	"	Like Sheep	Isaiah 53:6
23	"	Oppressed and Afflicted	Isaiah 53:7
24	"	A Lamb to the Slaughter	Isaiah 53:7
25	"	Imprisoned	Isaiah 53:8
26	"	Grave of a Rich Man	Isaiah 53:9
27	"	The Pleasure of the LORD	Isaiah 53:10
28	"	Many Justified	Isaiah 53:11
29	"	Divide the Spoil	Isaiah 53:12

12th Month in a Normal Year (Adar) or 13th Month (Adar 2) in a Leap Year – usually falling in February/March/April

Day	Main Title	Sub-Title	Text
1	Israel's Enemies	Haman's Lot	Esther 3:7
2	"	The Amalek Spirit	Numbers 24:20
3	"	A Controversy with the Nations	Jeremiah 25:31
4	"	David and Goliath	1 Samuel 17:45
5	"	Jehoshaphat Prevails	2 Chronicles 20:15
6	"	A Confederacy	Psalm 83:4, 5
7	"	Edom	Numbers 24:18, 19
8	"	On the Mountains of Israel	Ezekiel 36:5
9	"	God's Justice	Deuteronomy 32:43
10	"	Gog and Magog	Ezekiel 38:18, 19
11	Esther's Fast	For Such a Time as This	Esther 4:13, 14
12	"	Who Will Be Worshipped?	Esther 6:6
13	"	The Third Day	Esther 9:1
14	Purim	Resting, Feasting and Gladness	Esther 9:17
15	Shushan Purim	Complete Rest	Esther 10:3
16	Ephraim and Judah	The Scattered Tribes	Ezekiel 37:19
17	"	Made One	Hosea 1:10b, 11
18	Elijah the Prophet	The Coming of Elijah	Malachi 4:5
19	"	The Hearts of Fathers and Children	Malachi 4:6
20	"	Fathers	Luke 2:49
21	"	Spiritual Fathers	1 Kings 16:31
22	"	The Famine	1 Kings 17:1
23	"	The Contest on Mount Carmel	1 Kings 18:21
24	"	The Rain Comes	1 Kings 18:41
25	The Latter Rain	The Call to Repentance	Joel 2:23
26	"	He Will Come	Hosea 6:3
27	"	The Fig Tree and the Vine	Joel 2:22
28	The Lion of God	The Lion of the Tribe of Judah	Revelation 5:6
29	"	The Lion Roars	Amos 1:2
30	"	The Lion is the Lamb	Revelation 5:6

Colossians 2:16 'So let no one judge you in food or in drink, or regarding a festival or a new moon or sabbaths, which are a shadow of things to come, but the substance is of Christ.

NISAN

1st Day of the 1st Month
Abib – also called Nisan, usually falling in March/April
Biblical New Year
The Lamb of God

This month shall be your beginning of months; it shall be the first month of the year to you. *Exodus 12:2*

The first mention of biblical New Year is found in Exodus 12:2 with the first Passover. In the first month of the biblical Year, the Hebrew men were instructed by God to take a 'Lamb' without blemish for their households, and to paint its blood on the door posts and lintels of their houses. The blood was the 'sign' which would cause the angel of death to 'pass over' their house and leave their family unscathed, enabling them to escape slavery.

Yeshua is the 'spiritual' Passover Lamb through whom we find redemption and deliverance from sin. He is the Son of God who existed before time began. Through Him all things were created. (John 1:1–3) He is the 'beginning and the end', the 'Alef and the Tav', (the first and the last letters of the Hebrew alphabet) and in Greek, the 'Alpha and the Omega'. (Revelation 1:8) The Alef and the Tav together spell the little Hebrew word 'et' which occurs mysteriously even in the first verse of the Bible. When the Hebrew letter 'vav' ('and') is placed between the Alef and Tav we have the word 'ot' which means 'sign'. Yeshua's blood, shed at the cross, is the 'sign' received on our lives by faith, so that God's judgement can 'pass over' our lives, and we can escape death and hell, like the Israelites who escaped the plague of death. Yeshua is the doorway through whom we pass to Heaven.

Yeshua is the Lamb, 'slain before the foundation of the world' (Revelation 13:8), provided just as God promised Abraham. (Genesis 22:8, 14) He was with the Father and the Holy Spirit from the beginning. (Isaiah 48:16) John said, 'Behold! The Lamb of God who takes away the sins of the world.' (John 1:29) We 'look at Him' to be saved. (Isaiah 45:22)

Meditate on Yeshua, 'slain' before the foundation of the world, and worship Him.

Readings: Exodus 12, 1 Peter 1:18–21, Genesis 22:1–14, Revelation 5

2nd Day of the 1st Month
Abib – also called Nisan, usually falling in March/April
The Biblical New Year
The Flood Dried Up

And it came to pass in the six hundred and first year, in the first month, the first day of the month, that the waters were dried up from the earth... *Genesis 8:13*

At biblical New Year, the flood dried up. The flood waters speak of God's judgement of sin. Mankind became corrupted by wickedness after Adam's 'fall' into sin at the Garden of Eden. God had to purge and cleanse the earth. In the midst of judgement, however, God showed mercy, not destroying the human race completely, but saving out of it a family from a righteous man, Noah, whose name means 'rest'. God would send His own Son, to save out of the earth, people who had been 'cleansed' by Him. God's cleansing work would be complete in their lives. They would be found holy in His sight. The flood of God's judgement would dry up. A price would be paid, a sacrifice given, to dry up the 'waters' of God's wrath. God would send His Son, Yeshua, to remove His judgement from our lives.

Genesis 5 lists the generations between Adam and Noah. When we translate the Hebrew names into English we understand the prophetic message they convey: (Adam) Man, first blood, (Seth) appointed, (Enosh) mortal, (Cainan) sorrow, (Mahalalel) God is who praised, (Jared) shall come down, (Enoch) teacher, (Methuselah) His death shall bring, (Lamech) weary, (Noah) rest. That is to say; 'Man, from the first blood has been appointed to mortality, suffering sorrow. But God, who is praised shall come down to earth as a teacher, and His death shall bring the weary rest.' (Genesis 5) This reminds us of the teaching of Yeshua; 'Come to Me, all you who labour and are heavy laden, and I will give you rest. Take My yoke upon you and learn from Me, for I am gentle and lowly of heart, and you will find rest for your souls, for My yoke is easy and My burden is light.' (Matthew 11:28–30)

What is Yeshua saying to you through Matthew 11:28–30?

Readings: Genesis 5–8:13, Psalm 32, 2 Peter 3:1–9

3rd Day of the 1st Month
Abib – also called Nisan, usually falling in March/April
Biblical New Year
Moses set up the Tabernacle

And it came to pass in the first month of the second year, on the first day of the month, that the tabernacle was raised up.

Exodus 40:17

The next mention of biblical New Year is when Moses set up the tabernacle in the wilderness. God gave Moses the written Law for the nation of Israel to live by, and to be His special people. The Israelites constructed the tabernacle (tent) of God's presence, according to God's precise instructions, so God could dwell among them, as their King. They were to live under God's government as His kingdom, obeying His laws and living His way.

Living in God's kingdom demanded perfect purity, wholeness, completion, cleanliness and justice. Anything polluted, incomplete or damaged, was unacceptable in God's holy presence. But the Israelites failed and broke God's holy laws. Like all of us they sinned and fell short of the glory of God. (Romans 3:23) They needed the penalty for their sin and shortcomings to be paid for by a perfect substitute, to reconcile them to God. So God gave them a system of animal sacrifices to enable His holy presence to dwell among His imperfect people. Each time there was sin or uncleanness, another sacrifice was needed. This demonstrated the need for a perfect sacrifice to take away sin forever. No animal could do that. Only God could provide the perfect sacrifice to take away the sins of mankind.

The sacrifices offered at the tabernacle were mere shadows of the sinless sacrifice God provided through Yeshua, who 'put away sin by the sacrifice of Himself'. (Hebrews 9:26) On the first day of the Biblical Calendar, the tabernacle was set up to show that God would provide the way for us to live under His Kingship with His holy presence in our midst.

Consider the fact that our mighty, Holy God wants you to dwell with Him in His kingdom.

Readings: Exodus 40, Romans 3:21–31, Hebrews 9:1–10:14

4th Day of the 1st Month
Abib – also called Nisan, usually falling in March/April
Biblical New Year
The Glory Filled the Tabernacle

Then the cloud covered the tabernacle of meeting, and the glory of the LORD filled the tabernacle. *Exodus 40:34*

On the first day of the first month, Moses not only set up the tabernacle in the wilderness among the tribes of Israel, but he placed all the furnishings in their correct places. He put the bread on the table, he lit the lamps on the lampstand, he burned the sweet incense, he hung the screen, and he burnt the offering and the grain offering on the altar, and set up the court. All these items are shadows and pictures of Yeshua, the Son of God.

When Moses finished the work, the cloud of God's glory filled the tabernacle, making it impossible for him to enter. When Yeshua died on the cross, as the sacrifice to take away our sins, He completed the work of the tabernacle. He cried out 'It is finished' (John 19:30), and the veil in the temple was torn in two, creating access to the holiest place of God's presence. Access was created to God's throne so that we no longer need to live separated from the love of God. Our guilt for breaking God's holy laws, our punishment, our condemnation, and the wall of separation from God, was torn apart, and the way was opened up for us to enter 'Eden' in our hearts, to come into the presence of Almighty God.

When Moses ministered in the tabernacle, the cloud of God's holy presence descended on the first day of the first month. When we put our faith in Yeshua, repenting of our sins and trusting in His sacrifice to make us right with God, we allow Yeshua to open the way for God's love to 'fall upon us'. Now nothing in heaven or on the earth will 'be able to separate us from the love of God which is in Christ Jesus our Lord.' (Romans 8:39)

God's presence rests above Yeshua's sprinkled blood. His love abides over your heart.

Readings: Hebrews 10:15–25, Romans 8:31–39, Psalm 100, Psalm 51, 1 John 4:8

5th Day of the 1st Month
Abib – also called Nisan, usually falling in March/April
Biblical New Year
Hezekiah re-dedicated the Temple

Now they began to sanctify on the first day of the first month, and on the eighth day of the month they came to the vestibule of the LORD. So they sanctified the house of the LORD in eight days, and on the sixteenth day of the first month they finished. *2 Chronicles 29:17*

We come now to the time when the temple, built in Jerusalem by King Solomon, replaced the tabernacle. The Israelites had chosen to have a man as a king, instead of depending on God alone. The cloud of God's presence rested above the temple, just as it had rested previously above the tabernacle of Moses. (2 Chronicles 7:1–3) However, over time, idolatrous kings ruled in Israel, and the temple became desecrated. King Ahaz 'encouraged moral decline' (2 Chronicles 28:19) and led the people into idolatry. He 'cut in pieces the articles of the house of God, shut up the doors of the house of the LORD, and made for himself altars in every corner of Jerusalem.' (2 Chronicles 28:24)

King Hezekiah, the son of Ahaz, was better than his father. He undertook the task of cleansing and restoring the temple. When he succeeded to the throne, he opened the doors of the temple and repaired them. He gathered together the Levites and commanded them to come back and serve in the temple. They had to sanctify themselves and clear out all the rubbish. Once cleansed, the temple was re-dedicated to God, and the lamps and incense burned again. The first 'inner part' of the temple took eight days to clear out, and then the outer part took another eight days. Eight is the number for new beginnings, sixteen is the day of the resurrection. The Apostle Paul wrote 'Do you not know that you are the temple of God and that the Spirit of God dwells in you? If anyone defiles the temple of God, God will destroy him. For the temple of God is holy, which temple you are.' (1 Corinthians 3:16, 17)

How do the details of this story correspond to your life?

Readings: 2 Chronicles 28, 29, Romans 12, 2 Corinthians 6:14–7:1

6th Day of the 1st Month
Abib – also called Nisan, usually falling in March/April
Biblical New Year
Ezra left Babylon

On the first day of the first month he began his journey from Babylon and on the first day of the fifth month he came to Jerusalem. Ezra 7:9

In the days of Rehoboam, son of King Solomon, the Land was divided into two; a northern kingdom and a southern kingdom. A succession of evil kings led to the downfall of the northern kingdom of Israel, and to its being led into captivity by the Assyrians in 722 BC. The southern kingdom of Judah also fell into idolatry, and was taken into exile in Babylon.

God's covenant with Moses clearly stated that Israel's ability to live in God's Land would depend on their obedience to God's laws. (Deuteronomy 28) If they rebelled against God's government, they would be cast out of the Land. However, a remnant would always be restored back to the Land, because of God's mercy and faithfulness. God has never broken His covenant with Abraham to give his descendants the land of Canaan as an everlasting possession. (Genesis 17:8) It is an everlasting covenant. (Psalm 105:10, 11)

The southern kingdom of Judah was taken away captive, by the Babylonians in 586 BC. After 70 years, God restored the Jews back to their Land, and at the biblical New Year, Ezra the scribe began his journey home with the returning exiles. Ezra brought the people back to their holy city of Jerusalem so that they could be restored to God through reading the Scriptures, repenting of their sins and worshipping God at the temple. When they did so, they discovered they had a destiny to fulfil. Their tribe had to remain intact because the Scriptures prophesied the Messiah would be born from among them. (Genesis 49:10) Now God brings us back too, from 'exile' in sin, to discover and fulfil His purpose for our lives.

Have you been in an 'exile' due to sin? Consider returning from 'exile' to find your destiny.

Readings: Deuteronomy 28–30, Ezra 7–10, Psalm 105

7th Day of the 1st Month
Abib – also called Nisan, usually falling in March/April
Biblical New Year
The Future Sanctuary is Cleansed

Thus says the Lord God. "In the first month, on the first day of the month, you shall take a young bull without blemish and cleanse the sanctuary..." *Ezekiel 45:18*

The prophet Ezekiel saw in a vision, a great temple, and he described it in detail. This temple has not yet physically existed on earth. It is still a mystery, much as the Church was a mystery in Old Testament times, not to be understood until the Holy Spirit was poured out on the disciples, 50 days after the resurrection of Yeshua.

It is quite possible that the temple described in Ezekiel 40–44, is a future temple that will exist when Yeshua has returned to earth to reign from Zion. Revelation 20 prophecies the 'millennium' kingdom of the Lord which we also read about in Isaiah 2:1–4, Isaiah 11–12, Zechariah 14 and Micah 4:1–5. At that time, people and animals will live in complete peace and harmony. Isaiah 2:2 and Micah 4:1 describe the future Messianic kingdom saying: 'Now it shall come to pass in the latter days that the mountain of the Lord's house shall be established on the top of the mountains, and shall be exalted above the hills; and all nations shall flow to it...' The disciples asked Yeshua when the kingdom would be restored to Israel but He would not say when this will come to pass. (Acts 1:6, 7)

Though there is much that we do not understand yet, we have the assurance of the cleansing from sin even in the age to come, in the millennium of Revelation 20. Yeshua cleanses the sanctuary of our lives. He completely washes away all uncleanness through the power of His pure blood, shed for us. Cleansed by Him, Yeshua graciously serves us by washing our feet from the uncleanness we pick up daily along the path. (John 13)

How does Yeshua want you to keep your 'sanctuary' clean? Ask Him to 'wash your feet'.

Readings: Ezekiel 43–45, John 13, Ephesians 5:25–27

8th Day of the 1st Month
Abib – also called Nisan, usually falling in March/April
The Covenant-Keeping God
The Blood Covenant

And when eight days were completed for the circumcision of the Child, His name was called JESUS. (Yeshua) *Luke 2:21*

Yeshua, a physical descendant of Abraham, was circumcised on His eighth day according to God's covenant with Abraham over 1900 years earlier. God said, 'My Covenant shall be in your flesh for an everlasting covenant.' (Genesis 17:10, 13)

A covenant is a solemn vow, pact or agreement between two people, and in ancient times it was sealed with blood to signify the death of the person who broke the covenant. Melchizedek, King of Salem gave Abraham bread and wine (Genesis 14:18) before Abraham went on to receive a mysterious blood covenant from God. (Genesis 15) God instructed him to cut certain animals and birds in half and to lay the pieces opposite each other on the ground. Then a deep sleep, horror and great darkness fell upon Abraham. As he slept, a flaming torch and smoking oven supernaturally passed between the pieces. God Himself walked between the pieces, signifying that He alone would take the full responsibility for keeping the covenant. He would become the Passover Lamb whose blood would be shed to pay the price of the covenant, to release Abraham's descendants from bondage to Pharoah (Satan), and bring them back into the Land He had covenanted to them (being joined to Him).

At Passover, Yeshua gave His disciples the bread and wine, symbols of the New Covenant in His blood. Then He went out and knelt in the Garden of Gethsemane. There His soul passed through agony, like the deep darkness and horror witnessed by Abraham. God Himself, sinless Man, walked through death in our place to redeem us back to Himself.

Thank Yeshua for taking upon Himself the responsibility to keep His Covenant.

Readings: Genesis 14:17–17:27, Deuteronomy 10:12–16, Luke 22, 23

NISAN

9th Day of the 1st Month
Abib – also called Nisan, usually falling in March/April
Preparation for Passover
Mary anointed Yeshua

Mary took a pound of very costly oil of spikenard, anointed the feet of Jesus, and wiped His feet with her hair. And the house was filled with the fragrance of the oil. *John 12:3*

Six days before the final Passover of His earthly ministry, Yeshua came to Bethany, a village on the Mount of Olives. He had special friends there. Martha would busily prepare Him food, while her sister Mary would sit at Yeshua's feet, feeding on all His life-giving words. And when their brother Lazarus had died, Yeshua raised him from the dead.

Mary had a very precious possession, an alabaster box containing the fragrant oil of spikenard – a rare plant which would have been gathered and carried from the highest mountains on earth. Spikenard was worth more than its weight in gold.

Yeshua returned to Bethany before His death and Mary came to Him bearing her alabaster box. Breaking it open, she poured its fragrant contents over her saviour. The pungent aroma filled the whole house, saturated Yeshua's skin and clung to her hair. When the men reprimanded her action Yeshua defended her saying, "Let her alone; she has kept this for the day of My burial..." (John 12:7).

Song of Songs speaks of the fragrance of spikenard. It is one of the distinctive fragrances hidden within the enclosed garden of the bride. Sweet love, devotion, worship, sacrifice, service and commitment are nurtured in her heart for Him alone. The bride comes to the bridegroom full of her pleasant fruits and fragrances. She exclaims, 'Awake, O north wind, and come, O south! Blow upon my garden that its spices may flow out. Let my beloved come to his garden and eat its pleasant fruits.' (Song of Songs 4:16)

Invite Yeshua to 'walk in your garden' and enjoy your love.

Readings: John 12:1–8, Song of Songs 4:6–5:1, Luke 24:1

10th Day of the 1st Month
Abib – also called Nisan, usually falling in March/April
Preparation for Passover
Yeshua entered Jerusalem

The next day a great multitude that had come to the feast, when they heard that Jesus was coming to Jerusalem, took branches of palm trees and went out to meet Him. *John 12:12, 13*

On the tenth day of the first month, the children of Israel crossed over the Jordan River and entered the Promised Land from the east. (Joshua 4:19) Later, also on this date the Prophet Ezekiel received the vision of the mysterious temple (Ezekiel 40–44). He saw the eastern gate of the temple shut up, not to be opened, because 'the LORD God of Israel has entered by it'. (Ezekiel 44:2)

And we also see from the gospels that it was on the tenth day of the first month that Yeshua entered Jerusalem from the east, riding a young donkey colt down the Mount of Olives. (John 12:1, John 12:12) The people joyfully proclaimed Him Messiah, quoting Psalm 118:25, 26. The messianic prophesy of Zechariah 9:9, was fulfilled. (John 12:12–16)

Yeshua's 'entry' to Jerusalem was a perfect example of humility. He came as the servant Messiah to suffer and die, not to conquer and rule. Now, raised from the dead, He is the King of Glory, the King of Israel, and His Kingship will be revealed to all when He returns. (Zechariah 9:10) On this date the Passover lambs were to be selected (Exodus 12:3). They had to be male, young and without blemish. Thousands were checked for blemishes before being led to the temple for slaughter at Passover. Yeshua, the Lamb of God, lived among Israel and was observed to be truly 'without blemish' (Isaiah 53:7). The multitude proclaimed 'Save us! Blessed is He who comes in the name of the LORD! The King of Israel!' (John 12:13)

Meditate on the purity and humility of Yeshua the Lamb of God, and worship Him.

Readings: Exodus 12:1–11, John 12:9–16, Matthew 21:1–16, Psalm 118:19–29

NISAN

11th Day of the 1st Month
Abib – also called Nisan, usually falling in March/April
Preparation for Passover
Yeshua taught about His death

"...Most assuredly, I say to you, unless a grain of wheat falls into the ground and dies, it remains alone; but if it dies, it produces much grain..." *John 12:24*

The biblical feasts of 'Pesach', 'Shavuot' and 'Succot' are all connected with harvest time. 'Pesach' (called 'Passover' in English) and its seven days of 'Unleavened Bread' contain the 'Feast of First Fruits'. This was when the first sheaf of the barley harvest was gathered in, and waved before the Lord as an offering to God, to return to Him the first part of the harvest. The 'Feast of First Fruits' is now always kept on the third day of 'Pesach', though in Leviticus 23:10, 11 it fell on the day after the Sabbath during the feast.

Fifty days (seven weeks) after the 'Feast of First Fruits', comes the 'Feast of Shavuot' (Weeks). 'Shavuot' marks the 'First Fruits' of the wheat harvest, when the first wheat sheaf was gathered in and offered to the Lord. Later, in the seventh month, comes the 'Feast of Succot', (called 'Tabernacles' in English). 'Succot' is called the 'Feast of Ingathering' in Exodus 23:14–16, because it marks the end of the harvests, when all the grain has been harvested and the grapes have been gathered and pressed. (Deuteronomy 16:13)

In His final week, before dying on the cross, Yeshua taught his disciples that it would be necessary for Him to die. He likened Himself to a grain of wheat which has to fall into the ground and die for the new plant to grow and produce a harvest of multiplication. In His earthly body Yeshua could not physically meet everyone, but now in His risen body, Yeshua can meet with all who come to Him. Everyone who repents and believes, turning to Him, can receive the harvest of seeing and knowing Yeshua, and become His harvest for eternity.

How is God speaking to you through the picture of the grain 'dying' in the ground?

Readings: Exodus 23:14–16, John 12:17–36, Mark 8:34–38

12th Day of the 1st Month
Abib – also called Nisan, usually Falling in March/April
Preparation for Passover
Those who didn't believe

But although He had done so many signs before them, they did not believe in Him.... *John 12:37*

Though many of the Jewish people believed that Yeshua was truly the Son of God, the temple authorities did not believe in Him. There were many among the rulers who believed that Yeshua was the Messiah but they didn't want to be put out of the Synagogues by the Pharisees. So they did not confess their belief in Him. 'They loved the praise of men more than the praise of God.' (John 12:43) They hid their faith. They concealed their hearts.

The hearts of those who did not believe in Yeshua had been hardened so that they could not 'see' who He was. As spiritual beings, our ability to understand the things of God is linked to the condition of our hearts. The Pharisees were an example for us, and a warning not to become more concerned about the 'external' things of religion than the condition of our hearts. If they had understood the importance of faith and humility of heart towards God, they would have been able to spiritually discern the Son of God. Yeshua taught that we must humble ourselves and believe like little children, discerning with our hearts. (Luke 18:17)

Two days before Passover, the chief priests and elders of the people gathered in the palace of the High Priest and surreptitiously made plans to put Yeshua to death. (Matthew 26:1–4) They were afraid that if all the people followed Yeshua they would lose the nation to the Romans. But God caused Caiaphas, the High Priest that year, to prophecy, saying "You know nothing at all, nor do you consider that it is expedient for us that one man should die for the people, and not that the whole nation should perish." (John 11:49, 50) God was still speaking to them, if they would only listen to what He was saying.

Ask God to show you any areas of unbelief in your heart and to help you discern who He is.

Readings: John 12:37–50, Luke 18:9–17, Isaiah 6, Matthew 10:24–42

NISAN

13th Day of the 1st Month
Abib – also called Nisan, usually falling in March/April
Preparation for Passover
The New Covenant

And He took bread, gave thanks and broke it, and gave it to them, saying, "This is My body which is given for you; do this in remembrance of Me". Likewise He also took the cup after supper, saying, 'This cup is the New Covenant in My blood, which is shed for you...." Luke 22:19, 20

At twilight, Yeshua reclined at the table and ate the Passover meal with His disciples. But instead of using the meal as simply the God-ordained remembrance of the deliverance of the Israelites from Egypt (Exodus 12:25–27), Yeshua took up the unleavened bread and the wine, and gave them to His disciples in remembrance of Himself. He would not eat the Passover again until it comes to its fulfilment in the kingdom of God. (Luke 22:16)

The unleavened bread represents more than the bread baked in haste in Egypt. Yeshua made it represent Himself, the Lamb of God, His body broken for us so that we can 'feed on Him'. Yeshua is the 'Bread of Life' (John 6:35), the 'Lamb slain from the foundation of the world'. (Revelation 13:8) The Israelites ate the Passover lambs to receive strength for their flight from Egypt. Now we 'eat' the bread and receive by faith, the life that flows from Yeshua to deliver us from sin, sickness, death and judgement. (John 6:33–58)

Yeshua took up the Passover cup of wine after the supper and said, "This cup is the New Covenant in My blood, which is shed for you..." (Luke 22:20) When we drink the juice from the fruit of the vine in this way, we receive into ourselves the power of Messiah's risen life, cleansing us from sin and redeeming us from the curse of the law. When we eat the bread and drink the cup, we proclaim the Lord's death till He comes. (1 Corinthians 11:26)

What are we to remember when we partake of the New Covenant Meal of bread and wine?

Readings: Luke 22:7–37, John 6:33–58, 1 Corinthians 11:23–32, Psalm 118

14th Day of the 1st Month
Abib – also called Nisan,
usually falling in March/April
Passover – 'Pesach'
The Sacrifice of Yeshua

> Then they took Jesus and led Him away. And He, bearing His cross, went out to a place called the Place of a Skull, which is called in Hebrew, Golgotha, where they crucified Him.... *John 19:16b–18a*

Twilight on the 14th day of the 1st month is the 'LORD's Passover'. (Leviticus 23:5) After the Passover meal Yeshua went out to the Garden of 'Gethsemane' (which means 'oil press') on the Mount of Olives. There, Yeshua took upon Himself the complete wrath of God against every sin ever to be committed in all time. In great anguish, pressed down like olives in an oil press, He prayed, sweating great drops of blood. His disciples slept, Judas betrayed Him, He was imprisoned by the temple authorities, and He was denied by Peter.

At Passover the Jews could have a prisoner released by the Romans. They chose a rebel, Barabbas, to be freed, while their innocent King willingly became the 'scapegoat'. As Passover sacrifices were being slaughtered nearby in the temple, Yeshua's own holy blood was shed. Mocked, beaten, spat upon, scourged and finally nailed to a cross, the Lamb of God became the perfect sacrifice, taking upon Himself the sins of the whole world.

There is no sin too great which cannot be forgiven through turning to Yeshua's death on the cross. There is no sickness, pain, disease or wound that cannot be healed because of His wounds. As Yeshua died, He cried out 'It is finished', bowed His head and gave up His Spirit. The sky went dark, the earth quaked, graves of holy men opened up and the veil in the temple was torn from top to bottom, opening the way to the Holy of Holies. A Roman soldier standing opposite Yeshua said, 'Truly this Man was the Son of God!' (Mark 15:39)

Meditate on Yeshua's perfect sacrifice to reconcile you to God, and respond to Him.

Readings: Leviticus 23:4–8, Matthew 26:17–27:56, Isaiah 53, Psalm 22

15th Day of the 1st Month
Abib – also called Nisan,
usually falling in March/April
**The Feast of Unleavened Bread
– 'Hag HaMatzot'**
Yeshua in the Grave

Now in the place where He was crucified there was a garden, and in the garden a new tomb in which no one had yet been laid. So there they laid Jesus, because of the Jews' Preparation Day, for the tomb was nearby. *John 19:41, 42*

The fifteenth day of the 1st month is the Feast of 'Matzot' (Unleavened Bread). For seven days unleavened bread is to be eaten. (Numbers 28:17) On this day, the Israelites left Egypt having eaten the Passover lamb the night before. (Numbers 33:3) They did not have time to let yeast in their bread rise, because they had to escape hastily. They had to eat quickly baked, unleavened bread, and the lamb they had eaten sustained them.

On the 'Feast of Unleavened Bread', the dead body of Yeshua lay in a new tomb, placed there hastily because it was a Sabbath day of rest when no work could be done. On this day, all yeast and leavening agents have to be removed from homes. (Exodus 12:15) The yeast or leavening is a picture of sin, which permeates our whole nature. Yeast ferments and decays, representing sin and death. It can only be removed because Yeshua died in our place.

Yeshua's body in the grave never decayed. (Psalm 16:10, Acts 2:25–31) There was no leaven of sin in Him. He was the pure 'offering'. He was to rise from the dead. When we receive Him in our hearts, the leaven of our old nature is removed from our spirit, as though we never sinned or broke any of His commandments. The presence of Yeshua increases in our hearts, and the desire to sin decreases. (Romans 7, 8) The Apostle Paul told the believers 'purge out the old leaven, that you may be a new lump, since you truly are unleavened. For indeed Christ, our 'Passover', was 'sacrificed for us.' (1 Corinthians 5:7)

Consider the true significance of eating the unleavened bread of Yeshua's uncorrupted life.

Readings: Exodus 12:14–20, 29:1–3, Leviticus 2:1–13, Matthew 27:57–66, 1 Corinthians 5

16th Day of the 1st Month
Abib – also called Nisan,
usually falling in March/April
**The Sheaf of the First Fruits –
'HaBikkorim'
The Resurrection of Yeshua**

"Why do you seek the living among the dead? He is not here but is risen!" *Luke 24:5b, 6a*

On the first day of the week an angel descended from heaven, rolled back the massive stone from the entrance to the tomb and sat on it. Leaving behind the grave clothes, Yeshua rose alive from where His dead body had lain. He physically rose from the dead, never to die again. This was the first ever resurrection. When he rose from the dead, Yeshua fulfilled the prophetic sign of Jonah. (Matthew 12:39, 40) Jonah's body had lain in the belly of the whale dead, only to be brought back alive (resuscitated) onto dry land after three days. (Jonah 2)

The resurrection occurred on the 'Feast of First Fruits', the day that the first sheaf of the barley harvest was gathered, brought into the temple, and waved as an offering to God. (Leviticus 23:9–15) The first portion of the harvest belongs to God and is given back to Him as an offering. (Deuteronomy 26:1, 2) This ensures God's blessing on the rest of the harvest. When Israel came into their inheritance (the Land) they had to bring the first fruits of the new country to God. Yeshua's resurrection is the 'first fruits' of the harvest of God. The rest of the harvest will be gathered when those who die 'in Christ' are resurrected from the dead. Yeshua became the 'first fruits' of the harvest gathered to the Father. (John 20:17) Ascended and offered to the Father, the rest of the harvest of souls yet to be gathered into eternal life is guaranteed. 1 Corinthians 15 explains that those who are Christ's will be raised at His coming – His return. The rest will be raised later to judgement when all things have been put 'under His feet' and Yeshua delivers the restored kingdom to God the Father. Everyone will live for eternity. Where we spend it depends on our response to Yeshua.

Praise God for His victory over death and thank Him for the hope of the resurrection.

Readings: Leviticus 23:9–15, Matthew 28:1–9, Acts 24:15, 1 Corinthians 15, Revelation 20, 2 Chronicles 29:17

NISAN

17th Day of the 1st Month
Abib – also called Nisan, usually falling in March/April
Resurrection Appearances
Yeshua appeared to Mary Magdalene

...she turned around and saw Jesus standing there, and did not know that it was Jesus. *John 20:14*

Mary Magdalene was the first person to see the risen Lord on the morning He rose from the dead. Yeshua had cast out seven demons from her and she became one of His faithful followers. Now she went to the tomb very early in the morning with the other women, to put spices on the body of her Lord and master, as was the burial custom. When the women arrived they found the stone rolled away. An angel spoke to them saying, "Do not be alarmed. You seek Jesus of Nazareth, who was crucified. He is risen! He is not here. See the place where they laid Him...." (Mark 16:6)

Peter and John arrived and witnessed the linen cloths lying in the tomb before returning to their homes. But Mary Magdalene stayed outside the tomb weeping. As she wept, she stooped down and looked in. There she saw two angels sitting, one at the head, the other at the feet where the body had lain. They said to her, "Woman, why are you weeping?"

She said to them, "Because they have taken away my Lord, and I do not know where they have laid Him." Now when she had said this, she turned around and saw Jesus standing there, and did not know that it was Jesus. Jesus said to her, "Woman, why are you weeping? Whom are you seeking?" (John 20:13–15)

She supposed Him to be the gardener but Yeshua said to her "Mary!" She turned and said to Him "Rabboni" (teacher). She wanted to cling to Him but she couldn't because He had to return to the Father. He was the 'first fruits' of the resurrection. He belonged to Him.

Do you think you always recognise the voice of Yeshua when He speaks to you?

Readings: Luke 8:1–3, Matthew 27:55, 56, John 19:25, John 20:1–18, John 18:37

18th Day of the 1st Month
Abib – also called Nisan, usually falling in March/April
Resurrection Appearances
The Men on the Road to Emmaus

Now behold, two of them were travelling that same day to a village called Emmaus, which was seven miles from Jerusalem. And they talked together of all these things which had happened. So it was, while they conversed and reasoned, that Jesus Himself drew near and went with them... *Luke 24:13–15*

Later, on the same day that Yeshua rose from the dead, He made His second appearance as the risen Lord. It happened as Cleopas and his companion walked along the road to Emmaus. They were questioning and reasoning about the events that had just occurred in Jerusalem, when Yeshua Himself drew near and walked beside them, joining in their conversation and speaking with them. But they did not recognise Him.

The disciples had checked that the tomb was empty, as the women had said. Cleopas and His companion expressed their disappointment in events because they had hoped Yeshua would be the one who would redeem Israel. The men had studied the Scriptures, but the true meaning remained closed to them. They had not understood how all the Law, Prophets and Writings reveal Yeshua. Now, the author and inspiration of the Holy Scriptures, the Word of God, walked and talked with them, awakening them to the truth.

Their hearts burned within them as they began to understand God's plan of redemption, why the Messiah had come. Then at supper He 'broke the bread'. Suddenly they recognised Him. Their eyes were opened, like Adam and Eve's when they ate the fruit of the tree of the knowledge of good and evil. Suddenly they discerned the true 'bread of life' in their midst, broken for them. When they 'saw', He disappeared from their eyes.

Do you 'see' with your spirit or just with your eyes? Do you discern the bread of life?

Readings: Luke 24:1–35, 1 Corinthians 2, 11:27–32, Romans 11:25, Zechariah 12:9, 10

NISAN

19th Day of the 1st Month
Abib – also called Nisan, usually falling in March/April
Resurrection Appearances
Yeshua Appears to His disciples

Then the same day at evening, being the first day of the week, when the doors were shut where the disciples were assembled, for fear of the Jews, Jesus came and stood in the midst, and said to them, "Peace be with you". *John 20:19, 20*

After Yeshua departed from Emmaus, He appeared to His disciples where they were gathered behind locked doors. The doors were locked because the temple authorities were angry at claims that Yeshua had risen from the dead. So the disciples, whose lives were in danger, hid themselves. Already afraid for their lives, they were troubled to see Yeshua appear in their locked room. They thought they were seeing a ghost.

Yeshua reassured His disciples, saying, "Peace be with you!" and "Peace to you!" He breathed on them, and they received the Holy Spirit. (John 20:19–23) He asked them why they were troubled, and rebuked them for doubting the reports of the others who had seen Him. (Mark 16:14) He invited them to see the nail wounds in His hands and feet, and He ate a piece of broiled fish and some honeycomb to prove He was not a ghost. (Luke 24:36–43)

Yeshua's risen body is more solid than walls and doors. He moves in dimensions beyond the three dimensions of the natural world. He moves easily between earth and heaven. Yeshua demonstrated the physical reality of the supernatural realm beyond our own experience, which makes the natural world seem unsubstantial in comparison. Thomas was unable to believe that Yeshua was alive until he saw Him with his eyes. Yeshua said to him, "Thomas, because you have seen Me, you have believed. Blessed are those who have not seen and yet have believed." (John 20:29) You are blessed when you believe in Him.

Is your faith shaped by what you perceive naturally or by what is revealed in the Scriptures?

Readings: John 20:19–31, 1 Corinthians 2:9, Isaiah 26:3, John 14, 1 Peter 1:6–9

20th Day of the 1st Month
Abib – also called Nisan, usually falling in March/April
Resurrection Appearances
Yeshua and the Great Catch of Fish

After these things Jesus showed Himself again to the disciples at the Sea of Tiberias.... *John 21:1*

This is the fifth recorded appearance of Yeshua after the resurrection and His third appearance to the disciples. Six of Yeshua's disciples had accompanied Simon Peter back home to the lake in Galilee and back to their fishing, back to where Yeshua had called them to follow Him and let Him make them into Fishers of Men. (Matthew 4:19, Luke 5:10)

On that occasion Yeshua had taught the multitude gathered on the shore from Simon Peter's boat. He had told Simon Peter to launch out into the deep and let down his nets for a catch. (Luke 5:4) Simon had not caught any fish all night, but when the fishermen let down the net in obedience, they caught so many fish the net began to break, and the boat began to sink under the weight of all the fish. Now, again, Simon Peter was back on the lake with the disciples, once again fishing and catching nothing. Yeshua appeared and called the disciples from the shore to ask if they had any food. They had nothing. So He called out: "Cast the net on the right side of the boat and you will find some." (John 21:6) They cast the net and couldn't draw it in. There were 153 large fish and yet the nets didn't break.

On the shore, Yeshua had a small fire burning, with fish and bread laid out on it, ready for their breakfast. Hope began to dawn. Perhaps Yeshua still had a good future for him after all. Perhaps Peter was not the complete failure that he felt. Three times he had denied being Yeshua's disciple. Now Yeshua asked Peter three times if he loved Him and he replied assuring his Lord and master that of course He did. Yeshua responded with a new commission for Peter – to feed His lambs and tend and feed His sheep. (John 21:1–19)

In what way can you identify with Simon Peter? Hear what the Lord has to say to you.

Readings: Luke 5:1–11, Luke 22:31–62, John 21

21st Day of the 1st Month
Abib – also called Nisan, usually falling in March/April
The Final Day of Unleavened Bread
Coming up from Egypt

...on the seventh day there shall be a feast to the LORD. Unleavened bread shall be eaten seven days. And no leavened bread shall be seen among you, nor shall leaven be seen among you in all your quarters. And you shall tell your son in that day, saying, 'This is because of what the LORD did for me when I came up from Egypt.' *Exodus 13:6–8*

This is the seventh and final day of eating unleavened bread in memorial of Israel 'coming up' out of slavery in Egypt. Egypt symbolises slavery to sin. Israel had to be 'redeemed' by the Passover Lamb – to come up from exile in Egypt into the Promised Land. Yeshua the Passover Lamb redeems us from sin to bring us up 'out of Egypt' and 'across the Red Sea' into eternal life. Now we can live a life ruled by the Spirit, free from bondage.

The seventh day of eating unleavened bread is a Sabbath day of rest and of 'convocation'. (Exodus 12:16) The Hebrew word for 'convocation' – 'miqre', also means a 'rehearsal'. It foreshadows a future or a spiritual reality. This convocation at the end of seven days eating unleavened bread 'rehearses' our complete and total freedom from the bondages of sin. Seven days represent completion. When we 'completely' eat the unleavened bread of the life of Yeshua, it manifests in every part of our lives, our mind, will, emotions and behaviour, not just our spirit. Eating 'His Word' will completely renew us.

Yeshua identified with us by spending His early years in exile in Egypt until Herod died. (Matthew 2) Now, with Him, we journey across the Red Sea (identifying with His death, cleansed through His blood). The word 'Hebrew' means 'crossed over ones'. For us it means that we have crossed over from the slavery of a self-ruled life, to freedom in God.

Thank God for the joy of crossing over from death to life through His gift of grace to you.

Readings: Exodus 13–15, Hosea 11:1–9, Matthew 2, John 3, Galatians 2:20, Romans 8:1–17

22nd Day of the 1st Month
Abib – also called Nisan, usually falling in March/April
Times and Seasons
Winter is Past, Spring has Come

My beloved spoke, and said to me: "Rise up, my love, my fair one, and come away, for lo, the winter is past, the rain is over and gone. The flowers appear on the earth, the time of singing has come..."
Song of Songs 2:10–12

The book 'Song of Songs', also known as 'The Song of Solomon', is set at this time of year with the arrival of spring in the Land of Israel. The 'latter' spring rains are over and gone. Swathes of scarlet anemones and poppies give way to bright yellow blossoms, pink cyclamen, narcissus and luscious lilies. The warmth causes the birds to sing and coo, and the fig tree and vine start to put forth their first little fruits.

It is time for each one of us to come 'out of hibernation' from the cold and the rain, and heed the invitation of Yeshua, the Bridegroom, to come away with Him. The Song of Songs can be interpreted as the love song between God and Israel or between a man and a woman, but ultimately it is the story of Yeshua wooing his beloved – his Bride. His Bride is all those who, like the Shulamite, learn to rise up and come away into relationship with Him, to know and love their Lord and saviour personally in their hearts.

At first she realises that she has neglected her own relationship with God in her busyness. But her lover persists in calling her into fellowship with Himself in the secret place, in the secret 'chambers' of her heart. She has to overcome her tendency to make excuses to not spend time in His presence, but finally she learns how to draw close to Him and enjoy His fellowship. She becomes mature and equipped to help her 'little' sisters – those who do not yet know the Lord – to grow up and become secure in Him.

Can you perceive the call of Yeshua, to come away and spend time getting to know Him?

Readings: Song of Songs 1–8, John 17:3

23rd Day of the 1st Month
Abib – also called Nisan, usually falling in March/April
Times and Seasons
God's Kingdom Plan

Jesus answered, "My kingdom is not of this world. If my kingdom were of this world, My servants would fight, so that I should not be delivered to the Jews; but now My kingdom is not from here."

John 18:36

God's kingdom is a heavenly kingdom which will not be fully manifest until Yeshua has returned to earth to rule and reign. (Isaiah 2:1–4, Micah 4:2–5) God's kingdom (also called the 'kingdom of heaven') has God as its King, and its citizens obey God's kingdom laws and government, and, as one preacher said, causes us to 'live in God's world God's way'. His kingdom is established in our hearts as we obey Him. (Matthew 7:21–23)

The fact is that this world is not living under God's kingship. Since Adam and Eve listened to Satan and ate from the tree of the knowledge of good and evil, they were cast out of the Garden of Eden. They had disobeyed God their King, (Genesis 3) and Satan became Prince of this world. (John 12:31) In God's kingdom plan He called out the nation of Israel to be His own people on earth to worship Him and keep His laws. Israel however rejected God as their only King, choosing instead to have an earthly king like other nations. (1 Samuel 8:6, 7) But God turned this to good by coming Himself in the lineage of their king, David, to become the King of Israel, not by force, but by bringing hearts, not only of Israel but of people from all nations, into submission to Him as King and to obey His commandments.

It is only God's abundant grace and loving kindness that enables us to walk uprightly under His kingdom rule. He is mighty to forgive our transgressions and empower us to live aright in His kingdom. His kingdom brings righteousness, peace and joy in the Holy Spirit.

Do you submit to God as your King and seek His kingdom above all else? (Matthew 6:33)

Readings: Romans 14:17, Matthew 4:7–10, 4:23–5:20, 6:31–34, 27:37, Revelation 19:16

24th Day of the 1st Month
Abib – also called Nisan, usually falling in March/April
Times and Seasons
God's Kingdom Order

For I am not ashamed of the gospel of Christ, for it is the power of God to salvation for everyone who believes, for the Jew first and also for the Greek. *Romans 1:16*

God's kingdom is 'ordered'. We are to respect God's order in our relationships. This makes for peace and stability. We are to obey and pray for our earthly masters and national governments. (1 Timothy 2) Children are to obey their parents, and wives are to obey their husbands. Husbands are to obey Yeshua. (Ephesians 5:17–6:18) Godly obedience comes from a free will that is submitted to God, not to ungodly control or manipulation.

God's government requires that we all find our security in God's love and not in a 'role' or 'position'. The fear of God in our lives will displace the fear of man. (Daniel 6:6–10) Yeshua always obeyed the Father and He is our example of humble obedience and servanthood. (John 13:14, Philippians 2:1–11) It is as we live securely in acceptance of the place God has given us at this time in our life that we find freedom. In God's kingdom many who are first shall be last and the last first. (Matthew 19:30) God does not show partiality to our 'status' but regards our godliness and submission in the position He has given us. In God's kingdom, humility and obedience receive a greater reward than lording it over others.

When we understand God's order and government in our lives we are able to understand God's order with Israel and the Jewish people. Israel is God's servant for the restoration of His kingdom on earth. The gospel is 'for the Jew first and also for the Greek'. (Romans 1:16, 2:9–11) That doesn't make Gentiles less valuable in God's sight. It is simply a matter of God's calling. On this day, Daniel's humility was rewarded. (Daniel 10:4, 12)

Meditate on the greatness of God's love for you which is unaffected by your natural 'status'.

Readings: Romans 1, Philippians 2:1–11, Ephesians 5, 6, Romans 11:25–29, Daniel 10:4–12

25th Day of the 1st Month
Abib – also called Nisan, usually falling in March/April
Times and Seasons
God's Plan for Israel

...at this present time there is a remnant according to the election of grace. *Romans 11:5*

Israel began, as it were, as a 'proto-type' of God's kingdom on earth, and remains to us a sign of the hope of the return of the King of the Jews, to rule and reign from Jerusalem. The Apostle Paul esteemed, valued and cared deeply about His people the Israelites, because he said, to them pertain 'the adoption, the glory, the covenants, the giving of the Law, the service of God, and the promises, of whom are the fathers and from whom according to the flesh, Christ came who is over all, the eternally blessed God.' (Romans 9:4, 5)

God has not forsaken His people Israel. When the Jews did not believe with faith in Yeshua their Messiah they were cast out of their Land and dispersed across the earth just as Yeshua and the Scriptures had prophesied. (Deuteronomy 30:1, Matthew 26:31) The temple was destroyed in 70 AD by Roman armies, and the land remained barren and desolate while the majority of the Jews and the tribes of Israel were dispersed among the nations. (James 1:1) This was for a purpose. The 'time of the Gentiles' had begun so that the Gentile nations could receive the kingdom too. Israel was cut off in their unbelief so that the Gentiles could hear the gospel and be saved through faith. (Romans 11:19)

But this will not continue forever. (Romans 11:23) Yeshua said, "Jerusalem will be trampled by Gentiles until the times of the Gentiles are fulfilled". (Luke 21:24) A time would come when Jerusalem would be restored to the Jews. Israel will one day be able to welcome back their Messiah, Yeshua, to their Land, saying, (in Hebrew) 'Baruch haba be Shem Adonai' – 'Blessed is He who comes in the name of the LORD!' (Matthew 23:39)

Thank God that His abundant grace, which preserves and keeps Israel, also keeps you.

Readings: Luke 21, Matthew 23:37–24:31, Romans 11:13–15, Ezekiel 36, Revelation 7

26th Day of the 1st Month
Abib – also called Nisan, usually falling in March/April
Times and Seasons
Gentiles 'grafted in'

And if some of the branches were broken off, and you, being a wild olive tree, were grafted in among them, and with them became a partaker of the root and fatness of the olive tree, do not boast against the branches. But if you do boast, remember that you do not support the root, but the root supports you. *Romans 11:17, 18*

Paul likened Israel to a specially cultivated olive tree. Its roots and trunk come from the faith of Abraham and God's covenants with His people. When Jews reject their Messiah Yeshua through unbelief, they get cut off from the very fulfilment and completion of the tree whose life and fruit is salvation through faith. Abraham was made righteous through faith. (Genesis 15:6) Meanwhile, Gentiles who believe in Yeshua, 'come into' faith and are like branches from a wild tree grafted into the cultivated olive tree. They immediately receive the fruits of salvation which have come through God's New Covenant with Israel (Jeremiah 31:31) sealed through the broken body and shed blood of the Jewish Messiah, Yeshua. They receive from the Jewish Scriptures. Gentile 'branches' are supported by 'Jewish roots'.

This is all because of God's grace, not because of any self-generated righteousness. Therefore Gentiles must not be arrogant and boast against the Jews. Gentiles are to show respect to the Jewish 'roots' of their faith which sustain them, and remember that the Jews were 'cut off' the tree of faith because of their unbelief so that they as believing Gentiles could be grafted in. If Gentiles are blessed in their faith, how much more blessed will be the Jews when they come to faith in Messiah Yeshua, and are grafted back into their own 'olive tree'. The Apostle Paul wrote of the Jews, 'If their being cast away is the reconciling of the world, what will their acceptance be but life from the dead?' (Romans 11:15)

What attitude of heart should Gentiles have towards Jews? Pray about any failures in this.

Readings: Genesis 12:1–3, 15:1–6, Romans 4, Romans 9–11

NISAN

27th Day of the 1st Month
Abib – also called Nisan, usually falling in March/April
Holocaust Memorial Eve
The Persecution of Israel

And they also, if they do not continue in unbelief, will be grafted in, for God is able to graft them in again. For if you were cut out of the olive tree which is wild by nature, and were grafted contrary to nature into a cultivated olive tree, how much more will these, who are natural branches, be grafted into their own olive tree? *Romans 11:23*

The Apostle Paul wrote to the Church in Rome explaining that they must not boast against the Jews, but must remember that, as Gentiles, they have received the roots of their faith from the Jews. (Romans 11:18) Sadly, history has demonstrated that many generations of the Gentile Church have failed to heed Paul's advice, and going further than boasting, they have actually persecuted the Jews, expelling them from different nations and murdering them. This evening a siren sounds in Israel to mark a two minutes' silence at the beginning of 'Holocaust Memorial Day' or 'Yom HaShoah' as it is called in Hebrew. This is the anniversary of the Warsaw Ghetto Uprising of spring 1943, and it is the official day chosen by the Israeli Knesset to remember the Nazi Holocaust when over six million Jews perished. This day has come about in modern times, but is in keeping with the solemn days of mourning and remembrance found in Scripture. (Lamentations 2:10) Many Jews, like Yeshua, went in silence to the slaughter. (Isaiah 53:7) Those who inflicted suffering on them were unknowingly afflicting Yeshua, and will be judged by God. (Matthew 25:31–46)

False teaching that the Church has replaced Israel in God's plan has been prevalent in Christian churches since the Early Church Fathers, teaching that Israel's 'divine election' has been revoked. But Paul wrote that the Jews are beloved for the sake of the fathers and the gifts and calling of God are irrevocable. (Romans 11:25–36)

What does the irrevocability of God's gifts and callings on His people show us about God?

Readings: Romans 11:19–36, Matthew 24:3–13, Matthew 25:31–46, 2 Thessalonians 2:5–16

28th Day of the 1st Month
Abib – also called Nisan, usually falling in March/April
Holocaust Memorial Day
Israel's Travail

"For I have heard a voice as of a woman in labor, the anguish as of her who brings forth her first child, the voice of the daughter of Zion bewailing herself; She spreads her hands, saying, 'Woe is me now, for my soul is weary because of murderers!' Jeremiah 4:31

Israel is the servant of God's kingdom on earth (Isaiah 40–66) and Yeshua is the 'suffering servant' of Isaiah 53 who suffered to bring God's kingdom to the earth. Yeshua suffered so that when everything is finally restored and fulfilled, He will be able to hand the kingdom over to the Father. (1 Corinthians 15:24) He suffers because God's kingdom is opposed. Satan's kingdom of darkness attacks God's servants. There is travail to bring about God's purposes on earth. Yeshua suffered, died and was raised from the dead to bring us new birth. Israel, as the suffering servant of Isaiah 44:21 is also experiencing the 'labour pains' of God's kingdom.

Isaiah prophesied the travail of Yeshua, with these words: 'He shall see the labour of His soul and be satisfied. By His knowledge My righteous Servant shall justify many for He shall bear their iniquities.' (Isaiah 53:11)

Israel travailed 'after' the birth of Yeshua when the babies and children of Bethlehem were killed by Herod. (Matthew 2:16–18, Jeremiah 31:15) Isaiah prophesied, 'Before she was in labour, she gave birth, before her pain came, she delivered a male child.' (Isaiah 66:7) cf. Revelation 12:5. Israel's travail in the holocaust immediately brought forth the State of Israel. 'Shall the earth be made to give birth in one day? Or shall a nation be born at once?' (Isaiah 66:8). Israel's travail continues and intensifies as she draws closer to her spiritual re-birth and the return of her King. And in all their afflictions, Yeshua is afflicted. (Isaiah 63:9)

Which travail and suffering would Yeshua have you share with Him to bring His kingdom?

Readings: John 16:19–22, Micah 4:10–11, 5:3, Isaiah 49:13–26, 66:7–13, Psalm 102

NISAN

29th Day of the 1st Month
Abib – also called Nisan, usually falling in March/April
Israel and the Nations
Israel's Re-birth

"...Shall I bring to the time of birth, and not cause delivery?" says the LORD. *Isaiah 66:9*

Isaiah describes God's servant Israel being comforted in Jerusalem. (Isaiah 66:12, 13) She will not have gone through all the pain and travail for nothing. God promised His servant Israel that they would bring glory to Him once again in the sight of the nations, being once again established in Jerusalem. (Isaiah 66)

The Prophet Ezekiel uses the statement (or one similar) – 'then they will know that I am Lord' – over sixty times. (e.g. Ezekiel 28:24, 26) God will vindicate His name among the nations by showing that He has not forgotten His Covenant people, His Covenant Promises or His Covenant Land. If God never restored Israel to Himself or never judged her enemies, it would look as though God were weak and unable to keep His Covenants. (Ezekiel 36)

It is therefore God Himself who is bringing about Israel's natural re-birth for the vindication of His name in the sight of the rebellious and mocking nations. (Ezekiel 36) The re-birth is happening in stages. The first stage is the re-gathering of His people from the nations back into their Land. (This began to accelerate in the 19th Century.) The second is making them one nation in their Land (which happened with the San Remo Treaty in 1917 and the formation of the state of Israel in May 1948). The third stage is their spiritual re-birth when the remnant of Israel will be cleansed and healed and receive Messiah Yeshua. Ezekiel prophetically saw Israel's dry bones rising to new life in the end times. (Ezekiel 37) God's remnant, His people Israel will be truly restored. Yeshua will receive His Bride, the New Jerusalem, and He will rule and reign until He has put all His enemies under His feet.

How is God demonstrating that He is Lord, through your life?

Readings: Ezekiel 28:25, 26, Ezekiel 36, 37, Jeremiah 23:3–8

30th Day of the 1st Month
Abib – also called Nisan, usually falling in March/April
Israel and the Nations
God's Call to Return

The remnant of Israel! Behold I will bring them from the north country, and gather them from the ends of the earth, among them the blind and the lame, the woman with child, and the one who labours with child, together a great throng shall return there, they shall come with weeping, and with supplications I will lead them.

Jeremiah 31:7b–9

Jeremiah, Isaiah and Ezekiel all prophesied the return of Israel to their Land in the end times. In the Law of Moses their return from exile was promised if they would turn back to God. (Deuteronomy 30) Daniel and Nehemiah repented of the sins of their people, (Daniel 9, Nehemiah 1) and Israel experienced national repentance and a return to the Law of God once they returned to the Land. (Nehemiah 9) God was faithful to His covenant to Israel. He had promised that Messiah was to be born to them, in the tribe and land of Judah. (Micah 5:2) In our day too, Jews are returning to Zion because of God's covenant and His prophetic plan. Now in these days God is calling the Jews and the scattered tribes of Israel back from the countries where they have been dispersed, through an unexplainable inner urge that could only come from God, as well as through people either encouraging them, or persecuting them, like the fishers and hunters of Jeremiah 16:14–17. Jeremiah 31:7b–9 is a clear prophecy of the boats and aeroplanes that have headed for Israel, full of 'olim' (Jewish immigrants), 'making aliyah' (going up) to Israel from all over the world, in recent decades.

The process will be completed in the fulfilment of Yeshua the Messiah's kingdom. The day is yet to come when people from all the nations will come and sit with Yeshua in His kingdom. (Luke 13:29, 22:30) Yeshua will return to 'take up' His people and dwell in Zion.

How is your future hope tied into the prophetic hope of the Jews returning to Mount Zion?

Readings: Daniel 9:1–21, Nehemiah 1, Isaiah 43:1–6, Jeremiah 33:25, 26, Luke 13:22–30

1st Day of the 2nd Month
Ziv – also called Iyar, usually falling in April/May
Israel and the Nations
The Numbering of Israel

As the LORD commanded Moses, so he numbered them in the
Wilderness of Sinai.... *Numbers 1:19*

On the first day of the second month in the Wilderness, the Lord spoke
to Moses, commanding him to 'take a census' of all the children of Israel,
by their families. And so on that very day, the day of the monthly new
moon celebration, when no work could be done, Moses assembled the
congregation and each family recited their ancestry. (Numbers 1)

The numbering was not just 'counting'. It had to do with 'ownership'.
Each person was 'numbered' because they mattered as individuals.
They belonged to the children of Israel, pertained to the Covenants of
God, and were known personally to Him. They were numbered on the
first day of the lunar month, when Israel rejoices in God's everlasting
covenant faithfulness to them. The Lord instructed Moses that when
the people of Israel are numbered by a census, every man should give
a silver half-shekel ransom for himself, as an offering to the service of
God's Tabernacle, to make atonement for himself. It brought them under
God's protection. Otherwise a plague would break out among them.
(Exodus 30:11–16) Every individual soul needs a ransom payment to
be made to redeem them from sin.

King David sinned against God by numbering Israel without God's
command, and without the payment, so a plague broke out. God's
people cannot be numbered. (Genesis 13:16) An angel stopped the
plague at the threshing floor of Ornan the Jebusite. David then bought
that threshing floor on Mount Moriah for 50 silver shekels and 600
shekels of gold, and there Solomon built the temple. (2 Samuel 24:16,
1 Chronicles 21:15–26) On that same mountain, Yeshua, 'numbered
with the transgressors', paid the price for you. (Isaiah 53:12)

*Consider the 'value' that Yeshua has placed on every individual, paid for
with His own life.*

Readings: Numbers 1, Exodus 30:11–16, 2 Samuel 24, Mark 15:25–39,
1 Kings 6:1, Ezra 3:8

2nd Day of the 2nd Month
Ziv – also called Iyar, usually falling in April/May
Israel and the Nations
Israel, a blessing to the Nations

Now Solomon began to build the house of the LORD at Jerusalem on Mount Moriah, where the LORD had appeared to his father David, at the place that David had prepared on the threshing floor of Ornan the Jebusite. And he began to build on the second day of the second month in the fourth year of his reign. *2 Chronicles 3:1, 2*

On this day, King Solomon began to build the temple on Mount Moriah in Jerusalem, where King David had bought the threshing floor. The indescribable splendour and majesty of Solomon's kingdom is a picture for us of the glory of God's kingdom. Solomon himself, however, fell into apostasy, when his many foreign, pagan wives turned his heart away from God. Only the pure and holy Lamb of God is fit to be King of the kingdom of God.

Solomon's prayer of dedication for the newly built temple included a blessing for the foreigners who would go and pray at the temple, saying "when they come and pray in this temple, then hear from heaven Your dwelling place, and do according to all for which the foreigner calls to You, that all peoples of the earth may know Your name and fear You, as do Your people Israel...." (2 Chronicles 6:32, 33) All nations could pray to God in Israel.

The Queen of Sheba visited King Solomon and 'all the kings of Arabia and governors of the country brought gold and silver to Solomon'. (2 Chronicles 9:14) The kingdom of Israel was famous, favoured and mighty among the nations with Solomon as king, (whose name means 'peaceful'). The kingdom of God is ruled by Yeshua, Prince of Peace, and He will be worshipped by people from all nations. Israel does not just bless the earth with her abundance of fruit (Isaiah 27:6), but with spiritual blessings to the nations. (Zechariah 8:13)

Meditate on Zechariah 8:20–23. Thank God for the blessing Israel already is to the nations.

Readings: 2 Chronicles 3–9, Zechariah 8, 14:16–19, Isaiah 60

3rd Day of the 2nd Month
Ziv – also called Iyar, usually falling in April/May
Israel and the Nations
Nations Judged on Account of Israel

"For behold, in those days and at that time, when I bring back the captives of Judah and Jerusalem, I will also gather all nations, and bring them down to the Valley of Jehoshaphat; and I will enter into judgement with them there on account of My people, My heritage Israel, whom they have scattered among the nations, they have also divided up My land..." *Joel 3:1, 2*

The name 'Jehoshaphat' means 'The Lord judges', and the Valley of Jehoshaphat is a real place in Israel, now called the Kidron Valley, in Jerusalem. Because God chose Israel as His covenant people He will judge the nations according to their treatment of His people, for scattering them among the nations and for dividing up their Land. The nations' attitude to Israel reflects their attitude to His Word, and to God Himself. When the nations do not acknowledge God as their King they disregard His priorities and perspective. Today many nations are intent upon appeasing the nations that are hostile to Israel, for the sake of oil and commercial interest. In human terms the Land of Israel has little to commend it. It is very small (the size of Wales) in comparison to the vast oil-rich nations of the Middle East.

In these days the nations are trying to do precisely what Zechariah foretold – divide up God's Covenant Land. The nations are pressurising Israel to appease those nations which hate her for simply existing, and which hatefully slander her. But God's Word clearly states that He will judge the nations which divide up His land. (Joel 3:2) Genesis 12:3 states that God will bless those who bless Israel and curse those who curse Israel. We need to be careful not to adopt the philosophies of men, which seek peace by human means and disregard God's Word concerning Israel.

What do you listen to? The Word of God, or the slanderous tongues of Israel's enemies?

Readings: Joel 3, Zechariah 12:1–9, Haggai 2:6–9

4th Day of the 2nd Month
Ziv – also called Iyar, usually falling in April/May
Remembrance Day
The Day of the Vengeance of God

And it came to pass, when Joshua was by Jericho, that he lifted his eyes and looked, and behold, a Man stood opposite him with His sword drawn in His hand. And Joshua went to Him and said to Him, "Are You for us or for our adversaries?" So He said, "No, but as Commander of the army of the LORD I have now come."

Joshua 5:13, 14

Today restored Israel remembers the fallen soldiers of all the wars and the victims of terrorism in recent times. It is estimated that in 1948 alone at least 6000 Israelis out of a population of 650,000 gave their lives to defend the tiny fledgling State against an army of one and a half million from five surrounding hostile nations.

Back around 1240 BC, the LORD appeared to Joshua as a Man – the commander of the army of the LORD – and gave him instructions to defeat the city of Jericho and begin to possess the Land for His kingdom plan, for His inheritance. Israel obeyed and took the city just as God said. (Joshua 5:10 – 6:27) God does not take sides for or against nations for their own sake. He stands for His kingdom plan and purpose, and Joshua is a picture of Yeshua who, on the Day of God's vengeance, will secure God's promised inheritance, vindicate His people and judge those who, when they came up against Israel, warred against Him.

Isaiah 61:2, 3 prophesies the 'Day of vengeance of our God' when God will 'comfort all who mourn, to console those who mourn in Zion, to give them beauty for ashes and the oil of joy for mourning.' The Lord will trample the winepress of His wrath (Isaiah 63:1–4, Revelation 19:11–21) and bring justice for His afflicted ones. Those who grieve in Zion will be comforted. God's enemies will be destroyed and His faithful ones vindicated.

Meditate on Romans 12:19 – 'Vengeance is mine, I will repay' says the Lord.

Readings: Joshua 5:10 – 6:27, Isaiah 61:1–3, 63:1–6, Revelation 19:11–21

5th Day of the 2nd Month
Ziv – also called Iyar, usually falling in April/May
Independence Day
Back in the Land

And it shall come to pass in the place where it was said to them 'You are not My people', there it shall be said to them, 'You are sons of the living God.' *Hosea 1:10b*

On the fifth day of the second month (which in 1948 was 14th May), the Jewish leaders of Israel made their declaration of Independence from British rule, and the State of Israel was formed. Under the British Mandate the Land was called Palestine, a continuation of the name 'Palaestina' given by the Roman Emperor Hadrian in the 2nd Century AD, in an attempt to erase the Jewish heritage of the Land. On this day in 1948 the Land was re-named Israel, and the State of Israel was born, fulfilling Isaiah 66:8: 'Shall the earth be made to give birth in one day? Or shall a nation be born at once?' The Hebrew language was revived as Israel's pure spoken language, preserved for 2000 years in the Scriptures. (Zephaniah 3:9)

Israel's restoration is a sign to the nations that God is real, and that His covenant with Abraham, confirmed to Isaac and Jacob – to give them the Land, is as Scripture says, 'an everlasting covenant'. (Genesis 17:7, 8, Psalm 105:7–12) It is also the sign that Israel's spiritual re-birth will come to pass as prophesied in Ezekiel 36:24–38, and Hosea 1:8–11. Hosea took back to himself his adulterous wife. God is taking back and restoring Israel to Himself. Israel's restoration is a sign to the Gentiles that God can bring anyone, including them into His kingdom. He can restore anyone to Himself. (Acts 15:12–17, Amos 9:11, 12) God's people, the tribes of Israel, are returning to the Land, and when Yeshua returns in glory His kingdom will be fully revealed. God spoke to the House of Israel: 'I will take you from among the nations, gather you out of all countries, and bring you into your own Land. Then I will sprinkle clean water on you, and you shall be clean...' (Ezekiel 36:24, 25)

If God is faithful to preserve and restore Israel, He is faithful to do that for you. (Psalm 121)

Readings: Genesis 17:1–8, Ezekiel 36:22–38, Hosea 1, 2, Psalm 105

6th Day of the 2nd Month
Ziv – also called Iyar, usually falling in April/May
Israel and the Nations
The Apple of God's Eye

For thus says the LORD of hosts: "He sent Me after glory, to the nations which plunder you; for he who touches you touches the apple of His eye. For surely I will shake My hand against them, and they shall become spoil for their servants. Then you will know that the Lord of hosts has sent Me." *Zechariah 2:8*

In this passage the pre-existing Son of God speaks through the prophet Zechariah. He prophesies His being 'sent' by the Father, to be the Lord of 'hosts' – literally 'armies', to execute vengeance on the nations who meddle with or harm Zion. The nations which touch Zion, touch the apple, or 'pupil', of the Father's eye. Consequently Yeshua will 'bring down' the might of all the nations that plunder and oppose Zion, causing them to be plundered themselves by their former servants. The reason He is doing this now is so that Zion can testify that the Lord fulfils His Word, and that this is from Him, it is His doing.

The Father sent Yeshua to focus His ministry on Israel. Israel was and still is the 'apple of His eye' – the central focal point of His activity in the earth, into which everything else relates. In John's Gospel, Yeshua says over forty times that He had been sent by the Father, and in Matthew 15:24 He explains even more specifically that His mission was to the Jews, saying that He had been sent to the lost sheep of the house of Israel. He never even left the land of the tribes of Israel during His ministry on earth. The plundering of Israel's plunderers is, and will continue to be, a sign to all Jews that God loves them and is carrying out His vengeance and justice on their behalf. Yeshua is Israel's Messiah. Gentile believers in Yeshua are 'grafted in' to the Commonwealth of Israel. (Ephesians 2:12, 13)

Consider– Israel is the 'pupil' of God's eye through which He looks at you.

Readings: Zechariah 2, Matthew 15:21–28, Isaiah 14, Ezekiel 38, 39

IYAR

7th Day of the 2nd Month
Ziv – also called Iyar, usually falling in April/May
Israel and the Nations
Not Reckoned among the Nations

And from the hills I behold him: There! A people dwelling alone, not reckoning itself among the nations. *Numbers 23:9*

The Gentile seer, Balaam had been hired by the King of Moab to curse the 'camp' of the Israelites as they journeyed to the Promised Land. But Balaam exclaimed to the king that he could not curse Israel since he could not curse what God had not cursed (Numbers 23:8), and that there is no sorcery against Jacob or divination against Israel. (Numbers 23:23) He went on in his fourth prophetic oracle to prophecy the appearance of a ruler, Messiah, a star from the midst of Israel. (Numbers 24:17) A star indeed appeared shining brightly in the sky at the birth of Yeshua, and was seen among the nations. (Matthew 2:1–12) Seeing the star, Magi came from the East and worshipped Him.

Whilst Israel wandered in the wilderness, the Lord taught them about their unique destiny: to bring forth the Messiah and to be victorious in the midst of their enemies. (Numbers 24:15–19) Moses taught them that they were to be separate from the nations, set apart and holy, belonging to God (Exodus 33:16, Leviticus 20:26), God's 'special treasure', His 'treasured possession'. (Exodus 19:5, 6, Psalm 135:4, Deuteronomy 7:6, 14:2, 26:18)

Yeshua, God's Servant came to 'restore the preserved ones of Israel' and also to be a light to all the Gentiles. (Isaiah 49:3–6) In the temple, Simeon beheld the infant Yeshua and worshipped God saying, "My eyes have seen Your salvation which you have prepared before all peoples, A light to bring revelation to the Gentiles and the glory of Your people Israel". (Luke 2:30–32) The Messiah of Israel is Israel's glory and a light to the nations.

Consider the work of Yeshua – restoring Israel and bringing forth His Bride from the nations.

Readings: Numbers 23, 24, Isaiah 49, Luke 2:25–38, 1 Peter 2:9, 10

8th Day of the 2nd Month
Ziv – also called Iyar, usually falling in April/May
Israel and the Nations
Ishmael and Isaac

Then God said: 'No, Sarah your wife shall bear you a son, and you shall call his name Isaac; I will establish My covenant with him for an everlasting covenant, and with his descendants after him.'

Genesis 17:19

The story of the birth of Abraham's son Isaac is a picture for us of how to obtain the salvation of our souls. Abraham's wife Sarah was unable to have children, but God had promised them countless descendants. As the years passed and Sarah grew old, she gave up faith and hope in having children herself, and tried to 'make it happen' by her own means, apart from trusting God, by giving her slave girl Hagar to Abraham to try and obtain a son.

Hagar bore Abraham a son, named Ishmael. But God said the promise would come to pass through the son born to Abraham's wife, Sarah. Finally, miraculously in her old age, after the Lord had met with Abraham, Sarah had a son, Isaac. Isaac became the father of Jacob, and Jacob was renamed Israel, and from his descendants Yeshua was born.

The 'slave girl' Hagar is a picture for us of the Covenant of the Law given to Moses at Mount Sinai. This covenant highlights our 'slavery' to sin and our inability to perfectly keep God's laws through our own 'works'. But God has a better covenant for us, one born by the faith of the 'free woman', the wife. The Bride of Yeshua is freed from sin and its penalty, by faith in the New Covenant forgiveness of sins. Only belief and trust in the righteous sacrifice of Yeshua will set us free from 'bondage' to sin and give us the 'freedom' to receive God's gift of His righteousness. We have a choice – to live an Ishmael life of our own making, or an Isaac life of dependency on God for our righteousness through faith in Him.

Meditate on what it means, like Abraham, to 'cast out' Ishmael and live by faith in God.

Readings: Genesis 12:1–3, Genesis 15 – 18:15, Genesis 21, 22, Galatians 4:21–31

9th Day of the 2nd Month
Ziv – also called Iyar, usually falling in April/May
Israel and the Nations
Law and Grace

I do not set aside the grace of God; for if righteousness comes through the law, then Christ died in vain. *Galatians 2:21*

The Covenant of the Law given to Moses at Sinai serves two purposes. Firstly, it convicts us, showing that we have all broken God's holy standards. It legally proves that 'all have sinned and fall short of the glory of God'. (Romans 3:23) Secondly, it teaches that to be reconciled to God and have our sins forgiven, a perfect payment is needed. The life blood of animal sacrifices could never take away sin once and for all. We need the perfect sacrifice of a substitute, a perfect human being to take the death penalty that we deserve, in our place.

The only sinless human being who has ever lived is Yeshua, the Son of God. Yeshua perfectly kept and perfectly fulfilled the Law of God. He said, "Do not think that I came to destroy the Law and the Prophets. I did not come to destroy but to fulfil...." (Matthew 5:17) His shed blood is the perfect sacrifice of the New Covenant, which takes away our sins, cleanses us and makes us righteous in God's sight, when we put our faith and trust in Him.

The Law is good and serves a purpose, but that purpose is always to lead us to God's grace. In our pride we would think we are able to make ourselves righteous. But when we have humility and brokenness we know that we need another, more perfect than ourselves. We need the spotless Lamb of God who takes away the sins of the world. His grace will change us from the inside out, but only when we come to Him in our brokenness, repentance and dependence on Him. When pride gets in the way we try to prove our own righteousness to God. But God welcomes all who repent and know that without Him they are lost sinners.

Deep in your heart do you strive to prove your righteousness or do you receive His grace?

Readings: Matthew 5:17–20, Romans 4:13 – 8:17, Galatians 5:13–18

10th Day of the 2nd Month
Ziv – also called Iyar, usually falling in April/May
Israel and the Nations
Circumcised Heart

For in Christ Jesus neither circumcision nor uncircumcision avails anything, but faith working through love. *Galatians 5:6*

In the Early Church the majority of believers in Yeshua were Jewish, and the males would have been circumcised at eight days of age according to God's covenant with Abraham. For them there was no conflict between being a circumcised Jew and being a follower of Yeshua. But then as time passed more and more Gentiles became saved and joined what was perceived at that time to be a sect of the Jews. The question arose for them as to whether Gentiles should be circumcised like their Jewish brethren who had been circumcised as infants.

The clear answer in Paul's letter to the Galatians is 'no'! Gentile believers do not have to become circumcised on conversion to Yeshua. Here is the principle of the natural preceding the spiritual. (1 Corinthians 15:46) First we have a natural body, but in the resurrection we will have a spiritual body. The first Adam gave birth to the natural human race. The second Adam, Yeshua, brought us new birth. The natural came before the spiritual. So it is with circumcision. It was the sign of God's covenant with Abraham, of belonging to the natural family of Israel. Now, on entry to God's spiritual kingdom, the sign of the 'natural' Israel is not necessary. Only the sign of the 'spiritual' kingdom is necessary. The spiritual sign is the circumcision of the heart.

In the natural the 'physical flesh' is cut away. In the spiritual the 'soulish flesh' is cut away. These are the vices listed in Galatians 5:19–21. God must cut them out of our hearts.

Read Galatians 5:16–26 and examine your heart. Crucify the flesh and live by the Spirit.

Readings: Genesis 17:9–27, Deuteronomy 30:1–6, Romans 2:25 – 4:12

11th Day of the 2nd Month
Ziv – also called Iyar, usually falling in April/May
Israel and the Nations
All One in Yeshua

There is neither Jew nor Greek, there is neither slave nor free, there is neither male nor female; for you are all one in Christ Jesus.

Galatians 3:28

Jewish followers of Yeshua and Gentile followers of Yeshua are all one in the kingdom of God. Natural differences are transcended. Externals such as male and female, slave and free, Jew and Gentile, though integral to our natural identity are not important in our spiritual identity. What matters in the kingdom of God is our identification with Yeshua. He looks for humble, faith-filled hearts where He can dwell.

Before Yeshua brought the spiritual kingdom of God and His Kingship to our hearts, the realm of the natural was most important. Our whole identity was wrapped up in our 'natural' self. But when we are born again by the Spirit, we become spiritually alive. We no longer simply know people according to the natural, but according to the spiritual. The Lord told Samuel "...the LORD does not see as man sees, for man looks at the outward appearance, but the LORD looks at the heart." (1 Samuel 16:7) God regards the spirit, through the Spirit.

Entry to the kingdom of God is by one door, Yeshua. He is the same door – for both Jews and Gentiles, men and women, slaves and free. There is no room for either pride or inferiority in the company of others. Instead we are to 'in lowliness of mind let each esteem others better than himself.' (Philippians 2:3) The dividing wall of hostility, which kept Gentiles out of the Jewish temple, has gone. The kingdom of God and the Messiah is now available to all who simply look to Yeshua for salvation. (Isaiah 45:22) Believing Gentiles become spiritually one with believing Jews to form 'One New Man'. (Ephesians 2:15)

Does your sense of who you are come from your natural 'status' or abiding in Christ and from the assurance given by the promises of God in His Word and the work of the Holy Spirit?

Readings: Ephesians 2, 3, Galatians 3, 1 Corinthians 12:12–31

12th Day of the 2nd Month
Ziv – also called Iyar, usually falling in April/May
Israel and the Nations
God's Appointed Times

And the LORD spoke to Moses, saying, "Speak to the children of Israel, and say to them: 'The feasts of the LORD which you shall proclaim to be holy convocations, these are My feasts....'" *Leviticus 23:1, 2*

The word translated 'feast' is the Hebrew word 'moed', which means 'appointed time'. The 'feasts' of Israel are God's –'appointed times' when God meets especially with His people. They are the specific times of spiritual blessing and God's activity in the earth as we take time to meet with Him. Of course we can always draw near to God, but these are special times that God has ordained for meeting with Him. These times were not arranged by man, but were commanded by God through Moses, most particularly in Leviticus 23. They are specific to Israel but now Gentile believers who have been 'grafted in' to the 'Jewish root' of the olive tree can also be blessed through their meeting with God on these days too.

The 'moedim' – 'appointed times' occur over a seven-month period beginning with Passover and ending with tabernacles. There are seven 'moedim' and they can be divided into two main groups – spring and autumn. Yeshua fulfilled the symbolism of the spring 'moedim' on their exact days. The autumn 'moedim' can be seen to represent the end-times and Yeshua's second coming. The multi-dimensional symbolism of the 'moedim' points to God's perfect plan of redemption, that He may receive His Bride and Israel may be restored.

There is great blessing in aligning with God's 'appointed times'. Through them we have a picture of God's perfect plan of redemption in the first and second comings of Messiah and a picture of His plan for His kingdom before and after His return.

Consider how God's 'appointed times' bring us into alignment with His eternal plan.

Readings: Leviticus 23, Numbers 28, 29, Deuteronomy 16, Ezekiel 45–48

IYAR

13th Day of the 2nd Month
Ziv – also called Iyar, usually falling in April/May
Israel and the Nations
Sons of Zion, Sons of Greece

For I have bent Judah, My bow, fitted the bow with Ephraim, and raised up your sons, O Zion, against your sons, O Greece, and made you like the sword of a mighty man. *Zechariah 9:13*

This verse describes the conflict between two opposing forces represented by the sons of Zion and the sons of Greece. Yeshua will return to defend the sons of Zion, save them and restore double to them. (Zechariah 9:10–17) He came to set the captives free.

This conflict was foreseen in the visions of Daniel and the words of the Angel Gabriel, concerning the 'time of the end'. (Daniel 8:17, 10:14, 11:40) Daniel wrote of 'appointed times', for future events. (11:27, 29, 35) He foresaw the rise of the kingdom of Greece, the rise of Alexander the Great (356–323 BC) and the rise of Antiochus Epiphanes (186 BC) (Greek for 'god manifest') who ruled the Seleucid Empire – a remnant of Alexander the Great's world kingdom. (Daniel 8:8–14 and Daniel 11) These events 'foreshadowed' end-time events, which will culminate in the appearance of the evil and blasphemous 'king' (Daniel 11:36–39), the invasion of the Land, and Jacob's Trouble. (Daniel 11:40 – 12:1)

The Greek world empire was one of the 'world powers' depicted in Daniel's vision of the 'beasts'. (Daniel 7) The Hellenistic (Greek) world-view and culture spread through the ancient world and encroached upon Jewish culture and religion. The Epicurean philosophy that pleasure was the chief goal of life was in total opposition to the morality set forth in the Hebrew Scriptures, and it enticed many people. Two world-views were in opposition – a 'man-centred (humanistic) existence' versus the 'God-centred' Hebraic world-view. Yeshua will return to defend and save the sons of Zion. (Daniel 12:1–3, Zechariah 9:10–17)

Ask God to help you identify what is born from 'Greece' and what is born from 'Zion'.

Readings: Zechariah 9:11–17, Daniel 8, Habakkuk 3, Isaiah 8:11 – 9:7, Matthew 24:30, 31

14th Day of the 2nd Month
Ziv – also called Iyar, usually falling in April/May
The Second Passover
A Second Chance

Then the LORD spoke to Moses, saying, "Speak to the children of Israel, saying: 'If anyone of you or your posterity is unclean because of a corpse, or is far away on a journey, he may still keep the LORD's Passover. On the fourteenth day of the second month, at twilight, they may keep it...' *Numbers 9:9–11*

On this day, the Israelites who were unable to keep Passover in the first month, either because they were away on a journey, or because they were defiled by touching a corpse, were given a second chance to partake of the Passover Meal. King Hezekiah and his people kept the Passover on this day when they had completed their cleansing of the temple. (2 Chronicles 30:2) The temple and the priests had to be ritually clean in order to perform the Passover sacrifice. Anyone who had touched a corpse in the days preceding Passover was rendered unclean by God's Law and unable to partake of the Passover.

When Yeshua died, His body was placed in a tomb at Passover. The High Priest Caiaphas and his servants had been reluctant to condemn Yeshua to death at Passover because they needed to be ritually clean in order to 'eat the Passover'. (John 18:28) But Yeshua's body did not defile anybody. He is the Passover sacrifice, through whom we are sanctified and made holy. We are not sanctified 'in order' to receive Yeshua, but after. We cannot make ourselves 'clean' for Passover. We come to Yeshua, the Passover Lamb, as we are and He makes us 'clean' and purifies us from all sin. We have all been on a 'journey' away from God, and we have all touched 'death' and 'defilement' through our sin. But He invites us to 'draw near' to Him (Matthew 11:28) to come to Him like the prodigal son who returned to his father from a distant land. He will not refuse anyone. (Luke 15:11–24)

When you feel 'unclean' or 'away from God', return quickly to your Father who loves you.

Readings: Numbers 9:1–14, Luke 15:11–24, 1 Corinthians 11:23–34, 2 Chronicles 30

15th Day of the 2nd Month
Ziv – also called Iyar, usually falling in April/May
Testing in the Wilderness
Israel Entered the Wilderness

And they journeyed from Elim, and all the congregation of the children of Israel came to the Wilderness of Sin, which is between Elim and Sinai, on the fifteenth day of the second month after they departed from the land of Egypt. *Exodus 16:1*

On this day, the children of Israel entered the wilderness. They departed Egypt at Passover, crossed the Red Sea, and journeyed on to Elim – the place of twelve wells and seventy palm trees. There they camped, received physical refreshment and fresh hope before entering the next phase of their journey to the Promised Land. Elim was a picture of God's grace and the rest that we find in Him and in His kingdom.

The actual distance between Elim and the Promised Land was not great. The children of Israel could have arrived in probably less than a month. But they needed to pass through the wilderness on the way because God had many things to teach them. If they had entered the Land immediately, they might have been destroyed by their enemies. When the nation of Israel crossed the Red Sea, they were 'baptised' into Moses. (1 Corinthians 10:1, 2) In the wilderness they would learn through Moses, and through their trials and temptations, that their hearts were sinful, unbelieving and rebellious against God. Similarly, we need to be convicted by the truth of God's Law and His holy standard before we can appreciate and enter into the true riches of His mercy and grace.

Israel spent forty years being tested in the wilderness. Of the generation that left Egypt, only two out of the original 600,000, Joshua and Caleb, actually entered the Land. Joshua and Caleb entered the Promised Land because they had faith in God.

Have you experienced wilderness wanderings? What do you need to bring you through?

Readings: Exodus 15 – 16:1, Numbers 14:26–38, Mark 1:12, 13, Hebrews 12:1–11

16th Day of the 2nd Month
Ziv – also called Iyar, usually falling in April/May
Testing in the Wilderness
God Calls Us into the Wilderness

Who is this coming up from the wilderness, leaning upon her beloved?
Song of Songs 8:5

In the Song of Songs the Shulamite grows in her relationship with her bridegroom and her love matures and changes over time. In the final chapter where she has grown to maturity and the ability to express selfless love, she comes 'up from the wilderness, leaning on her beloved'. (Song of Songs 8:5) Clearly her time in the wilderness has brought her to the place where she no longer pursues her own interests or relies on her own labours and resources. Now she leans totally on the Lord and depends on Him. She has learnt from her wanderings in the wilderness and now she walks leaning on Him, on her beloved.

In the first chapter she prayed the prayer we can all pray: 'Draw me away! We will run after you!' (Song of Songs 1:4) She submitted herself to His leadership in her life, to take her where He wanted. He brought her face to face with her own disobedience and lack of love, to the place where, wooed by His love, she could let go of all her frantic and zealous working for Him, and concentrate instead on developing her relationship with Him and learn to be intimate with Him, to know Him. Yeshua calls us to be still and quieten our hearts, to draw near to Him in the secret place, and learn to enjoy being close to Him and in His Word.
The disciple John learned to lean on the Lord. (John 13:23) He felt safe in His presence. Psalm 56:8 says, 'You number my wanderings; put my tears into Your bottle; are they not in Your book?' God sees our wanderings and our tears of pain, but He is merciful and He remembers us. We come to a place where we prefer to lean totally on God and submit to His will for our lives. We no longer try to work out everything for ourselves.

What does it mean for you to come up from the wilderness leaning on your beloved?

Readings: Psalm 23, Song of Songs: 1–8, Psalm 56:8–11, James 1:22–25

IYAR

17th Day of the 2nd Month
Ziv – also called Iyar, usually falling in April/May
Testing in the Wilderness
He Humbles and Tests Us

And you shall remember that the LORD your God led you all the way these forty years in the wilderness, to humble you and test you, to know what was in your heart, whether you would keep His commandments or not. *Deuteronomy 8:2*

Crossing the 'Red Sea' was Israel's baptism into the Law of Moses. The children of Israel were led by God into the wilderness to find out what was truly in their hearts. They thought they could obey God's commandments. But God humbled them and tested them. In the wilderness they discovered that their hearts were unbelieving and rebellious.

When we have crossed over the 'Red Sea' of receiving salvation through faith, God continues to test our hearts. We may think we have the strength and willpower to live a good Christian life. But quickly we learn through God's testing, that actually we are totally dependent on the power of the Holy Spirit in us to maintain our relationship with Him and to keep His commandments. God wants us to give Him the whole of our lives, for us to make Yeshua our Lord and master, to take up our cross (surrender to Him), and follow Him. (Matthew 16:24) Yeshua said, "If you love Me, keep My commandments." (John 14:15) In His wilderness dealings God tests us so to know our hearts. God wants to change us, heal us, and make us into people who believe the truth about Him; that He is good, loving and able to do all that He promises, so that we love Him and obey His commandments. His tests reveal where we have roots of sin, bitterness, pride, fear, pain and rebellion. If when we see our hearts, we humble ourselves in repentance and forgiveness, His words will set us free. His words are 'manna', truth about God and ourselves, which sets us free. (John 8:32, 17:17)

What have you learnt about your heart? Humble yourself in repentance and hear His truth.

Readings: Deuteronomy 8:1–5, Matthew 16:24–27, 18:4, John 8:28–36, Psalm 106

18th Day of the 2nd Month
Ziv – also called Iyar, usually falling in April/May
Testing in the Wilderness
He Provides for Us

Your garments did not wear out on you, nor did your foot swell these forty years. *Deuteronomy 8:4*

God provided for the physical needs of the nation of Israel while they were in the wilderness. He provided water out of the rock, manna from heaven and their clothes did not wear out. Their bodies were kept strong and well nourished.

Despite these blessings, the Israelites did not please God because they lusted for more than He had given them. God provided them with enough to not only survive but to be strong. What they didn't have was luxury. There were no new clothes, nor was there a tasty variety of foods. There was nothing to pamper their flesh.

Consequently the people complained and grumbled to God, wanting Him to satisfy their craving for meat. So He sent them quail to eat. But 'while the meat was still between their teeth, before it was chewed, the wrath of the LORD was aroused against the people, and the LORD struck the people with a very great plague.' (Numbers 11:33) The people who yielded to the craving of the flesh died and were buried. The same happened with those who committed sexual immorality. (1 Corinthians 10:1–13)

We are not to complain bitterly when our fleshly desires are not met. We are not to reluctantly remember the pleasures of our former life. Instead we are to learn to 'feed on' Yeshua and find Him as our greatest delight. (John 6:47–51) He says, 'Delight yourself also in the LORD, and He shall give you the desires of your heart.' (Psalm 37:4) The Apostle Paul wrote, 'Now godliness with contentment is great gain.' (1 Timothy 6:6) We are not to pursue earthly pleasures and riches, but seek the true riches of Heaven. (Matthew 6:19, 20)

Have you fully put your trust in God as your provider, your treasure and delight?

Readings: 1 Corinthians 10:1–13, Numbers 11, 1 Timothy 6:6–10, John 6:47–51

IYAR

19th Day of the 2nd Month
Ziv – also called Iyar, usually falling in April/May
Testing in the Wilderness
He Speaks to Us

So the LORD spoke to Moses face to face, as a man speaks to his friend. The wilderness is a place where God speaks to us. The wilderness was the place where the LORD spoke directly with Moses. The word for wilderness in Hebrew is 'Midbar' which also means 'speech'. It is the quiet place where we learn to hear God's voice. *Exodus 33:11*

In the wilderness Israel could hear the voice of God. His voice was not 'drowned out' by Egyptian slave masters and all the 'tasks' of Egypt. In the wilderness there were just miles of sand, rocks and a few small shrubs. It was silent and empty. The 'Tabernacle of God's Presence' was situated in the middle of the camp. This is like us when we lay aside distractions and wait on Him alone in the secret place of our hearts with God at the centre.

Moses was able to hear the voice of God. More than that, we are told that when Moses stood at the door of the tabernacle, the Lord spoke with Moses face to face. He knew the manifest presence of God and had a relationship with him. On the instruction of the Lord, Moses ascended Mount Sinai and there he received the 'Torah' (which means 'Instruction or Teaching') for the nation. The glory of the Lord passed by as Moses stood in the cleft of the rock and Moses was permitted to see His back. (Exodus 33:22, 23)

Now Yeshua takes His Bride into the wilderness so she will learn to recognise His presence and rise up and respond to His voice. She too is hidden 'in the clefts of the rock' to meet with God in the secret place. He says to her, 'Let me see your face, let me hear your voice; for your voice is sweet, and your face is lovely.' (Song of Songs 2:14) He longs to hear your songs and your prayers. Your relationship with God can be like that of Moses.

Consider how He delights in hearing your voice and speaking to you. (Song of Songs 2:14)

Readings: Exodus 33, Numbers 27:15–17, John 10:1–16

20th Day of the 2nd Month
Ziv – also called Iyar, usually falling in April/May
Testing in the Wilderness
He Leads Us

Now it came to pass on the twentieth day of the second month, in the second year, that the cloud was taken up from above the tabernacle of the testimony. And the children of Israel set out from the Wilderness of Sinai on their journeys; then the cloud settled down in the Wilderness of Paran. *Numbers 10:11, 12*

On the day that Moses first raised up the tabernacle (biblical New Year), the cloud of God's presence covered the tent. In the darkness the cloud appeared as fire. Whenever the cloud rose up from the tabernacle, the children of Israel would move to the place where it settled. It was on this day, that the cloud was taken up and moved on, leading the children of Israel to a new place. They lived in tents so that they could keep moving on and not be more loyal to a place than to God. Obedience to His voice and commandments, wherever He takes us, will keep us close to Him.

Yeshua our 'Bridegroom' is like the pillar of cloud. He journeys with us in the wilderness. (1 Corinthians 10:4) In the Song of Songs the Bride thought for a time that she was alone but He was there all the time because He is observed 'coming out of the wilderness like pillars of smoke, perfumed with myrrh and frankincense, with all the merchant's fragrant powders.' (Song of Songs 3:6) His sweet presence is always near. It is us who neglect to draw near. He would have our hearts ready to respond and come away with Him, to spend time with Him any moment He calls. But we quickly feel distanced if we fail to respond.

In our hearts we are to always be willing to move on where He leads and not get stuck in a place of our own choosing. Yeshua goes with us to provide water from the rock.

Are you following the call of Yeshua, to go with Him wherever He leads?

Readings: Numbers 9:15 – 10:36, Song of Songs 2:10, 5:2–13, 7:11, 12, Revelation 3:20, 21

21st Day of the 2nd Month
Ziv – also called Iyar, usually falling in April/May
Testing in the Wilderness
He Heals Us

"If you diligently heed the voice of the LORD your God and do what is right in His sight, give ear to His commandments and keep all His statutes, I will put none of the diseases on you which I have brought on the Egyptians. For I am the LORD who heals you." *Exodus 15:26*

Just three days after the children of Israel had crossed the Red Sea, they had no water apart from some that was so bitter they could not drink it. So the Lord showed Moses a tree and when he cast it into the water it was made sweet and drinkable. (Exodus 15:22–25)

The people were complaining bitterly because they were thirsty. The 'tree' that Moses used to heal the water is a picture of the cross. Yeshua's forgiveness makes our hearts sweet with God's love so that His fresh water can flow through us. We can be freed from the accumulated roots of bitterness and the suppressed pain that came from our wounds, from our not truly forgiving from our heart. When we receive Yeshua's forgiveness and when we forgive those who wounded us, our bitterness is removed and healed. (Isaiah 53:5) Abiding in His love keeps and protects us.

Love for God and love for our neighbour as ourselves brings health to the body, mind and spirit. Keeping His commandment to love protects us. In contrast, hatred is like bitter poison. When Israel complained bitterly against God, snakes bit them. They were cursed. (Genesis 3:14) But when Moses put a bronze snake on a pole, the people looked at it and were healed. (Numbers 21:4–9) Bronze symbolises judgement. Yeshua 'became' sin and took our curse upon Himself, in our place, when He died on the cross. (Galatians 3:13)

Whenever you are in sickness and pain, the cross is there for you to be healed.

Readings: Exodus 15:22–27, Numbers 21:4–9, Galatians 3:13, Psalm 107.

22nd Day of the 2nd Month
Ziv – also called Iyar, usually falling in April/May
Testing in the Wilderness
He Prepares Us

"Now, O Israel, listen to the statutes and the judgements which I teach you to observe, that you may live, and go in and possess the land which the LORD God of your fathers is giving you...." *Deuteronomy 4:1*

The children of Israel had to experience forty years of humbling and testing in the wilderness before they were ready to enter the Promised Land. Similarly the Lord takes us through 'wilderness experiences' to discipline and train us so that we can learn to walk in humility, grace, faith and love, and bring more pleasure to Him. In the Song of Songs, it was only when the beloved had come up from the wilderness, 'leaning on her beloved' (Song of Songs 8:5) that she was really able to help her younger sister, because now she asked for and received direct wisdom from the Lord. (Song of Songs 8:8–14)

God's dealings in our lives through the things we suffer, teach us to obey and respond to the Lord. Only He is able to break our 'self-sufficiency' and independent spirit. Even Yeshua who had no sin learned obedience through the things He suffered. (Hebrews 5:8)

King David spent many years in the wilderness being prepared for kingship by God. Tending the sheep, he became brave and fearless, progressing from killing lions and bears to killing Goliath. In the wilderness he became skilful on the harp, mighty in battle, and humble and godly in his attitude to King Saul.

Israel made many mistakes in the wilderness, but they reached the point where they could enter the Promised Land. God's purpose for their time in the wilderness was complete. 'Weeping may endure for a night, but joy comes in the morning.' (Psalm 30:5)

Ask the Lord to take your 'wilderness experiences' and make something beautiful from them.

Readings: 1 Samuel 17:26–54, Psalm 25, Hebrews 5, 6

IYAR

23rd Day of the 2nd Month
Ziv – also called Iyar, usually falling in April/May
Testing in the Wilderness
He Tests Our Faith

But My servant Caleb, because he has a different spirit in him and has followed Me fully, I will bring him into the land where he went, and his descendants shall inherit it. *Numbers 14:24*

Moses sent 12 men from the tribes of Israel into the Land of Canaan, the Promised Land, to spy out the Land they were to enter and inhabit once their wanderings in the wilderness were over. But of those 12 men, only two, Joshua and Caleb, returned believing that God's promise of conquering the Land was possible. The rest of the spies thought it would be too difficult because they saw the people as giants. The Israelites chose to listen to the bad report of the 10 spies, and subsequently the people all perished in the wilderness because of their unbelief.

Hebrews warns us: 'Brethren, beware, lest there be in any of you an evil heart of unbelief in departing from the living God.' (Hebrews 3:12) The Israelites hardened their hearts in unbelief, not trusting God. They did not really believe in God's goodness and sovereign power and ability to give them victory, or the truth and reliability of His Word. God was looking for hearts that were 'soft' towards Him, believing and trusting in His great love, kindness, faithfulness, compassion and power. Instead they thought the task impossible because of their enemies the Amalakites, Hittites, Jebusites, Amorites and Canaanites.

Joshua and Caleb, the two believing and courageous spies, saw the good things of the Land and said, 'If the Lord delights in us, then He will bring us into this Land and give it to us, a land which flows with milk and honey.' (Numbers 14:8) They believed God's promise. God delighted in their faith and took them into the Land and enabled them to conquer it.

Which is greater, the truth of God's words in Scripture, or the giants that you perceive?

Readings: Numbers 13, 14, Hebrews 3, 4, Isaiah 30:15–18

24th Day of the 2nd Month
Ziv – also called Iyar, usually falling in April/May
Testing in the Wilderness
He Reveals Himself

What is your beloved more than another beloved, O fairest among women? What is your beloved more than another beloved?

Song of Songs 5:9

When Israel was in the wilderness they received a revelation of God that was not given to any other nation. When they went astray it was because they failed to remember the loving kindness the Lord had shown them; how He had taken them like a child by their arms, healing them and drawing them with gentle cords, bands of love, taking the yoke from their neck, stooping and feeding them. (Hosea 11:1–4) They failed to continue in His love.

Now the Lord is calling His Bride of true believers from all nations, to come apart with Him and to receive a special revelation of Him like Israel did in the wilderness. Yeshua promised that the Son will reveal Himself and the Father to all those who seek Him. (Matthew 11:27, Matthew 7:7) He wants us to know Him as the 'lover of our souls'.

In the Song of Songs, the Daughters of Jerusalem – who represent the believers who have never pursued a relationship with Yeshua – ask the Shulamite why her bridegroom is better than anyone else. The Shulamite replies in intimate detail explaining, 'My beloved is white and ruddy, chief among ten thousand. His head is like the finest gold; his locks are wavy, and black as a raven. His eyes are like doves by the rivers of waters, washed with milk, and fitly set. His cheeks are like a bed of spices, banks of scented herbs. His lips are lilies, dripping liquid myrrh....' 'Yes, He is altogether lovely. This is my beloved, and this is my friend, O daughters of Jerusalem!' (Song of Songs 5:10–16) The Bride knows and loves Yeshua because she has drawn close to Him. The wilderness is where we get to know Him.

Do you 'know' Yeshua? Take time to draw near to Him, in His word and prayer.

Readings: Hosea 11:1–4, Song of Songs 5:9–16, Matthew 7:21–23, John 14:8–11

25th Day of the 2nd Month
Ziv – also called Iyar, usually falling in April/May
The 40th Sheaf Gathered In
Yeshua is 'taken up' to Heaven

He also presented alive after His suffering by many infallible proofs, being seen by them during forty days and speaking of the things pertaining to the kingdom of God. *Acts 1:3*

Today is the fortieth day since Yeshua rose from the dead on the 'Feast of First Fruits'. On this day, forty days after His resurrection, our risen Lord was physically 'taken up' away from the disciples into Heaven in a cloud, like the first sheaf of the barley harvest which is 'taken up' from its field and offered as a wave offering to the Lord.

Forty is the number for testing. (Hebrews 3:9) For forty days Israel saw and tested the infallible proofs of Yeshua's resurrection. (Acts 1:3, 1 Corinthians 15:3–8) The infallible proofs convinced many Jews of the fact of the resurrection, but the Jewish nation as a whole still chose to reject the 'risen' Messiah. Yeshua's disciples wondered before He departed if He was about to 'restore the kingdom to Israel'. (Acts 1:6) But He told them that it was not for them to know the times and seasons. Only the Father knows when, by His own authority.

Yeshua came to earth to receive a harvest and a kingdom from all nations. The disciples needed to wait in Jerusalem until they had received the Holy Spirit. Then they would be empowered to go out from Jerusalem as His witnesses into all the earth, to gather in the rest of the harvest of souls into the kingdom of God. Yeshua promised His disciples that just as He was taken up from them, so too He would return to His people. He had prophesied through Hosea: 'I will return again to My place till they acknowledge their offense. Then they will seek My face; in their affliction they will earnestly seek Me.' (Hosea 5:15) The day is coming when Israel will acknowledge their offence, that they rejected their Messiah.

Ask God to help you to never 'miss' how God is fulfilling prophetic scripture in your day.

Readings: Acts 1:1–14, Hosea 5:10 – 6:3, Luke 24:44–53, Mark 16:14–20

26th Day of the 2nd Month
Ziv – also called Iyar, usually falling in April/May
10 Days Waiting in Jerusalem
Wait for Baptism in the Holy Spirit

And being assembled together with them, He commanded them not to depart from Jerusalem, but to wait for the Promise of the Father, "which," He said "you have heard from Me; for John truly baptised with water, but you shall be baptised with the Holy Spirit not many days from now." *Acts 1:4, 5*

Before His ascension to Heaven, Yeshua instructed His disciples to wait in Jerusalem until they received the Baptism in the Holy Spirit. John the Baptist had prophesied the baptism given by Yeshua, saying, "...I indeed baptised you with water, but He will baptise you with the Holy Spirit." (Mark 1:8) The disciples followed Yeshua's instruction and waited in Jerusalem until they received the Holy Spirit on the 'Feast of Shavuot', ten days later.

Baptism by John the Baptiser had been by total immersion in flowing water. (Leviticus 22:6) The Jewish custom at the time, and today also, was total immersion in a pool of flowing water, a 'mikveh' for ritual cleansing. At the preaching of John the Baptiser, many Jewish people repented of their failure to keep the Law of God and re-dedicated their lives back to Him. This prepared them to receive Yeshua, who alone can cleanse us from sin.

The Hebrew word for baptism, 'hatbalah', is found in Exodus 12:22, Leviticus 4:16, 17, and Leviticus 14:6, 16, 51, when the priest 'immersed' his finger or some hyssop in the blood of the sacrifice for ritual cleansing. Now we are to be immersed and filled with the life of Yeshua through the Holy Spirit. The blood of Yeshua 'cleanses' us from sin when we are 'baptised' into His death for cleansing, and we 'die' to our 'self-life'. We rise to new life in the Spirit, cleansed and empowered on the inside, to live with and for God.

Consider the fact that we need two baptisms, immersion in water and in the Holy Spirit.

Readings: Mark 1:1–11, Leviticus 14:1–9, Romans 6, Ezekiel 36:24–30, Psalm 42:7

27th Day of the 2nd Month
Ziv – also called Iyar, usually falling in April/May
10 Days Waiting in Jerusalem
Prayer in One Accord

These all continued with one accord in prayer and supplication, with
the women and Mary the mother of Jesus, and with His brothers.

Acts 1:14

Yeshua's disciples gathered together where they were staying in Jerusalem,
in the upper room of a house, together with the women and Yeshua's
mother and brothers. They continued in prayer and supplication in one
accord, waiting for the gift of the Holy Spirit. They had unity in their
thoughts, prayers and actions. Previous disputes and conflicts over who
would be greatest in Yeshua's kingdom had passed away. (Mark 9:34)

They did not wait passively. They were in prayer and supplication.
Yeshua had taught that we are to ask Him for the Holy Spirit, because
our loving heavenly Father 'gives the Holy Spirit to those who ask Him.'
(Luke 11:13) Their prayers were important for receiving the Holy Spirit,
but so was their unity. Psalm 133 promises God's blessing where brothers
dwell in unity – His blessing is poured down like the precious anointing
oil on the head of Aaron the High Priest. It comes down from the head,
the heavenly High Priest Yeshua, in heaven, on His body, the Church on
earth. The Holy Spirit cannot bless division, warring and strife.

The Apostle Paul exhorted the Philippians, 'If there is any consolation
in Christ, if any comfort of love, if any fellowship of the Spirit, if any
affection and mercy, fulfil my joy by being like-minded, having the same
love, being of one accord, of one mind. Let nothing be done through
selfish ambition or conceit, but in lowliness of mind let each esteem
others better than himself.' (Philippians 2:1–3)

*Meditate on Philippians 2:1–3. Do you pursue this type of accord with
fellow believers?*

Readings: Acts 1:12–26, Matthew 18:19, 20, Luke 11:5–13, Psalm 133

28th Day of the 2nd Month
Ziv – also called Iyar, usually falling in April/May
Jerusalem Day
Unified Jerusalem

Pray for the peace of Jerusalem: "May they prosper who love you. Peace be within your walls, prosperity within your palaces."

Psalm 122:6, 7

Today is Jerusalem Day, the day when the modern Jewish State of Israel recalls the re-unification of Jerusalem on this day, in June 1967. This was the culmination of the Six Day War when the Israelis took back the eastern part of Jerusalem from the Jordanians, who had taken it during the 1948 War of Independence, after the end of the British Mandate.

Jerusalem has been the capital city of the Jewish people for over 3000 years (2 Samuel 5:7) even though it has been destroyed, conquered and trampled by different empires and peoples for over 2000 years. Yeshua prophesied the trampling of Jerusalem by Gentiles – until 'the times of the Gentiles are fulfilled'. (Luke 21:24) In 1967 Jerusalem came completely under Jewish rule, signalling the dawn of a significant fulfilment of prophecy.

The nations still resist treating Jerusalem as the capital city of Israel by refusing to put their embassies there. But we know that God has an allotted time to fulfil Zechariah 14. The 'fiery' 'governors of Judah' (Zechariah 12:1–7) are probably the Knesset, as the nations try to divide Jerusalem in a man-made attempt to create a (false) 'peace'. (Ezekiel 13:10–16)

The Hebrew name for Jerusalem, pronounced 'Yerushalayim' or 'Yerushalem' contains within it the root letters of the Hebrew word 'shalom' meaning 'peace'. Strong's Concordance suggests that the name means 'founded peaceful' and that the former part of the name comes from the root word 'yara' which means to throw an arrow or flow like a river. The words 'Torah' (Law, Instruction) and 'Moreh' (Teacher) also come from this root word.

Reflect on and respond to the command in Psalm 122 to 'pray for the peace of Jerusalem'.

Readings: Psalm 122, Isaiah 2:2–3, Psalm 137, Psalm 48, Zechariah 12–14, Revelation 21

29th Day of the 2nd Month
Ziv – also called Iyar, usually falling in April/May
Jerusalem
Melchizedek, King of Salem

Melchizedek, King of Salem, brought out bread and wine; he was the priest of God Most High. *Genesis 14:18*

Abraham pursued and defeated Chedorloamer and three other evil kings in order to rescue his nephew Lot whom they had taken captive. Then he returned to the 'King's Valley' where he was met by Melchizedek, King of 'Salem' – 'Shalem' in Hebrew. The name of this good king means 'King of Righteousness'. The Hebrew word 'shalem' means peaceful and perfected. It contains the notion that a payment has been made to create peace.

Melchizedek, the King of Righteousness and the King of Peace, brought to Abraham bread and the wine, which became through Yeshua, the symbols of the New Covenant. Melchizedek also received Abraham's tithe as a Priest would. This was before the Law of Moses was given, in which a man could not be a King and a Priest. But this man was both King and Priest. (Hebrews 7) Melchizedek, the King of 'Shalem' represents Yeshua our High Priest and King who paid the ultimate payment in Jerusalem, through the New Covenant, to redeem man back to God, and defeat Satan, who has taken captive men's hearts. Psalm 110 is a prophecy about Yeshua, our King and Priest after the order of Melchizedek. (Matthew 22:41–46) Psalm 110:1, 2 prophesy His first coming and verses 3–7 His second coming. This is explained further in Hebrews 5 – 7. In Jerusalem our Righteous King made the ultimate priestly sacrifice in order to purchase 'peace' between God and man so that His kingdom can come. He will come again to judge the earth and rule over the nations, in righteousness and peace, from Jerusalem. (Isaiah 2:1–4, Zechariah 14:9)

Meditate on the kingship of Yeshua shown in Psalm 110. Worship Him as Priest and King.

Readings: Genesis 14, Psalm 110, Matthew 22:41–46, Revelation 5

1st Day of the 3rd Month
Sivan, usually falling in May/June
Jerusalem
The City of David

I have chosen Jerusalem, that My name may be there, and I have chosen David to be over My people Israel. *2 Chronicles 6:6*

Today is the first day of the third lunar month. The first day of a month is called in Hebrew 'Rosh Hodesh' (Head of the Month). The word 'hodesh' (month) is related to the word 'hadash', meaning 'new, rebuild', after the appearance of the new moon. God gives 'new beginnings' but He also faithfully keeps His everlasting promises. (Jeremiah 31:35–37) God chose Jerusalem to be the place where His name would dwell forever, fulfilling Deuteronomy 12:5, and He chose David to be His king to reign over Israel from Jerusalem. Before he was king, David customarily feasted at King Saul's table at the time of the new moon feast. (1 Samuel 20:5) But it would be from David's seed that God would bring forth a heavenly King. God said, 'I will set up your seed after you, who will be of your sons; and I will establish his throne forever' '...And I will establish him in My house, and in My kingdom forever, and his throne shall be established forever.' (1 Chronicles 17:10b–14)

Yeshua was born in Bethlehem, the ancestral home of King David, of which it was prophesied: 'Out of you shall come forth to Me the One to be Ruler in Israel.' (Micah 5:2, Matthew 2:6) Not everyone would immediately recognise Yeshua as King, but David composed the prophetic Psalm about Yeshua being His Lord, even before He came. (Psalm 110:1, Matthew 22:41–46) King David's love and tears for Saul, Jonathan and Mephibosheth abide as a picture for us of Yeshua's undying love for the Jews and Jerusalem. (2 Samuel 1:17–27, 9:13, Luke 19:41, 42) King David established his throne in Jerusalem.

Meditate on the fact that Yeshua is established King on the Jewish throne of King David.

Readings: 2 Samuel 7, Isaiah 11:1–5, Revelation 3:7, 5:5, 22:16

SIVAN

2nd Day of the 3rd Month
Sivan, usually falling in May/June
Jerusalem
His Dwelling Place

For the LORD has chosen Zion; He has desired it for His dwelling place: "This is My resting place forever; here I will dwell, for I have desired it." *Psalm 132:13, 14*

The specific place of God's presence among the children of Israel was the 'Cloud of His Presence', which rested above the Ark of the Covenant. This was concealed within the Holy of Holies section of the tabernacle, sometimes called in Hebrew the 'mishcan' from the root word 'to dwell'. This was the place where His name dwelt. (Deuteronomy 14:23) The tabernacle went with Israel through the wilderness, and into the Promised Land.

When Saul was king in Israel the Ark of the Covenant was abandoned. (1 Samuel 6, 7) King David received the news that the Ark was to be found in woodland at Kirjath Jearim, so he brought it back with much joy to Mount Zion. (Psalm 132, 2 Samuel 6, 7) There King David established worship with musical instruments. David's tabernacle foreshadows the second coming of Yeshua when Zion will be His dwelling place. (Joel 3:17, 21, Amos 9:11)

King David's son Solomon built the glorious temple in Jerusalem to be the 'house' where God could put His 'name' (1 Chronicles 22:10, 2 Samuel 7) and the glory of God's presence 'dwelt' there until the glory of God's presence departed (1 Kings 8:29, 9:3, 2 Chronicles 7:14, Ezekiel 11:23), and both the First and the Second Temple were destroyed.

Now the temple for our worship is our hearts, as we worship Him, 'in spirit and truth'. (John 4:3–24, Galatians 4:26) But a day is coming when Yeshua will return again to Jerusalem, (Isaiah 4:4, Ezekiel 43:1–7) and in that day, Jerusalem will be the place of His throne and He will 'dwell in the midst of the children of Israel forever.' (Ezekiel 43:7)

How can you worship God in 'spirit and truth' and provide a dwelling place for Him?

Readings: Psalm 132, 2 Samuel 6, John 4:3–26, Galatians 4:26, Ezekiel 43:1–7, Amos 9:11

3rd Day of the 3rd Month
Sivan, usually falling in May/June
Jerusalem
The Messiah's Kingdom

Now it shall come to pass in the latter days that the mountain of the LORD's house shall be established on the tops of the mountains and shall be exalted above the hills; and all nations shall flow to it.

Isaiah 2:2

Isaiah 2:2–4 describes the kingdom of Messiah, which will be established on the earth by Yeshua when He returns. His kingdom will be established on the mountain of the LORD's house. The mountain of the LORD's house is where the temple once stood and where the 'Temple Mount' remains situated in Jerusalem today. King Solomon built the temple on Mount Moriah, on the land purchased by his father David from Ornan the Jebusite. (2 Chronicles 3:1) Many years earlier, Abraham had offered his son Isaac to God, in the same 'land of Moriah' (Genesis 22:2), and since the term 'land of Moriah' indicates a larger area, it is probable that the place where Yeshua became our sacrifice for sin was also in the 'land of Moriah'.

Mountains in Scripture represent kingship, authority, government and power. In Psalm 2 the Father speaks of the kingship of Messiah, His Son, in His coming kingdom, saying, 'I have set My King on My holy hill of Zion.' (Psalm 2:6) Mount Zion is a mountain in the land of Moriah where King David had his throne and seat of government in Jerusalem. Satan will be 'bound' during Messiah's kingdom reign. (Isaiah 11:1–9, Revelation 20:2–4) Messiah's kingdom is described in Daniel as being like a stone, not cut by human hands, which will strike down all previous human empires and become a great mountain, which will fill the earth. (Daniel 2:35, 44) Yeshua will return and bring true peace to the whole earth from Jerusalem and His rule and reign is described in Psalm 72:1–19.

Since for now, the kingdom exists in our hearts, how can we demonstrate His kingdom?

Readings: Isaiah 2:2–4, Daniel 2, 7, Psalm 72, Matthew 5:1–12, Hebrews 12:22–29

SIVAN

4th Day of the 3rd Month
Sivan, usually falling in May/June
Jerusalem
A Cup of Trembling

"Behold, I will make Jerusalem a cup of drunkenness to all the surrounding peoples, when they lay siege against Judah and Jerusalem..." *Zechariah 12:2*

Any nation which lays siege and comes against the Jews and Jerusalem will stagger and reel with trembling as though intoxicated. The nations which try to divide the Holy Land and city will be judged by God. (Joel 3:1–3) He will make Jerusalem 'a very heavy stone for all peoples; all who would heave it away will surely be cut in pieces, though all nations of the earth are gathered against it.' (Zechariah 12:3) The nations will not prevail against Jerusalem in the end times because it is God's city and He will judge them for their actions.

Isaiah prophesied a time when God says to Jerusalem, 'See, I have taken out of your hand the cup of trembling, the dregs of the cup of My fury: You shall no longer drink it. But I will put it into the hand of those who afflict you.' (Isaiah 51:22, 23) Jerusalem will no longer be under the judgement of God for missing 'the time of their visitation' (Luke 19:44), but those who oppose the capital city of Israel will come under His judgement instead.

The repeated destructions of Jerusalem over the millennia by Gentile nations were the outworking of God's curse brought about by Israel's unfaithfulness. (Deuteronomy 28) But now that Israel is back in the Land, His righteous judgements are beginning to fall upon the Gentiles who trample Jerusalem and fail to recognise His plan for her. (Isaiah 51:23) Yeshua will see that Jerusalem is rebuilt and her opposition scattered (Zechariah 1, 2) because He Himself will dwell in Zion. (Joel 3:17) The opposing world systems and powers will 'drink the cup' of the wine of the wrath of God. (Revelation 14:10, 15:7, 16:1, 19, 18:3)

Consider the seriousness of this message and the need to warn people so they understand.

Readings: Zechariah 1, 2, 12:1–3, Joel 3, Isaiah 51, Revelation 14–18

5th Day of the 3rd Month
Sivan, usually falling in May/June
Jerusalem
A City Not Forsaken

And you shall be called Sought Out, A City Not Forsaken.

Isaiah 62:12

The city of Jerusalem was forsaken for centuries. The writer Mark Twain visited in 1867, and described the desolation of the land, devoid of vegetation and human population. Isaiah prophesied of Zion, 'You shall no longer be termed Forsaken, nor shall your land any more be termed Desolate; But you shall be called Hephzibah (My love in her) and your land Beulah'. [Married] (Isaiah 62:4) The Jewish people are 'married' to Zion by God's Covenant.

First, the Jewish people were 'betrothed' to God at Mount Sinai. God was like a husband to them and they were the consenting wife when they agreed to obey God's laws. (Jeremiah 31:32) When they broke the covenant with God, broke His laws, and rejected their Messiah, God cast them away from the Land, leaving it desolate. Jerusalem was like a forsaken wife, bereft of her people. But now God is calling His people back to the Land saying, 'Return, O backsliding children' 'for I am married to you. I will take you, one from a city and two from a family, and I will bring you to Zion.' (Jeremiah 3:14)

Israel is like an 'adulterous wife' to God. But Hosea shows us how God desires to draw her back to Himself. (Hosea 3) God says He will bring His people into the New Covenant. He said, 'I will put My law in their minds and write it on their hearts; and I will be their God and they shall be My people.' (Jeremiah 31:33) Then Jerusalem shall be called 'The Throne of the Lord' (Jeremiah 3:17). God's glory over Zion will be like a wedding canopy. (Isaiah 4:4, 5) He will not leave Zion desolate. Yeshua will return to be united with His Bride from the nations, and Jerusalem will be 'a praise' in the earth. (Isaiah 62:7)

Consider becoming a 'watchman' for Jerusalem (Isaiah 62:6, 7) to bring God praise.

Readings: Isaiah 62, Hosea 3, Isaiah 54, Isaiah 4:3–6

6th Day of the 3rd Month
Sivan, usually falling in May/June
The Feast of Weeks – 'Shavuot'
Firstfruits of the Wheat Harvest

> Count fifty days to the day after the seventh Sabbath; then you shall offer a new grain offering to the LORD. You shall bring from your dwellings two wave loaves of two-tenths of an ephah. They shall be of fine flour, they shall be baked with leaven. They are the firstfruits to the LORD. *Leviticus 23:16, 17*

Seven weeks of seven days have passed since Yeshua was raised from the dead on the 'Feast of Firstfruits', the day when the first sheaf of the barley harvest was offered up to God. Yeshua, the 'firstfruits' of the resurrection guarantees the resurrection from the dead. Seven Sabbaths have now passed and we have come to the 'Feast of Weeks' also known as the 'Feast of Firstfruits', the firstfruits of the later wheat harvest. On this day, the 50th day, 'Pentecost', the disciples who had waited in Jerusalem to receive the Holy Spirit as Yeshua commanded them, received the Baptism in the Holy Spirit and the Church was born. (Acts 2)

The Law of Moses commanded that on the 'Feast of Shavuot' two loaves of fine flour be waved before the Lord. Bread represents life for our mortal bodies. The loaves are white to represent righteousness. We have eaten the unleavened bread of Yeshua – the bread without leaven – without sin. Now we present ourselves to God as sons of God made righteous, filled with the new leaven of the Holy Spirit in us. We are offered to the Father 'leavened' with the new righteous nature of Yeshua, two loaves, One New Man in Messiah.

To manifest this new nature in our lives we need to be continually filled with the Holy Spirit. We are like the seven branched lampstand of Zechariah 4:2 which needs to have the oil of the Holy Spirit flowing through us, burning brightly to shine God's light into the world.

Meditate on Ephesians 1:13, 14 and the Holy Spirit, the guarantee of our inheritance.

Readings: Leviticus 23:15–21, Acts 2:1–13, Ezekiel 1, Zechariah 3, 4, Revelation 1.

7th Day of the 3rd Month
Sivan, usually falling in May/June
The Congregation of Believers
The Holy Spirit

But this is what was spoken by the prophet Joel: 'And it shall come to pass in the last days, says God, that I will pour out My Spirit on all flesh...' *Acts 2:16, 17*

In his first ever sermon, on the day of Pentecost, the Apostle Peter quoted the words of Joel concerning the Holy Spirit being poured out on all flesh, Jewish and Gentile, male and female, young and old. (Joel 2:28, 29) The Holy Spirit transforms us from the inside out, enabling us to know God's love and to love with His love. (Galatians 5:22) The Holy Spirit is God. He brings the presence of the Father and the Son, the One true God into our hearts. He comes and abides in our spirits when we invite Him in. (Luke 11:13) He is our lover, comforter, and counsellor. In Hebrew every verb concerning the Holy Spirit is written in the feminine form, since the Holy Spirit is the one who gives new birth.

The outpouring of the Holy Spirit at Shavuot was the completion and perfection of Yeshua's work of salvation to bring forth His Congregation of Believers, and prepare His Bride. The Law of Moses was unable to change hearts and make us righteous, but the Holy Spirit in us writes God's commandments on our hearts so we may fulfil His will. (Jeremiah 31:31–33) The Holy Spirit will come to all who call on His name, right up until the 'day of the Lord', the great tribulation, when people will be calling on God for salvation. (Joel 2:32)

Yeshua was the firstfruits to be filled with the Holy Spirit. He was the perfect harvest pleasing to God. (Luke 3:22, 4:1) Only the Holy Spirit abiding in us can bring forth a fruitful harvest, as He gives us the boldness we need to share the gospel, and the supernatural gifts of the Holy Spirit to make us effective in the work of reaching souls. (1 Corinthians 12)

How are you able to keep your 'lamp' full of the oil of the Holy Spirit? (Matthew 25:1–13)

Readings: Joel 2:28, 29, Luke 11:9–13, John 15, Acts 2:14–36, 1 Corinthians 12–14

8th Day of the 3rd Month
Sivan, usually falling in May/June
The Congregation of Believers
The Redeemed Congregation

And they continued steadfastly in the apostles' doctrine and fellowship, in the breaking of bread, and in prayers. *Acts 2:42*

When the Holy Spirit came and filled the disciples who were waiting in Jerusalem, there was a loud sound of rushing wind, and tongues of fire appeared on each of their heads. They spoke in tongues and appeared drunk with joy. The Holy Spirit gave them great boldness to preach the gospel, including the Apostle Peter who preached boldly to the crowds of Jews in Jerusalem, telling them that Yeshua was their Messiah, and that they needed to repent of their sins and be baptised. 3000 people believed Peter's message, repented and were baptised, quite probably in the temple 'mikvot' (ritual baths). Those first 3000 people were God's redeemed 'qahal' or 'congregation' because it was in this month, the third month of the year, that the Israelites had responded to God's call to become His own 'special treasure' – His own 'people' and accept the call to obey His Law. (Exodus 19:3–8)

That first congregation of Israelites quickly broke their word. When Moses was up Mount Sinai receiving the Commandments of God, they fell into idolatry and worshipped a calf engraved out of gold. (Exodus 32:8) On that occasion 3000 people died out in the desert at the hands of the sons of Levi. The Law demonstrated to them that they failed to reach God's standard, but the Holy Spirit ministered God's forgiveness and righteousness to them. The new Congregation of Believers, the Early Church, met daily in the temple in one accord and in their houses they broke bread together, worshipping in simplicity of heart, giving to the poor and having all their possessions in common.

Read the description of the Early Church. (Acts 2:37–47) What can you learn from this?

Readings: Acts 2:37–47, Exodus 19:1–9, Exodus 32, Colossians 1:18, 1 Corinthians 14

9th Day of the 3rd Month
Sivan, usually falling in May/June
The Congregation of Believers
The Rock of the Church

Simon Peter answered and said, "You are the Christ, the Son of the living God." Jesus answered and said to him, "Blessed are you, Simon Bar-Jonah, for flesh and blood has not revealed this to you, but My Father who is in heaven. And I also say to you that you are Peter, and on this rock I will build My church, and the gates of Hades shall not prevail against it." *Matthew 16:16–18*

This conversation between Yeshua and Peter is one of only two references in the Gospels to the 'ekklesia' – translated 'church'. (Matthew 16:18, Matthew 18:17) It took place at Caesarea Philippi in northern Israel at the place where the Greek god of forests and meadows, 'Pan', was worshipped. Niches carved in a large cliff face contained images of the pagan gods and Herod the Great built a pagan temple dedicated to Caesar Augustus. Later Philip the Tetrarch named it after himself. For that reason it is called Caesarea Philippi.

In Caesarea Philippi men and idols contended for the status of 'gods'. But it was here that Peter confessed that Yeshua is the Christ (Messiah), the Son of the living God. Consequently Yeshua gave Simon the name Peter – Greek 'Petros' (a piece of rock). And Yeshua called Himself the Rock – Greek 'Petra' (a mass of rock). (Strong's Concordance)

Yeshua is not like the idols that were placed in niches in the rock. He is the biggest and greatest rock of all. Yeshua is the rock that was with Israel in the wilderness (Exodus 17:6, 1 Corinthians 10:1–4). He is the Chief Cornerstone and foundation (Isaiah 28:16, Psalm 118:22) and the Rock of the kingdom of God (Daniel 2:35). We are His body on earth and He is the Head. He is in us and we are in Him. All that we build must be built on Him.

Consider the standing and authority Yeshua gives you as part of His body, the Church.

Readings: Matthew 16:13–19, 1 Peter 2:4–10, 1 Corinthians 3:9–17, 1 Corinthians 12

10th Day of the 3rd Month
Sivan, usually falling in May/June
Ruth
The House of Bread

Then she arose with her daughters-in-law that she might return from the country of Moab, for she had heard in the country of Moab that the LORD had visited His people by giving them bread. *Ruth 1:6*

In Leviticus, the instructions for keeping the 'Feast of Shavuot' are immediately followed by instructions for gleaning grain. (Leviticus 23:22) An example of someone who gleaned grain is Ruth, the Moabite woman, a Gentile. She lived in the time when the judges ruled Israel and a famine came upon the Land. Elimelech, an Israelite, and his wife Naomi, left Bethlehem (which means 'House of Bread') because there was no bread to eat, and they went to settle in the land of Moab among the Gentiles. One of their sons married Ruth.

When Elimlech and his two sons died, Naomi and Ruth were left as widows. When Naomi heard that God had visited His people Israel by giving them bread, she decided to return to her home in Bethlehem. Ruth decided to leave her own people and accompany her mother-in-law to Bethlehem, despite Naomi's persuasion not to. Ruth said to Naomi, "Your people shall be my people, and your God, my God. Where you die, I will die, and there will I be buried." (Ruth 1:16, 17) She was prepared to die, and be buried like a grain of wheat in the ground, for the sake of her loyalty to the God of Israel. (John 12:24–26)

Her reward was a great harvest. She not only found a harvest and bread, but she also found the owner of the fields, Boaz, who was to become her husband. Similarly, God visited Israel by giving them bread, the bread of life, Yeshua the Messiah. (Ruth 1:6, John 6:33–35) Yeshua said, "I am the bread of life. He who comes to me shall never hunger..." (John 6:35)

What type of bread do you pursue? How do you feed on Yeshua?

Readings: Ruth 1, John 6, John 12:24–26

11th Day of the 3rd Month
Sivan, usually falling in May/June
Ruth
The Friend

But Ruth said: "Entreat me not to leave you, or to turn back from following after you; for wherever you go, I will go; and wherever you lodge, I will lodge; your people shall be my people, and your God, my God. *Ruth 1:16*

The name Ruth means 'friend'. Ruth was a Gentile from Moab who had a choice – to go with her Jewish mother-in-law to Israel or to stay home and marry a Gentile. Ruth's sister-in-law 'Orpah' – whose name means 'nape' or 'back of the neck' – turned her back on Israel. She represents the people and nations which 'turn their back' on Israel, and the God of Israel especially in these last days. Orpah worshipped false gods.

Ruth on the other hand was a friend to Naomi the Israelite and she even accompanied Naomi to Israel. Boaz the owner of the harvest fields represents Yeshua. Boaz showed favour to Ruth and gave her grain because of the kindness she had shown to her Israelite mother-in-law. Yeshua shows His kindness to Gentiles who bless Israel. (Genesis 12:3)

Yeshua was born in Bethlehem, where Boaz had his fields and gave grain and bread to Ruth. Yeshua's family line came from Bethlehem. Gentiles coming to faith in Yeshua are like Ruth as they join themselves to the God of Israel through the New Covenant and are joined to His people by faith. When Gentiles receive of Yeshua, the Bread of life, they partake in a Jewish covenant. Yeshua made the New Covenant with the bread and wine with the Jews. (Jeremiah 31:31–33) Gentiles are invited to partake as friends – like Ruth did, when she joined herself to Israel. (2 Timothy 4:17, Acts 10:45) All who come into the New Covenant, Jew and Gentile, are made children of the God of Israel.

How can Gentiles show practically that they are friends of Israel and the God of Israel?

Readings: Ruth 1:11–22, Acts 10, Isaiah 42:1–9

12th Day of the 3rd Month
Sivan, usually falling in May/June
Ruth
Gleaning

And when she rose up to glean, Boaz commanded his young men, saying, "Let her glean even among the sheaves, and do not reproach her. Also let grain from the bundles fall purposely for her; leave it that she may glean, and do not rebuke her." *Ruth 2:15, 16*

Ruth gleaned grain in the fields of Boaz. She gathered the grains that had been left on the ground according to the law given in Leviticus and the instructions for Shavuot. Leviticus 23:22 states, "When you reap the harvest of your land, you shall not wholly reap the corners of your field when you reap, nor shall you gather any gleaning from your harvest. You shall leave them for the poor and for the stranger; I am the LORD your God."

Shavuot is a picture of the great harvest, the harvest of the Bride of Yeshua, who will prepare for His return. Ruth, a Gentile woman, is a picture of the Gentile participation in the Bride of Yeshua. His Bride is called forth out of all nations, not just the Jews. In Israel, the poor and the strangers could gather any surplus grain that was left behind in the fields after harvesting. Boaz went further than Leviticus 23 by not restricting Ruth to gleaning the corners of the fields. She could glean among the sheaves. She received grace and favour.

To partake of the Passover you had to be Jewish, or become Jewish by circumcision. This was because God's redemption began and came from the Jews. (Exodus 12:43) But a Syro-Phoenecian woman who talked with Yeshua recognised that Gentiles could also receive from God saying, "even the little dogs under the table eat from the children's crumbs." (Mark 7:28). Yeshua is like Boaz. He shows extravagant grace and favour to Gentiles who partake of His New Covenant until 'the end of the barley and wheat harvest.' (Ruth 2:23)

Boaz poured grain into Ruth's lap. Consider God's abundant grace to Ruth, friend of Israel.

Readings: Ruth 2, Leviticus 23:16–22, Mark 7:24–30, Romans 1:16

13th Day of the 3rd Month
Sivan, usually falling in May/June
Ruth
The Redeeming Relative

> Naomi said to her, "This man is a relation of ours, one of our close relatives." *Ruth 2:20*

Naomi, the Israelite, returned from Moab destitute. The land that had belonged to her husband Elimelech was sold when famine hit Bethlehem. She returned to Bethlehem with nothing apart from her Gentile daughter-in-law Ruth. Ruth also had nothing – no husband, no land and no security. This is a picture of us when we are 'lost' in our sins.

The Torah makes provision for situations like this by ensuring justice for those hit by adversity. The land can be restored back to the person who previously owned but lost the land. Brothers were to marry their brother's widow to ensure that the widows were provided for and the name of the dead not forgotten. (Numbers 27:10, 11) The close relative is the man who has the right to buy the land and property back into the family and marry the wife. It was the relative Boaz who took up his responsibility to redeem Ruth and the land.

This is a picture of how God redeems us. Yeshua became our relative, our brother, taking the form of a Man to purchase us back to the Father. The ancient right of redemption can also be seen where Jeremiah had the right to 'redeem' or buy back into the family His cousin's field. (Jeremiah 32:6–15) The 'deeds' of ownership were kept in two scrolls, one sealed and one left open. (Jeremiah 32:14) Yeshua redeemed back the whole earth, paying with His blood. The title deed of His ownership of our hearts is sealed with the Holy Spirit for the day of redemption. (Ephesians 4:30) The title deed of the ownership of all creation is sealed up in Heaven. Only Yeshua is worthy to open the seal of the scroll in Heaven and reclaim the whole earth and the Bride because He is our redeeming relative. (Revelation 5:9)

Thank Yeshua for paying the price to redeem you back to Himself, to make you His Bride.

Readings: Ruth 3, Jeremiah 32:6–15, Revelation 5

14th Day of the 3rd Month
Sivan, usually falling in May/June
Ruth
The Threshing Floor

Now Boaz, whose young women you were with, is he not our relative?
In fact, he is winnowing barley tonight at the threshing floor. *Ruth 3:2*

Naomi told Ruth to wash and anoint herself and put on her best garment
and go down to Boaz at midnight to the threshing floor to request that
she come 'under his wing.' (Ruth 3:9) She was asking him to marry her.
Now we approach Yeshua to make us His own. Her arrival at 'midnight'
symbolises that final moment when Yeshua will return. (Matthew 25:6)

Ruth went to Boaz at the threshing floor. This is the patch of ground
where the barley or wheat that has been harvested, is gathered in from
the fields, and where the valuable grain is separated from the worthless
chaff. The grains are trampled under the feet of a donkey or ox, which
walks round and round on the threshing floor pulling a heavy and brutal
threshing sledge behind it. The threshing sledge wrongly used could
maim or even kill.

The threshing floor is a picture of God's judgements on the nations and
individuals who oppose His will and come against the nation of Israel.
(Micah 4:13, Habakkuk 3:12) God deals with the nations according to
how they treat Israel. Their actions to divide or destroy her will return
upon their own heads. 'For the day of the LORD upon all the nations is
near; as you have done, it shall be done to you; your reprisal shall return
upon your own head.' (Obadiah verse 15) God will 'thresh' the nations.
(Isaiah 41:15, Jeremiah 51:33)

When Yeshua returns, He will separate people as a shepherd divides
his sheep from his goats. The sheep will be those who come to the
assistance of Yeshua's 'brethren' in their tribulations, and the goats will
be those who do not. (Matthew 25:40)

*Pray for your nation, and the church in your nation, that it be found to
stand with Israel.*

Readings: Ruth 3:1–9, Matthew 3:11–12, Matthew 25:31–46,
Revelation 14:14–20

15th Day of the 3rd Month
Sivan, usually falling in May/June
Ruth
Marriage and Covering

And he said, "Who are you?" So she answered, "I am Ruth, your maidservant. Take your maidservant under your wing...." *Ruth 3:9*

When Ruth approached Boaz at the threshing floor, she uncovered his feet, lay down and requested his covering. Boaz had already recognised that Ruth had come to the Land seeking refuge 'under the wings' of the God of Israel, for God to 'cover her' with His provision and protection. (Ruth 2:12) Now she came to Boaz seeking his covering too. This is a spiritual principle. The Ark of the Covenant was covered with the wings of cherubim, heavenly creatures. (Exodus 25:20) Winged creatures stand continually before the throne of God in Heaven, and they cover themselves with two sets of wings because of God's glory and to move with Him. (Ezekiel 1:22–25) Men come under the angels, then under men, women. (1 Corinthians 11:10) All are covered by submission to God and obedience to Him.

Jewish men cover themselves with their 'talit' (prayer shawl) when they pray, as Yeshua would have done, as a Jewish man. The prayer shawl has tassles at its corners, with knots tied as a reminder to obey God's commandments. (Numbers 15:37–41) Ruth wanted to come under the 'covering' of Boaz since he was himself covered by God. Ruth was willing to put herself under his covering because he was a man submitted to God.

We are covered when we stay under the protection of Yeshua. When sin exposes us to the molestations of the devil we need to quickly come back under the safe covering of His cleansing blood and forgiveness. We need to abide under the shadow of His wings (Psalm 91:4), submitting to God and those in authority over us, and keeping His commandments.

Ask God to show you if you are living your life under the covering of His wings. (Psalm 91)

Readings: Matthew 8:4–13, 1 Corinthians 11:1–16, Ephesians 5:17 – 6:13, 1 Peter 3

16th Day of the 3rd Month
Sivan, usually falling in May/June
Ruth
The Marriage of Ruth

And all the people who were at the gate, and the elders, said, "We are witnesses. The LORD make the woman who is coming to your house like Rachel and Leah, the two who built the house of Israel...."
Ruth 4:11

The marriage of Ruth to Boaz was her second marriage. Her first marriage was to one of Naomi's two sons – Mahlon and Chilion. The names Mahlon and Chilion mean 'sickness' and 'death'. Ruth's first marriage can be seen to represent 'marriage' to the first covenant of Israel – the Law. Laws only serve to reveal our sin. Without grace to cover our failures we are only headed for sickness and death, the penalty for breaking the Law. Like Ruth, we need to come into the second 'marriage', to our Boaz, Yeshua, who gives us His unmerited grace and favour through the New Covenant.

Boaz legally redeemed Ruth at the city gate, the place of public legal transactions so that the name of the dead would not be 'cut off'. God is a God of redemption. He does not want us to remain and die in our sins. He came to bring us out of the consequences of our departure from God and bring us back to Himself in intimate relationship, the intimacy of knowing God in our hearts. This is even more intimate than human marriage. For this reason all believers, male or female can identify themselves as 'married' to Yeshua. As His Bride filled with the Holy Spirit, believers know the intimacy of receiving His love in their hearts and hearing and knowing His voice. He is totally committed to you.

Boaz and Ruth married and gave birth to Obed, ancestor of King David and of Messiah Yeshua. Yeshua brings forth new life, not sickness and death.

What inheritance have you received – like Ruth, upon entering into covenant with Yeshua?

Readings: Ruth 4, Hebrews 8:7–13, 9:15, Matthew 19:28, 29, Revelation 19:1–10

17th Day of the 3rd Month
Sivan, usually falling in May/June
The Ancient Jewish Wedding
The Chosen Bride

"You did not choose Me, but I chose you and appointed you that you should go and bear fruit...." *John 15:16*

The marriage of Ruth leads us now to look at the ancient Jewish wedding customs we find in Scripture and how they are a picture for us of God's plan for our relationship with God. The Apostle Paul wrote that marriage is a picture of the relationship between Yeshua and His Church. (Ephesians 5:30–32) The first thing we can learn concerns the choice of the Bride. Abraham (who represents Father God) sent his servant to find a bride for Isaac. (Genesis 24) This is a picture of the Holy Spirit who is sent by the Father to select the Bride of Yeshua.

In Genesis 24, Rebekah responds to the call of the servant (the Holy Spirit) to arise, leave everything and come away to become the bride of Isaac. Similarly Yeshua wants us to respond willingly, receptively and with a trusting, generous heart, to His invitation to receive His love and grace, to rise up, come away and become His Bride. The Holy Spirit draws our hearts to God and listens for our consent to rise up and become His Bride. (Genesis 24:58)

Like the bridegroom of ancient Israel, the Bridegroom Yeshua is the initiator of the relationship. We may think that we have 'found' Yeshua, but He has in fact pursued us first by sending the Holy Spirit to touch our hearts. We responded to His 'drawing'. (Song of Songs 1:4) We love Him because He first loved us. (1 John 4:19) The Holy Spirit knocks on the doors of our hearts inviting us to know Yeshua. 'Many are called but few are chosen' because few respond to this call to radical obedience. (Matthew 22:1–14, 20:1–16).

Read Genesis 24. What can Rebekah's attitude, choices and actions teach you?

Readings: Genesis 24, Matthew 22:1–14, 20:1–16, Matthew 7:13–27, John 14:15–15:27

18th Day of the 3rd Month
Sivan, usually falling in May/June
The Ancient Jewish Wedding
The Bride Price

Or do you not know that your body is the temple of the Holy Spirit who is in you, whom you have from God, and you are not your own? For you were bought at a price; therefore glorify God in your body and in your spirit, which are God's. *1 Corinthians 6:19–20*

In ancient Israel, the bridegroom had to pay a price or a 'dowry' to the father of his intended bride. This not only compensated for the cost to the father of bringing up a daughter in his home, but it ensured the high value that the bridegroom was prepared to pay for her. He had to really love her. The girl could not just be 'bought'. She had to give her consent to marry the intended bridegroom.

In Genesis 24 the transaction took place before Rebekah met her husband. She gave her consent and went to become Isaac's bride even before she met him. (Genesis 24:58) We too have to consent in faith to become Yeshua's Bride, trusting that one day we will see Him face to face. He does not force us to become His own. We are not 'bought' against our will.

When Jacob looked for a wife in the land of his forefathers, he fell in love with Rachel and said to Laban, "I will serve you seven years for Rachel your younger daughter." (Genesis 29:18) In the end Jacob served a total of fourteen years to pay for Rachel. He loved the second bride, Rachel, whose name means 'ewe' (female sheep). She represents the second covenant, the New Covenant, beautiful and loved by Yeshua, His precious flock.

Yeshua paid a very high price, His own life blood shed on the cross, to purchase His Bride from the Father. (Acts 20:28) She gives herself to Him in response to His great love.

How should we live when we know that we are not our own but have been bought at a price?

Readings Genesis 29, 1 Corinthians 6:9–20, 1 Corinthians 7:20–24, 1 Peter 1:13–25

19th Day of the 3rd Month
Sivan, usually falling in May/June
The Ancient Jewish Wedding
The Betrothal

For I am jealous for you with godly jealousy. For I have betrothed you
to one husband, that I may present you as a chaste virgin to Christ.

2 Corinthians 11:2

The Apostle Paul had godly jealousy for the Church in Corinth, desiring
that they not be pulled away from their pure devotion to Messiah by a
false gospel. He had 'betrothed' the Corinthian Church to Yeshua as a
chaste virgin, and he didn't want their pure devotion to Messiah to be
tainted by any false preaching, false beliefs or false spirit.

Betrothal was an important part of the Jewish wedding in ancient Israel.
It was the first part of a two part marriage ceremony. Modern Jewish
weddings put the Betrothal and the Marriage into one ceremony, but in
ancient times they could be up to a year apart. The Betrothal Ceremony
is the legal part of the marriage, and the later Marriage Ceremony is
the spiritual giving of the bride and groom to each other, after which
they have sexual intimacy and live together. They had to remain chaste
between the Betrothal and the Marriage Ceremony. The story of Mary
and Joseph illustrates this point. (Matthew 1:18–25)

At the Betrothal Ceremony the bride and groom exchanged vows and
the legal document – the 'ketubah' – was signed before witnesses. The
'ketubah' is the certificate on which the bridegroom commits to provide
for all the practical needs of the bride. The Betrothal Ceremony is a
powerful picture for us of becoming born again. Matthew 6:28–33 is
like the marriage 'ketubah', where Yeshua promises to provide for those
who 'seek first the kingdom of God'. The groom would then return to
live with his father until the wedding day when he would return to marry
his bride. Yeshua will return to 'marry' His betrothed Bride.

*Do you see yourself as a chaste virgin betrothed to Yeshua, waiting for the
wedding day?*

Readings Hosea 2:19, 20, Matthew 1:18–25, Matthew 6:24–34, Song
of Songs 7:10

20th Day of the 3rd Month
Sivan, usually falling in May/June
The Ancient Jewish Wedding
The Cup

> Then He took the cup, and gave thanks, and said, "Take this and divide it among yourselves; for I say to you, I will not drink of the fruit of the vine until the kingdom of God comes." *Luke 22:17, 18*

The two parts of the ancient Jewish wedding – the Betrothal and the Marriage Ceremony, both had the sharing of a cup of wine by the bride and bridegroom as a symbol of their marriage covenant. Yeshua gave His disciples the cup of wine at the Last Supper, the Passover, the night before his death. This cup was the 'seal' of the New Covenant in His blood, which was prophesied in Jeremiah 31:31–33. It was like the cup drunk at a Betrothal.

Yeshua taught His disciples, "This cup is the New Covenant in My blood, which is shed for you." (Luke 22:20) God's covenant with Abraham had been sealed with blood. (Genesis 15:10) The New Covenant is sealed with the sinless DNA of the blood of the Son of God. The Hebrew word for bridegroom is 'chatan' which means 'given in covenant'. The Bridegroom gives himself in His covenant to His wife. Paul wrote to the Ephesians: 'Husbands, love your wives, just as Christ also loved the Church and gave Himself for her, that He might sanctify and cleanse her...' (Ephesians 5:25, 26)

Yeshua was the Bridegroom who gave Himself in covenant to receive for Himself a pure, spotless bride. The seal – 'chotam', was in His blood. When we partake of the Cup of the New Covenant we remember His Betrothal to us through His death. But Yeshua promised He will drink the cup again when He comes again in His kingdom. (Luke 22:18). This is like the second cup which will be shared with the Bride when He returns for her.

Remember to partake of the cup of the New Covenant, thankful for all that it signifies.

Readings: Luke 22:14–20, Jeremiah 31:31–33, Ephesians 5:25–33

21st Day of the 3rd Month
Sivan, usually falling in May/June
**The Ancient Jewish Wedding
Gifts for the Bride**

Then the servant brought out jewellery of silver, jewellery of gold, and clothing, and gave them to Rebekah. *Genesis 24:53*

When Abraham's servant selected Rebekah to be Isaac's bride, he gave her beautiful and precious gifts to wear. This is a picture of the Holy Spirit giving the Bride of Yeshua His gifts to beautify her and prepare her to meet Him face to face. Yeshua is preparing a Bride adorned with the beauty of holiness, the beauty He gives us, His beauty. (Genesis 24:51–53)

Abraham's servant put a golden nose ring and bracelets on Rebekah to identify her as the one God had chosen to become Isaac's bride. (Genesis 24:12–23) In the same manner God anoints us, 'sealing us' with the Holy Spirit in our hearts as a guarantee (2 Corinthians 1:22) and then He confers on us and increases in us the 'ministry gifts' for the purpose of maturing and beautifying the body of Messiah Yeshua. (Song of Songs 8:8, 1 Corinthians 12:8–11, Romans 12:3–8)

The Father will beautify our character as we show forth the fruit of the Holy Spirit in our lives, causing us to more and more resemble Yeshua. (Galatians 5:22) This was prophesied by Isaiah: "as a bride adorns herself with her jewels"... so "the Lord God will cause righteousness and praise to spring forth before all the nations." (Isaiah 61:10–11) Ezekiel 16 describes how God selected, washed and clothed Israel with fine clothes and sandals of badger skin. These remind us of the coverings of the tabernacle. God adorned Israel with the jewels and clothes of a bride, but she 'trusted in her own beauty and played the harlot.' (Ezekiel 16:15, 16). But through the New Covenant God covers us and beautifies us.

Are there any ways you can identify with Israel's experience when you read Ezekiel 16?

Readings: Ezekiel 16, Isaiah 61, Ephesians 4

22nd Day of the 3rd Month
Sivan, usually falling in May/June
The Ancient Jewish Wedding
The Bridal Baptism

He who believes and is baptised will be saved; but he who does not believe will be condemned. *Mark 16:16*

Immersion in water is part of the Jewish Wedding. New Testament baptism is similar to the total immersion of the bride immediately before her wedding. Jewish brides, today as in ancient times, immerse themselves in the 'mikveh', the pool of running water, to cleanse and purify themselves, before dressing in white for the wedding and coming to the bridegroom in the wedding ceremony. A bride's 'baptism' (tevilah) marks her 'death' to her old life and her former status as a single person. She rises from the water cleansed and ready to adopt her new life and new status as a married person under the authority of her husband.

This is a picture for us of the spiritual cleansing and baptism we pass through to become Yeshua's Bride. When John the Baptiser was baptising in the River Jordan, he saw Yeshua approaching and joyfully declared Him to be the 'Lamb of God who takes away the sin of the world!' (John 1:29) Yeshua baptises us completely, washing away all the uncleanness of our sin, inside and out. John was not jealous that his followers transferred their allegiance and left him to go and follow Yeshua. Rather, he rejoiced knowing that they rightfully belong to Yeshua, the Bridegroom. "He who has the bride is the Bridegroom; but the friend of the Bridegroom who stands and hears him, rejoices greatly because of the Bridegroom's voice." (John 3:29) John recognised the bridal significance of baptism.

Baptism is part of becoming a disciple of Yeshua. We leave behind our old life in the waters of baptism and rise to new life with Him. We are cleansed and set apart for Him.

Meditate on the full significance of baptism, as preparation for life with Yeshua.

Readings: John 1:1–34, John 3, Acts 19:1–7, Colossians 2:11 – 3:17

23rd Day of the 3rd Month
Sivan, usually falling in May/June
The Ancient Jewish Wedding
The Bridegroom Prepares a Place

"In My Father's house are many mansions; if it were not so, I would have told you. I go to prepare a place for you...." *John 14:2*

Yeshua used the analogy of the Jewish wedding to prepare His disciples for His departure back to Heaven. He told them it was necessary for Him to go back to His Father so that He could prepare a place for them. In His Father's house are many mansions. He had to prepare a place for them before He could fetch them away to be with Him forever. (John 14:1–4) Yeshua is now away, preparing a place for His Bride in Heaven.

This is like the time, of up to a year, between the Betrothal and the Marriage Ceremony when the bride and bridegroom could not see each other. The bridegroom had to prepare a bridal chamber for the consummation of the marriage and for their life together. He could not return to take his bride away with him until he had completed the bridal chamber for her. He carefully constructed and prepared this special place as an 'add on' to his father's house. The father would not permit his son to return to fetch his bride and complete the second part of the wedding until the bridal chamber was completely ready. Only when the father said so, could the son return for his Bride, and initiate the Marriage Ceremony.

This is a picture for us. Yeshua will return for His Bride when His Father says so. He could not tell His disciples the timing of His return. Only the Father knows that. (Matthew 24:36) It would be to their advantage that He went away because then He could send them the Holy Spirit to be their Helper while He was away. And while He is still away He is preparing a place for us in Heaven, a place uniquely designed for us that we cannot imagine.

What matters more, your earthly home or your heavenly home? (Luke 18:22–30)

Readings: John 14–17, Psalm 45:10–17, Matthew 9:15–17

24th Day of the 3rd Month
Sivan, usually falling in May/June
The Ancient Jewish Wedding
The Waiting Bride

"...But the Helper, the Holy Spirit, whom the Father will send in My name, He will ~~...~~ embrance all things that ~~...~~ ace I give to you; not as ~~...~~ 26, 27a

Just like the br ~~...~~ egroom has departed, leavi ~~...~~ e the Bride waits for His ap ~~...~~ the waiting time. She can ~~...~~ urn of her bridegroom, or shc ~~...~~ ther things.

While we wait for the ~~...~~ ed to think it will be a long time before ~~...~~ ur lifetime. But Scripture tells us that His retu ~~...~~ en we don't expect it, like a thief in the night. (2 ~~...~~ we need to be careful how we live, as a bride ready to ~~...~~ at anytime. She needs to keep full of the Holy Spirit (John 14:25–~~...~~, and not go off with other 'lovers'.

[Handwritten note: John 14~2 .. In my Father's House are many mansions. if it were not so I would have told you . I go to prepare a place for you . ... Jesus come but went back to prepare a place for us —]

The Bible tells us that in the last days many scoffers will come, walking according to their own lusts, and saying, "Where is the promise of His coming?" (2 Peter 3:3, 4) They will forget that "with the Lord one day is as a thousand years, and a thousand years as one day". (2 Peter 3:8) In these last days it is clear that many, including the Church, have forgotten that the Bridegroom can return for His Bride at any time. The Bride is the 'kallah' which can be translated 'enclosed one'. She needs to free herself from distractions and become like a "garden enclosed" (Song of Songs 4:12) with a single focus like 'doves' eyes' for her Bridegroom. (Song of Songs 2:14, 4:1)

What lifestyle and spiritual disciplines do you need to adopt to be ready for Yeshua's return?

Readings: Matthew 24:32–51, Song of Songs 2:14, 4:12

25th Day of the 3rd Month
Sivan, usually falling in May/June
The Ancient Jewish Wedding
The Return of the Bridegroom

"Watch therefore, for you know neither the day nor the hour in which the Son of Man is coming...." *Matthew 25:13*

The Jewish bride in ancient times didn't know when her bridegroom would return to carry her away to the wedding. The return of the bridegroom at midnight (Matthew 25:6), symbolises the final hour, the time of judgement (Exodus 12:29), when people are sleeping. (Ruth 3:8) The bride would have continued her daily business after her betrothal, but she would have been continually listening for the sound of the imminent return of her bridegroom for the marriage ceremony. When he did return for her, while he was still some distance off, he and his companions made a great noise; lots of loud cries and a trumpet call to wake her up and warn her that he was coming. When she heard the sound of his approach in the distance, she quickly prepared herself and made herself ready to meet him on his arrival.

In the parable of the ten virgins, all ten slept, but only five were ready with sufficient oil for their lamps when they awoke, to go and meet the bridegroom. (Matthew 25:1–13) The five foolish virgins awoke without enough oil, and had to go and get some more. When they tried to enter the wedding, the door was already closed, and it was too late to enter. Similarly, when the Lord returns, those who are ready will be allowed into the 'marriage supper of the lamb'. (Revelation 19:6–9) The rest who are not ready will be shut outside.

Yeshua told us to watch for His return. He used the parable of the fig tree. When it has leaves, we know it is nearly the summer. The fulfilment of prophecy concerning the 'fig tree' – Israel – is a clear trumpet call to the Bride that His return is near. (Matthew 24:32–35)

Do you watch the fulfilment of biblical Prophecy to prepare for Yeshua's return?

Readings: Matthew 25:1–13, Mark 13:28–37, 1 Thessalonians 4:1 – 5:10, 1 Corinthians 15:52

26th Day of the 3rd Month
Sivan, usually falling in May/June
The Ancient Jewish Wedding
The Bridal Chamber

Beloved, now we are children of God; and it has not yet been revealed what we shall be, but we know that when He is revealed, we shall be like Him, for we shall see Him as He is. *1 John 3:2*

In ancient times the Jewish bridegroom would only return to fetch his betrothed bride when the construction and preparation of the bridal chamber was complete. Once the time of preparation was over, he would go and take up his bride in his arms, or in a palanquin, and carry her away to his father's house where the guests were waiting for the Marriage Ceremony. Similarly Yeshua will one day soon 'catch' His Bride up into the air. (1 Thessalonians 4:17) At the wedding seven wedding blessings were pronounced, and the bride and groom drank together from the 'second' cup of wine. (Luke 22:18)

Having performed the ceremony, the bride and bridegroom would then go alone to the bridal chamber to consummate the marriage. The friend of the bridegroom rejoiced when he heard the bridegroom's voice (John 3:29) which signalled that the guests could commence the feast. The bride and bridegroom would dwell together in their chamber for a whole week. Jacob gave Leah her 'week' despite the fact she was not the bride that he desired. (Genesis 29:27) There is another more troubling week mentioned in Daniel 9:27.

The wedding chamber is both wonderful and frightening for the bride, because the works she has done in her lifetime pass through the fire of His pure and loving eyes. Her sins are forgiven but the quality of her works will be revealed. She will receive her reward but works done independently of Him will be 'burned up'. (1 Corinthians 3:9–15)

What do you want Yeshua to see when you meet Him face to face?

Readings: Genesis 29:20–30, 1 Corinthians 3:9–15, 2 Corinthians 5:1–10, Luke 19:11–26

27th Day of the 3rd Month
Sivan, usually falling in May/June
The Ancient Jewish Wedding
The Marriage Supper

"...Let us be glad and rejoice and give Him glory, for the marriage of the Lamb has come, and His wife has made herself ready." And to her it was granted to be arrayed in fine linen, clean and bright, for the fine linen is the righteous acts of the saints. Then he said to me, "Write: 'Blessed are those who are called to the marriage supper of the Lamb!'" *Revelation 19:7–9*

Yeshua told a parable about a wedding to describe the kingdom of heaven. Those who were chosen, had to have responded to the invitation to come to the wedding, and they had to wear a wedding garment. We too must respond to Yeshua's invitation and wear His wedding garment of righteousness. Many are called but few are chosen. (Matthew 22:1–14) The Marriage Supper of the Lamb of God comes in Revelation 19, before the binding of Satan, and the millennial rule of Yeshua on earth for 1000 years. (Revelation 20, Zechariah 14) At this time the Bride will have been purged and cleansed by meeting Yeshua, and clothed in the 'fine linen' of righteousness. (Revelation 19:7–9)

On the third day of His ministry, Yeshua attended a wedding feast in Cana of Galilee. (John 2:1–11) The Hebrew name 'Cana' means to 'purchase, recover, redeem, surely, verily'. The wine at the wedding ran out, so Yeshua had the six ritual purification water pots filled with water, and He turned the water into wine, the 'best wine' which comes last. The later wine of the New Covenant 'second cup' will be drunk in His kingdom at the Marriage Supper of the Lamb. It will be the 'seventh vessel'. The 'wine of the kingdom' will be drunk on the 'seventh day' of Sabbath rest. Then when all things have been completely redeemed and restored, Yeshua will hand the Kingdom back to the Father. (1 Corinthians 15:24–28)

Do you desire joy in earthly marriage? With Yeshua the greatest joy is yet to come!

Readings: Matthew 22:1–14, Revelation 19–21, John 2:1–11, 1 Corinthians 15:20–28

28th Day of the 3rd Month
Sivan, usually falling in May/June
Israel the Wife
The Lord her Husband

Then she will say, 'I will go and return to my first husband, for then it was better for me than now.' *Hosea 2:7*

Yeshua will return for His betrothed Bride of the New Covenant but the Scriptures also speak of Israel 'the wife'. This is because the New Covenant fulfils the marriage covenant God made with Israel at Mount Sinai, when Israel agreed to enter into His Covenant of the Law. Gentiles have been included into the Jewish New Covenant, whereas Jews are fulfilled and redeemed back into their own New Covenant. (Jeremiah 31:31, Romans 11:24)

Israel is the wife according to God's covenant with Moses. At Mount Sinai she said 'I do' (Exodus 19:8) and consented to keep God's commandments. She was cleansed, washed and purchased by God. (Psalm 74:2, Ezekiel 16:8, 60) She was set apart, made holy, betrothed (Jeremiah 2:2), and loved by God. (Deuteronomy 33:3) When Israel strayed like an unfaithful wife (Hosea 2:5, Ezekiel 16, Jeremiah 3:14), God let her go (Jeremiah 3:8), but with His 'chesed' – mercy and loving kindness, He drew her back to Himself. (Jeremiah 3:14, Hosea 11:4) He promised her a new marriage covenant. (Jeremiah 31:31–34) Like the prodigal son she realises that she needs to return to God. (Hosea 2:7) Hosea 5 describes the incurable wound of Israel. She has rejected her Messiah, her husband. But in her affliction Israel will seek God and return to Him. (Hosea 5:15) This will happen 'on the third day'. This 'third day' reminds us of the wedding at Cana (John 2:1) when the saved remnant of Israel will once again be married to the Lord (Hosea 6:2) and she will be healed of her backsliding. (Hosea 14:4) Israel, the first wife, will return to the Lord.

Pray for the restoration of anyone you know who has 'backslidden' from faith in the Lord.

Readings: Hosea 11:7, 8, Hosea 14, Ezekiel 16:60–63, Revelation 7:4, 17

29th Day of the 3rd Month
Sivan, usually falling in May/June
Israel the Wife
Comfort

*"Comfort, yes, comfort My people!" says your God. "Speak comfort
to Jerusalem, and cry out to her, that her warfare is ended, that her
iniquity is pardoned; for she has received from the* Lord's *hand double
for all her sins." Isaiah 40:1, 2*

God's people Israel received double from the Lord's hand for all their
sins. Israel is God's special inheritance. She not only receives special
blessing, but special responsibility. God said of Israel, "...I will repay
double for their iniquity and their sin, because they have defiled My
land; they have filled My inheritance with the carcasses of their detestable
and abominable idols," (Jeremiah 16:18) and 'double destruction' was
foretold in Jeremiah 17:18. Israel had vowed to obey God's Laws. They
were responsible before God for their actions. Under the Law, thieves
had to restore double as compensation. (Exodus 22:4, 7, 9) Israel had
to pay double for her sins. Her temple was destroyed twice, her people
exiled twice, and she has received untold sufferings in her travail as
God's chosen people.

God is the God of justice, but He is also the God of mercy. Israel
carried the greater responsibility but also receives the greater comfort.
Zechariah 9:12 speaks of being restored 'double' because of the blood
of the covenant. Isaiah 61:7 says 'Instead of your shame you shall have
double honour, and instead of confusion they shall rejoice in their
portion. Therefore in their Land they shall possess double: everlasting
joy shall be theirs.' Yeshua first comforted the people of Israel at His first
coming, healing bodies and souls and bringing salvation. Now the Holy
Spirit is the Comforter. (John 14:16) Israel's double comfort will come
at Yeshua's second coming when she will be fully restored to the Land,
and He will rule and reign from Zion. On the day of His vengence
He will comfort Zion. (Isaiah 61:2)

*How can you 'speak comfort' to Israel in these days while she is being slandered
and hated?*

Readings: Isaiah 40, 57:16–19, Isaiah 61, John 14:15–18, Revelation
18:2–8

30th Day of the 3rd Month
Sivan, usually falling in May/June
Israel the Wife
The Vineyard

For the vineyard of the LORD of hosts is the house of Israel, and the men of Judah are His pleasant plant. *Isaiah 5:7*

Israel is likened in Scripture to a vineyard. Isaiah 5 describes Israel as the 'vineyard of the LORD', and begins with a song between the Father and the Son regarding 'His vineyard'. (Isaiah 5:1) The love in the Godhead looks for fruit, the fruit of lives yielded to Him. The Song of Songs uses the same imagery of the Vineyard. The Beloved in the Song of Songs (1:6) began by neglecting her own vineyard (relationship with God), but ends with her vineyard bearing so much fruit that the owner of her vineyard (the king) and those who have invested in her, receive fruits from her life. The reason she bears fruit is that she has developed her relationship with God. (Song of Songs 8:12)

The vineyard that God planted, Israel, was planted with love and care by God Himself. He placed her in a good land which promised a good harvest. (Numbers 13:27) God watched over His nation Israel and He looked for a harvest of love and righteousness, a nation that would honour Him as King and obey His commandments. He expected Israel to bring forth good fruit, but she only brought forth wild grapes. (Isaiah 5:2) She committed many sins and much wickedness. When Yeshua came, He came to His own vineyard. He told a parable. (Luke 20:9–20) The owner of the vineyard leased out his vineyard to vinedressers, but when he sent his servants to them they beat them and treated them badly. (This is how Israel treated the Prophets.) Then the owner sent His beloved son. Instead of receiving Him they killed Him. (The temple authorities rejected Yeshua and He died at their hands.) So now the Father gives the kingdom to others, to the ones who will receive Yeshua.

If you receive Yeshua, He looks for a good harvest in your vineyard. How do you treat Him?

Readings: Isaiah 5:1–7, Isaiah 27:2, 3, Song of Songs 1:6, 8:11, 12, Luke 20:9–20

1st Day of the 4th Month
Tamuz, usually falling in June/July
The Fruit of the Holy Spirit
Love

Then He said, "Take now your son, your only son Isaac, whom you love, and go to the land of Moriah, and offer him there as a burnt offering on one of the mountains of which I shall tell you."

Genesis 22:2

Today is the first day of the fourth month, the month in which the heat of Israel's summer sun is ripening the fruit on the trees. On the first day of the month we return to worship the Lord, the only one who can bring an abiding, lasting harvest in our lives. His truth is planted like seed in our hearts and minds through the revelation of His Word and the Holy Spirit. Just as people may look to see how the fruit is ripening on the trees, so too we can look to see if we are bringing forth the fruit of the Spirit in our lives – fruit of 'love, joy, peace, patience, kindness, goodness, faithfulness, humility and self-control'. (Galatians 5:22)

The first fruit is love. The first mention of 'love' in Scripture comes when Abraham is asked to offer up his son Isaac whom he loves. (Genesis 22:2) This is a picture of the love in the Godhead between the Father and the Son, and for us, that He would offer up His only Son to die in our place. 'God so loved the world that He gave His only begotten Son that whoever believes in Him should not perish but have everlasting life.' (John 3:16)

We are only able to truly love God and others because He has first loved us. (1 John 4:19) God is love. Now you show your love for God by obeying Him and keeping His commandments. (John 14:15) He commands us to love Him with all our heart, soul, mind and strength and to love our neighbour as ourselves. (Mark 12:29–31) His Holy Spirit in us and His truth in our minds will set us free to love as we should, with His love.

Read 1 Corinthians 13 and see if you are living a life of love. Ask Him to help you.

Readings: Genesis 22, 1 Corinthians 13, 1 John

2nd Day of the 4th Month
Tamuz, usually falling in June/July
The Fruit of the Holy Spirit
Joy

If you keep My commandments, you will abide in My love, just as I have kept my Father's commandments and abide in His love. These things I have spoken to you, that My joy may remain in you, and that your joy may be full. John 15:10, 11

The second fruit of the Holy Spirit is joy and it is not your own joy or worldly joy. It is the joy of Yeshua Himself abiding in you. To receive this joy you are to abide in His love – like the branches of the vine. To abide in His love we need to obey His voice. If we are not obeying the still small voice of the Holy Spirit in our hearts and conscience, and in accordance with Scripture, we will stray from abiding in God's love. In the Sermon on the Mount (Matthew 5:3–12), Yeshua taught us how to live in His 'blessedness' – or 'happiness'.

Yeshua never stops loving us, and His grace is always available to us when we return to Him. It is only when our hearts do not condemn us that we have confidence before God. (1 John 3:21) God would not have us coming under the heaviness of condemnation because of our failures. Condemnation is not from Him. When we slip up we are to come straight back to Him in repentance and receive His grace and thank Him for His love and forgiveness.

The Apostle Paul tells us there is no condemnation now 'to those who are in Christ Jesus, who do not walk according to the flesh, but according to the Spirit.' (Romans 8:1) When the Jews returned to Jerusalem from the exile in Babylon, they were grieved because they had broken God's Laws. But Nehemiah exhorted them to not grieve, but to rejoice because it was the 'Feast of Tabernacles'. This feast represents our 'rest' from the warfare caused by sin. Now the 'Joy of the Lord is your strength'. (Nehemiah 8:10)

How can you walk consistently in God's joy? Is the 'joy of the Lord' your strength?

Readings: Matthew 5:3–12, John 17:9–26, Nehemiah 8, Philippians 4:4

3rd Day of the 4th Month
Tamuz, usually falling in June/July
The Fruit of the Holy Spirit
Peace

Peace I leave with you, My peace I give to you; not as the world gives do I give to you. Let not your heart be troubled, neither let it be afraid.
John 14:27

The fruit of peace in our lives is the peace that Yeshua gives us. This is not the same as the peace that the world gives. It is not a mere absence of conflict, but it is the powerful peace of God's presence ruling and reigning in our hearts, eliminating and destroying every negative emotion. True peace is where the source of all chaos has been totally defeated by God and His truth reigns in our hearts. His peace comes when we forgive, love and trust.

Yeshua gives us His peace – firstly peace with God, then peace in every situation in our lives. We have to receive it. We must not let our hearts be troubled or afraid. We are to put our total confidence in the goodness and faithfulness of God, trusting Him to deliver us.

Whenever the storms come, we can be confident that God is with us in the boat. (Mark 4:37–41) Great storms will come on the earth in the end times as Yeshua prophesied. He said that on the earth there will be "distress of nations, with perplexity, the sea and the waves roaring, men's hearts failing them from fear and the expectation of those things which are coming on earth, for the powers of the heavens will be shaken..." (Luke 21:25, 26) But we are to 'look up' and lift up our heads because our redemption is near. We can experience peace knowing that God will redeem us. He is our Saviour. He is in the boat with us and He says "Peace, be still!" over every storm in our lives. (Mark 4:39) Even the wind and the rain obey Yeshua who has 'bought' our 'shalom' – peace.

'Cast all your care upon Him, for He cares for you.' (1 Peter 5:7) Choose to walk in peace.

Readings: Isaiah 26:3, Psalm 131, Mark 4:35–41, John 20:19–23.

Lord help me to apply these
words & truths into my own
life regarding my son Paul & his
family as I find it so difficult
to not be anxious for them all
I surrender them all over to
you Lord and put my trust in
you ... I love them & forgive them
of not keeping me informed about
their lives and health and their
whereabouts — Thank you
Lord. Amen
26/7/12

Peace. John 14 : 27 Peace I
leave with you. My peace I give to
you, not as the world gives do I
give to you. Let not your heart be
troubled, neither let it be afraid.
His peace comes when we forgive
love and trust.   (SHALOM)
1st peace with god
and peace in every situation in
      our lives.
We have to receive it though!
& not be troubled & afraid.
      page 120

4th Day of the 4th Month
Tamuz, usually falling in June/July
The Fruit of the Holy Spirit
Long-Suffering

"We must through many tribulations enter the kingdom of God."

Acts 14:22

The fruit of long-suffering is the God-given ability to endure and persevere for a long time, doing the will of God despite encountering difficulties, trials and tribulations. It could also be called patience. It involves overcoming and being victorious in the face of suffering and even persecution. God never promises us an easy life. But He has promised to be with us and help us in our trials, giving us the Helper, the Holy Spirit. (John 15:18–27)

If the world hates us we are to remember that the world hated Yeshua first. Yeshua told His disciples, "...In the world you will have tribulation, but be of good cheer, I have overcome the world." (John 16:33) He gives us His strength and overcoming power. If we are abiding in the vine, resting in the love of God and obeying His voice then we can trust too in the words of Romans 8:28, 'And we know that all things work together for good to those who love God, to those who are called according to His purpose.'

We have a choice when we are suffering – either to become 'bitter' or 'better'. Suffering is like a refiner's fire. If we stand firm according to God's Word in our trials, then we will come out of the fire refined and purified. Peter wrote: 'you have been grieved by various trials, that the genuineness of your faith, being much more precious than gold that perishes, though it is tested by fire, may be found to praise, honor and glory at the revelation of Jesus Christ...' (1 Peter 1:7) The 'fire' we experience here prepares us to pass through the fire of seeing Yeshua face to face. When we suffer for Yeshua, God suffers in us and with us as we share His sufferings. We are not alone. This is the time to become intimate with Him.

Do you rejoice in your sufferings knowing that you share them with Him? (1 Peter 4:13)

Readings: 1 Peter, John 15:18–27, 2 Corinthians 1:3–7, Psalm 40:1–3

5th Day of the 4th Month
Tamuz, usually falling in June/July
The Fruit of the Holy Spirit
Kindness

> But when the kindness and the love of God our Saviour toward man appeared, not by works of righteousness which we have done, but according to His mercy He saved us.... *Titus 3:4, 5*

The kindness of God is His mercy which does not treat us according to what our sins deserve. When we have received His kindness then we are able to demonstrate the same kindness to others. In fact this is what the Lord requires of us.

Yeshua told the parable of the unforgiving servant. (Matthew 18:21–35) In this parable, He shows why we must have compassion and mercy toward those who require our forgiveness. It is because we ourselves received the great compassion and mercy of God, when He forgave our own great debt of sin. We must therefore extend that same kindness and mercy to others, forgiving them when they sin against us. Yeshua told Peter that we are not to forgive just a small amount – up to seven times – but seventy times seven – an infinite amount. This is a direct reversal of Genesis 4:24 where Lamech declared seventy-sevenfold vengeance. Only God can perform true vengeance with justice. Yet He offers forgiveness.

Kindness shows goodness to others regardless of how they treat us or what they can give us in return. Our greatest example of kindness is God Himself. He is just to punish sin, but kind to forgive, when we come to Him in repentance to receive forgiveness through the blood of His Son. He is the Lord, 'merciful and gracious, longsuffering, and abounding in goodness and truth, keeping mercy for thousands, forgiving iniquity and transgression and sin, by no means clearing the guilty...' (Exodus 34:6, 7) Now we too are to demonstrate the mercy and loving kindness of God to our neighbours, not treating them as their sins deserve.

Is there anyone that you need to demonstrate God's mercy and loving kindness towards?

Readings: Matthew 18:21–35, 2 Peter 1:2–9, Ephesians 2:4–10, Matthew 5:7

6th Day of the 4th Month
Tamuz, usually falling in June/July
The Fruit of the Holy Spirit
Goodness

Or do you despise the riches of His goodness, forbearance, and long suffering, not knowing that the goodness of God leads you to repentance? Romans 2:4

God has shown us amazing grace. Our response must be one of repentance with a humble and contrite heart. We must not trample His goodness underfoot by continuing in the same sins. The revelation of God's goodness should cause us to be good to others. We manifest the goodness of God in different ways – with the fruit of the Holy Spirit, with a good and loving attitude, with good deeds, with generosity and always believing the best of others. Goodness cannot be mean-spirited, spiteful or harsh, but instead blesses, encourages, gives generously, honours and serves others. Goodness is powerful to soften the hardest of hearts, by demonstrating the grace of God, and causing them to experience His goodness.

God is good to us all, and He does not readily cause us to pass through affliction. (Lamentations 3:31–33) Many of our afflictions have come through either our own sin and foolishness, or that of other people. Many times God gives us warnings to avoid paths that He knows will lead to pain He does not want us to experience. We are to trust that God is good to us and thank Him for His goodness. (Psalm 107:1, 8, 9, 21, 31) If we don't believe that God is good we will become negative, pessimistic and lacking faith to believe that He will keep His promises. God wants us to trust that He wants to be good to us – bless us, heal us, protect us, and provide for us. He wants us to put our faith in Him, trusting that He is a good and loving Heavenly Father. When we believe that our heavenly Father knows how to give good gifts to His children when they ask Him (Matthew 7:7–12), we can freely be good to others.

Do you really believe in your heart that God is good? Ask God to show you His goodness.

Readings: Exodus 33:14 – 34:7, Psalm 107, Luke 6:17–49, Matthew 7:7–12

7th Day of the 4th Month
Tamuz, usually falling in June/July
The Fruit of the Holy Spirit
Faithfulness

Through the LORD's mercies we are not consumed, because His compassions fail not. They are new every morning; Great is Your faithfulness. *Lamentations 3:22, 23*

God's faithfulness is great! Jeremiah was able to say this even in the midst of the great suffering that was coming upon Jerusalem. His mercy and compassion towards us are new every morning because He is faithful. He always remembers His covenant towards us – the covenant in the blood of His Son Yeshua, our Saviour. He is faithful because He did not leave us without help when Adam sinned. He promised that the seed of woman, (the Messiah), would bruise the head of Satan. (Genesis 3:15) And His heel would be bruised in the process. God would redeem us at cost to Himself. God did what He said.

God is completely faithful to His Word. He keeps His promises and covenants. He fulfilled the prophetic scriptures concerning the first coming of the Messiah. He has kept His promise to preserve the Jews and restore Israel. As long as the sun, moon and stars remain in the sky, Israel will not pass away (Jeremiah 31:35, 36), and as long as God's covenant with the day and night remain, He will not cast away the descendants of Jacob and David. (Jeremiah 33:19–26) God is even more dependable and faithful than the appearance of the sun in the sky every morning, and of the moon and stars at night.

When we believe and trust in God's faithfulness to His Word and His covenants, we too will be faithful to keep our word and promises: we will be faithful to the covenant commitment of marriage, we will keep our Word no matter the cost (Psalm 15:4), we will be faithful to God, family, friends and colleagues, and we will keep our commitments.

Are you faithful to keep your word – to God, to others and to your covenant commitments?

Readings: Psalm 15, Psalm 89, Jeremiah 33:19–26, Matthew 25:14–23

8th Day of the 4th Month
Tamuz, usually falling in June/July
The Fruit of the Holy Spirit
Gentleness

> You have also given me the shield of Your salvation, Your gentleness
> has made me great. You enlarged my path under me; so my feet did
> not slip. *2 Samuel 22:36, 37*

God is gentle with us. 'As a father pities his children, so the LORD pities
those who fear Him. For He knows our frame; He remembers that we are
dust.' (Psalm 103:13, 14) God knows everything about us. He knows
our weaknesses, our frailties, our faults and our sins. But He still loves
us like a loving parent loves their children – with unconditional love,
totally accepting us even while we still have all our faults and failings.

God does not treat us as we deserve, but with grace, mercy and
compassion. He deals with us gently, step by step, knowing how far
He can stretch us to make us grow, whilst not destroying us. 'God is
faithful, who will not allow you to be tempted beyond what you are able,
but with the temptation will also make the way of escape, that you may
be able to bear it.' (1 Corinthians 10:13) He does not want us to feel
bad about ourselves or be hard on ourselves. He does not put us down
or scorn us. When we fail He wants us to look to Him and delight in
His grace and loving kindness. He encourages us on, like a father with
his stumbling child who is learning to walk. He does not 'accuse' but
He gently corrects us.

Because God is gentle with us, the Holy Spirit in us will make us
patient and gentle with others. We will demonstrate unconditional love.
We will not readily point out people's faults to them or dwell on their
weaknesses. We will be humble and esteem others better than ourselves
(Philippians 2:3) and be sensitive to their feelings, not wanting to hurt
them. We will not lord ourselves over others, but humbly lift them up
and esteem them with love.

*Do you correctly perceive God's gentleness towards you? Are you gentle to
others?*

Readings: 2 Samuel 22, Philippians 2, 2 Corinthians 10:1, 2 Timothy
2:24

9th Day of the 4th Month
Tamuz, usually falling in June/July
The Fruit of the Holy Spirit
Self-Control

For God has not given us a spirit of fear, but of power and of love and of a sound mind. *2 Timothy 1:7*

God's Holy Spirit in us gives us the strength to be self-controlled. That means that our words, thoughts and actions can be determined by deliberate choice and the leading of the Holy Spirit, and not by uncontrollable impulses running wild. We can choose what we think about, and with our will we can reject and cast down wrong, sinful, and unscriptural thoughts, ideas and impulses. The soul consists of the mind, will and emotions. Following the Holy Spirit means that we discern the leading of the Holy Spirit in our spirit, and we choose to obey Him and do His will, and do what is right. God Himself always acts in accordance with His character revealed in the Word of God, and though He allows us to exercise our free will, He always wants us to choose rightly. In contrast, the emotional person is driven by soulish emotion and mere feelings, to do what they want even if it is clearly not right. Proverbs 25:28 says 'Whoever has no rule over his own spirit is like a city broken down without walls.'

The greatest example of self-control was given to us by Yeshua, in the Garden of Gethsemane, when He prayed to the Father, "Father, if it is Your will, take this cup away from Me; nevertheless not My will, but Yours, be done." (Luke 22:42) An angel strengthened Him to do the most difficult task that the Father has ever permitted any human being to go through. Similarly, when we make the choice to do God's will in a situation, He will strengthen us to carry out His will. An attitude of humble submission to God is needed. We are not to be like wild animals following lustful instincts. Our choices are to be ordered by God's leading in our spirit, which will always be in line with the Word of God.

Have you submitted your will to the will of God, to choose to do right and to obey Him?

Readings: Luke 22:39–46, Deuteronomy 30:19, 1 Timothy 3, Romans 6, Jeremiah 52:5, 6

10th Day of the 4th Month
Tamuz, usually falling in June/July
The Seven Species of Israel
A Harvest from God

And it shall be that if you earnestly obey My commandments which I command you today, to love the LORD your God and serve Him with all your heart and with all your soul, then I will give you the rain for your land in its season, the early rain and the latter rain, that you may gather in your grain, your new wine, and your oil.

Deuteronomy 11:13, 14

God wants us to have a harvest, a harvest of souls being saved through our witness and testimony, and to have fruit from our labours. This harvest cannot be gathered without His help and empowering. All good gifts, including the fruit of our labours, come from Him. It is He who makes our work successful. It is He who brings forth a harvest of souls into the kingdom of God. He provides for our needs and blesses us. We cannot do it without Him.

When Israel entered the Promised Land they had to live in dependence on God, and not how they had lived in Egypt. In Egypt they had sown their seed and watered the ground by foot, like a vegetable garden. The Promised Land had no big river or irrigation system. It was a land of hills and valleys that depended directly on the rain from heaven in its season. (Deuteronomy 11:10, 11) It couldn't be watered by man. Without rain there was famine.

God warned the Israelites to be careful not to let their hearts be deceived, nor turn to ask other gods to send the rain in its season. (Deuteronomy 11:8–21) Their security had to be in God who was watching over them and their land. If they would obey His commandments they would be blessed. He would send the rain in its season and give them a harvest. He was jealous for their love and devotion, as He is for ours. Yeshua said, 'You cannot serve God and mammon.' (Matthew 6:24) You must serve God alone, not money or earthly security.

Where do you place your security; in God, or the world's systems?

Readings: Deuteronomy 10:12 – 11:32, Matthew 6:19–34

11th Day of the 4th Month
Tamuz, usually falling in June/July
The Seven Species of Israel
Wheat and Barley

For the LORD your God is bringing you into a good land, a land of brooks of water, of fountains and springs, that flow out of valleys and hills; a land of wheat and barley, of vines and fig trees and pomegranates, a land of olive oil and honey.... *Deuteronomy 8:7, 8*

Moses wrote the book of Deuteronomy for the Israelites just before they entered the Promised Land. In Deuteronomy, God gave instructions about the manner in which they were to live in the Promised Land, in order to live fully in God's covenant blessings. The 'Promised Land' God brings us into when we obey His plan for our lives, is like the blessed Land of Israel. Israel is a good land, blessed with flowing water, valleys and hills, wheat, barley, vines, fig trees, pomegranates, olive oil and honey. (Deuteronomy 8:7, 8) The seven fruits listed here, or 'seven species', as they are often called, are part of God's covenant blessings for His people. The Jewish nation is bound to the Land of Israel through God's everlasting covenant with Abraham. (Genesis 15:7) The seven species, (Deuteronomy 8:8), mirror God's spiritual blessings, especially through the seven main feasts of Israel.

Wheat and barley, the first two of the seven species, remind us of Yeshua, the Bread of Life. To yield their harvest the whole plant of wheat or barley is cut down and dies. The seeds which die in the ground bring the multiplication of new plants, and the seeds which are ground to flour provide essential nutrients to sustain life. At 'Passover', Yeshua broke the bread which represented His body broken for us. On the 'Feast of Unleavened Bread', the following day, we remember His body, laid in the grave. The wheat could be seen to represent His living body, and His ministry through His sinless life, and His suffering on the cross, and the barley can be seen to represent His body given for us in death.

Meditate on the symbolism of the 'wheat and barley' that God blesses you with everyday.

Readings: Deuteronomy 8, 2 Kings 4:38–44, John 6, 1 Corinthians 11:17–34

TAMUZ

12th Day of the 4th Month
Tamuz, usually falling in June/July
The Seven Species of Israel
Grapevines

I am the true vine, and My Father is the vinedresser. *John 15:1*

The grapevine, the third of the seven species of Israel, represents the blood of Yeshua and the 'wine' of His kingdom. The juice from the grape is the powerful symbol of the New Covenant made in His blood. (Luke 22:20) The life is in the blood. (Leviticus 17:11) The third feast of the Biblical Calendar, the 'Feast of Firstfruits' is when Yeshua rose from the dead. His resurrection life gives us the hope of the resurrection from the dead. The life of God, made manifest at the resurrection of Yeshua, is the very same power which works in our lives. (Ephesians 1:7–21) Yeshua is the vine, we are the branches. His life is in us and we are in Him. His resurrection life flows through us and we are joined to Him, wrapped up in His life. The Land of Israel is filled with this symbol of the life of God. Before the Israelites even entered the Land, twelve spies returned carrying a massive bunch of grapes, so huge that it had to be carried on a pole between two men. (Numbers 13:23) The Land of Israel has vineyards and ancient winepresses, watchtowers, water cisterns and terraces in abundance.

Now Yeshua is 'the vine' and we are 'the branches'. Yeshua commands us to 'abide in Him'. (John 15:1–17) The branches have to be connected to the whole vine to produce grapes. The branches receive life–giving sap from the roots and trunk of the vine, Yeshua. God the Father is the vine dresser. He prunes the branches which don't bear fruit, and He prunes the branches that do bear fruit, so that they can bear more. When we abide in Him, we will be 'pruned' like a vine. We will be disciplined to produce more and better fruit for Him.

Have you been pruned? And are you receiving all the 'sap' you need to bear good fruit?

Readings: 1 Kings 21, Matthew 26:26–29, John 15:1–17

13th Day of the 4th Month
Tamuz, usually falling in June/July
The Seven Species of Israel
Fig Trees

I saw your fathers as the firstfruits on the fig tree in its first season.

Hosea 9:10

The fourth of the seven species, the fig tree is often taken to represent Israel. It was even present in the Garden of Eden. Hosea tells us that the fathers of Israel were like the firstfruits on the fig tree. The fig tree has two crops in two different seasons. The first crop in the first season is called the 'bikkore' which means 'firstfruits'. The firstfruits are the little hard figs which appear before the leaves of the tree open up. When Yeshua was walking through Bethany He saw a fig tree with leaves on it. The firstfruits would have come and gone. Being hungry He looked for fruit, but finding none He cursed it and it immediately withered and died. (Matthew 21:19, Jeremiah 8:13) The tree would never again have fruit.

This is like Israel, who failed to produce her crop of righteousness. Yeshua came and looked at the temple and the 'fig tree' of 'Israel'. (Mark 11:11–13) The first 'harvest' – the faith of Abraham, Isaac and Jacob had come and gone. (Mark 11:13) After the Patriarchs came the Law. The Law was not able to produce righteousness. The temple had become a den of thieves.

But the fig tree has a second season, from August and through the winter. (Mark 11:13) This fruit is much softer and sweeter than the early firstfruits harvest. The nature of firstfruits is that they guarantee the arrival of the later harvest. The second harvest of righteousness came through the New Covenant when God's Laws were written on our hearts through the Holy Spirit. At Shavuot, the fourth feast, our hearts are turned from stone to flesh, made soft and sweet like the second harvest of the fig tree, through the Holy Spirit.

Ask God to make your heart soft and sweet, through the Holy Spirit abiding in you.

Readings: Genesis 3:7, Mark 11:11–33, Matthew 21:17–46, Luke 13:6–9, Revelation 22:1, 2

TAMUZ

14th Day of the 4th Month
Tamuz, usually falling in June/July
The Seven Species of Israel
Pomegranates

Like a piece of pomegranate are your temples behind your veil.

Song of Songs 6:7

The fifth feast, the 'Feast of Trumpets' reminds us that Yeshua the Bridegroom will return for His Bride and the fifth of the seven species reminds us of the Bride of Yeshua, and her Heavenly Bridegroom. The top of the pomegranate fruit looks like a crown. This speaks of the lordship of Yeshua, lifted up over the heart of every believer. We will be lifted up to meet with Him. The shiny crimson peel of the fruit conceals a surprise, hundreds of seeds suspended in blood red juice. Each seed, covered in transparent and red flesh, represents an individual, a person who is part of Yeshua's Bride, washed through the water and the blood. Split open, the fruit resembles a heart, its chambers full of the sweet wine of love. In Song of Songs, the bride exclaims, "I would cause you to drink of spiced wine, of the juice of my pomegranate." (Song of Songs 8:2) Yeshua drinks joyfully the love of our hearts. He gave us the wine of His life. We give Him the wine of a devoted and worshipping heart.

The pomegranate reminds us of the beauty of holiness, without which we will not see the Lord. (Hebrews 12:14) Aaron the High Priest had little pomegranates sown around the hem of his priestly garment, alternating with little golden bells. (Exodus 28:33–35) The bells indicated to the people the movement of the High Priest when He was in the tabernacle. He could not go into the most holy place of God's presence without holiness. When Yeshua our High Priest died on the cross, His body was broken and the veil of the temple was torn in two, so that we may receive His righteousness and draw near to Him. (Matthew 27:51) The Song of Songs 6:8 says that the 'temples' of the bride's face are 'like a pomegranate split open behind her veil.' Now, as we look into His face, He sees His holiness reflected in us.

Look upon the beauty of Yeshua. Give Him sweet juice from the pomegranate of your heart.

Readings: Numbers 13:23, Exodus 28, Song of Songs 4:3, 13, 6:7, 11, 7:12, 8:2

15th Day of the 4th Month
Tamuz, usually falling in June/July
The Seven Species of Israel
Olives

...God anointed Jesus of Nazareth with the Holy Spirit and with power ... Acts 10:38

The olive groves of Israel abound with hardy, but humble looking little olive trees. Olive trees have extreme longevity and they are almost impossible to kill. They remind us of the permanence of God's covenants. In Romans 11:24, the Apostle Paul writes of the cultivated olive tree of the Jewish people, and the natural olive tree of the Gentiles, and how Gentile believers in Yeshua are like branches, grafted into the cultivated tree, through the New Covenant. The roots and the trunk of the cultivated tree – the Jewish nation – never die. God's covenant through Abraham is an everlasting covenant. (Psalm 105:8–11)

The olives of the olive tree are crushed to produce olive oil, and in the Scriptures olive oil is used as a symbol of the Holy Spirit, for the anointing of the prophets, priests and kings, and for the tabernacle and its articles. (Exodus 30:22–33) The word for 'anointed one' is the Hebrew word 'Meshiach', which means 'Messiah' and translated into Greek is 'Christ'. Yeshua, King of Israel was anointed with the Holy Spirit. (Acts 10:38) The olive is first mentioned in Genesis 8:11 when the dove brought a freshly plucked olive leaf back to Noah. The olive tree was the first thing which emerged from the floodwaters of God's judgements. This is a sign of hope. It can be seen to represent the survival of Israel through God's judgements which will come upon the earth at the end of the age in the tribulation. The olive reminds us of the sixth feast, the Day of Atonement, which foreshadows the day when God will pour out the Spirit of grace and supplication upon all the House of David and upon Jerusalem, and they will see their Messiah. (Zechariah 12:10)

Do you value and respect the anointing of the Holy Spirit, who empowers you to serve Him?

Readings: Isaiah 61:1–3, Exodus 27:20, 21, Exodus 30:22–33, Zechariah 4, Luke 7:37, 38

TAMUZ

16th Day of the 4th Month (Tamuz)
Tamuz, usually falling in June/July
The Seven Species of Israel
Honey

The next day a great multitude that had come to the feast, when they heard that Jesus was coming to Jerusalem, took branches of palm trees and went out to meet Him... John 12:12, 13

Honey, the seventh of the seven 'species' of Israel in Deuteronomy 8:8 represents the sweetness of Yeshua abiding among us. The word 'honey' – 'dvash' has two meanings. It can be used for honey from the honey bee and also for the sweet syrup that is made from dates, the fruit of the date palm. Since the previous species in the verse are all botanical species, the Jewish interpretation is that the seventh is also a botanical species – more specifically, the date palm.

The date palm is first mentioned at Elim (Exodus 15:27) where there are seventy palm trees at the oasis. These can be seen to foreshadow the seventh feast, the 'Feast of Tabernacles', when a total of seventy bulls were sacrificed. (Numbers 29) The date palm is next mentioned in God's instructions to Moses concerning the 'Feast of Tabernacles'. In Leviticus 23:40, the Israelites were commanded to take palm branches, along with branches of willow and branches from beautiful trees, and the fruit of beautiful trees, and wave them before the Lord with rejoicing. When Yeshua entered Jerusalem before His death on the cross, palm trees were waved before Him, as a prophetic sign that He is the coming King. He will return to earth to rule and reign and to live among us in His millennial kingdom.

When Yeshua returns He will judge the earth and rule with a rod of iron (Revelation 5:5, 6, 19:15), but His presence as King upon the earth will be sweet and bring perfect joy. The nations will no longer scorn Israel, but all creation will be at peace and in harmony.

Meditate on God's sweetness and strength and how He would demonstrate that in your life.

Readings: Judges 14, Ezekiel 3:1–3, Revelation 10:8–11, Song of Songs 4:11–5:1

17th Day of the 4th Month
Tamuz, usually falling in June/July
Redeemed from the Curse
The Fast of the Fourth Month

Judah has gone into captivity, under affliction and hard servitude; She dwells among the nations, she finds no rest; all her persecutors overtake her in dire straits. *Lamentations 1:3*

Today is the Jewish Fast day of the fourth month mentioned in Zechariah 8:19. Jewish history records that this is the anniversary of the cessation of temple sacrifices in 587 BC, due to the siege of Jerusalem by the Babylonians. Israel and Judah came under God's curses for breaking His Law as He had warned them in Deuteronomy 28. But this Fast Day, Zechariah tells us, will become a 'cheerful feast' for the Jews.

God had promised great blessings for Israel in the Promised Land if they would obey His voice and follow His commandments. If they didn't obey Him they couldn't live under His blessing. The curses for disobedience would come upon them and 'overtake them'. (Deuteronomy 28:15) Deuteronomy 28:52–57 prophesied the terrible calamities that would come on Jerusalem with the specific prediction of an enemy siege around the city and desperate or 'dire straits'. (Deuteronomy 28:57, Lamentations 1:3)

The siege of Jerusalem ended with the Jews being carried off into an exile in Babylon which lasted 70 years, after which they were able to return to their own land. Centuries later under persecution from the Romans, Apostomos set up an idol in the re-built temple on this very same day and burnt a Torah scroll. The curse for all who break God's Laws ultimately is death and hell. That is why it is so important that we repent and turn to Yeshua who redeems us from the curse. (Galatians 3:5–14) The curse for disobedience began in Eden. (Genesis 3) It will end in the New Jerusalem. (Revelation 22:3)

Read Galatians 3:5–14 and meditate on how Yeshua has redeemed you from the curse.

Readings: Deuteronomy 28, Galatians 3:5–14, 2 Kings 25, Jeremiah 38, Lamentations

TAMUZ

18th Day of the 4th Month
Tamuz, usually falling in June/July
Redeemed from the Curse
Broken Walls

And all the army of the Chaldeans who were with the captain of the guard broke down all the walls of Jerusalem all around. *Jeremiah 52:14*

The walls around Jerusalem are symbolic of the walls of protection around our lives. When the inhabitants of Jerusalem broke God's commandments, the effect of the curse was to expose them to their enemies by breaking down their walls of protection. They became vulnerable to the oppression of dark forces, physical and mental sickness and death. Jerusalem was surrounded and besieged by her enemies, the Chaldeans and the Babylonians.

Curses for breaking God's Laws last to the third and fourth generation, but the blessings for obedience pass on for a thousand generations of those who love Him and keep His commands. (Deuteronomy 5:9) Your descendants will reap the consequences of your choices, as indeed you have received good or bad things from your ancestors. Whether we have received good or bad, we can all come to Yeshua to be set free from every curse.

We can live under God's protection from Satan and the curses of living in a fallen world by abiding 'under the shadow of the Almighty', submitting to Him and walking with Him in His righteousness, obeying His voice. (Psalm 91) God Himself provides a 'hedge' of protection around us from the devil, who seeks to rob, steal and destroy. (Job 3:23) This doesn't mean bad things never happen to the righteous. We must actively claim the promises of Psalm 91. If, however, we deliberately forsake God and move into deliberate sin, then we cannot expect His walls of protection to surround us. We must run back into God. 'The name of the LORD is a strong tower; the righteous run to it and are safe.' (Proverbs 18:10)

Abide in the 'safe place' of Yeshua, trusting in Him who broke the curse for you.

Readings: Jeremiah 52, Psalm 51, Psalm 91, Micah 7:8–20

19th Day of the 4th Month
Tamuz, usually falling in June/July
Redeemed from the Curse
Rebuilding the Walls

Then I said to them, "You see the distress that we are in, how Jerusalem lies waste, and its gates are burned with fire. Come and let us build the wall of Jerusalem, that we may no longer be a reproach."

Nehemiah 2:17

Nehemiah poured out his heart and tears before God in prayer and fasting, because of the sins of the children of Israel, his own sins, and the sins of his father's house. (Nehemiah 1:6) He asked the Lord to show them mercy. And the Lord answered his prayer. He was allowed to return to Jerusalem to rebuild its walls and gates.

This is a pattern of the restoration that the Lord brings to our lives. We begin by hearing God's Word, and discerning where we and our family and nation have sinned; we respond to our sin with repentance and a request for the Lord's mercy; we receive His forgiveness and, together with Him, we rebuild the walls of protection around our life.

We do this by coming back to the Word of God. When we obey God's Word we stay within the walls of God's supernatural protection. When we step outside by disobedience, it is like moving outside our own city wall. Yeshua was crucified just outside the city. (John 19:20) When we step outside God's 'walls' for our life, the first thing we can encounter is our crucified and risen Lord. We can then be covered by His cleansing blood, and receive His forgiveness. That immediately brings us back inside the walls of His protection.

The walls of God's protection around our lives are rebuilt by forgiveness – when we receive God's forgiveness, when we forgive ourselves, when we forgive others, and when we humble ourselves to ask forgiveness of others. Then God's love can rebuild our walls.

What 'boundary walls' of behaviour and conduct has God highlighted to you from His Word?

Readings: Nehemiah 1 – 13

20th Day of the 4th Month
Tamuz, usually falling in June/July
God's Laws Written on Our Hearts
Who God Is

I am the LORD your God, who brought you out of the land of Egypt, out of the house of bondage. *Exodus 20:2*

Today we begin to look at the Ten Commandments and how we are to regard them in the light of the New Covenant. Breaking any one of the Commandments of God brings the curse of judgement and hell, and for Israel it resulted in their being taken captive into exile. The Jewish scribes and Pharisees became so afraid of breaking God's Law that they created many extra rules to act like a 'fence' around it. They made people live under even stricter rules than God had commanded, so they would not break God's Law by mistake. When Yeshua came they accused Him of breaking the Law, but it was actually their man-made rules that He broke. He kept God's Law as well as the 'spirit' of it. (Mark 7:7, 2:23–27) Yeshua taught His disciples to keep His Commandments. This would be the sign of their love for Him. (John 14:15) The difference was that they were not to try to make themselves righteous by keeping laws. Instead they were to experience a heart transformation through knowing who God is – their Redeemer – who would transform them from the inside out, so that their righteousness would exceed that of the 'law keepers', the scribes and the Pharisees. (Matthew 5:20) They would be empowered by God's love, as prophesied by Ezekiel: 'I will give you a new heart and put a new spirit within you; I will take the heart of stone out of your flesh and give you a heart of flesh. I will put My Spirit within you and cause you to walk in My statutes, and you will keep My judgements and do them.' (Ezekiel 36:26, 27) By His Spirit we can keep the first commandment and recognise who God is – the one who has redeemed us from the bondage to man-made laws.

Meditate on the fact that God's Ten Commandments begin with a revelation of redemption.

Readings: Exodus 20, Matthew 5, 15:1–20, Matthew 22:37–40, John 14, Revelation 22:14

21st Day of the 4th Month
Tamuz, usually falling in June/July
God's Laws Written on Our Hearts
Not Having Idols

You shall have no other gods before Me. You shall not make for yourself a carved image.... *Exodus 20:3, 4*

We continue to look at the Ten Commandments which were written on tablets of stone, but are now written on to our hearts. Under the Covenant of the Law, the Ten Commandments brought the conviction of sin leading to guilt and death. (2 Corinthians 7:10) Under the New Covenant of God's Grace through Yeshua, the Law is written on our hearts, fulfilled by and through Yeshua and the Holy Spirit living in us. Jeremiah prophesied, '...this is the covenant that I will make with the house of Israel after those days, says the LORD: I will put My law in their minds, and write it on their hearts; and I will be their God, and they shall be My people....' (Jeremiah 31:33)

The New Covenant, as prophesied by Jeremiah, would not only bring the complete forgiveness of sin, but the knowledge of God. God promised that through the New Covenant every individual can have a living relationship with God. (Jeremiah 31:34)

The second of the Ten Commandments forbade the worship of idols and any other gods apart from Him, the true God. Now, having the Holy Spirit in our hearts, it is possible for us to know God and desire Him more than anything else. John wrote, '...the Son of God has come and has given us an understanding, that we may know Him who is true; and we are in Him who is true, in His Son Jesus Christ. This is the true God and eternal life. Little children, keep yourselves from idols.' (1 John 5:20–21) Knowing God frees us from the grip of worshipping idols because He satisfies and delights us more than anything else.

Have you drawn near, to know God, so that you do not desire anything more than Him?

Readings: Exodus 20: 3–6, Jeremiah 31:31–34, Luke 14:25–35, Mark 10:18–31, John 12:25

TAMUZ

22nd Day of the 4th Month
Tamuz, usually falling in June/July
God's Laws Written on Our Hearts
Reverencing God's Name

You shall not take the name of the LORD your God in vain, for the
LORD will not hold him guiltless who takes His name in vain.

Exodus 20:7

Many religious Jews use the Hebrew word 'HaShem' – 'The Name' to
ensure they don't hold the Lord's name in vain even accidentally. The
four Hebrew letters of the Holy name of God are so holy that they are
translated in English Bibles by the word LORD written in capital letters.
The exact pronunciation of the holy name of God is not known. One
suggestion is 'Yahweh'. (Exodus 3:13, 14) 'Jehovah' is a derivation from
this. In the Law blasphemy is punishable by death. (Leviticus 24:16)
Yeshua was falsely accused and put to death under this law. (Matthew
26:63, 64)

The New Covenant releases us from bondage to anxious fear
concerning God's name, since Yeshua took the punishment for our
transgressions. But this does not give us licence to blaspheme or take
God's name in vain. The apostle Paul urged the respect of wives towards
their husbands as a picture of how the Church is to respect Yeshua.
(Ephesians 5:22–33) We are to respect and reverence our heavenly
'Bridegroom' Yeshua because we love Him and don't want to grieve
Him. We will naturally respect the one who loves us and died for us.

The Bible shows us that blasphemy will increase in the end times and
that the beast (the anti-Christ system) will blaspheme God. (Revelation
13:5–8) The blaspheming beast will make war against the saints who,
in contrast, fear God's name and His Holy character. But God's holy
ones will not go unrewarded. In Revelation 11, the twenty four elders
worship God, thanking Him that He rewards those who fear His name.
(Revelation 11:18)

*Will you stand against the world's anti-Christ system by loving and
reverencing God's name?*

Readings: Exodus 20:7, Leviticus 24:10–16, Ephesians 5:22–33,
Revelation 13, 19:7, 8

23rd Day of the 4th Month
Tamuz, usually falling in June/July
God's Laws Written on Our Hearts
Keeping Sabbath

Remember the Sabbath day, to keep it holy. *Exodus 20:8*

The Sabbath day, 'Shabbat' in Hebrew, is the seventh day of the week (Saturday). It is the weekly day of rest for all people because on the seventh day God rested after completing the six days of creation. (Genesis 2:1–3) Not only is it a day for all creation to rest from their labours, but God affirmed the importance of Sabbath to His people as a 'miqre' a holy convocation, literally a 'rehearsal' for the 'rest' we find through Him. (Leviticus 23:3) Yeshua called Himself the 'Lord of the Sabbath' (Mark 2:28) and He came ultimately to give us the 'rest' of being saved through faith (Hebrews 4), rather than through keeping the Law.

The problem for the Jews was that over time the 'law makers' made so many rules about what constituted 'work', that keeping the Sabbath became very complicated. Yeshua simplified it saying that the Sabbath was made for man, not man for the Sabbath. We are blessed when we keep 'Shabbat', it is good for us. We don't need to become obsessed with keeping rules. Yeshua has completed our salvation for us and He has 'sat down' at the right hand of the Father. The word sit 'shevet' is related to the word 'Shabbat'.

The Christian adoption of Sunday goes back to 7th March 321 AD when the Roman Emperor Constantine, who was opposed to anything practised by the Jews, made Sunday the Christian's day of rest and worship, not Saturday. This helped him integrate Christianity with Mithraism which worshipped the sun on 'Sun-day'. The Catholic Church changed the day from Saturday to Sunday at the Council of Laodicea (c.363 AD), (Convert's Catechism of Christian Doctrine), but nowhere in Scripture are we commanded to change the Sabbath.

How can you 'walk' daily in the Sabbath 'rest' of God, and 'sit' in Sabbath rest on Shabbat?

Readings: Exodus 20:8–11, Matthew 12:1–14, Luke 14:1–6, Mark 2:23–28, Hebrews 4

TAMUZ

God's Laws Written on Our Hearts
Honour your Parents

Honour your father and your mother, that your days may be long upon the land which the LORD your God is giving you. *Exodus 20:12*

This is the only one of the Ten Commandments to have a promise of blessing attached if you keep it. The word to honour 'kaved' means to 'glorify'. It is about our attitude to our parents and the way that we treat them. Its continued importance under the New Covenant is verified by Yeshua's affirmation of the commandment and also by the Apostle Paul.

Yeshua is our example of honouring parents. After the story of the young Yeshua teaching in the temple we have the comment that he returned with His parents to Nazareth and was 'subject' to them. Consequently He was blessed, increasing in wisdom and stature and in favour with God and men. (Luke 2:52) Later Yeshua confronted the hypocrites, the Pharisees and the Scribes, who through their man-made traditions and rules had nullified God's commandment. He rebuked them for finding an escape route, by means of their tradition, to avoid God's commandment to honour their father and mother. (Mark 7:1–13) Clearly for Yeshua, 'honouring' includes considering our parents' practical needs.

The Apostle Paul also affirmed this commandment in his instruction about family relationships. (Ephesians 6:1, 2) Writing to Timothy, he said that widows are to be provided for by their children or grandchildren. (1 Timothy 5:4) It is good to be thankful to God for our parents who gave us life. All children have to forgive their parents' mistakes and faults. When we honour our parents we can expect the blessing of a long life. Yeshua never broke this commandment, but He died young, aged 33, taking upon Himself our punishment for sin.

Examine with the Lord how you treat your parents and your heart attitude towards them.

Readings: Exodus 20:12, Luke 2:41–52, Mark 7:1–13, Ephesians 6:1–4, Malachi 4:4–6

25th Day of the 4th Month
Tamuz, usually falling in June/July
God's Laws Written on Our Hearts
Do Not Murder

You shall not murder. *Exodus 20:13*

Human life is very precious to God. From the moment a human being is conceived in the womb, to the moment that person dies, they are designed to receive God's grace and loving-kindness and to fulfil their individual destiny according to God's good plan. The blood pumping around the body, containing totally unique DNA, sustains our life. God breathed the soul into the body to make it live, and it is His alone to take away. (Genesis 2:7)

Leviticus tells us that the 'life of the flesh is in the blood'. (Leviticus 17:11) When Cain killed Abel, Abel's blood cried out to God from the ground for justice. (Genesis 4:10) God hears the cry come up to Him from all blood which has been spilt, whether in abortion, euthanasia, manslaughter, or murder. It cries out for vengeance. 'Whoever sheds man's blood, by man his blood shall be shed; for in the image of God He made man.' (Genesis 9:6)

Under the Law every premeditated murder is punishable by the death penalty. But under the New Covenant there is grace. Whether or not the death penalty is carried out is a matter for the law of your own nation or state. But before God the death penalty has already been paid by Yeshua. God's Law requires that the blood of the murderer be shed. Yeshua, the innocent Lamb of God, shed His blood in our place. He bled and died on the cross.

Now, sustained by God's grace, we are not only to refrain from murder, but from hatred. Yeshua's grace in our hearts will enable us to value and cherish life, for He said, "whoever is angry with his brother without a cause shall be in danger of the judgement." (Matthew 5:22) God's love frees us from our hatred, fear and murderous desires.

Thank God that the shed blood of Yeshua is able to silence the cries of blood for vengeance.

Readings: Genesis 4, Numbers 35, Matthew 5:21–26, Luke 22:20, James 4:1–3, 1 John 3

26th Day of the 4th Month
Tamuz, usually falling in June/July
God's Laws Written on Our Hearts
Do Not Commit Adultery

You shall not commit adultery. *Exodus 20:14*

According to the Law, the penalty for adultery is death. (Leviticus 20:10) This teaches us the seriousness of this sin and the destruction it brings. Proverbs 6:32 says, 'Whoever commits adultery with a woman lacks understanding; He who does so destroys his own soul.' When people commit adultery they do not realise that they are destroying themselves. They are committing violence against their own soul.

Now under the New Covenant, the law – not to commit adultery – has been written on our hearts by the Holy Spirit. Now we must live it. Out of reverence and the fear of the Lord, married men and women will be careful to not put themselves or others in tempting and compromising situations. They will be diligent to keep their covenant commitment of love and faithfulness to their spouse, a covenant which was made before God and is Holy in His sight. Singles should honour the covenant of marriage, and not 'separate' married people.

Yeshua taught, "You have heard that it was said to those of old, 'You shall not commit adultery.' But I say to you that whoever looks at a woman to lust for her has already committed adultery with her in his heart. If your right eye causes you to sin, pluck it out and cast it from you; for it is more profitable for you that one of your members perish than for your whole body to be cast into hell..." (Matthew 5:27–29) Job made a covenant with his eyes not to 'look upon a young woman'. (Job 31:1) The love of our Heavenly Bridegroom will strengthen our hearts to keep our minds pure. Yeshua did not condemn the woman who was caught in adultery but He said to her, "Go and sin no more." (John 8:11)

Receive God's grace to honour and reverently respect the covenant of marriage, and be pure.

Readings: Leviticus 20:10–21, Matthew 5: 27–32, John 8:1–11, 1 Corinthians 6:9–20

27th Day of the 4th Month
Tamuz, usually falling in June/July
God's Laws Written on Our Hearts
Do Not Steal

You shall not steal. *Exodus 20:15*

Leviticus 19:11 states, 'You shall not steal, nor deal falsely, nor lie to one another.' The eighth of the Ten Commandments concerns our righteousness in dealing with property. The Mosaic Law upheld honest and just dealings in buying and selling (Leviticus 19:35, 36), lending and borrowing, not permitting the greedy to exploit the needy, not even permitting usury (the taking of interest). (Leviticus 25:35–38) God's judgement comes on those who make dishonest gain. 'Are there yet treasures of wickedness in the house of the wicked, and the short measure that is an abomination? Shall I count pure those with the wicked scales, and with the bag of deceitful weights?' (Micah 6:10, 11)

Yeshua confronted the exploitation within the religious establishment at the temple, when he turned over the tables of the money-changers and sellers of sacrificial birds and animals. They were a 'den of thieves' making profit out of the visitors to the temple. (Matthew 21:12–13) If Yeshua were to visit some of our Christian ministries today, what would He do? Christian ministers must be careful not to exploit the flock or put undue pressure and manipulation on people to buy things or to give their 'love offerings'. (Jude 11)

Zacchaeus had committed extortion. But when He met Yeshua He made restitution four-fold, doubling the 'double' required by God's Law. (Exodus 22:9, Luke 19:1–10) Now all of us, like Zacchaeus, filled with gratitude for God's grace, find our hearts changed to become honest and cheerful givers, making restitution where necessary, joyfully giving to God's work over and above the tithe (Malachi 3:8–12), and blessing those in need.

Are you aspiring to be a 'giver' rather than a 'taker'? Are you honest with your finances?

Readings: Malachi 3:8–12, Exodus 22:1–4, Luke 19:1–10, Ephesians 4:28

TAMUZ

28th Day of the 4th Month
Tamuz, usually falling in June/July
**God's Laws Written on Our Hearts
Do Not Lie**

You shall not bear false witness against your neighbour. *Exodus 20:16*

The Law of God teaches that we must not tell lies about anyone. This means that we are to be careful how we talk about others not only in the Law Courts, but also in our daily lives. We are not to spread false tales about others or ourselves.

The New Covenant requires us to walk in even greater righteousness than the requirement of the Law through His grace. Yeshua taught us not even to judge and condemn others in our hearts. (Matthew 7:1–5) Satan is the 'accuser of the brethren' (Revelation 12:10) and we are not to collude with him. Yeshua would bring us into the truth about ourselves before He would show us any truth about others. (Matthew 7:1–5) We are to forsake lying and speak the truth with our neighbours 'for we are members of one another.' (Ephesians 4:25) We are to love one another as Yeshua has loved us. (John 13:34) His love and humility in our hearts will free us from pointing the finger of accusation at others.

Yeshua seeing Nathanael described him as "...an Israelite indeed, in whom is no deceit!" (John 1:47) And the Apostle Peter described Yeshua, saying, 'Christ also suffered for us, leaving us an example, that you should follow His steps: "Who committed no sin, nor was deceit found in His mouth."' (1 Peter 2:21, 22) Yeshua not only spoke the truth, but He is the truth. Yeshua said, "I am the way, the truth and the life...." (John 14:6)

Yeshua had false testimony spoken against Him, but like a sheep before its shearers He remained silent. (Isaiah 53:7) No deceit was in His mouth. (Isaiah 53:9) Now His grace enables us to walk like Nathanael – and like Yeshua, without deceit or guile.

Examine your speech and the motives behind it. Ask God to fill your words with His grace.

Readings: Jeremiah 17:9, Malachi 2:6, Isaiah 53:7–9, Acts 5:1–11, Colossians 4:6

29th Day of the 4th Month
Tamuz, usually falling in June/July
God's Laws Written on Our Hearts
Do Not Covet

You shall not covet your neighbour's house; you shall not covet your neighbour's wife, nor his male servant, nor his female servant, nor his ox, nor his donkey, nor anything that is your neighbour's.

Exodus 20:17

The Law of Moses requires us not to covet or 'selfishly desire' something for ourselves that belongs to someone else. We are not to be jealous of someone else's home, job, husband or wife, friends, possessions or status, wanting them for ourselves. This is very selfish and self-centred and fails to rejoice in all the good things that God has given us. We are to receive with thanks what God has given us and rejoice when others are blessed.

When we have a relationship with Yeshua, He would free us from comparison with others and feelings of inferiority. His merciful love and grace towards us would make us secure in who He has made us and what He has given us. Other people are no longer a threat to us because we know that God has a unique and good plan for our life, and infinite love designed especially for us as individuals. God has all the riches of heaven at His disposal to bless you and you do not need something that belongs to someone else. Perhaps you do not have something because you have not asked for it! (James 4:1–3) Or perhaps God has withheld something for your own good? Perhaps it is not the right time to have that thing you desire or perhaps you have not worked enough to earn the money you would need to buy it?

Secure in God's abounding love and provision for us we are able to go further than avoiding covetousness. We are able to release our own possessions to those who would ask for them. (Matthew 5:38–42) We are to lend freely and give, trusting in God's care for us.

Do you have the attitude that is more concerned to bless others than to be blessed?

Readings: Matthew 5:38–42, 1 John 2:15–17, Philippians 4:10–13, Acts 20:25–38

1st Day of the 5th Month
Av, usually falling in July/August
The New Month
Death of Aaron the High Priest

Then Aaron the priest went up to Mount Hor at the command of the
LORD, and died there in the fortieth year after the children of Israel
had come out of the land of Egypt, on the first day of the fifth month.

Numbers 33:38

We worship God on the first day of the new month at the time of the
new moon and thank God for His continued grace and mercy towards
us, and His faithfulness to His covenants. On this day, Ezra the scribe
arrived in Jerusalem, completing his journey back from exile in Babylon.
(Ezra 7:9) He began the journey at biblical New Year. But many years
before that, on the first day of the fifth month, Aaron the High Priest
and brother of Moses died at the top of Mount Hor in the 40th year of
Israel's wilderness wanderings. He ascended the mountain at the Lord's
command, and so it was that he died and was buried.

The name Mount 'Hor' simply means 'Mountain'. The death of
the High Priest of Israel on a mountain foreshadows the death of our
heavenly High Priest Yeshua who died on another mountain, in the
land of Moriah, in Jerusalem. Now our Heavenly High Priest Yeshua
is seated on His Heavenly Throne in the Mount Zion which is above
in Heaven where He ministers in a tabernacle not made with human
hands. (Hebrews 8:1, 2)

Aaron, the first High Priest, was a man with frailty and sin. He had
created the golden calf while Moses was up Mount Sinai and he had led
the people into idolatry. Consequently he could not enter the Promised
Land. However, he was made holy before the Lord in his office of High
Priest, so that he could foreshadow our perfect and sinless High Priest,
Yeshua. Through Yeshua we are able to enter the Promised Land of
eternal life with God.

*Thank Yeshua that He is the doorway of access to the heavenly Promised
Land. (John 10:9)*

Readings: Exodus 28–30, Numbers 33:38, 39, Hebrews 2:14–18, 9:6–28

2nd Day of the 5th Month
Av, usually falling in July/August
Israel Enters the Promised Land
Joshua

Moses My servant is dead. Now therefore, arise, go over this Jordan, you and all this people, to the land which I am giving to them – the children of Israel. *Joshua 1:2*

Joshua led the people of Israel in to possess the Promised Land. His name, 'Yehoshua' in Hebrew has the same Hebrew root as the name 'Yeshua' meaning 'Salvation'. Joshua is a picture of Yeshua, our salvation, who leads us into our inheritance. Yeshua was with Joshua to grant him success, causing him to inherit the Land. (Joshua 5:13, 14) He was a 'saviour' to the people of Israel, causing them to subdue their enemies and inherit the Land.

The Lord had promised Abraham that He would give his descendants the land of Canaan and drive out the peoples from it. Four generations would have to pass for the iniquities of the Amorites inhabiting the land to be complete. After that they could be defeated. (Genesis 15:16) God promised Moses that if Israel kept the Passover, then He would send an Angel before them to keep Israel in the way and to bring them into the place He had prepared. Moses told them, "Beware of Him and obey His voice, do not provoke Him, for He will not pardon your transgressions; for My name is in Him. But if you indeed obey His voice and do all that I speak, then I will be an enemy to your enemies and an adversary to your adversaries...." (Exodus 23:20–22) This was fulfilled in Joshua 5:10–15.

God led Israel into the Promised Land under Joshua's leadership, (Joshua 4:11–14). In the end times the 'time of the Gentiles' will be fulfilled, (Luke 21:24), and Israel will come into their inheritance of salvation through Yeshua. (Romans 11:26) Yeshua is Commander of the Army of the Lord. (Joshua 5:10–15) He will save and deliver His people Israel.

When you feed on Yeshua the Passover Lamb, He will lead you, defend and deliver you.

Readings: Genesis 13:14–17, Genesis 15:13–16, Exodus 23:14–24, Joshua 5:10–15

3rd Day of the 5th Month
Av, usually falling in July/August
Israel Enters the Promised Land
The Walls of Jericho

So the people shouted when the priests blew the trumpets. And it happened when the people heard the sound of the trumpet, and the people shouted with a great shout, that the wall fell down flat. Then the people went up into the city, every man straight before him, and they took the city. *Joshua 6:20*

Just as with Joshua, when the priests blew the trumpets and the walls of Jericho fell down on the seventh day so that they could take the city, so in Revelation we have the prophecy of the angels in heaven blowing seven trumpet blasts which release God's judgements onto the earth in the time of the Great Tribulation. (Revelation 8, 9, 11:15–19) After the seventh trumpet, loud voices in heaven say, "The kingdoms of this world have become the kingdoms of our Lord and of His Christ, and He shall reign forever and ever!" (Revelation 11:15) Yeshua will inherit the earth, as Israel inherited the Promised Land.

Jericho was taken in one day – which foreshadows the Day of God's Vengeance. (Isaiah 63:4) For six days the people circled the city in silence which represents the intercession of God's people for the kingdom of Messiah to come. (Revelation 8:1–5) The seven priests with the Ark of the Covenant represent Yeshua the Priest and God's Law which convicts the world of sin. On the seventh day the Israelites marched around the city seven times and the priests blew the trumpets. Then the people gave a great shout and the wall of the city fell down. The Israelites captured and utterly destroyed the city. Only Rahab and her family were saved because they stood with Israel and used the sign of the red ribbon, which represents the blood of Yeshua which will protect and save all those who call upon Him.

Meditate on Revelation 8:1–5 and the power of your prayers for God's kingdom to come.

Readings: Joshua 6, Revelation 8–11

4th Day of the 5th Month
Av, usually falling in July/August
Israel's Failure to Keep the Law
The Judges

They forsook the LORD and served Baal and the Ashtoreths. And the anger of the LORD was hot against Israel. So He delivered them into the hands of plunderers who despoiled them; and He sold them into the hands of their enemies all around so that they could not longer stand before their enemies. *Judges 2:13, 14*

When Israel had entered the land of Canaan, and Joshua and the elder generation died, Israel was left without new leadership. They had the priesthood and they were supposed to continue keeping God's Law and worshipping God as their King. But the next generation failed to obey God's commandments, they broke covenant, and they worshipped the false gods of the pagans who still remained in the land. Because of the disobedience of the Israelites, God allowed their enemies to remain as a test. The Israelites failed the test and went after the gods of the pagans, Baal and Ashtoreth, the male and female fertility gods. Instead of serving God, everyone did what was right in their own eyes. (Judges 17:6)

Consequently, God delivered the Israelites up to their enemies, to be plundered and despoiled. The curses for failing to keep the Law came into effect. The Israelites demonstrate to us the impossibility of keeping God's Law on our own apart from our King, Yeshua. When God punished the Israelites by letting them be overrun by their enemies, they called out to Him in repentance, and pleaded for His mercy. God raised up a succession of different 'judges' or 'deliverers' who drove back their enemies for them. These judges foreshadow for us Israel's perfect deliverer Yeshua. 'Whoever calls on the name of the LORD shall be saved, for in Mount Zion and in Jerusalem there shall be deliverance, as the LORD has said, among the remnant whom the LORD calls.' (Joel 2:32)

Pray for God to deliver you and your nation from evil and to keep you far from temptation.

Readings: Judges 1–3, Joel 2:28–32, Obadiah 17, Luke 4:18, Romans 5

5th Day of the 5th Month
Av, usually falling in July/August
Israel's Failure to Keep the Law
The Kings

And I will establish him in My house and in My kingdom forever; and his throne shall be established forever. *1 Chronicles 17:14*

After the Judges, the Israelites cried out to God for a King. And so Saul was appointed Israel's first ever King. But as king, Saul failed miserably. He disobeyed God and he presumed to do the job of the priest and make sacrifices. So he lost the anointing and eventually the throne passed to David, a man after God's own heart. (1 Samuel 13:14)

King David also failed. He was a warrior king who had many mighty achievements and was a good king. He brought the Ark of the Covenant to Jerusalem. But he had a big failure. He took another man's wife and had her husband killed. He failed morally.

After King David came King Solomon. King Solomon was famous for his God-given wisdom and for building the splendid First Temple in Jerusalem. He had a reign of peace but he fell morally and took hundreds of foreign wives who led his heart astray after pagan gods.

His son Rehoboam came to the throne but because of the sin of his father, the kingdom was divided into a northern and a southern kingdom. The behaviour of the kings affected the whole nation. Evil kings led the nation into idolatry and finally they were taken into exile. Jeconiah who was carried off to exile in Babylon was to become ancestor to Joseph, legal father of Yeshua. (Matthew 1:11) Yeshua was born into the royal lineage of King David. Yeshua, the King of kings, is the Son of God, sinless and untainted by the curses and failures of the royal blood line. His 'sceptre is righteousness'. (Psalm 45:6, 7)

Yeshua is Israel's only perfectly good and righteous King. He is your King too. (Psalm 45)

Readings: 1 Samuel 8, 2 Samuel 7, Matthew 1:1–17, Luke 23:38, Revelation 19:16

6th Day of the 5th Month
Av, usually falling in July/August
Israel's Failure to Keep the Law
The Prophets

I will utter my judgements against them concerning all their wickedness, because they have forsaken Me, burned incense to other gods, and worshiped the works of their own hands. *Jeremiah 1:16*

God's people Israel, every tribe, utterly failed to keep God's commandments. They became like an unfaithful wife, breaking their covenant promise to keep the Law. They 'committed adultery' by going after foreign gods. This is like us. When we know God's Laws, and how we 'should' be living, we find that our flesh wants to do exactly the opposite. We do what we know we shouldn't do. (Romans 7:7–8:1) Like Israel, we always fail when we depend upon our own efforts without knowing the grace of Yeshua. It is only when we have brought our failure and brokenness to the cross of Yeshua, and received His grace, mercy, forgiveness and unconditional love, that we are empowered to live righteously, through His righteousness in our hearts. When we have been forgiven much, we love much.

God raised up the prophets to confront the divided kingdoms with their grievous sins – their idolatry, occult child sacrifice, injustice, covetousness, and defilement of the temple. But each of the prophets also brought a message of hope. Though Israel would be punished for breaking God's Laws, in the end God would restore them by His grace alone. He will bring them back out of all the nations where they have been dispersed to their own land. He will give them the New Covenant. He will cause them to be blessed again – not because they deserve it but because of God's grace and faithfulness to His covenants. Israel will be restored, because that is God's will and promise.

Consider that, just as your hope is in God's grace alone, so too is God's nation Israel.

Readings: Jeremiah 33, Ezekiel 36, Hosea 14, Joel 3, Amos 9

7th Day of the 5th Month
Av, usually falling in July/August
Israel's Failure to Keep the Law
Nebuzaradan Arrived

And in the fifth month, on the seventh day of the month (which was the nineteenth year of King Nebuchadnezzar king of Babylon), Nebuzaradan the captain of the guard, a servant of the king of Babylon, came to Jerusalem. *2 Kings 25:8*

This is the day on which the instrument of God's judgements – Nebuzaradan – arrived in Jerusalem. He symbolised the arrival of God's judgements. Breaking God's Law always carries a penalty. We always reap what we have sown. (Galatians 6:7, 8) People have a choice: to continue their own way and carry the penalty themselves, which ultimately is hell, or to receive God's grace, because Yeshua has already paid the penalty on their behalf. Judgement will arrive sooner or later. It will not fail, because God is holy and just.

Sometimes God's grace will lead us to experience His chastisement. (Hebrews 12:1–11). He chastens us to bring us to the cross and His throne of grace, so that we may escape the judgement of our sin, and trust by faith that Yeshua has taken our punishment upon Himself. If we fail to come to His cross and don't live in the power of His love and grace, there is no other escape. Every day countless souls descend to hell because they never called upon the name of the Lord to be saved, but mistakenly trusted in their own 'righteousness'.

King Zedekiah chose to ignore the warnings of the Lord, brought to him through the prophet Jeremiah. Finally, the day came when it was too late. There was nothing he could do. He had not heeded the warnings. He was captured, his sons were killed and his eyes were gouged out. He was carried off into exile in Babylon. (2 Kings 25:1–9) There will be a judgement day. Therefore we must all 'look to Yeshua and be saved'. (Isaiah 45:22)

Has God been warning you about anything? Pray for people to repent before it is too late.

Readings: Isaiah 64:6, 7, Isaiah 45:21, 22, Jeremiah 52:1–11, 2 Kings 24, 25:1–8

8th Day of the 5th Month
Av, usually falling in July/August
Israel's Failure to Keep the Law
The City Burned

He burned the house of the LORD and the king's house, all the houses
of Jerusalem, that is, all the houses of the great, he burned with fire.

2 Kings 25:9

When Nebuzaradan arrived in Jerusalem he broke down the city walls,
and burned down the fine houses and the House of the Lord. Jerusalem
was to lie desolate for 70 years, before her exiles would return from
Babylon.

The Prophet Jeremiah warned King Zedekiah of Judah to surrender
to the king of Babylon otherwise Jerusalem would be burned with fire.
(Jeremiah 38:17–23) But Zedekiah ignored the warning and the fire
came. The horror of consuming, destroying fire, reminds us that the Bible
warns of a much worse fire, one which will last for eternity. Revelation
20 speaks of the lake of fire which has been prepared for the beast and
false prophet, (Revelation 19:20), for the devil (Revelation 20:10) and
for all those whose names are not found written in the Lamb's Book of
Life at the final judgement. (Revelation 20:11–15) Those who have
believed and trusted in Yeshua for their salvation have their name written
in the Book of Life. Your name was written in heaven the moment you
put your faith in Yeshua as your saviour.

After the millennial reign of Yeshua at the final judgement, the
unsaved dead will stand before the Great White Throne. All who have
gone to hell whose names are not found written in the Book of Life will
be cast into the Lake of Fire. (Revelation 20:11–15) On the day that
Yeshua is revealed from Heaven, God will take vengeance on all who do
not 'know God and on those who do not obey the gospel of our Lord
Jesus Christ.' (2 Thessalonians 1:3–10) But He is not willing that any
should perish, but that all should come to repentance.

*Ask God to show you how you can warn people about hell fire, and the
need to repent.*

Readings: 2 Thessalonians 1, Mark 9:38–50, Luke 16:19–31, Revelation
20:7–15

9th Day of the 5th Month
Av, usually falling in July/August
The Fast of the 5th Month
Fasts Will Become Feasts

'The fast of the fourth month, the fast of the fifth, the fast of the seventh, and the fast of the tenth, shall be joy and gladness and cheerful feasts for the house of Judah....' *Zechariah 8:19*

The ninth day of the 5th month is the traditional fast day mentioned in Zechariah 7:3 and 8:19, when Jews mourn the destruction of both the First and the Second Temples in Jerusalem, on this day. The First Temple was destroyed by the Babylonians in 586 BC, and the Second Temple was destroyed by the Romans in 70 AD. Both these events were preceded by a siege around the city walls and the starvation of the inhabitants within the walls. The tragic detail is described in the book of Lamentations, and the curses of Deuteronomy 28:45–68 clearly came into effect.

In Luke 19:41–44 Yeshua looked out over Jerusalem and wept. He prophesied the siege and destruction of the city and the temple that was to happen on this day in 70 AD. It would happen because His people did not know the time of their visitation. They had missed the one who could deliver them from the curse of breaking the Law. (Isaiah 43:25–28) Zechariah 8:19 lists the fasts of the 4th, 5th, 7th and 10th months saying that they shall be 'joy and gladness' and 'cheerful feasts'. Messiah will be in the midst of His people, wiping every tear from every eye. (Isaiah 25:8) The curse has been broken for all who repent, believe and trust in Him. (Isaiah 43:25) One day, this day will be a 'cheerful feast' because all of Israel's shortcomings will have passed away and the glory of the Lord will be in their midst. (Isaiah 11:9) When the Messiah has returned, Israel will be restored, and in the new heaven and the new earth the curse will have passed away. (Revelation 22:3)

Pray especially for Jewish people to find the grace, blessing and protection of Yeshua today.

Readings: Luke 19:41–48, 21:20–24, 2 Chronicles 36, Lamentations 1–5, Isaiah 25

10th Day of the 5th Month
Av, usually falling in July/August
The Exile
Hope in the Midst of Judgement

It came to pass in the seventh year, in the fifth month, on the tenth day of the month, that certain of the elders of Israel came to inquire of the LORD. *Ezekiel 20:1*

On this day, Nebuzaradan completed the destruction of Jerusalem and the temple and carried off the exiles (Jeremiah 52:13) and on this day, during the exile, the elders of Israel asked the Prophet Ezekiel for a word for them. (Ezekiel 20:1) God's response was to tell them the sins of their fathers. They had broken God's commandments and rebelled against Him, even when they were in the wilderness. God reminded them how far they and their forefathers had fallen short in keeping His Law, especially His Sabbaths. (Ezekiel 20) The holy days and the Sabbaths, which included the 'moedim', were a special sign between God and themselves that He was their Lord. Yet they had failed to keep the special Sabbaths of God. Once they had entered the Promised Land their fathers had worshipped idols and they had sacrificed their firstborn children to demons. They had committed all these abominations. That was the reason they were in exile and in bondage in Babylon.

But there was still hope. In Ezekiel 20:33, God spoke to Israel about their future re-gathering not just from Babylon but from a future exile among all the nations. Then they would be purified from their sins, and instead of bringing disgrace on God's name among the Gentiles because of the curse and God's judgements, God's name would be hallowed and reverenced, because God would have preserved Israel and sanctified them. (Ezekiel 20:39–44) God fulfilled His promise given through Jeremiah 29:10–14, and He brought the Jews home after 70 years. He is now regathering Israel. He is keeping His promise of hope.

Meditate on Jeremiah 29:11 and God's plans to give you a future and a hope.

Readings: Ezekiel 20, Jeremiah 29:10–14, Nehemiah 1:6–11, Luke 4:16–21

11th Day of the 5th Month
Av, usually falling in July/August
The Exile
The Remnant

And the remnant who have escaped of the house of Judah shall again take root downward, and bear fruit upward. For out of Jerusalem shall go a remnant, and those who escape from Mount Zion. The zeal of the LORD of hosts will do this. *Isaiah 37:31, 32*

When the southern kingdom and the residents of Jerusalem were carried off into exile in Babylon, some remained behind in the Land. God not only promised the return of the exiles, but He ensured that a small remnant stayed in the Land. One of the remnant left behind was the Prophet Jeremiah. Later, in the first century AD when the Jews were dispersed among the nations and the Romans occupied the Land, then too, a small remnant remained in the Land. More returned throughout the centuries, and a number were forced to convert to Islam or Christianity for fear of their lives, especially in the Middle Ages. God has never allowed the remnant in the Land to be totally destroyed. They are a picture of God's spiritual remnant, which believes in Yeshua, and is faithful and obedient to Him. Even when churches and nations fall into apostasy, God preserves a faithful remnant.

Isaiah 10:20–23 describes a remnant of the Jews returning to the Land and Isaiah 37:30–32 describes Jews being 'planted' in the Land again. There would be natural re-growth – like a tree that has been cut down but not completely destroyed. The fruit of the remnant that returned from exile in Babylon was the birth of the Messiah, and the Early Church. 'There shall come forth a Rod from the stem of Jesse, and a Branch shall grow out of his roots.' (Isaiah 11:1) Hosea promised the sprouts of new life from the tree of Israel. (Hosea 14:4–8) In the end-times God's remnant will return and be saved. (Romans 9:27, 28)

Has anything been 'cut down' in your life which He wants to revive to bear fruit? (Job 14:7)

Readings: Isaiah 1:9, Ezekiel 6:8–10, 11:14–21, Ezra 9:8–15, Matthew 12:20, Revelation 7

12th Day of the 5th Month
Av, usually falling in July/August
The Exile
Do Not Go to Egypt

The LORD has said concerning you, O remnant of Judah, 'Do not go to Egypt!' Know certainly that I have admonished you this day.
Jeremiah 42:19

The elite of Judah were carried off into exile in Babylon, where most lived in relative comfort for seventy years. There, they were able to establish homes, families and livelihoods. Even the exiled King Jehoiachin was brought out of prison, and ended up eating food at the table of the new king of Babylon. (2 Kings 25:27–30) This is like believers who manage to prosper in a world and system that is governed by godless powers.

But the situation was very different for the poorer 'remnant' left behind in Judah. They had the difficult task of surviving without their king and government. Their new governor Gedaliah, who had been appointed by the king of Babylon, was assassinated by rebels, and life was very difficult for them. The question was whether they would trust God to keep them, or whether they would trust in their own ways. They could either seek God, or try to work out their own strategy to make their lives better – without involving God.

The Prophet Jeremiah was one of those left behind in the Land, and so the people went to him for a word of guidance from God. But when the word came, still they didn't obey it. He said they were not to go to Egypt, but they wanted to go to Egypt to secure bread for themselves, and to be safe. Once in Egypt, their own supposed solution to the problem brought them into even more trouble. They became embroiled in the Egyptian pagan religion by burning incense to foreign gods, and many perished by the sword and famine, when king Nebuchadnezzar of Babylon invaded Egypt. Only a remnant escaped back to Judah.

What does this say to you about being part of God's faithful remnant?

Readings: Jeremiah 42–44, 46, Zechariah 10:9–12, Matthew 2:13–15, Hosea 11:1

13th Day of the 5th Month
Av, usually falling in July/August
The Exile
Babylon

By the rivers of Babylon, there we sat down, yea, we wept when we remembered Zion. We hung our harps upon the willows in the midst of it. *Psalm 137:1, 2*

The Jews wept during their 70 year exile in Babylon. They were far away from the temple on Mount Zion, Jerusalem, alienated from their Land, laws, customs, sacrifices, and under the discipline of God. Babylon, the small land on the plains of the river Euphrates, was the power centre of the massive Babylonian Empire which covered the whole of the fertile crescent of the Tigris and Euphrates Rivers and down into the land of the tribes of Israel.

Babylon itself was the probable site of the Tower of Babel. There the people had gathered together and said, "Come, let us build ourselves a city, and a tower whose top is in the heavens; let us make a name for ourselves, lest we be scattered abroad over the face of the whole earth." (Genesis 11:4) But God thwarted their plan and dispersed them abroad.

Abraham, in obedience to God, left the region of Babylon, leaving behind Ur of the Chaldeans. God called forth a family of Semites, through whom Messiah would be born, and He brought Abraham to the land of Canaan. God's plan was to establish His own holy nation which would glorify Him. The Land and nation of Israel, in covenant with God, with Jerusalem as its capital city, stands in direct contrast to Babylon, which represents the ruler-ship of man, independent of God. Babylon is the 'ancient capital' of the system of mankind which sets itself up apart from Israel's Messiah, Yeshua, – financially, politically and religiously, to govern and to control the world. Revelation 17 and 18 prophesy the re-emergence, and God's judgement of Babylon in the end-times.

How can citizens of God's kingdom keep separate from the 'world kingdoms' of Babylon?

Readings: Genesis 11:1–9, Genesis 12:1–9, 2 Corinthians 6:14–18, Revelation 17

14th Day of the 5th Month
Av, usually falling in July/August
Israel in Exile
Babylon is Judged

Call together the archers against Babylon. All you who bend the bow, encamp against it all around; let none of them escape. Repay her according to her work; according to all she has done, do to her; for she has been proud against the LORD, against the Holy One of Israel.

Jeremiah 50:29

In the Scriptures, the instruments of God's judgement are themselves judged by God. (Obadiah 1:15, 16) This happened to the Assyrians and the Babylonians. As they had done to the tribes of Israel and Judah, so it was done to them. They had been used by God to judge His people when they forsook Him, worshipped idols and broke His Laws. But the Assyrians and Babylonians were themselves cruel, brutal and godless, and in the end they too came under God's judgements for their brutality. (Isaiah 47, Jeremiah 50) There is a pattern here seen even to this day. Israel and the Jews are being shaken by the nations which come against them, so that they will turn from their sin and call out to Messiah, Yeshua, to be saved. But we know that the very nations which come against Israel are themselves being judged by God in the valley of Jehoshaphat. (Joel 3:1–3)

The nations are not to be proud. Assyria and Babylon were proud with their mighty powerful empires. But it is God's kingdom that will prevail. Today the nations are proud, judging and dividing Israel. But they forget that they will be judged for judging her. Ezekiel 26, 27 addresses the King of Tyre who gladly watched the fall of Jerusalem. The King of Tyre becomes a picture of Lucifer himself in Ezekiel 28. In the end times it is Satan himself who will be behind the conspiracy of the nations to divide up, give away, sell-off and finally to try to destroy Israel. But in Revelation 20:10 Satan is judged and cast into the lake of fire.

Consider Matthew 7:2, that you will receive the same judgement you judge others with.

Readings: Isaiah 41:11–13, Isaiah 47, Revelation 18, Haggai 2:22, Matthew 7:1–5

15th Day of the 5th Month
Av, usually falling in July/August
The Increase in Dew
A Celebration of Love

In fact, there is a yearly feast of the LORD in Shiloh ... therefore they instructed the children of Benjamin, saying, "Go, lie in wait in the vineyards, and watch; and just when the daughters of Shiloh come out to perform their dances, then come out from the vineyards, and every man catch a wife for himself from the daughters of Shiloh."

Judges 21:19, 20

The fifteenth day of the fifth month was the day of the yearly feast in Shiloh, north of Bethel, in the hills north of Jerusalem. Shiloh is symbolic of the Messiah from the tribe of Judah. (Genesis 49:10) Each year, on this feast the young women danced in the vineyards to attract husbands. One year, when the tribe of Benjamin had suffered judgement and slaughter because of their great sin, the remnant of the young men found new hope and joy, by taking wives for themselves from among the dancers of Shiloh. (Judges 21) Their situation was changed from judgement to dancing, from sorrow to joy. (Psalm 30:4, 5, 11)

This feast, not commanded of the Lord in Scripture, was a celebration of love and it coincides with the time the grapes swell on the vine and the white flower, the 'squill' appears across the whole land. It is symbolic of the season of the Bride and the Bridegroom. The dew suddenly increases, signalling the arrival of cooler nights and a change of season.

Dew in Scripture is a great blessing, sustaining life before the rainy season arrives. 'Dew' is promised to the Remnant of Israel and Judah. 'The seed shall be prosperous and the vine shall give its fruit'... 'The heavens shall give their dew – I will cause the remnant of this people to possess all these.' (Zechariah 8:12) As dew brings life, there will be resurrection from the dead. (Isaiah 26:19, Romans 11:15) The blessing of the dew will surely come.

Thank the Lord for the 'dew' of resurrection coming onto your life.

Readings: Judges 21, Isaiah 26:19, Zechariah 8:11–17, Song of Songs 5:1, 2, Psalm 30:11

16th Day of the 5th Month
Av, usually falling in July/August
The Increase in Dew
Understanding The Times

...of the sons of Issachar who had understanding of the times, to know what Israel ought to do, their chiefs were two hundred; and all their brethren were at their command.... *1 Chronicles 13:32*

King Saul had died, and at the Lord's command, David had gone to reside in Hebron. (2 Samuel 2:1) The men of the tribe of Judah made David King (2 Samuel 2:4), and the mighty men of valour, trained for battle, armed for war, valiant warriors from all the tribes, went to enforce the kingship of David, by bringing the kingdoms that had belonged to Saul, under David's authority. (1 Chronicles 12:23) The men from the tribe of Issachar were noted for their understanding of the times, knowing what Israel ought to do.

These mighty warriors, valiant men, knew that it was the time to come behind David as their new king, and that it was time to build up his kingdom. They knew that it was an important time, because if they had not enforced the kingship of David, some other person, not chosen by God, would have risen up and led a rebellion, particularly from the House of Saul, and led the nation of Israel astray. Their action meant that the tribes of Israel could unite behind David their king, fight his battles and strengthen their hold on the Land.

This is a picture for us. We are to be like the sons of Issachar who knew the times they were in and knew what Israel ought to do. They did not casually sit back. They arose and served their king with wisdom and understanding. Similarly we are to understand that we are in a spiritual battle between the kingdoms of light and the kingdom of darkness. We are to understand that Yeshua is King, the anointed Messiah on the throne of David, and be ready to obey His commands, and to know what to do to build up His kingdom.

Ask God to give you the understanding to know the times we are in, and to know what to do.

Readings: 2 Samuel 1 – 3, 1 Chronicles 13

17th Day of the 5th Month
Av, usually falling in July/August
Prophecies of Daniel for the Latter Days
Changing Times

"Blessed be the name of God forever and ever, for wisdom and might are His. And He changes the times and the seasons; He removes kings and raises up kings; He gives wisdom to the wise and knowledge to those who have understanding...." *Daniel 2:20, 21*

King Nebuchadnezzar in Babylon received a mysterious dream from God. He wanted the wise men to tell him his dream and its meaning, but they were unable to do so. But in answer to Daniel's prayer, God revealed King Nebuchadnezzar's dream, and its meaning, to him. Daniel exclaimed to the king, that God changes times and seasons, removes kings and raises up kings, and gives wisdom and knowledge to those who have understanding.

It is the Lord's will that we know what time and season we are in. When Yeshua was born King of the Jews and was laid in a manger in Bethlehem, a star appeared in the sky and wise men from the east saw it and came to worship Him. (Matthew 2:1, 2) These wise men saw the sign and knew the time they were in. It is possible that they came from the same royal court where Daniel had served over 500 years earlier. (Daniel 2:48) Daniel or his fellow Jews could have taught their ancestors what to look out for. When finally the star appeared in the sky, they knew it was the prophesied sign (Numbers 24:17), and they immediately went to worship the King of the Jews. The Jews in Jerusalem missed the sign! Similarly God has given us the prophecies of Daniel so that we can be like the wise men and understand the times that we live in. The book of Daniel was 'sealed up' until 'the time of the end'. (Daniel 12:4, 9) Through Daniel we will be able to discern kingdoms, kings, times and seasons, including the rise of the anti-Christ, and the soon return of Yeshua.

Ask God to help you discern the time and season we are in, and interpret prophesy correctly.

Readings: Daniel 1, 2, Matthew 24:32–35, Luke 12:35–56

18th Day of the 5th Month
Av, usually falling in July/August
Prophecies of Daniel for the Latter Days
The Final Persecuting World Powers

The fourth beast shall be a fourth kingdom on earth, which shall be different from all other kingdoms, and shall devour the whole earth, trample it and break it in pieces. *Daniel 7:23*

The picturing of world empires is explained in the interpretation of Daniel's dream of the four beasts. (Daniel 7) These beasts are heathen, Gentile, world powers, which will come against the Jews. The fourth beast will be different from all other empires – and its persecution of the 'saints' – believers, will happen in the last days. But God will be with them, as He was with Daniel in the fiery furnace. (Daniel 3:28) The fourth beast will be against (anti) Christ. (Daniel 7:19–22) It will devour and trample the whole earth.

Daniel received his prophecies whilst living and working in Babylon, the first great heathen, Gentile, world power. The 'spirit of Babylon' was passed through the great empires of Babylon, Medo-Persia, Greece and Rome. (Daniel 7:1–7) All these empires attempted to unite nations and peoples under a powerful leader or leaders, whilst rejecting the God of Israel. The Tower of Babel was an attempt by man to achieve greatness in rebellion against the creator God, to raise up a place that could not be submerged by God's floodwaters of judgement. But Jeremiah 51:42 says 'The Sea has come up over Babylon. She is covered with the multitude of its waves.' Ancient Babylon was eventually destroyed.

The final empire is the ten toes of the statue of Daniel 2:33, and the ten kings of Daniel 7:24. From it there will arise a different horn (leader) which is the final 'anti-Christ' personality. (Daniel 7:24, 25) But Daniel 2:34, 35 and Daniel 7:26, 27 show its demise and the full arrival of God's everlasting kingdom which will never be destroyed.

Give thanks that you belong to the kingdom of Messiah which will endure forever.

Readings: Daniel 3–7, Revelation 13

19th Day of the 5th Month
Av, usually falling in July/August
Prophecies of Daniel for the Latter Days
The Seventy Weeks

Seventy weeks are determined for your people and for your holy city, to finish the transgression, to make an end of sins, to make reconciliation for iniquity, to bring in everlasting righteousness, to seal up vision and prophecy and to anoint the Most Holy. *Daniel 9:24*

The seventy 'weeks' or 'seven-year periods', as they have been generally understood to mean, lay out future history for the Jews and Jerusalem. They present a time-line of set time-periods for certain events to happen, and the clock started ticking when the Babylonian Exile ended, and the command was given to rebuild Jerusalem (Ezra 1, Nehemiah 2:7, 8). The timing is specific and lasts until the end of this age, when the Messiah will return to rule and reign. The seventy 'sevens' represent the entirety and completion of God's redemptive history and purpose outlined in Daniel 9:24. The first period of seven sevens (49 years) took the Jews to the actual rebuilding of Jerusalem. The second period of sixty-two sevens (483 years) took them to the appearance of Yeshua, the Messiah who was 'cut off but not for Himself' in His sacrificial death on the cross. (Daniel 9:25, 26a)

After this there is a period of unspecified length which we are still in. This has included the second destruction of Jerusalem and the temple, and the time when the Land was left desolate (after 70 AD), and many subsequent desolations and wars. (Verse 26b) The final 'seven' will commence with the confirmation of a covenant for seven years. (Verse 27) This will be a covenant 'with many'. In the middle of the following week (after three-and-a-half years) the 'prince who is to come' will bring an end to sacrifice and offering (presumably in the rebuilt temple), and set up the 'abomination of desolation'. At the end of the seven years the consummation will come (with the return of Yeshua) destroying the 'desolation'.

What deception must we beware in these last days? (2 Thessalonians 2)

Readings: Daniel 9:24 – 11, 2 Thessalonians 2

20th Day of the 5th Month
Av, usually falling in July/August
Prophecies of Daniel for the Latter Days
A Covenant with Many

> And the people of the prince who is to come shall destroy the city and the sanctuary. The end of it shall be with a flood, and till the end of the war desolations are determined. Then he shall confirm a covenant with many for one week; but in the middle of the week he shall bring an end to sacrifice and offering. *Daniel 9:26b, 27a*

Daniel 9:25, 26 contains the clear prophecy of the first coming of the Messiah Yeshua, which was fulfilled after '69 sevens,' (483 years) and many writers claim to have worked out the exact dates, showing the accuracy of the prophecy. We have, in verses 25 and 26, the only two references in the Old Testament which actually use the word Messiah – 'Meshiach'. All other references are 'allusions' to the Messiah or metaphors. In the New Testament the word was also only used twice, both by John in John 1:41 and John 4:25.

Yeshua was 'cut off' or we could say 'put to death' – 'not for Himself', which indicates the sacrificial nature of His death as a substitute for us. (Daniel 9:26) Immediately after this, we have the prophecy of the destruction of the city (Jerusalem), and the sanctuary (the temple), which was fulfilled in 70 AD as prophesied, with a 'flood' (calamity). We are told that this would be done by the people of the 'prince who is to come', who only John names, calling him the 'anti-Christ' (1 John 2:18). The fourth 'beast' was probably the Roman Empire that destroyed Jerusalem in the 'spirit of Babylon', which overran it and imposed its own religion and politics. The prince 'who is to come', will come in the same spirit – see the characteristics in Daniel 7:25. He will make a covenant with many, possibly bringing a false peace. (1 Thessalonians 5:3) After three-and-a-half years the sacrifices and offerings of the Jews will cease, and the 'abomination of desolation' will be in evidence.

Is the 'prince who is to come' the 'anti-Christ' of 1 John 2:18? What does John teach us?

Readings: 1 John 2:18–29, 4:3, 2 John 7–11, Revelation 13, 19:19, 20

21st Day of the 5th Month
Av, usually falling in July/August
Prophecies of Daniel for the Latter Days
The Abomination of Desolation

And on the wing of abominations shall be one who makes desolate, even until the consummation, which is determined, is poured out on the desolate. *Daniel 9:27b*

The prophecies of Daniel contain references to 'abominations' which bring about, and are connected with, desolation. The word for abomination, 'Shiqquwts', is from the word meaning disgusting, filthy, idolatrous, abominable, filthy, idol, and detestable thing. The same word is used in 1 Kings 11:5, 7 and 2 Kings 23:13 for the idols and abominations of the Ammonites, Moabites, and the Sidonians who had fertility cults, and who practised child sacrifice. The 'abomination of desolation' is a blasphemous, idolatrous and detestable image, placed in the holy place in the temple in Jerusalem. This was possibly what happened in 175 BC when Antiochus Epiphanes set up an idol to Zeus (Jupiter) in the Holy of Holies and ordered the Jews to sacrifice pigs (which is a blasphemy). (Daniel 11:31)

Daniel prophesied abominations which would bring in desolation, until God comes and destroys them. He will pour out His judgement upon them. That will be the 'consummation' or the end of the 'seventy sevens'. Yeshua referred to Daniel's prophesy, when He sat on the Mount of Olives and spoke about the end times. He said, "When you see the 'abomination of desolation' spoken of by Daniel the prophet, standing in the holy place" (whoever reads let him understand), "then let those who are in Judea flee to the mountains." (Matthew 24:15) If this future 'abomination of desolation' follows the same pattern as that set up by Antiochus Epiphanes, and that of the Romans, then it will take place in a future re-built temple in Jerusalem. (Matthew 24:15–22, Mark 13:19–20) It will precipitate the greatest tribulation the earth has ever seen before Yeshua returns to rule and reign.

What 'abominations' which bring 'desolation' must we avoid today?

Readings: Daniel 8, 11:31 – 12:12, Matthew 24:15–22, Mark 13:3–23, 2 Peter 2

22nd Day of the 5th Month
Av, usually falling in July/August
Prophecies of Daniel for the Latter Days
The Time of Trouble and Deliverance for the Jews

At that time Michael shall stand up, the great prince who stands watch over the sons of your people; and there shall be a time of trouble, such as never was since there was a nation, even to that time. And at that time your people shall be delivered, everyone who is found written in the book. *Daniel 12:1*

This prophecy in the final chapter of the book of Daniel concerns the time of the Great Tribulation. At that time Michael shall stand up. Michael is the mighty Angel who watches over the Jewish people. (Daniel 10:21, Revelation 12:7) The Jews will enter the 'time of trouble', their greatest tribulation ever, greater even than the holocaust. At that time there will be deliverance for God's people who call upon Him and trust in Yeshua for their salvation, whose name is found written in the book of life. (Revelation 20:12)

The Prophet Jeremiah also prophesied this time of trouble which will come on God's people before Yeshua returns. He called it 'Jacob's Trouble'. (Jeremiah 30:7) The holocaust was a time of great trouble for the Jews, but after the holocaust and the Zionist struggle, the State of Israel was formed. This however, was not the prophesied deliverance through seeing Yeshua raised up as their King. This is yet to come to pass (Jeremiah 30:9), and will happen when Yeshua returns to deliver the Jews out of their trouble.

In Matthew 24:21–31 Yeshua prophesied the Great Tribulation which would precede His return. Daniel 11:40–45 spoke about the kings of the South and the North and one leader in particular invading the Land. Revelation 16:16 mentions Armageddon. But at the end, in the day of His vengeance, Yeshua will return and deliver His people. (Isaiah 63:1–6)

God is your deliverer. Whoever calls on the name of the Lord shall be saved. (Acts 2:21)

Readings: Daniel 11:40 – 12:3, Matthew 24:21–31, Isaiah 63:1–6

23rd Day of the 5th Month
Av, usually falling in July/August
Prophecies of Daniel for the Latter Days
Travel and Knowledge Increase

"But you, Daniel, shut up the words, and seal the book until the time of the end; many shall run to and fro, and knowledge shall increase."
Daniel 12:4

The book of Daniel was sealed until the time of the end. When we begin to understand the prophecies of Daniel concerning the time of the end, then we must be in the time of the end. As the time approaches, more and more details will make more and more sense, and fit with the times we are living in, showing us that we truly are in the time of the end.

One prophecy in the book of Daniel that would have been impossible to understand up until the 1990s is the 'increase of knowledge'. (Daniel 12:4) This prophecy has already been 'opened up' to us. Up until the use of personal computers and the internet, it was impossible to conceive the vast explosion and availability of knowledge that we have today. Who could have dreamed of the exponential multiplication in digital technology, satellites and mobile phones, and what it would mean for us today as it has changed our world. The Prophet Daniel also said that many shall "run to and fro". (Daniel 12:4) Previous generations could never have imagined the 'busy activity' of many people in our day, the distances and speed of commuting, and the extent of foreign travel available to many.

As the return of the Lord draws near we are to be 'wise and understand' the prophecies of Daniel. (Daniel 12:10) As we watch world events we need discernment from God so as not to interpret world events according to a worldly understanding from the media, or even false teaching in churches, but with understanding from Scripture and the Holy Spirit.

Do you seek to understand world events from the point of view of the Scriptures?

Readings: Daniel 12, Revelation 12:7–12, 13:14, Ecclesiastes 1:1–13, Psalm 119:105

24th Day of the 5th Month
Av, usually falling in July/August
Gospel Prophecies for the Latter Days
The Temple Destroyed

Then Jesus went out and departed from the temple, and His disciples came up to show Him the buildings of the temple. And Jesus said to them, "Do you not see all these things? Assuredly, I say to you, not one stone shall be left here upon another, that shall not be thrown down."

Matthew 24:1, 2

We go now to the key gospel passages about the end-times, in Matthew 24, Mark 13 and Luke 21. They take place on two separate occasions. Matthew's and Mark's accounts are of an occasion when Yeshua sat on the Mount of Olives looking across to the temple. Luke's version took place inside the temple. In Matthew's and Mark's gospels, Yeshua concentrates on the 'end of the end times' when many signs have already taken place, whereas Luke's gospel account includes the 'beginning of the end times', even with the destruction of Jerusalem – which was fulfilled in 70 AD. Excavations at the Temple Mount in Jerusalem have revealed the stones that were 'thrown down' just as Yeshua prophesied.

The Jewish followers of Yeshua who knew the prophecies of Yeshua were able at that time to escape Jerusalem, because He had warned them what to look out for and what to do. He said that when they saw Jerusalem surrounded by armies, they were to know that its desolation was near, and to let those in Judea flee to the mountains. (Luke 21:20, 21) Their opportunity for escape happened when there was a break in the siege of Jerusalem. In 68 AD Vespasian was made Emperor of Rome and he left his son Titus to make the final assault. During the hand-over there was a break in the siege. The Jewish followers of Yeshua fled with their lives because Yeshua had told them to and so they escaped the terrible destruction wrought by Titus in 70 AD.

What should residents of Jerusalem watch out for and do in the future? (Matthew 24:15–22)

Readings: Matthew 24, Mark 13, Luke 21

25th Day of the 5th Month
Av, usually falling in July/August
Gospel Prophecies for the Latter Days
False Messiahs and False Prophets

"Take heed that no one deceives you. For many will come in my name, saying, 'I am the Christ', and will deceive many...."

Matthew 24:4, 5

Yeshua warned the Jewish people of the danger from false messiahs and false prophets who would come before the end of the age. It has happened just as He said. Many personalities have arisen in Judaism claiming to be the Jewish Messiah. One example is Shabbatai Zevi (1626–1676), who had much charisma and even held a coronation for himself. He planned to liberate Palestine from the Ottomon Empire to form the Jewish State, but when the Muslims gave him the choice of converting to Islam or being tortured to death, he converted to Islam. Amazingly many Jews continued to believe in him.

Christians can be deceived too when they follow strong leaders without exercising their own discernment or checking the Scriptures to see if what they are taught is scriptural and true. Yeshua said, "Take heed that no one deceives you." (Matthew 24:4) The Bereans were a good example to us because they 'received the word with all readiness, and searched the Scriptures daily to find out whether these things were so.' (Acts 17:11)

Yeshua warned against false prophets, lawlessness, and peoples' hearts growing cold. (Matthew 24:11) He also said, "Beware of false prophets, who come to you in sheep's clothing, but inwardly they are ravenous wolves. You will know them by their fruits. Do men gather grapes from thorn bushes or figs from thistles? ..." (Matthew 7:15, 16) We are to check a person's character, whether the way they live and what they say is scriptural. We must be discerning so as not to be deceived, and be true to the true gospel. (Galatians 1:6, 7)

Ask God to increase your discernment. What must you beware of? (Mark 12:38–40)

Readings: Mark 13:21–23, 2 Corinthians 11, 2 Timothy 3, 2 Peter 2

Syria -
28/8/14

26th Day of the 5th Month
Av, usually falling in July/August
Gospel Prophecies for the Latter Days
Betrayals, Persecutions and Martyrdoms

And you will be hated by all for My name's sake. But not a hair of
your head shall be lost. By your patience possess your souls.
Luke 21:17, 18

The time will come when the true devoted believers in Yeshua will be
hated by all, be persecuted, betrayed and martyred. (Matthew 24:9)
This is already happening in certain parts of the world. But it will
increase. We are not to worry beforehand. Instead we are to trust our
heavenly father who loves us. Enemies of the gospel may be able to kill
our bodies, but we will immediately be with Yeshua so we cannot lose.
(Philippians 1:21) It is the persecutors who need to beware, because
unless they repent and turn to Yeshua, they will lose their souls in hell.
They need to hear the truth, and be given the opportunity to repent.

Jewish believers in Yeshua will be delivered up to the 'synagogues',
betrayed by friends and family. (Matthew 24:10) This is already
happening particularly among certain communities who completely
ostracise family, friends, husbands and wives, when they turn to Yeshua,
considering them to be no longer Jewish. That of course is not the case.

True believers in Yeshua who love the God of Israel, and obey the
Scriptures, will be persecuted by the apostate church in the last days.
There already is an increase in false doctrine, false teachings, and
deceiving, lying spirits and spiritual experiences in churches which
actually come from demons. The Apostle Paul warned, 'Evil men and
impostors will grow worse and worse, deceiving and being deceived.'
(2 Timothy 3:13) Believers must preach the truth of God's Word no
matter the cost, not seeking personal comfort. Yeshua said, "...whoever
loses his life for My sake and the gospel's will save it..." (Mark 8:35)

*Thank God for the promise of the help of the Holy Spirit in our hour of
need. (John 16)*

Readings: Matthew 5:10–12, Mark 8:34–38, 2 Timothy 4:1–8,
Revelation 12:11

27th Day of the 5th Month
Av, usually falling in July/August
Gospel Prophecies for the Latter Days
Wars, Pestilence and Famine

For nation will rise against nation, and kingdom against kingdom. And there will be famines, pestilences, and earthquakes in various places. All these are the beginning of sorrows. *Matthew 24:7, 8*

These traumatic world events prophesied by Yeshua are the 'beginning of sorrows'. The Greek word used here for sorrows – 'odin' means 'a pang or throe, especially of childbirth, pain, sorrow, travail.' These sorrows are the labour pains of the earth for the birth of God's kingdom reign on earth – when Yeshua returns.

The nature of labour pains is that they grow increasingly frequent and intense as the moment for birth draws near. This is what is happening in our day. Famines, wars, pestilences, natural disasters and earthquakes are increasing in frequency and severity. This is a sign of the times we are in, and of the imminent return of the Lord. (Revelation 6)

When Yeshua was born the angels joyfully sang "on earth peace, goodwill toward men!" (Luke 2:14) Yeshua brought peace between God and man. But the peace on earth prophesied in Isaiah 2:4 and Micah 4:3 will only come when Yeshua has returned to rule and reign on the earth for the 'thousand years' prophesied in Revelation 20. The complete fulfilment of peace on earth will come in His restored kingdom when Yeshua is ruling and reigning. (Isaiah 11:6–10). Therefore we are not to be troubled. The signs we see are the labour pains which have already been occurring for two thousand years, as Yeshua said they would. Unprecedented devastation is yet to be poured out on the earth with the arrival of the four horsemen of Revelation 6 during the Great Tribulation.

Read God's promise to Israel in Isaiah 43:1, 2 and receive it as God's promise for you too.

Readings: Psalm 23, Psalms 56, 57, Proverbs 3:25, 26, John 14:27, 28, Revelation 6

28th Day of the 5th Month
Av, usually falling in July/August
Gospel Prophecies for the Latter Days
Jewish Jerusalem

And Jerusalem will be trampled by Gentiles until the times of the Gentiles are fulfilled. *Luke 21:24*

Yeshua prophesied the desolation of Jerusalem (which happened in AD 70) and then He said that Jerusalem would be trampled by the Gentiles. This would be for a fixed, determined period of time which would come to an end when the times of the Gentiles are fulfilled. The implication is that after a period of time under Gentile rule, Jerusalem would come back completely under Jewish rule and then we would be in the time of the Jews.

After AD 70 Jerusalem was governed by a succession of Gentile rulers: Romans, Byzantines, various Muslim Dynasties, Crusaders, Mamluks, Ottomans, and finally the British Empire. In 1948 the State of Israel was formed and the War of Independence began when Israel was invaded by five Islamic nations. The war left half of Jerusalem (the east) in the hands of the Jordanians. But in 1967, in the Six Day War, the Israelis defeated the Jordanians, and Jerusalem came entirely under Jewish rule for the first time since the days of the kings of Judah. Jewish people knew this was significant and many believers saw this as the fulfilment of Yeshua's prophecy. In 1967 many Jews around the world suddenly came to salvation – particularly through the 'Jesus Movement'. Perhaps they were a sign that we were entering the 'time of the Jews', or perhaps they signalled the greater fulfilment yet to come.

While the United Nations and the Gentile nations of the world try to divide Jerusalem they are still, in a sense, 'trampling Jerusalem', trying to take East Jerusalem away from the Jews. But a time will come when Jerusalem will be trampled no longer. In the fullness of time the whole earth will enter 'the time of the Jews' and Yeshua will reign from Zion.

If you feel trampled upon for your testimony to God, the time of your blessing will come.

Readings: Luke 21:20–24, Zechariah 12, Isaiah 62

29th Day of the 5th Month ·
Av, usually falling in July/August
Gospel Prophecies for the Latter Days
The Return of the Lord

"Now learn this parable from the fig tree. When its branch has already become tender and puts forth leaves, you know that summer is near, so you also, when you see all these things, know that it is near – at the doors!..." *Matthew 24:32*

At the end of the Great Tribulation everything that can be shaken will have been shaken, including the powers of the heavens. There will be great signs in the sky. Then the Lord will be seen coming on the clouds. That is how He was caught up to heaven. He will return in the same manner as He was seen going into Heaven. (Acts 1:11) All the tribes of the earth will mourn when they see the Son of Man returning with 'power and great glory'. There will be a great sound from the trumpets of the angels and they will gather together God's 'elect'. Zechariah says He will return to the Mount of Olives. (Zechariah 14:3, 4)

Yeshua said that we must learn from the parable of the fig tree. When we look and see leaves on its branches we know that the summer is near. Similarly, when we see the signs that Yeshua prophesied for us – then we can know that all these things are about to come to pass. In Scripture, the fig tree is symbolic – most especially of Israel. The sign of the restoration of the Jews to Israel, the sign of Jewish Jerusalem, the sign of the false prophets, the 'abomination of desolation', the tribulations, all these things demonstrate the time and season. Nobody knows the exact timing of His return, but His people must be prepared, watching and waiting for Him. It is possible that the Bride will be 'caught up' to her Bridegroom anytime, even before the Great Tribulation comes to pass, because we need to be ready to be taken at any time. (Matthew 24:44, 50) Theologians call this the Pre-Tribulation 'rapture'. We do not know. What we do know is that we must be watching and ready.

Are you watching the 'fig tree' to know the time and season, and to be ready for the Lord?

Readings: Matthew 24:29–35, Mark 13:24–37, Luke 21:35–38

30th Day of the 5th Month
Av, usually falling in July/August
Gospel Prophecies for the Latter Days
An Unexpected Hour

Watch therefore, for you know neither the day nor the hour in which the Son of Man is coming. Matthew 25:13

Matthew 24 tells us that the Lord will return when people do not expect Him. He has warned us to be watching and ready, understanding the time and season that we are in. But just as all the people apart from Noah were taken by surprise by the sudden total devastation of the flood upon the whole earth, so too people will be caught out by the return of the Lord.

People will be living their lives as normal, even getting married when the Son of Man 'takes' the people who are His own. This is what people call 'the rapture', when the Bride is 'caught up' – 'raptured up' to God, possibly before the Great Tribulation and the 'Day of God's Vengeance', because people will be living normally and not expecting Him. We don't know when it will be. We must live expecting Him to return at any time. 1 Thessalonians 4:16, 17 says, 'the Lord Himself will descend from heaven with a shout, with the voice of an archangel, and with the trumpet of God. And the dead in Christ will rise first. Then we who are alive and remain shall be caught up together with them in the clouds to meet the Lord in the air....' 1 Thessalonians 5:2, 3 says '... the day of the Lord so comes as a thief in the night. For when they say, "Peace and safety!" then sudden destruction comes upon them....'

Yeshua tells us to be like the wise virgins who had enough oil in their lamps to go out and meet the Bridegroom when He returned. (Matthew 25:1–13) When a master returns to his house unexpectedly, he wants to find his servant working hard and behaving well. (Matthew 24:43–51) We are to guard ourselves, be sober, alert, obeying Him and His Word.

What does Yeshua require of you, if you are to be ready like the servant and the wise virgins?

Readings: Matthew 24:26 – 25:13, Luke 21:34–36, 1 Thessalonians 4:15 – 5:10

1st Day of the 6th Month
Elul, usually falling in August/September
Awaken the Believers
Building the House of God

In the second year of King Darius, in the sixth month, on the first day of the month, the word of the LORD came by Haggai the prophet to Zerubbabel the son of Shealtiel, governor of Judah, and to Joshua the son of Jehozadak, the High Priest.... *Haggai 1:1*

We return again to the first of the month, to the new moon, when the trumpets are blown. In this, the sixth month, the intense summer heat is beginning to subside and the olives are being gathered from the trees. We are only one month away from the culmination of the Levitical Feast Cycle with the autumn feasts which speak of end time events. It is therefore appropriate that this month we focus on God's activity amongst the congregation of believers, as He alerts the Bride, and He awakens her to prepare for Yeshua's return.

On this day, God's word came to the returned exiles from Babylon to fulfil God's command to build. Around 538–536 BC they had received Cyrus's decree to rebuild the temple in Jerusalem, but they had become discouraged, and given up. They needed a fresh word and encouragement to get them building again, to finish what they started, and rebuild the House of the Lord. The word came through the prophet Haggai. He reminded the people that the most important thing is to build God's house. They had all become preoccupied with rebuilding their own houses after their return from exile, and consequently they were not blessed, and the rains had not come. They needed to get back to work and not be afraid, because God was with them, and they had His Spirit. In their eyes the new 'House' was inferior to the old one that had been destroyed, but it was not so in God's eyes. The glory of the latter house would be greater than the first. Messiah would come! They would find peace with God and be blessed with harvests. They were home, they were no longer exiles.

Ask God to help you complete what you began in obedience to God. The best is yet to come!

Readings: Haggai 1, 2, Matthew 16:16–19, Revelation 1

2nd Day of the 6th Month
Elul, usually falling in August/September
The Church of Ephesus
Apostolic Church

"I know your works, your labor, your patience, and that you cannot bear those who are evil. And you have tested those who say they are apostles and are not, and have found them liars...." *Revelation 2:2*

This month we will look at the messages of Yeshua to each of the Seven Churches of Asia Minor (modern day Turkey) in Revelation 1–3. These 'letters' address the condition of the churches. The Seven Churches not only represent the varied state of churches around the world today, but they can also be categorised into distinct periods of history, from the earliest church up to our present day, when the condition of the seventh church, the Laodicean church is prevalent, especially in the West. The lessons can also be applied to individuals.

The letters are preceded by the glorious revelation of Yeshua Himself. The churches are meant to shine out the light of God into the world, through the Holy Spirit. Like the seven branched menorah (lampstand) which stood in the temple, Yeshua is the light of the world and each church receives a part of the revelation of Yeshua. If the Holy Spirit is grieved away, the church can no longer shine with God's light, and it will die spiritually.

The first of the Seven Churches, in Ephesus, can be seen to represent the early congregations from the time of the original apostles up until approximately 100 AD. The Early Church began full of fire, zeal and love for the Lord, but it also had to contend hard to establish correct doctrine, teaching and theology. As the first generation of apostles died, it was essential to discern who the new God-sent apostles were, and reject the false ones. Their discernment pleased the Lord.

Consider the importance to the Lord of discerning between true and false apostles.

Readings: Revelation 2:1–3, Acts 2:42, Acts 19, 20, Ezekiel 34:1–5, 1 Timothy 1:3, 4

ELUL

3rd Day of the 6th Month
Elul, usually falling in August/September
The Church of Ephesus
Recover our First Love

"Nevertheless I have this against you, that you have left your first love. Remember therefore from where you have fallen; repent and do the first works, or else I will come to you quickly and remove your lampstand from its place – unless you repent." *Revelation 2:4, 5*

Yeshua commended the Ephesian Church, because they tested the people who called themselves apostles, and rejected the false ones who were liars. There will always be people who want to lead churches and 'Christian movements', but they have not all been sent, or even called by God. We know the true apostles from the false ones, not only by their doctrine, but by the fruit of their lives, and their humble servant-hood.

The Ephesian Church laboured hard for the sake of the name of the Lord and had not become weary. Nonetheless, the Lord did have something against this church. They had left behind their first love. The earliest believers had received that first baptism of the Holy Spirit at the first Pentecost in Jerusalem. But now, some years later, out in Asia Minor, in a city with a strong pagan culture, somehow these believers in Yeshua 'relaxed' or 'let go' of their first love for the Lord. We too must guard against 'letting go' of the most important One whose presence we need to discern, the Lord Himself. Mary discerned the value of the presence of the Lord with her, while her sister was too busy serving, to come to receive from the One she most needed.(Luke 10:41, 42) We may need to repent if this describes us.

Yeshua our Heavenly Bridegroom wants our love. He longs for us to spend time in His presence, for us to share our hearts with Him, to love the beauty, fragrance, loveliness of His person. He is our Saviour. He wants us to receive His love and to just love Him in return.

Spend time drawing near to God, receiving His love and telling Him that you love Him.

Readings: Revelation 2:4–7, Luke 10:38–42, John 13:23, Song of Songs 8:5–7, John 14:15

4th Day of the 6th Month
Elul, usually falling in August/September
The Church of Ephesus
The Nicolaitans

"But this you have, that you hate the deeds of the Nicolaitans, which I also hate." *Revelation 2:6*

One of the things the Lord commended the Ephesian Church for, was their hatred of the deeds of the Nicolaitans. It is not known for certain who the Nicolaitans were. One theory is that they were a sect named after a man called Nicolas, who attempted to reconcile pagan religious practices with Christianity, and included pagan rituals and sexual immorality. Another theory is that it is the Greek version of the Hebrew 'Balaam', and therefore an allegorical illusion to an attempt to corrupt the Church with sexual immorality. A third possibility is that it comes from the Greek words 'nikao' (to conquer) and 'laos' meaning the 'laity' or the 'people' who are not the priesthood. Finally there is the possibility that it was the name of a Gnostic sect. The Gnostic belief was (and is) the belief that there is a hidden knowledge, that only a few privileged people can attain to (as in a secret society), and usually implicit in this is a denial of the virgin birth and divinity of Yeshua.

Actually all these views are compatible. The Early Church had to resist gnostic and pagan beliefs, and the sexual immorality that accompanied them. Just as a Babylonian-type political power system was passed on through the Medes, Persians, Greeks and Romans, to re-emerge in the end times, so the Babylonian religion has been passed down and blended into church practice. Many unbiblical church practices have roots in paganism and in a pagan-style priesthood, which sets itself above the laity, robbing people of the biblical 'priesthood of all believers'.(1 Peter 2:9) The Babylonian religion had Basilicas with high altars, robed and jewelled high priests wearing mitres, and a daily bread sacrifice. In contrast Yeshua is our only High Priest and He is interceding for us in Heaven. (Hebrews 7:24–28)

Thank God for Yeshua, your only High Priest, and that He is your example of servant-hood.

Readings: 1 Peter 2:1–10, Hebrews 7:11 – 9:28, Matthew 20:25–28, John 13:14

5th Day of the 6th Month
Elul, usually falling in August/September
The Church of Smyrna
The Martyred Church

"And to the angel of the church in Smyrna write, These things says the First and the Last, who was dead and came to life...."

Revelation 2:8

The second of the seven letters to the churches was written to Smyrna – whose name meant 'crushed myrrh'. Myrrh is the incense used in the preparation of bodies for burial. The wise men gave Yeshua Myrrh, (Matthew 2:11) and He was offered wine mingled with myrrh on the cross. (Mark 15:23) This church received no rebuke from the Lord, but received the instruction not to be afraid of the things they are about to suffer. This church represented the suffering and martyred church throughout the world and through the ages.

Yeshua revealed Himself to these believers as the one who overcame death through the resurrection, never to die again. Because He had overcome death Yeshua was able to tell the persecuted church not to fear what they were about to suffer, including prison. They may have been poor in worldly goods, but they were rich spiritually. They were persecuted by religious hypocrites who did not know God but actually did the bidding of Satan, to test them.

The tribulation this church was to suffer would last ten days. It is widely thought that the ten days represent the ten Roman Emperors who successively and viciously persecuted the Christians – beginning with Nero in 64 AD and ending with Diocletian in 310 AD. But Yeshua, King of kings, existed before any of these men were born, and He continued to live after they passed away. Faithfulness to the Everlasting King, even unto death will bring the reward of the crown of life. The lampstand of God's light and presence remained in place. They did not need to repent. Today Smyrna re-lives as part of the city of Izmir in Turkey.

Pray for the suffering and persecuted church around the world today. (Hebrews 13:3)

Readings: Mark 15:6–20, Revelation 6:9–11, 12:10–12, 20:4–6, 21:1–8

6th Day of the 6th Month
Elul, usually falling in August/September
The Church of Smyrna
Tribulation and Poverty

"I know your works, tribulation and poverty (but you are rich)...."
Revelation 2:9

Yeshua understood the suffering of His Church, their tribulation and poverty. In the eyes of the world they were poor and persecuted, but not in God's eyes. It is possible that in the end times, Christians will be forced out of a world economic system that they can no longer be part of, and suffer poverty. (Revelation 13:17) But God is rich.

Our treasure is where our heart is. (Matthew 6:19–21) If our heart is with the Lord, we have all the treasures of heaven at our disposal. In the last days it will be increasingly common, as greater tribulations come for believers, to experience the supernatural provision of food by angels. It is possible too, that if people can no longer afford normal travel, He will 'translate' us like He did Philip. (Acts 8:39, 40) Our true riches are in our relationship with God and all that Yeshua accomplished for us in His death on the cross. He has given us the riches of His divine favour and the inheritance of abundant eternal life and victory in Him. If we seek first the kingdom of God, and His righteousness, He will provide for all of our needs. (Matthew 6:31–34) But we are promised persecutions as well. (Mark 10:29, 30)

When the Apostle Paul was converted Yeshua showed him what he was to suffer for the sake of His name. (Acts 9:16) Paul came to suffer stoning, beatings, shipwrecks, sleeplessness, hunger, thirst, fastings, cold, nakedness and many journeys and perils. (2 Corinthians 11:24–28) Read these verses and consider how much Paul suffered. But who else contributed as many books to the Bible or had such influence as the Apostle Paul?

Thank God that though at this moment you may be poor and suffering, you are rich in God.

Readings: Matthew 16:24–28, Mark 10:17–31, Romans 8:18–39

7th Day of the 6th Month
Elul, usually falling in August/September
The Church of Smyrna
Do not Fear Suffering

"Do not fear any of those things which you are about to suffer."

Revelation 2:10

It would have been natural for the Church at Smyrna to become afraid, on hearing about the things they were about to suffer. But Yeshua told them not to be afraid. There was the eternal reward of the crown of life which awaited them if they would be faithful even unto death. (Revelation 2:10)

The suffering was not sent by God, but came from Satan to test them. This reminds us of how Yeshua told Simon, "...Indeed, Satan has asked for you, that he may sift you as wheat. But I have prayed for you, that your faith should not fail; and when you have returned to Me, strengthen your brethren." (Luke 22:31, 32) Peter failed the test - but His faith did not fail. He did return to Yeshua. And in the end he gave his life for the Lord. (John 21:18, 19) Another person who was 'sifted' or 'tested' by Satan was Job. The devil contested with God that, if Job suffered and lost everything, he would curse God to His face. (Job 1:11) After the test God restored double of everything to Job. (Job 42:10)

We have the Holy Spirit to help us to be faithful to God. In the moment of testing we have the Holy Spirit in us. He will carry us through, if we have already determined beforehand to stay faithful to Him. We have the warning from Yeshua, "whoever confesses Me before men, him I will also confess before My Father who is in heaven. But whoever denies Me before men, him I will also deny before My Father who is in heaven." (Matthew 10:32, 33) Yeshua also said, "Do not fear those who kill the body but cannot kill the soul. But rather fear Him who is able to destroy both soul and body in hell." (Matthew 10:28)

Thank God that you are not powerless over fear. Ask God to give you boldness and courage.

Readings: Matthew 10, Luke 22:31–46, 1 Corinthians 10:12–13

8th Day of the 6th Month
Elul, usually falling in August/September
The Church of Smyrna
Not hurt by the Second Death

"He who has an ear, let him hear what the Spirit says to the churches. He who overcomes shall not be hurt by the second death."

Revelation 2:11

God calls His people to be overcomers, so that they shall not be hurt by the second death. The second death comes in Revelation 20:14, where death and Hades are cast into the lake of fire. Every one whose name is not found written in the Book of Life at the final judgement, will be cast into the Lake of Fire with the devil and the fallen angels. Revelation 21:8 says that those who will suffer this eternal torment will be the 'cowardly, unbelieving, abominable, murderers, sexually immoral, sorcerers, idolaters and liars.' (Revelation 21:8)

In contrast, 'He who overcomes shall inherit all things, and I will be his God, and he shall be My son.' (Revelation 21:7) Those who believe in Yeshua and are made righteous in Him must overcome even to the point of death if necessary so as not to deny Yeshua. They may die, or even be put to death for their faith, but they will have made the choice for life in eternity with God.

When the persecutions did come on the Church at Smyrna, at the hands of the Roman Empire, believers were beheaded, burned alive and thrown to wild beasts. This man-made kingdom sought to destroy God's kingdom. To this day, countless numbers of believers around the world are dying for their proclamation of faith in Yeshua. We can pray that if persecution comes to us, His Holy Spirit in us will keep us faithful to the end. Yeshua is our example: who 'for the joy that was set before Him endured the cross, despising the shame, and has sat down at the right hand of the throne of God.' (Hebrews 12:2)

Consider the eternal consequences of overcoming, or not. Put your trust in God's help.

Readings: Hebrews 12:1–4, Revelation 20, 1 Corinthians 15:50–58

9th Day of the 6th Month
Elul, usually falling in August/September
The Church of Pergamos
The Paganised State Church

"And to the angel of the church in Pergamos write, These things says He who has the sharp two-edged sword...." *Revelation 2:12*

The two-edged sword of Yeshua which is revealed to the Church in Pergamos, (also known as Pergamon) reminds us of Isaiah 49:2: 'He has made My mouth like a sharp sword.' Yeshua's words are like a sword, which creates (John 1:1–14, Genesis 1:3), judges and divides. Hebrews 4:12 says, 'the word of God is living and powerful, and sharper than any two-edged sword, piercing even to the division of soul and spirit, and of joints and marrow, and is a discerner of the thoughts and intents of the heart.' This spiritual sword of God's Word is needed to separate and divide what is biblical in the Church from what is not.

The letter to the Church in Pergamos could be seen as representing the Church from the end of the Persecution by the Roman Emperors up until about 600 AD. The persecutions ended in 325 AD when the Roman Emperor Constantine 'married' the Christian Church to the pagan religion of the Roman Empire. The name 'Pergamos' contains the Greek word 'gamos', meaning marriage, and Pergamos was a centre of pagan idolatry and worship. Constantine brought together the pagan worship of the sun god Mithra with Christianity, creating a feast for the birth of Yeshua, on the feast day of the birth of the sun god Mithra, on 25th December as well as worship on Sun Day. Likewise the Isis/Ishtar/Ostre worship in the spring, part of a fertility cycle involving human sacrifice and re-birth was 'married to' the remembrance of the death and resurrection of Yeshua, superimposing it on a feast bearing the name 'Easter' – from the 'god' Ostre/Ishtar. The sword of the Word of God would separate us from paganism, freeing us to return to the biblical faith and feasts.

Ask God to use the sword of the Lord to free you from 'paganism' found in the Church.

Readings: Revelation 2:1–17, Mark 7:13, Colossians 2, Ephesians 6:10–20

10th Day of the 6th Month
Elul, usually falling in August/September
The Church of Pergamos
Satan's Throne Defeated

"I know your works, and where you dwell, where Satan's throne is."

Revelation 2:13

'Satan's throne' was in Pergamos. It is believed to be the white stone altar on which human sacrifices were made to Zeus. (Revelation 2:13) A German archaeologist excavated the altar and took it to a museum in Berlin. It is said that Hitler based the Nuremburg Stadium, from where he made speeches to Nazi rallies, on Pergamos and its altar. It is thought that the stone originally came from Babylon, and was moved to Pergamos in 487 BC. Babylon was where the Satanic Babylonian religion started. 'Nimrod' the mighty hunter is mentioned in Genesis 10:8 – 11:9 and it is thought he was the leader of the rebellion against God under the sway of Satan. (Revelation 12:7–9, 17:5) 'Nimrod' is from the word 'rebel'.

Babylonian religion is based on human lust, fertility and human sacrifice, but instead of coming under God's pure command to 'be fruitful and multiply' (Genesis 1:28), it involves death and idolatry. It manifests in various pagan myths, the essential element being an incestuous fertility cycle, with the exaltation of the 'madonna' with her child. This goddess is worshipped as the 'Queen of Heaven' (Jeremiah 44:15–19), Tammuz (Ezekiel 8:13–18), Ashteroth with Baal (Judges 2:13) and 'Mary'. The Babylonian fertility cycle of death and re-birth connects to the seasons. The biblical 'moedim', in contrast, exclude winter altogether, beginning and ending with the harvests of God, with no element of paganism.

Rome took on the Babylonian priesthood in 63 AD, and in 378 AD, Damasus, Bishop of the Christian Church in Rome was elected to the office of Supreme Pontiff of the Babylonian Order. But we are to be separate. God is light and in Him there is no darkness.

Sing praises and worship to Yeshua the light of the world, in whom there is no darkness.

Readings: 1 John 1 – 5, Luke 10:18–20, Genesis 10:1 – 11:9, Revelation 17:1–8

11th Day of the 6th Month
Elul, usually falling in August/September
The Church of Pergamos
The Doctrine of Balaam

"But I have a few things against you, because you have there those who hold the doctrine of Balaam, who taught Balak to put a stumbling block before the children of Israel, to eat things sacrificed to idols, and to commit sexual immorality." *Revelation 2:14*

Standing apart from satanic religion, cost the Church in Pergamos the life of God's faithful martyr Antipas. But despite this, the Church failed to deal with those among them who held to the doctrine of Balaam and the Nicolaitans. The name Balaam means 'without a people'. Balaam, a Gentile, straddled the fence. He failed to stand with Israel despite having received the revelation of God's chosen people to whom Messiah would come. Having spoken out the prophetic oracles about Israel, he laid them aside, and persisted in trying to bring Israel down, simply because he was being paid to do so. He cherished the wages that the King of Moab gave him for attempting to curse Israel more than he cherished the truth his prophecies contained. In the end he led Israel into trouble, by encouraging them to mix with the pagan Moabites who turned them astray, and encouraged them to adopt their pagan practices and sexual immorality. (Numbers 22–25)

This error is warned against in 2 Peter 2:15 and Jude 11, where covetousness, carousing, adultery, sexual sin and financial gain through the promotion of sin, are utterly condemned. Sexual immorality in churches often results in the tragedy of abortion. Some people are more concerned about their own desires, than in standing with God's people Israel, with biblical truth and morality. Yeshua calls on them to repent, otherwise He will fight against them with the sword of His mouth. In 716–717 AD Pergamos was attacked by Arabs and finally destroyed. This is a warning to many churches today which need to repent.

Pray for sexual purity and freedom from covetousness and idolatry in your church.

Readings: Numbers 25, 1 Timothy 4, 2 Peter 2, Jude, Ephesians 5:26, 27

12th Day of the 6th Month
Elul, usually falling in August/September
The Church of Pergamos
Hidden Manna

"He who has an ear, let him hear what the Spirit says to the churches. To him who overcomes I will give some of the hidden manna to eat. And I will give him a white stone, and on the stone a new name written which no one knows except him who receives it." *Revelation 2:17*

There is a reward for the overcomers, the people who do not succumb to the false doctrines of Balaam and the Nicolaitans, who don't eat the food sacrificed to idols, (participate in false religious customs), or indulge in sexual immorality. To these overcomers, who have had to live in a place so strongly influenced by the throne of Satan, God will give the hidden manna to eat.

The hidden manna is spiritual food which feeds our souls and gives us life. It is the life of Yeshua. (John 14:26) Manna was hidden inside the Ark of the Covenant, beneath the Mercy Seat. (Hebrews 9:1–4) We eat the hidden manna under the Mercy Seat. This is in contrast to any throne or habitation of Satan which brings death not life. The hidden manna is the life of Yeshua which we eat afresh every day, as we draw close to Him, to gather His word to us from His sweet presence, to sustain and strengthen. Yeshua said, "Your fathers ate the manna in the wilderness, and are dead. This is the bread which comes down from heaven, that one may eat of it and not die. I am the living bread which came down from heaven." (John 6:48–51) Overcomers who feed on this manna will live and never die.

They will learn their new name, written on a white stone, and known only to the one who receives it. God gives us our true identity and life in His love. There is no death in Him.

Ask the Father what your new name is, then guard it secretly in your heart and thank Him.

Readings: Exodus 16, Exodus 28:21, John 6:35–58, Hebrews 9:1–15

ELUL

13th Day of the 6th Month
Elul, usually falling in August/September
The Church of Thyatira
The Compromised Church

"And to the angel of the church in Thyatira write, These things says the Son of God, who has eyes like a flame of fire, and His feet like fine brass...." Revelation 2:18

Thyatira was where Lydia the seller of purple welcomed the Apostle Paul and his companions. (Acts 16:14) Yeshua looked upon this church with eyes flaming with love, holiness and godly jealousy for His people. Glory emanates from Him like fire, causing His feet to glow like shining fine brass. He knows their works, love, service, faith and patience.

Nevertheless there was a problem in the Church. The Church had compromised by allowing the woman Jezebel, who called herself a prophetess, to influence them by her teaching and by seducing God's servants to commit sexual immorality, and to eat things sacrificed to idols.

The Church of Thyatira can be said to represent the Church of the Middle Ages up until the protestant reformation in 1517 AD, when the papacy was the dominating world power. During those years most people had no access to the Scriptures and were held captive by a church system that had compromised with Babylonian Religion. Babylonian religion advocated food offered to idols – not just meat that was sold in the markets. There was a daily ritual offering of a bread sacrifice on the altar to idols. In churches, the bread offered at the daily 'mass' was believed to become the actual physical flesh of Yeshua (transubstantiation), and was actually a daily 'sacrifice' like the Babylonians practised. It wasn't until the reformation in 1517 AD, that the truth was recovered that salvation is received by faith in Yeshua's one perfect sacrifice offered for us once for all upon the cross.

Thank Yeshua for the fire in His eyes of love which releases you from any religious bondage.

Readings: 1 Corinthians 10:14–33, Romans 3:19 – 5:21, Titus 3:1–7, Ephesians 2:1–10

14th Day of the 6th Month
Elul, usually falling in August/September
The Church of Thyatira
Jezebel

"Nevertheless I have a few things against you because you allow that woman Jezebel, who calls herself a prophetess, to teach and seduce My servants to commit sexual immorality, and to eat things sacrificed to idols...." *Revelation 2:20*

The woman in their midst may actually have been called Jezebel or she may have been given this name because of her likeness to Jezebel, the wife of King Ahab of Israel. (1 Kings 18–21, 2 Kings 9) This Jezebel took it upon herself to advise her husband, and she had led him to stray from the God of Israel, and follow Baal, according to the pagan religion she had grown up with in the land of her birth. She actively opposed God's servants, massacring the prophets of the Lord (1 Kings 18:4). She encouraged sexual immorality, and she probably led the people to participate in pagan practice, by teaching them to eat food sacrificed to idols. As a consequence of her evil influence, the weak King Ahab set up an altar for Baal in the temple of Baal, together with an image. (1 Kings 16:32, 33)

The Church in Thyatira allowed a woman like this to operate in their midst. This is a warning to churches today, not to let a man or a woman with this controlling, manipulating spirit, to have any part in their church, causing people to commit sexual immorality and follow false teachings. Today false religion is not openly called Baal worship, but is seen in the syncretism with Babylonian religion: Paganism, New Age, cults, Free Masonry and worship of the 'moon god' of Arabia. Now, in our day, whole societies and people in churches worship the sex god 'Baal'. (2 Kings 17) Children are aborted, blood is spilt. The good news is that Elijah defeated the prophets of Baal. His victory foreshadowed the victory of Yeshua on the cross. (1 Kings 18) His eyes are burning fire, His feet, like brass.

Ask God to expose 'Baal' worship for what it is, in you, and in your church and nation.

Readings: 1 Kings 18–21, 2 Kings 9, 17, Revelation 17

15th Day of the 6th Month
Elul, usually falling in August/September
The Church of Thyatira
The Call to Repent

"And I gave her time to repent of her sexual immorality, but she did not repent." *Revelation 2:21*

God graciously gave Jezebel time to repent of her sexual immorality. Very often the roots of bondage to sexual sin lie in a deep wounding of the soul, particularly from childhood, and a love-deficit from parents. God understands our deep soul needs. But he wants us to be free from being controlled by sexual impulses and lusts. Sex is designed by God to be between a husband and his wife in marriage. Anything apart from that is sexual sin, and once indulged in, it creates a deeper bondage in the soul. In the Bible sexual sin invited the activity of demons. (2 Kings 23) God sets people free, through the power of the Holy Spirit who brings the fruit of self-control into our lives.

When we bring any sexual bondage to the cross, in repentance and open confession with another believer, then, in prayer we can be delivered. When sinful sexual behaviour has been allowed to run wild in a person it brings them into captivity in many different areas of their life. We are incapable of cleaning ourselves up. We have to come to Yeshua exactly as we are and let Him clean us up. When we draw near to Him in faith, to receive His forgiveness at the cross, He will wash us clean, and make us as pure as a virgin again on the inside. We are cleansed through the power of His blood which washes away all sin. His love and grace will wash your deep soul wounds clean, and heal your love deficit which caused the bondage in the first place. Yeshua said, "Those who are well have no need of a physician, but those who are sick. But go and learn what this means: 'I desire mercy and not sacrifice.' For I did not come to call the righteous, but sinners, to repentance." (Matthew 9:12, 13)

The moment you truly repent, God hears, and He forgives you. Forgive yourself and others.

Readings: Matthew 9:9–13, 1 Corinthians 5, 6, 2 Corinthians 7:5–16

16th Day of the 6th Month
Elul, usually falling in August/September
The Church of Thyatira
Power over Nations

"And he who overcomes, and keeps My works until the end, to him I will give power over the nations...." *Revelation 2:26*

Jezebel didn't repent, but there were plenty of people in the Church at Thyatira who did not participate in her sin and who were overcomers. To those who keep Yeshua's works until the end, He promises to give power over the nations.

The consequence of sexual sin and idolatry in an individual, church or nation, is always a weakening: 'sickness' either of the soul, body or church. Churches which are overtaken with actual sexual immorality, or have 'joined themselves' to false religion and doctrine, will eventually fall sick spiritually and die. Churches which have compromised lose their spiritual power, and when the Holy Spirit has been grieved away, more and more of God's people will also be grieved away. (Revelation 2:21–23) That does not mean the church will necessarily become small. It may just remain full of 'apostate' Christians who do not truly follow the gospel of Yeshua, or Christians who simply haven't noticed that the life has gone. Where there has been sexual sin there needs to be open repentance, not cover-up.

In Revelation 2:27 Yeshua quoted Psalm 2:9, promising overcomers ruler-ship with Him over nations. In the end times the nations will rise up and rebel against the Father and the Son, but the Father will set His Son, Messiah Yeshua, on His holy hill – Mount Zion. (Psalm 2:6) Then God's people will rule and reign with Him. Sin, especially sexual sin and abortions, brings a nation low, causing it to be trampled by other nations. (2 Kings 17) But in contrast 'righteousness exalts a nation.' (Proverbs 14:34)

Pray for God's mercy, cleansing and healing on your church and nation.

Readings: Psalm 2, Revelation 2:18–29, Isaiah 11:1–5

17th Day of the 6th Month
Elul, usually falling in August/September
The Church of Sardis
The Lifeless Church

"I know your works, that you have a name that you are alive, but you are dead...." *Revelation 3:1*

The Church in Sardis can be said to represent the church, particularly in Europe that emerged from the Protestant Reformation in 1517 AD, and continued up until about 1750 AD when the modern missionary movement began. It had the appearance of being alive because it was free from some of the elements of Babylonian Religion that had become part of the Roman Church. In this era the Protestant Church received the revelation preached through Martin Luther, that we are justified and saved through faith, and are not dependent on our own works – such as attending the mass or purchasing indulgences – to be saved. The problem was that they did not have the revelation of how to 'stay alive' in the Holy Spirit.

Yeshua revealed Himself to the Church in Sardis as the one who has the Holy Spirit, saying, "These things says He who has the seven Spirits of God and the seven stars." (Revelation 3:1) The seven-fold nature of the Holy Spirit is described in Isaiah 11:2 and Zechariah 4:2 and the seven stars represent the Seven Churches. Yeshua is the one who has the Holy Spirit to impart to the Seven Churches.

The Church in Sardis needed the Holy Spirit. It had the reputation for being alive, but actually it was dead. Yeshua knew their works. Probably many people knew their works. But He also knew their hearts. Churches and individuals can begin strongly, full of the Holy Spirit, but after a while they are still doing the same works but without the leading and empowering of the Holy Spirit. Their works have become dead rituals which are no longer led by a current quickening of the Holy Spirit.

Have you continued in any 'works' through habit but no longer in step with the Holy Spirit?

Readings: Revelation 3:1–6, Acts 2:38–41, Romans 8:1, 14, 2 Corinthians 3

18th Day of the 6th Month
Elul, usually falling in August/September
The Church of Sardis
Be Watchful

"Be watchful, and strengthen the things which remain, that are ready to die, for I have not found your works perfect before God."
Revelation 3:2

The Church of Sardis needed to repent. They needed to strengthen the little bit of life that remained before it died away. Their works were not perfect before God. Anything that we try to do in our own strength will not be perfect before God. Only what He initiates and performs through us, through the power of His Holy Spirit strength in us, is perfect before God. Works which proceed from our own flesh will always fall short. Only by abiding in Him can we bear fruit, and then it will come effortlessly because it will be a result of simply hearing His voice and obeying Him, through keeping in step with the Holy Spirit.

This is a solemn warning to all of us. We cannot live on old manna. We need to eat new manna every day. It is easy to set out doing something simply because it worked last time, or because it seems the right thing to do. But are we really spending time in prayer, hearing from God, and walking in His strength? Those works which came from our flesh will be burned up in the fires of judgement. Paul wrote, '...each one's work will become clear; for the Day will declare it, because it will be revealed by fire; and the fire will test each one's work, of what sort it is.' (1 Corinthians 3:13) The foundation of our work must be Yeshua the Messiah, and we must watch how we build on it. (1 Corinthians 3:10, 11)

The Lord also looks at our motives. The Church is warned to remember how they received and heard – and hold fast to the good and repent. We are all to watch the state of our hearts, so that we may be full of the Holy Spirit when He returns.

Which areas of your walk with God need strengthening, that you may be ready to meet Him?

Readings: Matthew 25, Matthew 13:1–30, 26:40, 41, Luke 12:35–48, 1 Corinthians 16:13, 14

19th Day of the 6th Month
Elul, usually falling in August/September
The Church of Sardis
White Garments

"You have a few names even in Sardis who have not defiled their garments; and they shall walk with Me in white, for they are worthy."

Revelation 3:4

The clean white garments worn by the overcomers in the Church in Sardis speak of righteous acts. These saints have not defiled their garments with sins and imperfect works. The wearing of 'clean white garments' is a heavenly gift of heavenly clothing.

Revelation 19:8 says of the marriage of the Lamb and His wife, 'And to her it was granted to be arrayed in fine linen, clean and bright, for the fine linen is the righteous acts of the saints.' The Bride of Yeshua is clothed and covered in His righteousness. Our own righteousness would be like 'filthy rags'. (Isaiah 64:6) The righteousness He clothes us with is His righteous acts; all that pertains to us through the cross, and all that He does through us. In Revelation 6:11, the martyrs in heaven are each given a white robe to wear. The Lord, the angels, the elders, the Bride and the martyrs in heaven, are all clothed in heavenly white raiment. The white garments of heaven are their reward and their name remains secure in the Book of Life, to be confessed by Yeshua before the Father and the angels.

Our 'work' is to believe and trust in Him, and then to walk with Him in the white robes of righteousness. In Zechariah 3:1–5, Joshua the High Priest has his filthy garments removed, before being clothed in rich robes and a clean turban. The blood of Yeshua washes our 'garments' clean. He Himself was lifted up, stripped bare, spat upon and bloodied, that we may become clothed, covered and clean. His robe was given up to a lottery, so that we may have conferred on us His pure robes of righteousness, and be ready for His return.

Are you conscious of wearing a 'pure' garment in the spirit, washed by the blood of Yeshua?

Readings: Genesis 3:7, 21, Matthew 6:28–30, Luke 23:34, Zechariah 3:1–10, Revelation 7:14

20th Day of the 6th Month
Elul, usually falling in August/September
The Church of Sardis
Overcomers

"He who overcomes shall be clothed in white garments, and I will not blot out his name from the Book of Life, but I will confess his name before My Father and before His angels." *Revelation 3:5*

Yeshua exhorts the churches to overcome, that they may receive their eternal reward, and their names not be blotted out of the Book of Life. Yeshua said, "He who overcomes shall inherit all things, and I will be his God and he shall be My son. But the cowardly, unbelieving, abominable, murderers, sexually immoral, sorcerers, idolaters and all liars shall have their part in the lake which burns with fire and brimstone, which is the second death." (Revelation 21:7, 8)

1 John 5:4, 5 states, 'For whatever is born of God overcomes the world. And this is the victory that has overcome the world – our faith. Who is he who overcomes the world, but he who believes that Jesus is the Son of God?' The word 'overcomes' is the Greek word 'nikeo' from 'subdue' meaning to conquer, overcome, prevail, get the victory. It is through our faith in Yeshua that Yeshua's victory is enforced in our lives. We are not to focus on our sin or problem, but on the finished work of Yeshua. His victory has already overcome our sin, sickness and poverty, to give us all we need. He said, "I have overcome the world." (John 16:33) Now we are 'more than conquerors through him that loved us,' and nothing can separate us from the love of God which is in Christ Jesus our Lord. (Romans 8:37, 39) The saints overcome their accuser by the blood of the Lamb, the word of their testimony, and not loving their lives unto the death. (Revelation 12:11)

Receive by faith the victory Yeshua has already won over your sin, sickness or problem.

Readings: John 17, 1 John 4:1 – 5:5, Revelation 12:10–12, 21:6–8

ELUL

21st Day of the 6th Month
Elul, usually falling in August/September
The Church of Philadelphia
The Loving Church

"And to the angel of the church in Philadelphia write, These things says He who is holy, He who is true, He who has the key of David...."
Revelation 3:7

Yeshua's letter to this church contains no rebuke, only praise because they have persevered, so He encourages them to keep hold of what they have, that no one may take their crown. They represent all that is good in the Church that we can aspire to. The Greek name of the church (Philadelphia) means 'brotherly love'. It can be said to represent the church that experienced the awakening after 1750 AD; the missionary sending church, full of the Holy Spirit, which loves their brothers the Jews and reaches the Jew first with the gospel.

Yeshua reveals Himself to this church as the one who has the key of David. This is a quote from Isaiah 22:22. Yeshua is the only one who has the key to open the hearts of the Jewish people. After around 1750 AD the Lord raised up mighty gospel preachers from among the Gentiles, who not only preached the gospel, but also had a revelation and understanding of God's plan and purpose for the Jewish people. The Wesley brothers, John Whitefield, Charles Spurgeon and William Wilberforce, all believed that God would soon restore the Jews to their own Land in what was then called Palestine, and that God was going to fulfil the Old Testament prophecies to the Jews. There has always been a small Jewish remnant believing in Yeshua, but Revelation 3:9 began to come to pass. Hebrew Christian movements began to grow and public figures such as Benjamin Disraeli the British Prime Minister and the Bishop Alexander, the first Anglican Bishop in Jerusalem, were raised up in the nineteenth century. At this time many missionaries went into remote places of the earth at great personal risk and cost, many laying down their lives to bring in God's harvest.

Consider the love of this church which keeps God's Word and does not deny His name.

Readings: Revelation 3:7–13, Isaiah 22:20–23, John 15:12–17, 2 Corinthians 10:14–16

22nd Day of the 6th Month
Elul, usually falling in August/September
The Church of Philadelphia
The Open Door

"I know your works. See, I have set before you an open door, and no one can shut it; for you have a little strength, have kept My word, and have not denied My name." *Revelation 3:8*

Yeshua is the one who opens and no one shuts, and shuts and no one opens. When Yeshua calls a believer in Him to go somewhere, He opens the door, though just because a door of opportunity is open doesn't always mean it is right to go through it. (2 Corinthians 2:12, 13) Governments may try to keep Christians and the gospel out of a certain location, but no human door is a barrier to Yeshua. He has a way to reach every person on this planet who is seeking after the truth. He will reach them through visions and dreams if necessary. Christians must take the gospel to the world, to the Jew first, then the Gentile. (Romans 1:16)

Yeshua miraculously opened the door to what was called Palestine when the Ottoman Empire fell in the First World War, and the British Mandate was granted by international directive to create a homeland for the Jews. But tragically the British betrayed the Jews especially during the Second World War, when they placed a limit on the number of Jews who could enter Palestine, turning many desperate Jews back to Europe, only to die in the concentration camps. At the same time they let many Arabs into the Land to reside. But the door those British men tried to close could not remain closed. Yeshua wanted it open, and by 1948 it was truly open as the newly formed State of Israel. The opening of the door of Israel in 1948, and of the territories regained in 1967, coincided with the outpouring of the Holy Spirit in the charismatic renewal. Yeshua is the open door to salvation and all the benefits He gave us when He died on the cross. We pass through Yeshua, the door, by faith to enter the blessings of Paradise. He gives us access to every spiritual blessing and eternal life.

Come to Yeshua, the door to His blessings. What door is He opening to you at this time?

Readings: John 10:1–10, Matthew 16:16–20, Acts 12:1–17, 14:27, 16:16–40

ELUL

23rd Day of the 6th Month
Elul, usually falling in August/September
The Church of Philadelphia
Persevere

"Because you have kept My command to persevere, I also will keep you from the hour of trial which shall come upon the whole world, to test those who dwell on the earth. Behold, I am coming quickly! Hold fast what you have that no one may take your crown."

Revelation 3:10, 11

The Church of Philadelphia had already passed through trials and been known to persevere. Those believers had been tested and proved faithful so the Lord had already rewarded them with the crown of life. Saint James wrote, "Blessed is the man who endures temptation; for when he has been approved, he will receive the crown of life which the Lord has promised to those who love Him." (James 1:12) When the Lord has given us the crown of life, because we have persevered and passed the test, we must watch that we do not backslide or be defeated by any future trials. We must not let anyone take our crown from us. Many would try to make us avoid the narrow way, the difficult path, to take an easier one – a path of compromise and disobedience. We must hold fast, and remember that He is coming soon. We must not relax or give up or give in.

Verse 10, about being kept from the hour of trial, is used to support the theology of the rapture of the Church before the Great Tribulation. It is said that believers, who have already persevered through their own testing, will be exempted from the hour of testing that is to come on the whole world. Yeshua gave the encouragement that He is coming quickly. This might mean that the 'Philadelphian' type of believers will be 'raptured' – that is 'caught up to heaven' (Greek – 'harpazo' cf. 2 Corinthians 12:2, 1 Thessalonians 4:17, Revelation 12:5) suddenly before the Greatest Tribulation takes place. We need to be prepared for this possibility, though we cannot know for sure that this is the correct interpretation of this verse.

Are you persevering in obedience to God even through trials, letting no one take your crown?

Readings: Matthew 7:13, 14, Luke 21:34–36, 1 Thessalonians 4:13–18, James 1

3/7/16

4/9/18

13/9/20

24th Day of the 6th Month
Elul, usually falling in August/September
The Church of Philadelphia
Pillars in the Temple

"He who overcomes, I will make him a pillar in the temple of My God, and he shall go out no more. I will write on him the name of My God and the name of the city of My God, the New Jerusalem, which comes down out of heaven from My God. And I will write on him My new name." *Revelation 3:12*

The overcomers of the Church of Philadelphia are part of the Bride identified with the New Jerusalem which comes down out of heaven from God. In Revelation 21:2 the holy Jerusalem is described coming down from heaven as a bride adorned for her husband. The believers who have been caught up to Heaven to become the Bride of Yeshua will bear the name of the heavenly city, which will come down from the new heaven to the new earth. Their new name and their identity in God will pertain to the New Jerusalem. They will build up the throne of God with their praises. They will be pillars in His temple. They will glorify and lift up His name in His presence forever more.

It is hard to imagine the bliss of living permanently in the manifest presence of God, though sometimes we have little foretastes of His intense love and awesome holiness when we draw near to Him. Psalm 84:10 says, 'For a day in Your courts is better than a thousand. I would rather be a doorkeeper in the house of my God than dwell in the tents of wickedness.' Revelation 21 and 22 picture for us the indescribable glories of the new heaven and earth.

The Church at Philadelphia kept God's Word and didn't deny His name. Despite frequent earthquakes and invasions, it remained a Christian city until 1390. Today it is the modern Turkish town of Alaşehir, which means 'City of God'.

Alaşehir

Meditate on the glorious heavenly benefits of being found to be an overcomer.

Readings: Revelation 21, 22, Psalm 84, 1 Peter 4:7–19

Philadelphia = means Brotherly Love

25th Day of the 6th Month
Elul, usually falling in August/September
The Church of Laodicea
The Apostate Church

"And to the angel of the Church of the Laodiceans write, These things says the Amen, the Faithful and True Witness, the Beginning of the creation of God...." *Revelation 3:14*

Yeshua reveals Himself to the Church of Laodicea as the one whose word can be trusted, the one through whom everything proceeds and was created. The Church at Laodicea was disgusting to him, like something you swallow and immediately vomit up because it is so distasteful. Everything would make Him want to reject this church, and yet, in his mercy, He still calls them to repent and to allow Him into their lives, that they may change and become overcomers, ready to rule and reign with Him in His kingdom.

The Laodicean church represents the apostate church which has emerged from the early twentieth century onwards. These churches have lost confidence in the truth of God's Word, in the pre-eminence of Yeshua, and in God as Creator, particularly through the Liberal Theology introduced by German Theologians at the beginning of the twentieth century. This so dulled the churches' senses that they were ready to embrace false beliefs, such as evolution and eugenics, to the extent that the Nazi holocaust became possible. The churches which teach Replacement Theology allegorize Scriptures about Israel, saying that they now apply to the church so that people don't understand God's plan and misguidedly resist God's purposes, even standing against His People and Land. Churches concentrate on being 'people-friendly', rather than a call to radical and costly obedience and discipleship to God. 'Laodicean' churches embrace various human philosophies but reject the supreme and higher wisdom of God's Word. Such churches become materialistic, humanistic, rationalistic, and lawless. As they have rejected God's truth, so too God will vomit them out.

Affirm your trust in God's revealed Word even if your 'mind' cannot yet comprehend it.

Readings: Revelation 3:14–22, Colossians 1:15 – 2:10, John 8:12–59

26th Day of the 6th Month
Elul, usually falling in August/September
The Church of Laodicea
Lukewarm

"I know your works, that you are neither cold nor hot. I could wish you were cold or hot. So then, because you are lukewarm, and neither cold nor hot, I will vomit you out of My mouth." *Revelation 3:15*

When people set themselves above God's revealed Word in the Scriptures, they cannot receive the fullness of who God is. They are, in a sense, trying to make themselves 'God' and judging Him by judging His Word. These people have never truly had a revelation of their own utter sinfulness and need for God's grace. They practise religion like a hobby, or to earn their way to heaven. They take what they like and reject what they don't like from the Scriptures, and create their own religion that suits them. Then they try to draw others around them to join their churches. But instead of preaching the complete truth of the gospel, they give them what they think people will like to receive, including a religious experience that pleases the flesh rather than putting the flesh to death. They do religious things like praying and worshipping, but they have never surrendered their life to Yeshua to be their Lord, or totally depended on His grace.

Laodicea had lukewarm water. It had to be brought to the city from the springs through long stone pipes. When the water arrived in the city it was lukewarm. It was neither refreshing like cold water, nor cleansing like hot water. It was tepid. That is what the church at Laodicea was like. The Laodicean Church did the things expected of a church, but it was neither alive nor dead, neither hot nor cold. Likewise there are people and churches which call themselves 'Christian' and look like Christians, but who have no revelation of sin and the need for God's grace, and have no relationship with Yeshua through the Holy Spirit.

Is any part of your life with God lukewarm? Your eternal destiny depends on Him.

Readings: Mark 4:1–20, Psalm 42, Psalm 49, Psalm 52

ELUL

27th Day of the 6th Month
Elul, usually falling in August/September
The Church of Laodicea
Buy Gold Refined in the Fire

Because you say, 'I am rich, have become wealthy, and have need of
nothing' – and do not know that you are wretched, miserable, poor,
blind, and naked – I counsel you to buy from Me gold refined in
the fire, that you may be rich; and white garments, that you may be
clothed.... *Revelation 3:17, 18*

The Church in Laodicea thought they were rich because they were a
wealthy trading city and had great riches, but in the eyes of God they
were wretched, miserable, poor, blind and naked! This is in striking
contrast to the church in Smyrna that suffered poverty, but was in fact
rich in God, having found spiritual riches in Him.

This is a warning to many comfortable Christians who feel financially
secure. Laodicea had a wealthy banking system, ample trade, and was
on a prosperous commercial route. Everything looked good from the
material point of view, which is why maybe they were content to drink
lukewarm water. Yeshua counselled these financially secure Christians
to recognise their true condition. Their gold was full of dross. They
needed to invest their time in developing a relationship with the Lord,
in being refined by Him. Gold represents the divine nature. They
needed to have their nature changed in His presence to resemble Him.
In heaven even the streets are paved with gold. We are to invest richly
in God's kingdom.

Yeshua told a parable of a rich man, who built a bigger barn to store
his crops, but then God said to him, "Fool! This night your soul will be
required of you; then whose will those things be which you have provided?
So is he who lays up treasure for himself, and is not rich towards God."
(Luke 12:20, 21) We need to invest in the right place.

*Read Acts 20:17–38. What can you learn from Paul's attitude to ministry
and money?*

Readings: Proverbs 23:23, 2 Corinthians 4:1–5:11, 1 Corinthians 3:9–15

28th Day of the 6th Month
Elul, usually falling in August/September
The Church of Laodicea
The Knock at the Door

Behold, I stand at the door and knock. If anyone hears My voice and opens the door, I will come in to him and dine with him, and he with Me. *Revelation 3:20*

Because God loves us, He chastens us, rebukes us and calls us to repent. The Laodiceans were famous for their medicines and eye salve. But they needed to receive God's own healing 'eye salve' so that they could 'see' spiritually. Their own 'cures' in the end were not what they needed. They needed to let Yeshua into their church.

Yeshua stands at the door of each one of our hearts. He is knocking and waiting for us to invite Him in. There are churches where He is left standing outside, not allowed into the service. There are many believers who leave Him standing outside in the cold, not inviting Him in to fellowship with them in their hearts. Some are afraid. Some are too busy. Some don't hear His knock. Some think He'll be like someone who didn't treat them well. Some are unable to open the door and allow Him fully to come in because of walls of bitterness and unforgiveness. Some are too busy trying to make their own way to heaven on their own and they don't want Him to come in and discredit all their efforts. Some are afraid of what He will ask them to do if they give themselves completely to Him. Some are afraid that He will not like what He will see and will find them imperfect and unworthy.

Yeshua already knows us inside out. He wants us to let Him in to fellowship with us in our hearts through the Holy Spirit. He promises that to those who hear Him knock, and open the door, He will come in and dine with them. Yeshua is always ready, willing and waiting to be invited in and to fellowship with you, if you will just open the door to Him.

Have you opened the door of your heart to let Yeshua in to dine and have fellowship with you?

Readings: Song of Songs 5:2–6, Matthew 19:23–30, Ephesians 3:14–19

29th Day of the 6th Month
Elul, usually falling in August/September
The Trumpet Call
Wake-up Call

Blow the trumpet in Zion, Consecrate a fast, call a sacred assembly.

Joel 2:15

As we draw near the close of this sixth month, we have looked at Yeshua's letters, or messages, to seven churches. Each type of church presented us with a challenge – a challenge to purity of faith, courage, purity of doctrine, zealousness and love for the Lord, and a willingness to suffer for His sake – even to death if necessary. He promises eternal rewards to all those who overcome and He calls us to repentance – for our sin, for being lukewarm, for compromise, for worldliness, immorality, idolatry and wrong doctrine.

We can respond on an individual level and we can respond on a corporate level. To respond on a corporate level requires a trumpet call – the preaching of God's truth. The trumpet needs to be blown loudly and clearly, so that people will understand, and so they can respond. Paul wrote, 'for if the trumpet makes an uncertain sound, who will prepare for battle?' (1 Corinthians 14:8) People need to sound God's call to repentance and holiness in the Church, for God's people to wake up spiritually, to repent, fast and pray. Then God can forgive and avert His judgements. God's prophets call people to repent and turn back to God. God sends warning signs upon the earth to bring people to repentance. The prophet Amos wrote, 'If a trumpet is blown in a city, will not the people be afraid? If there is calamity in a city, will not the LORD have done it? Surely the Lord GOD does nothing, unless He reveals His secret to His servants the prophets.' (Amos 3:6, 7) God is not willing that any should perish but desires that all come to repentance. The Church is in a battle for truth and holiness. If we sound the alarm, God will fight for us. (Nehemiah 4:20)

What trumpet call have you heard from God? How will you respond?

Readings: Joel 2, Amos 4:6–8, Nehemiah 4:15–23

30th Day of the 6th Month
Elul, usually falling in August/September
Eve of Blowing Trumpets
A Memorial

Then the LORD spoke to Moses, saying, "Speak to the children of Israel, saying: 'In the seventh month, on the first day of the month, you shall have a Sabbath rest, a memorial of blowing of trumpets, a holy convocation.'" *Leviticus 23:23, 24*

This evening at sundown the 'moed' – 'appointed time' for blowing trumpets begins. Leviticus 23 says that this is a day of Sabbath rest, a memorial of blowing trumpets and a holy convocation. So today, during the day, is a time to prepare and get ready for this special day, which will mark the beginning of the autumn feasts, and the seventh and final month of the 'moedim'. After sundown you can get out a 'shofar' (ram's horn) or any form of trumpet and blow it, and make a noise to the Lord in your worship to God. The blowing of the 'shofar' releases a spiritual atmosphere. It sends forth God's heavenly spiritual activity into the earth. The blowing of trumpets is a memorial. It makes us remember God's heavenly trumpet call and the holiness of His presence. The trumpet of God was first heard when God met with Moses on Mount Sinai at the giving of the Law. (Exodus 19:16–20) It brought a manifestation of God's holy presence with awesome signs, with quaking, smoke, fire, thundering and lightning, a thick cloud, and an extremely loud sound. Moses ascended the mountain to meet with God, and the people gathered trembling at the base of the mountain, unable to ascend into God's holy presence. (Exodus 19:16–20) Now, because of God's grace, we do not tremble with Israel at the base of the mountain, but come to Mount Zion and the heavenly Jerusalem. God will once again shake all things to remove what can be shaken. But God's kingdom cannot be shaken. Our God is a consuming fire. (Hebrews 12:18–29)

At this 'Feast of Trumpets', blow the trumpet to proclaim the awesome holiness of God.

Readings: Exodus 19, Exodus 32:15–35, Hebrews 12:18–29

1st Day of the 7th Month
Tishrei, usually falling in September/October
The Feast of Blowing Trumpets
A Holy Convocation

'In the seventh month, on the first day of the month, you shall have a Sabbath rest, a memorial of blowing of trumpets, a holy convocation. You shall do no customary work on it; and you shall offer an offering made by fire to the LORD.' *Leviticus 23:24, 25*

Today is the first day of the seventh month, and it is the 'moed' – God's 'appointed time' called 'Zicron Truah' – translated, a 'Memorial of Blowing'. It is a 'miqre kodesh' – a 'holy convocation' (rehearsal), a gathering of God's people for a holy day of Sabbath rest, to come before God with 'an offering made by fire to the LORD.' Our offerings today are not burnt sacrifices, but we can bring our worship to God, and blow trumpets to Him.

The blowing of Trumpets reminds us to listen and respond to the Word of God, like Nehemiah and the returned exiles in Jerusalem, who listened attentively to the Scriptures on this day. (Nehemiah 8:2, 3) In Ezra 3:6, this was the day burnt offerings were resumed in Jerusalem after the return from exile. The Israelites brought an offering made by fire as a shadow of the perfect sacrifice of Yeshua made once, for all time. Sacrifices will resume in the millennium, as a memorial of Yeshua's finished work upon the cross. (Ezekiel 45:21–24).

The first trumpet call of God, which sounded at Sinai, heralded the arrival of the Law, which brings conviction of sin and death. The future trumpet call of God will be redemption for the saved Bride when Yeshua returns for her. (1 Corinthians 15:52, 1 Thessalonians 4:16) At the last trumpet the saved dead will be raised, and the living will be caught up to God and will in an instant be changed with resurrection bodies. The rest of the dead will rise to the judgement, after the millennium, at the second resurrection. (Revelation 20:11–15)

Read Philippians 3:7–21 and consider Paul's attitude to the first resurrection from the dead.

Readings: 1 Corinthians 15, 1 Thessalonians 4:15–18, Philippians 3:7–21

2nd Day of the 7th Month
Tishrei, usually falling in September/October
The Seven Trumpets of Revelation
God's Judgements Released

And I saw the seven angels who stand before God, and to them were given seven trumpets. *Revelation 8:2*

The 'Feast of Trumpets' reminds us of the trumpet of God at Mount Sinai, and the future trumpet of God which will be blown at the rapture. In Scripture trumpets are also blown by men – at Jericho (Joshua 6), and by angels (Revelation 8). In Revelation the seven trumpets begin to be sounded by angels in heaven, each one in turn releasing God's judgements onto the earth. This happens in response to the prayers of the saints, which blend with the incense rising from the golden altar before the throne. God answers their cry for justice and to perform vengeance for them. In John's vision, an angel took the censer, filled it with fire from the altar, and threw it to the earth. And there were noises, thundering, lightning, and an earthquake. (Revelation 8:5) These all remind us of Exodus 19 and the mighty sounds and the earthquake, when God blew His trumpet at Mount Sinai.

When each trumpet is sounded in the time of the Great Tribulation, a plague of God's judgement falls upon the earth. The plagues of hail, blood, bitter waters, darkness, demonic locusts, and demonic armies all remind us of Egypt in Exodus 7 – 11; but, like Pharoah, the wicked of the earth do not repent. (Revelation 8, 9) The seventh angel sounds his trumpet in Revelation 11:15, and the temple of God opens in Heaven, with lightning, noises, thundering, an earthquake and great hail. God will bring His justice, and reward His saints. Zechariah 9:14–17 says, 'Then the LORD will be seen over them, and his arrow will go forth like lightning. The Lord GOD will blow the trumpet, and go with whirlwinds from the south. The LORD of hosts will defend them....The LORD their God will save them in that day.'

Thank God for His perfect justice and that He hears and responds to the cry of His saints.

Readings: Joshua 6:15–21, Revelation 4, 5, Revelation 8 – 11

TISHREI

3rd Day of the 7th Month
Tishrei, usually falling in September/October
The Fast of Gedaliah
A Broken Nation

Then Ishmael the son of Nethaniah, and the ten men who were with him, arose and struck Gedaliah the son of Ahikam, the son of Shapham, with the sword, and killed him whom the king of Babylon had made governor over the land. *Jeremiah 41:2*

Today is the Jewish fast day when Jews mourn the assassination of their Governor Gedaliah during the Babylonian Exile. The Jewish Governor of the remnant of Jews left behind in Judah, was brutally attacked and killed by a small group of his own people. It was a tragic incident. But this fast day, like the fast days in the fourth, fifth and tenth months will one day become a day of feasting and rejoicing, when God restores the remnant of Israel with Messiah their King. (Zechariah 8:18, 19)

The assassination of Gedaliah is a picture for us of Israel's failure to receive the King of kings. Yeshua came to His own people, who failed to receive Him as their King and gave Him over to death. But God's ultimate plan came to pass for Judah when He brought good from failure, victory from defeat, and five centuries later Messiah was born.

Gedaliah was executed, and a large part of the remnant of the Jews went down into Egypt and exile in the nations. But despite their failure, God had a plan to restore them and bring them back from exile to their Land. God brought forth Yeshua the King of the Jews from the restored remnant. The failure of the Jewish elite to receive Gedaliah as Governor, – Ishmael was from the Royal Family and his fellow conspirators had been officers of the king – foreshadows the failure of the Jewish religious elite to receive Yeshua. But one day Yeshua will reign as King, and be served by His re-gathered remnant from among the Jews.

Ask God what 'failure' in your life He wants to turn around to bring you into His plan.

Readings: Jeremiah 40–46, Romans 8:28–39

4th Day of the 7th Month
Tishrei, usually falling in September/October
Atonement
The Cloud and the Mercy Seat

And the LORD said to Moses, "Tell Aaron your brother not to come at just any time into the Holy Place inside the veil, before the mercy seat which is on the ark, lest he die; for I will appear in the cloud above the mercy seat." *Leviticus 16:2*

We are now in the days preceding 'Yom Kippur' or the 'Day of Atonement' which will fall on the tenth day of this month and which is the day when we reflect on the power of the blood of the sacrifice of Yeshua to atone for the sins of Israel and all who will receive it.

The word 'atonement' means 'expiation, forgiveness and covering'. The aspect of 'covering' comes from the root word meaning 'bitumen' or 'pitch'. Noah used pitch to make the wood of the Ark watertight. (Genesis 6:14) It kept out the waters of judgement to preserve alive those contained within. In the Holy of Holies a covering was needed. Aaron could not enter this part of the tabernacle whenever he wanted because the holy cloud of God's presence rested over the Ark of the Covenant containing the tablets of the Law. The Ark of the Covenant needed a covering. It had a permanent covering – the 'kapporeth' – the Mercy Seat. It had a covering of gold (over the wood), and it had a covering of the wings of the cherubim over the Mercy Seat. But those coverings were not sufficient for sinful man to safely enter where the cloud of God's presence rested. Once a year, on the Day of Atonement, blood was sprinkled on the Mercy Seat which covered the tablets of the Law. Only the blood of the sacrifice could atone for, or cover, the sins of Israel, placed between the tablets of the Law and the holy cloud of God's presence, paying the death penalty with the shedding of blood. The blood of the Lamb is now sprinkled on the Mercy Seat in heaven to cover and atone for our sins, so that we can live in God's holy presence. (Hebrews 12:24)

The blood sprinkled on the Mercy Seat, breaks the curse of having broken the Law, for you.

Readings: Genesis 6:13–22, Leviticus 16, Exodus 40:34, 35, Romans 5:6–11

5th Day of the 7th Month
Tishrei, usually falling in September/October
Atonement
The Blood of the Bull and the Ram

Thus Aaron shall come into the Holy Place with the blood of a young bull as a sin offering, and a ram as a burnt offering. *Leviticus 16:3*

Aaron the High Priest could not enter the Holy of Holies without the blood of the sacrifice. Likewise we cannot enter the presence of God, into the Holy of Holies, without the blood of Yeshua. The blood represented the laying down of life because 'the life of all flesh is in the blood'. (Leviticus 17:11) The blood of the sacrifice was sprinkled on the Ark of the Covenant. It did not have to be poured over or smeared over. Just drops sprinkled were sufficient, such is the power of the life of Yeshua laid down for us. (Hebrews 9:6–28)

The blood of the bull always represents the offering for sin. In Leviticus, we learn about the different animals and types of sacrifices and offering that took place at the tabernacle, and later at the temple. Each represents a specific aspect of the work of Yeshua, and each different type of sacrifice and offering served a different functión, as the work of Yeshua in our lives is multi-faceted to save, cleanse and heal our body, soul and spirit.

Under the sacrificial system the blood of the bull took away sin. The strongest animal was needed to carry away sins. But only Yeshua was strong enough to carry away the punishment of our sin once for all time. He bore it away, more powerfully than any bull, by 'becoming sin' for us. The other atoning sacrifice, the burnt offering of the ram reminds us of Yeshua our substitute. God provided a ram. Abraham knew prophetically that God would provide a lamb. (Genesis 22:8) We are like sheep which have transgressed and wandered astray. But Yeshua the innocent Lamb died in our place. (Genesis 22:13)

Meditate on how you need Yeshua the sin offering (the bull) and the burnt offering (the ram).

Readings: Leviticus 16:3, Genesis 22:1–14, Hebrews 9, 1 Peter 1:17–19

6th Day of the 7th Month
Tishrei, usually falling in September/October
Atonement
The Priest and the Holy Place

He shall put the holy linen tunic and the linen trousers on his body; he shall be girded with a linen sash, and with the linen turban he shall be attired. These are holy garments. Therefore he shall wash his body in water, and put them on. *Leviticus 16:4*

The High Priest Aaron's two sons died because they offered profane fire to the Lord. They had failed to submit themselves to God's order and instructions concerning the worship in the tabernacle, not realising that everything must be done according to God's commands. This teaches us that we can only come to God through the way that He has made available to us, through trusting in the sacrifice of Yeshua our High Priest, and not presuming to trust in our own works of righteousness, which are like filthy rags. (Isaiah 64:6) Sin and holiness cannot mix. The sinner must be made righteous to enter God's presence.

God's instructions for the priests to enter the Holy Place of His presence, teach us to draw near boldly to God and live in relationship with Him. The priests had to wear special linen clothes to enter the Holy Place of the tabernacle. (Exodus 39:27) Linen represents God's righteousness covering us, making us acceptable in His presence. The priests had to wash in water then put on special clean linen clothes. They also had to go sprinkled with the blood of the sacrifice (Leviticus 8:30), and on the Day of Atonement, sprinkle the blood on the Mercy Seat. (Leviticus 16:14, 15) We are washed through repenting of our sins and receiving forgiveness through Yeshua. Now we can enter the holy place of intimacy with God, washed by His forgiveness, and 'sprinkled' in the blood of Yeshua our High Priest. The sprinkled blood on our lives proclaims in the spirit that the death penalty has been paid. His life was given in exchange for ours so we can live. We are atoned for, covered, saved.

Thank God for His pure blood that cleanses you from all sin. Pray for Israel to receive it.

Readings: Hebrews 10:16–25, John 13:8, 1 John 1:7–10

TISHREI

7th Day of the 7th Month
Tishrei, usually falling in September/October
Atonement
The Two Goats

Then Aaron shall cast lots for the two goats: one lot for the LORD and the other lot for the scapegoat. *Leviticus 16:8*

On the Day of Atonement two kids, young goats, became part of the sin offering. Lots were cast and one goat was killed as the sin offering, and the other goat became the scapegoat. The goat that was killed as the sin offering represents Yeshua who 'took the penalty' for sin. The other goat 'carried away' the reminder of our sin, its remembrance, alive into the wilderness; this scapegoat was presented alive before the Lord. It made atonement for sin because the guilt of the sin of the people of Israel was laid upon it. It carried their sins in its own body out of God's sight, away from the tabernacle, never to be seen again. God no longer remembers our sin. We continue living but the living God has no more remembrance of our sin. It has been 'taken away'!

This is a powerful truth to comprehend. Whenever the devil comes back and reminds you of your sins, you can remind yourself that you have received the forgiveness of your sins by faith in Yeshua's blood, you have been cleansed by His word and truth, you have been clothed in His righteousness. There is no more memory of your sin in God. It was carried away out of God's sight by Yeshua at the cross. He bore your sins. (Isaiah 53:11) It has gone, because, like the goat, it has been carried far away from the Holy of Holies, so that we too can forget about it. We may need to make reparation (compensate those hurt by our sin) in some way, but we can never atone for our sin. Only Yeshua could do that. Yeshua completely fulfilled the requirements of the sin offering, and the scapegoat, so that no sacrifice is needed anymore.

Rejoice and thank God that you are completely free from your sins. They have gone forever.

Readings: Psalm 103, Micah 7:19, Jonah 1–4, Matthew 12:39–41

8th Day of the 7th Month
Tishrei, usually falling in September/October
Atonement
Sweet Incense

And he shall put the incense on the fire before the LORD, that the cloud of incense may cover the mercy seat that is on the Testimony, lest he die. *Leviticus 16:13*

Sweet incense burned continually in the tabernacle, on the little golden altar of incense placed on the northern side of the Holy Place. Every day, the priest entered the tabernacle to keep the incense burning so that the tabernacle was always filled with the sweet fragrance. In Scripture incense represents the acknowledgement of God's holy presence (Malachi 1:11), and the intercession of the saints. (Revelation 8:1–5)

On the Day of Atonement, the High Priest entered the Holy of Holies, behind the thick curtain, the veil of the tabernacle, with his hands full of sweet incense beaten fine, and with burning coals, gathered from the golden altar. He approached the Ark of the Covenant and sprinkled the incense on the hot coals to make it give off its sweet-fragranced smoke and placed it before the Ark so that the sweet incense cloud covered the Mercy Seat.

Sweet incense entered the Holy of Holies on the Day of Atonement, foreshadowing the day when Yeshua would make intercession for us to the Father, standing in the gap, bearing our sins upon Himself, so that we may be reconciled with God, no longer alienated from His holy presence. Now Yeshua's sacrifice makes intercession between us and the Father so that we can come into His manifest presence and so that our prayers may ascend to the throne of God. Yeshua continually intercedes for us before the Father (Hebrews 7:25), like the incense from the golden altar and He made intercession for us once for all time on the cross. (Isaiah 59:16)

Because Yeshua's intercession is like sweet incense, your prayers are like incense to Him.

Readings: Leviticus 16:11–14, Revelation 8:1–4, Romans 8:26, 27, Hebrews 7:25, Isaiah 53

TISHREI

9th Day of the 7th Month
Tishrei, usually falling in September/October
Eve of the Day of Atonement
Afflict Yourselves

It shall be a Sabbath of solemn rest, and you shall afflict your souls; on the ninth day of the month at evening, from evening to evening, you shall celebrate your Sabbath. *Leviticus 23:32*

The Day of Atonement begins this evening, and ends tomorrow evening. It is a day 'to make atonement for you before the LORD your God.' (Leviticus 23:28) It is the day which contained all the rituals that we have already looked at over the past few days. No work is done on this day. It is a day totally set apart to God when the Jewish people 'afflict their souls'.

The word 'afflict' – 'anah' also means 'poor'. It means to 'look down, browbeat, abase, afflict or chasten oneself'. It means to 'deal hardly with oneself, to submit and weaken oneself'. Yeshua said we must humble ourselves and become like little children to enter the kingdom of God. (Matthew 18:4) He said, 'Blessed are the Poor in spirit, for theirs is the kingdom of heaven.' (Matthew 5:3) It was not the proud, self-righteous Pharisee who found favour with God, but the repentant tax collector (fraudster). (Luke 18:9–14) On this day, we can humble our souls with fasting. (Psalm 35:13) Most observant Jews begin a twenty-five hour fast after a late afternoon meal, and mourn over their sins.

One day the Jewish people will mourn for another reason. Zechariah prophesied, 'And I will pour on the house of David and on the inhabitants of Jerusalem the Spirit of grace and supplication; then they will look on Me whom they pierced. Yes, they will mourn for Him as one mourns for his only son and grieve for Him as one grieves for a firstborn. In that day there shall be a great mourning in Jerusalem....' (Zechariah 12:10, 11)

Pray for Jewish people today, that they may 'look on' Yeshua, their sacrifice, and be saved.

Readings: Isaiah 45:22, Zechariah 12:10–14, Isaiah 30:12–19, Luke 18:9–14

10th Day of the 7th Month
Tishrei, usually falling in
September/October
**The Day of Atonement
– Yom Kippur**
The Jubilee Trumpet

> Then you shall cause the trumpet of the Jubilee to sound on the tenth day of the seventh month; on the Day of Atonement you shall make the trumpet to sound throughout all your land. *Leviticus 25:9*

Today is the Day of Atonement. It is the day when we not only focus on Yeshua who has atoned for our sins, but on God's atonement of the nation and Land of Israel. In Bible times, every 50 years, on the Day of Atonement a trumpet was sounded and the year of Jubilee commenced. (Leviticus 25) The fiftieth year marked the end of seven sevens of years. Every seventh year was a Sabbatical year of Sabbath rest, when no sowing, reaping or harvesting could take place. After seven sevens were completed the Jubilee began.

In the Jubilee year properties were restored to their original owners, and slaves were freed from their masters. All Israelites who had become poor, impoverished, or had suffered loss were restored. Oppression was broken and justice restored on the Day of Atonement. The children of Israel who had been cast off the Land were able to return and repossess it.

The Jubilee defies the world system of accumulation of wealth for selfish means. The Jubilee principle recognises that the Land of Israel belongs permanently to God and is allotted to His people for their inheritance and for His inheritance. (Exodus 15:17, 18) God is bringing His people back to His Land in fulfilment of the Jubilee, and when Yeshua returns as King, His ownership of Israel, the Land and the People, will be acknowledged. The 'earth shall be full of the knowledge of the LORD, as the waters cover the sea,' (Isaiah 11:9) and God's righteousness and justice will be seen in all the earth.

Praise God that He will return to His Land and people and cover them with His glory.

Readings: Leviticus 25, Isaiah 4, Isaiah 2:1–4, Ezekiel 11, 39:21–29, Matthew 23:37–39

TISHREI

11th Day of the 7th Month
Tishrei, usually falling in September/October
Joseph and His Brothers
The Ingathering

Now Joseph had a dream, and he told it to his brothers; and they hated him even more. So he said to them, "Please hear this dream which I have dreamed. There we were, binding sheaves in the field. Then behold, my sheaf arose and also stood upright; and indeed your sheaves stood all around and bowed down to my sheaf." *Genesis 37:5–7*

We now enter the four days which precede the final feast and 'moed' on the Biblical Calendar, the 'Feast of Tabernacles'. This feast concludes the seven-month cycle of God's 'appointed times' as given in the Torah – the first five books of the Bible, written by Moses. The 'Feast of Succot', called 'Hag HaAsif' – 'Feast of Ingathering' in Exodus 23:16, comes at the end of the agricultural year when the final fruits of the harvest have been gathered in to the storehouses, and the grapes have been pressed. The word 'asif' is also used to describe the 'gathering of souls' to their forefathers in death. (Genesis 35:29, Deuteronomy 32:50) The entry of a soul to Paradise is likened to a sheaf of wheat being gathered into the barn.

In Genesis we have the story of Joseph, whose name in Hebrew 'Yosef' is a form of the verb from the same root 'asif', meaning 'let him add'. The story of Joseph concerns the story of the favourite son of Jacob rising to become Prime Minister in Egypt, and how he gathered seven years of harvests into storehouses and so saved the lives of entire nations during the following seven years of famine. Joseph is a picture of Yeshua who saves and gathers souls, harvesting them into the kingdom. If the story were to end with the salvation of the Egyptians because of the storehouses, it would be as though just the Gentiles are saved. But in Joseph's dream the sheaves of his Jewish family finally bowed down to him. They came to him for grain. Yeshua's Jewish brothers are the final part of the harvest.

Meditate on Yeshua's desire (like Joseph) to gather in the harvest. (Luke 10:1–12)

Readings: Exodus 23:14–16, Genesis 37, Luke 10:1–12, Romans 11:25, 26

12th Day of the 7th Month
Tishrei, usually falling in September/October
Joseph and His Brothers
Joseph among the Gentiles

Then Midianite traders passed by; so the brothers pulled Joseph up and lifted him out of the pit, and sold him to the Ishmaelites for twenty shekels of silver. And they took Joseph to Egypt. *Genesis 37:28*

Aspects of the story of Joseph remind us of Yeshua who like Joseph, experienced the rejection of his brothers. The brothers in the story represent the tribes of Israel, the Jewish people. Jacob presumed that Joseph was dead because of lies told by the brothers. Today many Jewish people, who do not know that Yeshua is their Messiah, think He is dead. Another similarity is that Joseph was stripped of his special tunic. So was Yeshua (Genesis 37:23, John 19:23, 24). Joseph was given over to the Gentiles for twenty shekels of silver. Yeshua was handed over for thirty shekels of silver. (Genesis 37:28, Matthew 26:15) A goat was killed and the brothers dipped Joseph's tunic in it. (Genesis 37:31) In Revelation 7:14, the robes of the tribulation saints are washed white in the blood of the Lamb.

Jacob mourned his son for many days. (Genesis 37:34) God the Father has already waited two thousand years for the Jewish people. Joseph was delivered up to the Gentiles as was Yeshua in His death. When Joseph lived in Egypt he married a Gentile woman. For the last two thousand years Yeshua's Bride – the Church – has been predominantly Gentile. Joseph in Egypt suffered temptations, denial and persecution (Genesis 39, 40) but his fame increased until finally the nations came to him to be saved from the famine. Yeshua suffered and died, and now His Bride is coming to Him to be saved from many nations, including Egypt. Joseph was 'Lord of the Harvest'. Yeshua is 'The Lord of The Harvest of Souls'.

Yeshua's Bride comes from all nations. Pray for God's harvest in the Gentile nations today.

Readings: Genesis 39–41, Mark 12:1–12, Ruth 1:1–7

TISHREI

13th Day of the 7th Month
Tishrei, usually falling in September/October
Joseph and His Brothers
Joseph reunited with His Brothers

When Jacob saw that there was grain in Egypt, Jacob said to his sons, "Why do you look at one another?" And he said, "Indeed I have heard that there is grain in Egypt; go down to that place and buy for us there, that we may live and not die." *Genesis 42:1, 2*

Jacob and Joseph's brothers back in the land of Canaan experienced the famine. In the end times famine and tribulation will come upon the whole earth. Joseph's brothers heard that Egypt had storehouses of grain where they could go and buy grain: so driven by need they went down to Egypt. When they arrived they met Joseph but did not recognise him as their brother. For a start they didn't expect him to be alive, but also he didn't look Jewish. He had Egyptian clothes, hairstyle, language and accent. He looked totally Egyptian. He was the Egyptian Prime Minister! (Romans 11:25)

This has been the experience of many Jewish people. When Jews see 'Jesus' as presented by the Gentile believers and the Gentile church, they encounter a Gentile culture, not a Jewish one. The Christian feasts of Christmas and Easter are far removed from the biblical feasts, and artistic representations often show a Gentile-looking Jesus with blond hair and blue eyes, not a Jewish looking Messiah. Gentile church rules and regulations, such as 'no wine and no dancing' are alien to Jewish culture. Even the name 'Jesus' disguises Him, because His Hebrew name is Yeshua, which to a Hebrew speaker means 'Salvation'.

Joseph showed special grace to his younger brother Benjamin. This foreshadowed the Jewish believers who are now being saved by God's grace. When Joseph's brothers proved their remorse, he revealed himself to his brothers, alone, with many hugs and tears.

Imagine the emotion when Yeshua finally reveals His identity, to His Jewish brothers.

Readings: Genesis 42–50, Zechariah 12:10, Revelation 7:4–8

14th Day of the 7th Month
Tishrei, usually falling in September/October
Eve of the Feast of Tabernacles – 'Erev Succot'
Sabbath Rest

Then the LORD spoke to Moses, saying, "Speak to the children of
Israel, saying: The fifteenth day of this seventh month shall be the
Feast of Tabernacles for seven days to the LORD. On the first day there
shall be a holy convocation. You shall do no customary work on it."

Leviticus 23:33–35

This evening at nightfall the most joyous of the Levitical feasts will begin,
the 'Feast of Succot' which means 'Tabernacles'. The 'Feast' will last for
seven days, but the first day and the eighth days are days of Sabbath rest
when no work can be done. The beginning and the end of the 'Feast of
Tabernacles' are Holy Convocations which prophecy the Sabbath rest
of the kingdom. 'On the fifteenth day of the seventh month, when you
have gathered in the fruit of the land, you shall keep the feast of the
LORD for seven days; on the first day there shall be a Sabbath rest, and
on the eighth day a Sabbath rest.' (Leviticus 23:39)

Today is the last day of preparation for the day when no work can
be done. For Jews this means building and preparing a 'tabernacle' or
'booth' to dwell in, and preparing palm branches and other branches
and fruit of trees to wave before the Lord. Under the New Covenant
we are reminded of Yeshua's teaching that a time is coming when His
work and all work will be complete. He said, "I must work the works
of Him who sent Me while it is day; the night is coming when no one
can work." (John 9:4) These are the days when we are to gather the
harvest. In the days immediately prior to the 'Feast of Tabernacles' the
grapes are harvested and pressed in the wine press. This is a picture of
the time of tribulation when the earth will be trampled in the wine press
of God's judgements. (Revelation 14:19, 20, 19:15) Our works will be
over. Returning, He will bring Sabbath rest in His kingdom.

*How does the anticipation of the end of the harvest affect the way you live
today?*

Readings: Matthew 9:37, 38, John 4:34–38, John 9:4, Isaiah 40,
Revelation 14:19, 20

15th Day of the 7th Month
Tishrei, usually falling in
September/October
**The Feast of Tabernacles–
'Succot' Day 1
Waving Palm Branches,
Leafy Branches and Fruit**

And you shall take for yourselves on the first day the fruit of beautiful trees, branches of palm trees, the boughs of leafy trees, and willows of the brook; and you shall rejoice before the LORD your God for seven days. *Leviticus 23:40*

Today is the first day of the 'Feast of Tabernacles', a solemn, yet joyful 'holiday'. On this day, and for the rest of the seven days, Jewish men take a cluster of leafy branches and a fruit (the yellow etrog) in their hands, and wave them before the Lord. Rejoicing with the palm, willow and myrtle branches is symbolic of welcoming the coming King. The waving of palm branches happened spontaneously when Yeshua entered Jerusalem before His death. The people shouted, "Hosanna! (Save now, I pray!) Blessed is He who comes in the name of the LORD!" (John 12:13) The people were quoting from Psalm 118:25, 26.

John saw the waving of palm branches before the throne of God in Heaven. Revelation 7:9, 10 describes the throng of the redeemed from all nations, peoples, tribes and tongues 'clothed with white robes, with palm branches in their hand, and crying out with a loud voice, saying, "Salvation belongs to our God who sits on the throne, and to the Lamb!"'

The waving of palm branches is a reminder not only that Yeshua came to earth as the King of the Jews to save souls, but that He will come again to save Israel and establish His millennial kingdom reign on the earth, when He will be seen to rule and reign victoriously. The fruit waved at Succot must come from beautiful, majestic trees, fit for the King. The branches from willows by the brook remind us that a river will flow out of Jerusalem carrying fresh water, surrounded by the tree of life, for the healing of the nations. (Revelation 22:1–5)

Consider how leafy trees can also be symbolic of us. (Psalm 92:12–14, Hosea 14:4–8)

Readings: Leviticus 23:33–44, Exodus 15:22–27, Matthew 21:1–11, Revelation 7:9–17

16th Day of the 7th Month
Tishrei, usually falling in September/October
The Feast of Tabernacles – 'Succot' Day 2
Sacrifice and Offerings

For seven days you shall offer an offering made by fire to the LORD.
On the eighth day you shall have a holy convocation, and you shall
offer an offering made by fire to the LORD. It is a sacred assembly,
and you shall do no customary work on it. *Leviticus 23:36*

The sacrifices at the 'moedim', like all the other sacrifices throughout the
year had their symbolism fulfilled through Yeshua, the perfect sacrifice.
The sacrifices at the 'Feast of Tabernacles' were numerous. A total of
70 bulls would be sacrificed over the eight days. These are documented
in Numbers 29:12–39. The number seventy is a large, but perfect and
complete number. It is completion fulfilled in the government of the
earth. It demonstrates the kingdom spread into all creation. People
have suggested that God created 70 nations and that 70 represents all
the inhabitants of the earth. (Genesis 10, 1 Chronicles 1)

Other occurrences of the number 70 would be the number of
disciples Yeshua sent out to evangelise (Luke 10:1–20), the seventy
palm trees (Exodus 15:27), the seventy elders of Israel (Exodus 24:1),
the years Israel was in Babylon (Daniel 9:2), the seventy sevens of
Daniel (Daniel 9:24), and the 'infinite amount of time' forgiveness is
to be offered – seventy times seven. (Matthew 18:22) There are also
seventy holy days in the Biblical Calendar – fifty two regular Shabbats
and eighteen 'moedim'. In Ezekiel 45:21–25 Passover and Tabernacles
continue into the millennial reign of Yeshua on earth after His return,
though the sacrifices will be different in quantity from under the Law
of Moses. Shavuot will have passed away but Passover and Tabernacles
will continue. One day creation will be restored and perfected. Wars
will have ceased. Everything will be complete.

Rejoice in the fact the LORD will perfect everything that concerns you.
(Psalm 138:8)

Readings: Numbers 29, Isaiah 49:6, 55:1–5, Philippians 2:1–11

17th Day of the 7th Month
Tishrei, usually falling in September/October
The Feast of Tabernacles – 'Succot' Day 3
Dwell in Tabernacles

"...You shall dwell in booths for seven days. All who are native Israelites shall dwell in booths, that your generations may know that I made the children of Israel dwell in booths when I brought them out of the land of Egypt: I am the LORD your God." *Leviticus 23:42, 43*

This feast is called the 'Feast of Tabernacles' because for seven days Jews are commanded to 'dwell' in tabernacles. They build a booth outside their home or on their balcony, and eat their meals and socialise in it. Ideally they would completely live in it. Back in the spring the 'Feast of Passover' reminded us of Israel's release from slavery in Egypt. Now, at the 'Feast of Tabernacles' we remember the reality for the children of Israel once they had left Egypt. Dealing with cool evenings and mosquitoes, and not having comfortable chairs to sit on, these seven days remind us of the reality of coming out from an oppressive but 'secure' godless civilisation, to dwell in the wilderness, guided and directed by God, living in temporary dwellings, always ready to 'move on' at His command.

For the children of Israel this was not a comfortable experience. They grumbled and complained about the physical trials and difficulties of living and moving around a barren wilderness. Now when you sit in the 'succah' – the homemade 'tabernacle' – to eat dinner or chat with family and friends, it is a different experience. It is joyful and pleasurable. It is decorated with ornaments, and you can see the stars through the gaps between the branches of the roof. It reminds you that heaven is not so far away. Earth is just a temporary home, and the Creator of the stars in space has existed for eternity. In the succah, the distractions of modern living are left behind in the house, and in the simplicity of the booth you can meet with God, and recall that you are now God's 'dwelling place'. (Colossians 1:27)

Are you willing to live in 'tents' and move where He says, if He calls you to?

Readings: Exodus 13:17–22, Numbers 9:15–23, Hebrews 11:8–10

(Tabernacle means to dwell)

18th Day of the 7th Month
Tishrei, usually falling in September/October
The Feast of Tabernacles – 'Succot' Day 4
Yeshua Dwelt Among Us

And the Word became flesh and dwelt among us, and we beheld His glory, the glory as of the only begotten of the Father, full of grace and truth. *John 1:14*

At 'Succot' we can also remember that Yeshua 'tabernacled' among us. God came as man to 'dwell' among us on earth. The Greek word for 'dwelt' is 'skenoo' which comes from the word 'to tent' or 'to encamp, to occupy, or to reside as a symbol of protection or communion'. The Son of God left the glories of Heaven and humbled Himself, taking on a simple dwelling – the human frame, like a 'tent' to dwell among us. Paul described the immensity of God becoming man, saying that Yeshua, 'being in the form of God, did not consider it robbery to be equal with God, but made Himself of no reputation, taking the form of a bondservant, and coming in the likeness of men...' (Philippians 2:6–8)

Yeshua 'tabernacling' with us enabled mere mortals to behold His glory, the glory of the only Son of God the Father, full of grace and His truth. Meeting Him, some people were totally unaware they were meeting the Son of God, He was so human. Yet this man was the doorway to Heaven, and He lived in continual communion with His Father in Heaven.

Now, our spiritual dwelling place is above, seated with Him in Heavenly places, and Yeshua abides in our hearts through His Spirit. (1 John 3:24) Yeshua was transfigured for a brief moment and His heavenly glory was seen in shining radiance at the top of the mountain. (Matthew 17:1–4) Peter suggested making three tabernacles, one each for Yeshua, Moses and Elijah, but that was not necessary. One day He will 'tabernacle' and dwell in glory among us.

Meditate on the privilege of having the Spirit of the King of the Universe abide in your heart.

Readings: Genesis 28:10–17, 32:1, 2, Matthew 17:1–8, John 1, John 7:1–36, Revelation 21:3

TISHREI

19th Day of the 7th Month
Tishrei, usually falling in September/October
The Feast of Tabernacles – 'Succot' Day 5
Rejoice at the Sacred Feast

Seven days you shall keep a sacred feast to the LORD your God in the place which the LORD chooses, because the LORD your God will bless you in all your produce and in all the work of your hands, so that you surely rejoice. *Deuteronomy 16:15*

All of the Jewish people were commanded to rejoice during the seven day 'Feast of Tabernacles' in the place God would chose, which was to be Jerusalem. It is a joyous feast when the threshing at the threshing floor and the pressing at the wine press are over. It is joyous because of God's promise to bless all the produce and all the work of their hands.

People around the world look at the Jewish people and wonder how despite trials and persecutions, they end up prospering and being blessed again and again. There is a blessing when God is with you because of His Covenant faithfulness. This is not just for the Jews, but Gentiles too. Yeshua is 'Emmanuel' – 'God with Us'. When your work is undertaken with Him, He will bless it and prosper it. There is a feast at the end of the work of the harvest.

At the Last Supper, the Passover Meal, Yeshua took the bread and the wine and told His disciples, "you are those who have continued with me in My trials. And I bestow upon you a kingdom, just as My Father bestowed one upon Me, that you may eat and drink at My table in My kingdom, and sit on thrones judging the twelve tribes of Israel." (Luke 22:28–30) That Passover night was mingled with deep sadness for the disciples when they failed. But the 'Feast of Tabernacles' is one of victory, and ruling and reigning with Yeshua in His kingdom. The harvest will have been gathered in and a day is coming when He will wipe all tears from our eyes and we will live in everlasting joy. (Isaiah 51:11, Revelation 7:14–17)

Are you conscious of the Lord with you, blessing and helping you in your work?

Readings: Deuteronomy 16:13–17, 28:1–15, Luke 14:7–35, 22:13–30, 1 Corinthians 6:1–3

20th Day of the 7th Month
Tishrei, usually falling in September/October
The Feast of Tabernacles – 'Succot' Day 6
The Nations come up to Jerusalem

And it shall come to pass that everyone who is left of all the nations which came against Jerusalem shall go up from year to year, to worship the King, the LORD of hosts, and to keep the Feast of Tabernacles.
Zechariah 14:16

Zechariah 14 prophesies the return of the Lord, when Yeshua will fight against the nations which have battled against Jerusalem, and when His feet will stand on the Mount of Olives. (Zechariah 14:3, 4) Then He 'shall be King over all the earth' (verse 9) and all the nations which remain, will come up every year, to worship Yeshua, the Lord of hosts, in Jerusalem, and to keep the 'Feast of Tabernacles'. (Verse 16)

Revelation 20 calls this time the millennium. Other scriptures which appear to prophesy the reign of Yeshua on earth are Isaiah 2:1–4, Isaiah 11, 12 and Micah 4:1–8. The millennium is sometimes referred to as the 'Latter Days'. (Isaiah 2:1, Micah 4:1) In that time the nations will come to Jerusalem to learn the ways of the LORD, His Word and His Law. Zion will be recognised as the seat of the authority of Yeshua in all the earth. Yeshua will reign with justice and righteousness, bringing peace on earth. At the end of the thousand years, Satan, who had been bound, will be released for a short time and deceive the nations again. This time of trouble will end with Satan being cast into the lake of fire for ever.

The nations which come up to Jerusalem during the millennium, to worship the Lord at the 'Feast of Tabernacles', will be blessed with rain. Those that fail to come up to Jerusalem at the 'Feast' will receive no rain, and a plague will strike them. It is important that our nations do not fail to worship the King of kings in Jerusalem! (Zechariah 14:16–19)

If you go up to Jerusalem for the 'Feast of Tabernacles', you are 'rehearsing' for the King!

Readings: Zechariah 14, Isaiah 2:1–4, Isaiah 11, 12, Micah 4:1–8, Revelation 20

21st Day of the 7th Month
Tishrei, usually falling in September/October
The Feast of Tabernacles – 'Succot' Day 7
The Desire of All Nations

For thus says the LORD of hosts: "Once more (it is a little while) I
will shake heaven and earth, the sea and dry land; and I will shake all
nations, and they shall come to the Desire of All Nations, and I will
fill this temple with glory," says the LORD of hosts...." *Haggai 2:6, 7*

This prophecy came through the prophet Haggai, on this the twenty-
first day of the seventh month. (Haggai 2:1) The name Haggai means
'festive, feast day, sacrifice and solemnity'. Today, as we approach the
end of the 'Feast', we look forward to the glory of God's House during
Yeshua's millennial reign. In Haggai 2:1–5 and Zechariah 4:6–10 the
returned exiles were encouraged by God to finish rebuilding the temple
in Jerusalem. Zechariah prophesied the coming grace of Messiah, and
of the Holy Spirit in the temple. Haggai 2 looked forward to the future
glory of the 'latter house' that will be 'greater than the former' house, and
the true peace that God will give in that place. (Haggai 2:9)

The word 'aharon' means 'afterward, following, last, latter and utter
most'. This latter temple is associated with the second coming of Messiah
when God has shaken the nations and Yeshua has become 'The Desire
of All Nations'. Multitudes will have come to the Lord during the
shaking, and when Yeshua returns as King, the nations will come up to
the Messiah's temple in Jerusalem. It truly will be full of the glory of
God. Yeshua will bring true peace. However it seems from Scripture that
before Yeshua returns and establishes His 'latter house', another temple
will be built in Jerusalem, probably under a 'false peace' created by the
'counterfeit messiah'. In Daniel 9:27, the sacrifices which have resumed,
are ended by the 'prince', the anti-Christ. After the millennium in the
new heaven and new earth, there will be no temple, for the Lamb is its
temple. (Revelation 21:22, 23)

*Consider – the nations are being shaken so that multitudes will 'come up'
to the 'Feast'.*

Readings: Haggai 1, 2, Zechariah 4, 1 Corinthians 15:24–28, Revelation
21:9 – 22:5

22nd Day of the 7th Month
Tishrei, usually falling in
September/October
**The Eighth Day of Assembly –
'Shmini Azeret'
Final Sabbath Rest**

On the last day, that great day of the feast, Jesus stood and cried out, saying, "If anyone thirsts, let him come to Me and drink. He who believes in Me, as the Scripture has said, out of his heart will flow rivers of living water." *John 7:37, 38*

Today is the final 'moed' and 'miqre' (convocation/rehearsal), called in John 7:37 'the last day, that great day of the feast'. It is the climax or the culmination of the Levitical feasts, and prophetically, it rehearses the arrival of eternity at the end of the millennium reign of Yeshua, described in Revelation 21 and 22. Then Yeshua will hand the kingdom back to the Father. (1 Corinthians 15:24–28) The 'Feast' ends on the eighth day, which begins a new week, and speaks of a new beginning, of the new heaven and the new earth. On this day, Nehemiah completed the reading of the Torah, the Law, to the people. In Israel, today is called 'Simchat Torah' (Joy of Torah), when the scrolls are wound back to the beginning.

In the time of the Second Temple, Jewish history records that the priests would pour out a water libation on the altar and petition God for rain on the great day of assembly at the end of the feast. On this day, Yeshua cried out in a loud voice to invite anyone who thirsts to come and drink of Him. He gives us the Holy Spirit, who will fill us and flow out through us.

Zechariah 14:8 prophesies 'And in that day it shall be that living waters shall flow from Jerusalem, half of them toward the eastern sea and half of them toward the western sea; in both summer and winter it shall occur. And the LORD shall be King over all the earth. In that day it shall be – "The LORD is one," and His name one.' In Revelation 22:1 a pure river of water of life flows from the throne of God and of the Lamb. All life comes from Him.

If you are thirsty, come to Yeshua and drink, and let His life flow out effortlessly to others.

Readings: Nehemiah 8:18, Isaiah 12:3, John 7:37 – 53, Zechariah 14:6–9, Revelation 22:1–5

TISHREI

23rd Day of the 7th Month
Tishrei, usually falling in September/October
God's Word
Yeshua Teaches in the Temple

Now early in the morning He came again into the temple and all the
people came to Him; and He sat down and taught them. *John 8:2*

On this day, according to John's Gospel, Yeshua went back into the
temple, having stayed the night on the Mount of Olives, and he sat down
and taught the people. His loud exclamation the day before, proclaiming
that He is the source of living water, led many in the crowd to recognise
Him as the Messiah. The scribes and Pharisees could not understand
how someone from Galilee could be the Messiah. They did not realise
He had been born in Bethlehem. So they set up a test and brought to
him a woman caught in adultery.

Yeshua demonstrated wisdom and grace, by saying to them, "He who
is without sin among you, let him throw a stone at her first." (John
8:7) He released her from her bondage to sin whilst convicting the
religious people of their own sin. Yeshua shone the light of the Word,
His holiness, His wisdom, into their hearts so that they could all see
themselves aright. Then Yeshua taught the people saying, "I am the light
of the world. He who follows Me shall not walk in darkness, but have
the light of life." (John 8:12) Light was a familiar symbol to them at
the 'Feast of Tabernacles', since Jewish history records that there would
have been great illuminations in the temple precincts over the 'Feast of
Tabernacles'. Light is also mentioned, like the water, in Zechariah 14.
(Zechariah 14:6, 7)

We are to sit and listen to Yeshua teach us through His Holy Spirit
as we read the Scriptures. He sheds His light on them and teaches us so
we can understand. (1 John 2:27) On this day King Solomon sent the
people home from the 'Feast' joyful for all God had done.

Ask the Holy Spirit to open up the Scriptures for you. He is the light to
illuminate them.

Readings: 2 Chronicles 7:10, John 8:12, 9:1–7, Zechariah 14:6, 7,
Revelation 21:23–27, 22:5

24th Day of the 7th Month
Tishrei, usually falling in September/October
God's Word
Returning to the Scriptures

Now on the twenty-fourth day of this month, the children of Israel were assembled with fasting, in sackcloth, and with dust on their heads. Nehemiah 9:1

On the 24th Day of the seventh month Ezra the Scribe read the Torah scrolls to the returned Jewish exiles and all the children of Israel. They met together in the open square in Jerusalem by the water gate, a symbol of the Holy Spirit, and they listened attentively to the scriptures being read to them. They bowed their faces to the ground and worshipped God. Ezra, Nehemiah and the Levites explained the meaning of the Scriptures to them.

When the people heard the Scriptures read out loud on the first day of the seventh month, they realised how disobedient their ancestors, priests and kings, had been to God's holy Law, and they wept and mourned. But they couldn't keep mourning because it was a holy day, the 'Feast of Trumpets', and they had to rejoice, knowing that the joy of the LORD was their strength. Then they built booths and they kept the 'Feast of Tabernacles', joyfully. It wasn't until the 24th day that they were able to assemble again with fasting and repentance before God, as they listened to the Book of the Law being read to them. The time had come once again, to apply themselves to the truth of the Scriptures and to repent of their sins.

The fact that they had to rejoice and keep God's feasts before they turned to self-examination foreshadows for us the truth of God's grace. Before we have even been convicted of our sins through hearing the Word of God, He has already provided the answer through His sovereign grace. We celebrate the feasts knowing the end from the beginning, and experiencing the kindness and grace of God leads us to repentance. (Romans 2:4, 5)

Let the Scriptures convict you of sin, so you can repent and change in the light of his grace.

Readings: Nehemiah 8:9 – 9:38, 2 Corinthians 7:8–10, Romans 2:4, 5, Psalm 19

25th Day of the 7th Month
Tishrei, usually falling in September/October
God's Word
Understanding the Word

So they read distinctly from the book, in the Law of God; and they gave the sense, and helped them to understand the reading.

Nehemiah 8:8

Nehemiah actually listed in his account, the names of the men who 'read distinctly' the Book of the Law and 'explained' the readings. The men were worthy of note! The children of Israel needed Bible teachers to help them understand the sense of the readings that were read to them. Nehemiah's Bible teachers were skilled because they helped the people to understand the true meaning of the Scriptures, and to respond accordingly. Good Bible teachers will help the people to understand what the Bible actually says, not manipulate it to say something else that they want it to say.

In Nehemiah 8:8 the word for understand is 'biyn' which means to 'separate, mentally distinguish, attend, consider, be cunning, diligently direct, discern...' To understand means to correctly divide and discern between the true meaning and false interpretations. We have to ask whether the Scriptures are taught correctly, skilfully and with diligent discernment in our churches. Paul praised the people of Berea because, when they heard Paul teaching and preaching, they went back to the Word of God, and checked the Scriptures, to see if what he said was true and could be found in the Word. (Acts 17:10, 11) They saw for themselves that what Paul said was verifiable from Scripture, and so they opened their minds and hearts, and gladly believed the gospel of Yeshua. Unlike many people they did not close their minds to the truth, preferring to hold onto their pre-conceived ideas. They were 'fair minded', willing to be challenged and changed by God's Word. They were diligent and made the effort to check the truth and then submit to it.

Are you careful to 'divide and discern truth' according to Scripture when you listen or teach?

Readings: Acts 17:1–14, 2 Timothy 1 – 4, Colossians 1:9–14, Proverbs 2

26th Day of the 7th Month
Tishrei, usually falling in September/October
God's Word
Yeshua, the Word of God

In the beginning was the Word, and the Word was with God, and the Word was God. He was in the beginning with God. All things were made through Him, and without Him nothing was made that was made. *John 1:1–3*

Yeshua is the Word of God. When we read Scripture the presence and power of Yeshua speaks His Word directly to us and ministers to us. His words are powerful and spiritual. When He speaks whole galaxies come into existence. The atoms and molecules of the world around us and in us, respond to the Word of God. Yeshua holds together all the whizzing atoms and molecules so they don't fly into chaos. He creates order and life by the Words of His mouth. Psalm 33:6 says 'By the word of the LORD the heavens were made, and all the host of them by the breath of His mouth.' God spoke: '"Let there be light," and there was light.' (Genesis 1:3) When we speak out Scripture it carries His creative life.

2 Timothy 3:16, 17 says that 'all Scripture is given by inspiration of God, and is profitable for doctrine, for reproof, for correction, for instruction in righteousness, that the man of God may be complete, thoroughly equipped for every good work.' Yeshua said, 'Assuredly, I say to you, till heaven and earth pass away, one jot or one tittle will by no means pass from the law till all is fulfilled.' (Matthew 5:18) Even the smallest letters and punctuation marks in the original language convey spiritual truth, and not one is to be lost, even if we don't yet understand it. The Scriptures enable us to receive the infinitely profound, multi-dimensional, life-giving truth of God. The Holy Spirit abiding in you 'quickens' or 'makes alive' His Word to you personally. His Word abides and dwells in you by His Spirit and by the Word that you hear, receive and believe, you will grow in Him.

Invite the Holy Spirit to reveal new depths from His Word to you and through you.

Readings: John 1:1–3, John 8:25–59, John 15:11–15, John 16, 17, 2 Peter 3:5, Hebrews 11:3

TISHREI

27th Day of the 7th Month
Tishrei, usually falling in September/October
God's Word
The Fruitfulness of the Word

For as the rain comes down, and the snow from heaven, and do not return there, but water the earth, and make it bring forth and bud, that it may give seed to the sower and bread to the eater, so shall My word be that goes forth from My mouth; it shall not return to Me void, but it shall accomplish what I please, and it shall prosper in the thing for which I sent it. *Isaiah 55:10, 11*

These verses liken the Word of God to rain and snow which come down and water the earth. Where the rain falls life springs forth. In Israel the un-irrigated hills of Judea, Samaria and Galilee are brown and withered through the summer drought, but it seems that almost the moment the rain arrives everything turns green, and by the time spring arrives, the flowers have budded, blossomed and seeded. The rain brought forth life out of apparent deadness.

So it is with our lives. We can feel dead and dry spiritually, but if we keep reading the Word of God, we can trust that it is like drops of rain watering our soul. God's promise is that in due season the Words that you read will bring forth life and fruit, in and through you. In fact it cannot fail to do so! These verses are a promise that God's Word will bring fruit for God in whatever they are sent to do. So if you need healing – read scriptures about healing, if you need help, read scriptures about God's help, if you need wisdom, read scriptures about wisdom. We can also be channels of God's Word to other people, sending it into their lives. In Psalm 107:20 the people cried out to God for help and 'He sent His Word and healed them.' God's Word has an answer to every situation. If we ask the Lord, He will guide us to the scriptures we need and speak His Word into our hearts to bring forth fruit.

Which scripture are you receiving into your heart in these days for your situation?

Readings: Isaiah 55, Psalm 107, Mark 4

28th Day of the 7th Month
Tishrei, usually falling in September/October
God's Word
A Lamp

Your word is a lamp to my feet and a light to my path. Psalm 119:105

God's Word enlightens our path to show us the truth about where we are and where we are going. Without light on our path we stumble and fall. We take wrong turnings and we make mistakes. But when we keep reading the Scriptures every day, along with listening to the Holy Spirit, He opens our understanding so that His Word will be like a lamp, showing us the way to go, and what to do.

Yeshua is the 'Light of the World'. (John 8:12) We receive His light through the Scriptures together with His Holy Spirit in our hearts. His Word is relevant to every situation we will ever face in life. God has so constructed the Scriptures, that there is an answer for everything you will ever face in your life, contained within its words.

Psalm 119 is the Psalm which extols the benefits of God's Word. A study of this Psalm shows that it is an acrostic. It consists of 22 eight-verse sections, one section for each letter of the Hebrew alphabet. The first word of each verse begins with that letter of the alphabet. Each letter of the Hebrew alphabet comes from a practical picture from life. The first letter, the Aleph, is the picture of the head of an ox and it stands for strength, leadership and going first. The first verses of Psalm 119 express the blessedness that belongs to those who make God first in their life by putting His commandments first in their life. Even the Hebrew letters are assembled together in Words, so as to give a pictorial explanation of their meaning. If Hebrew letters and words have such a practical, physical foundation, how much more is God concerned that His Word meets your practical, everyday needs?

Are the Bible and the Holy Spirit the first place you turn for advice and guidance?

Readings: Psalm 119, Ecclesiastes 12:9–14, James 1:22–25, 2 Timothy 3:16, 17

TISHREI

29th Day of the 7th Month
Tishrei, usually falling in September/October
God's Word
Preach the Gospel

How then shall they call on Him in whom they have not believed? And how shall they believe in Him of whom they have not heard? And how shall they hear without a preacher? And how shall they preach unless they are sent? *Romans 10:14, 15*

The truth of the Scripture is not just meant to reach our hearts and lives. It is meant to overflow out of each one of us to the people around us. Each one of us is called to 'preach' the gospel and share the Word with others. We do not necessarily need a pulpit, a ministry or a title. And we must not forget to teach the Scripture to little children either. Yeshua said, 'Whoever receives one little child like this in My name receives Me.' (Matthew 18:5) We are to teach the young the ways of the Lord, so that they can grow up knowing their saviour.

In Ephesians 6:15 Paul wrote that we are to have our feet shod with the preparation of the gospel of peace. When we set out of the door, we need to be prepared to share the gospel, just as we prepare our feet to walk outdoors. Isaiah 52:7 says, 'How beautiful upon the mountains are the feet of him who brings good news, who proclaims peace, who brings glad tidings of good things, who proclaims salvation, who says to Zion, "Your God reigns!"' Yeshua sent His disciples out to preach, two by two. He sent them out to preach the kingdom of Heaven/God, (Luke 9:60), demonstrating it by healing the sick, cleansing the lepers, raising the dead and casting out demons. (Matthew 10:7) They were to preach the gospel, making disciples of all nations, baptising them and teaching them to obey His commandments. (Matthew 28:19) Paul teaches that the gospel is for the Jew first then the Gentile. That means that when you go to a new place you are to find the Jews first and share the gospel with them. When you have done that you can go to the Gentiles. (Romans1:16)

Where would Yeshua have you preach the gospel?

Readings: Luke 10, Luke 24:44–49, 1 Corinthians 1:11 – 2:16, 1 Corinthians 9

30th Day of the 7th Month
Tishrei, usually falling in September/October
In the Beginning
A Saviour Promised
Torah Portion 'Beresheet' – Genesis 1:1 – 6:8

I will put enmity between you (the serpent) and the woman, and between your seed and her seed. He shall bruise your head and you shall bruise His heel. *Genesis 3:15*

We are now beginning a series looking at the Hebrew Torah Portions, to see how Yeshua, God incarnate as man, was prophesied and spoken of in the Hebrew Scriptures. (John 5:39) These Torah portions are still read in synagogues today and are the same as would have been read in Synagogues on Shabbat two thousand years ago.

Genesis 1:1 tells us that in the beginning God created the heavens and the earth. Yeshua is the Word who spoke the command. (John 1:1–5) Adam and Eve, the parents of 'Mankind', were created by God, in the image of God, on the sixth day. After raising their sons Cain and Abel, they had other sons and daughters who married each other and the human race grew. (Genesis 5:1–4) Life-spans were long before death entered through sin.

Satan tempted Adam, who 'fell' into sin, bringing upon himself, his descendants, and all creation The Curse. (Genesis 3:16–19). But God prophesied a 'Messiah', who would be the seed of the woman (born by virgin birth without the seed of a man).The heel of this man would be 'bruised' – 'shuwph' meaning 'snap at, to overwhelm, break, bruise, cover'. But He would 'shuwph' the head of Satan. (Genesis 3: 15) This was fulfilled through Yeshua born to the virgin Mary, (Luke 1:26–35, 2:4–21) when He died on the cross and rose again. Satan is a defeated foe. In the tribulation, Satan fights the 'woman' – Israel, who gave birth to the 'Child', Yeshua. (Revelation 12) Satan is cast into the lake of fire. (Revelation 20:10)

Whilst you must beware the tactics of the devil, you can rejoice that he is a defeated foe.

Readings: Genesis 1:1 – 6:8, Isaiah 7:14, Romans 16:20, Hebrews 2:14–18, Revelation 12

1st Day of the 8th Month
Bul – also called Heshvan, usually falling in October/November
In the Beginning
God's Covenant with Noah
Torah Portion 'Noach' – Genesis 6:9 – 11:32

Thus I will establish My covenant with you: Never again shall all flesh be cut off by the waters of the flood; never again shall there be a flood to destroy the earth. *Genesis 9:11*

Today is the first day of the 8th month, the month when King Solomon finished building the temple (1 Kings 6:38), and Zechariah began to prophesy. (Zechariah 1:1) In Israel the first rains arrive, and the wheat and barley are sown during this month.

In the Torah Portion 'Noach', there had been intermarriage between spiritual beings (demons) and humans, to create hybrids (Genesis 6:2–4), and all flesh had been corrupted. The earth was filled with violence. God had to judge the earth, but in the midst of judgement God showed grace to righteous Noah, saving him and his family so that the Messiah could be born, a human being, and allow God's grace to enter the human race, through the Son of God.

Noah, a righteous man, followed God's instructions to build the ark. Noah's long-living grandfather was named 'Methuselah', and his name meant 'his death shall bring'. Nobody could imagine what would actually happen when Methuselah finally did die. God flooded the whole earth, killing every living creature, apart from those who had entered the safety of the ark. The flood represents death and judgement, and the ark is a picture of salvation entered through the 'door' of Yeshua. A day is coming when the 'door' will be closed, and it will be too late for anyone left outside. After the flood God made a covenant with Noah, never again to destroy mankind with a flood. The next judgement of the whole earth will be with fire, at the end of the age. (2 Peter 3:5–7)

God's kindness to Israel and to you is as certain as His covenant with Noah. (Isaiah 54:7–10)

Readings: Genesis 6:9 – 11:32, Hebrews 11:7, Isaiah 54:7–10, 1 Peter 3:18–22, 2 Peter 2, 3

2nd Day of the 8th Month
Bul – also called Heshvan, usually falling in October/November
The Patriarchs
God's Covenant with Abraham
Torah Portion – 'Lech Lecha' – Genesis 12:1 – 17:27

Then He brought him (Abraham) outside and said, "Look now toward heaven, and count the stars if you are able to number them." And He said to him, "So shall your descendants be." *Genesis 15:5, 6*

In this Torah portion, Abraham became the 'father of faith'. When he received God's covenant that his descendants would be numerous like the stars in heaven, he believed God and became our example of faith. Abraham believed God, despite the fact he had no child, and so because of his faith, he was counted by God as righteous. (Genesis 15:6) Then God showed him that he would inherit the Land. The sign God gave him, to prove that Abraham's descendants would inherit the land of Canaan was a covenant made in blood.

This covenant involved killing a heifer, a goat, a ram, a turtledove and a young pigeon. Abraham brought them to God and cut them in two (apart from the birds). The ox speaks of Yeshua our servant, the ram, the submissive One, the goat, the sin-bearing One, the dove, the innocent One. He poured out His blood, and the burning oven, that supernaturally passed through the pieces shows that the responsibility for keeping the covenant unto death is kept and maintained through the zeal and power of God alone. Yeshua passed through death to bring Abraham's descendants of faith into their heavenly inheritance through grace.

Abraham believed God, that having left Ur, God was able to give him a heavenly city, the New Jerusalem. He didn't see the fulfilment with His own eyes, but died believing that God would bring it to pass. (Hebrews 11:8–16) Yeshua would make the way.

Read Romans 4 and reflect on Abraham's example of righteousness received through faith.

Readings: Genesis 12:1 – 17:27, Romans 4, Hebrews 11:8–16

3rd Day of the 8th Month
Bul – also called Heshvan, usually falling in October/November
The Patriarchs
The Seed of Abraham
Torah Portion – 'Vayeira' – Genesis 18:1 – 22:24

In your seed all the nations of the earth shall be blessed because you have obeyed My voice. *Genesis 22:18*

Abraham's obedience to God's voice enabled God's plan of redemption to take place through His descendants. God said that in Abraham's seed – all nations would be blessed. The promised 'Seed' of Abraham is his descendant Yeshua the Messiah.

The word 'seed' – 'zera' first appeared in Genesis 1:11 where the plants were given seeds to reproduce themselves. Reproduction through seeds means that all living creatures are descended from God's original creation according to His original design. The theory of evolution from one species to another is an attempt to discredit this principle. God's creation is designed so that every living creature reproduces through genes, after 'its own kind'. God's Seed, Yeshua, gives righteousness through the 'adopted spiritual gene' of faith.

In Genesis 3:15 we saw that the Messiah would be the seed (child) of a woman, but in Hebrew thought the 'seed' is usually recorded through the male line. The genealogies of Yeshua in Matthew's and Luke's gospels record Joseph's ancestral line as the adoptive father. God's view of adoption is that the adopted child receives the ancestry and lineage of the adoptive father as his own. Joseph the adoptive father of Yeshua, is a proven descendant of Abraham. To bring forth this lineage, Abraham had to walk a path of faith and obedience. It would be His obedience in the test regarding offering up his son Isaac that proved his faith in God to keep his promise, that God would bless His descendants, even sending Messiah.

How do you demonstrate the 'works' of obedience to accompany faith? (James 2:14–26)

Readings: Genesis 18:1 – 22:24, Galatians 3:16–19, Hebrews 11:17–19, James 2:14–26

4th Day of the 8th Month
Bul – also called Heshvan, usually falling in October/November
The Patriarchs
God gives Isaac a Wife
Torah Portion 'Chayei Sarah' – Genesis 23:1 – 25:18

...and he (Isaac) took Rebekah and she became his wife, and he loved her. *Genesis 24:67*

Isaac was the son born to Abraham because of faith. But Isaac was not able to bless all the nations as God had promised. The fulfilment of God's promise would come through a descendant of his, the Messiah. To produce descendants he needed a wife, but not just any wife. His wife needed to have been born into the family of Abraham, and be a descendant of Abraham's father, the man who was originally called to leave Ur of the Chaldeans, and travel to the Promised Land, though he never made it there himself. (Genesis 11:31, 32)

The wife had to be selected supernaturally. She had to belong to the 'family of faith' and her selection had to take place through the sovereignty and leading of the Holy Spirit. So Abraham's servant (a picture of the Holy Spirit) went to Abraham's family, and God's angel was with Him. (Genesis 24:40) The servant found the girl chosen by God, Rebekah, at the well where she drew water. The servant tested her, saying, 'Please give me a little water from your pitcher to drink.' (Genesis 24:45, 46) She passed the test by saying, 'Drink, and I will give your camels a drink also.' Isaac received His chosen wife, a wife full of God's grace.

Yeshua is seeking 'a wife' – believers who will respond to His call to leave behind their old life to follow and serve Him, to love and obey Him. Yeshua went to Jacob's well in Samaria. (John 4:6) There he saw a woman, and he said to her the same as Abraham's servant had said to Rebekah: 'Give me a drink'. The Bridal Church of Yeshua draws water for Him from His well of salvation, and receives from Him the living water of eternal life.

Consider the necessary qualities to become the 'Bride of Messiah Yeshua'.

Readings: Genesis 23:1 – 25:18, John 4:1–42, Isaiah 12:3, 1 Peter 3:1–6

5th Day of the 8th Month
Bul – also called Heshvan, usually falling in October/November
The Patriarchs
Jacob and Esau
Torah Portion 'Toldot' – Genesis 25:19 – 28:9

"Two nations are in your womb, two peoples shall be separated from your body; One people shall be stronger than the other, and the older shall serve the younger." *Genesis 25:23*

Jacob's wife Rebekah gave birth to twins – Jacob and Esau. The name Jacob comes from the Hebrew word for 'heel' because at birth he grabbed his brother's heel. Jacob, the younger twin, was pre-destined to inherit God's covenant to Abraham, despite the fact that it would normally fall to the elder son. Jacob usurped his older brother to receive the blessing of the elder son, to become an illustration of the true nature of faith and what pleases God.

The word 'heel' also reminds us of the heel of the prophesied Messiah, which would be bruised by Satan. (Genesis 3:15) Satan usurped the authority of God in the kingdoms of the world, bruising His heel, but Yeshua came and defeated him when He died on the cross and rose again, bruising Satan's head. Satan, the deceiving snake was crushed under Yeshua's feet. Satan thought he had won. But he was crushed under Yeshua's feet.

God said, 'Jacob I have loved, But Esau I have hated.' (Romans 9:13, Malachi 1:2, 3) God, in His Divine sovereignty, was establishing a principle and a lesson –that we become His children by faith in God, not by works of our own flesh, or by our birthright. The elder brother failed to value God's blessing, thinking it was by the merit of who he was in the natural, like Satan. Satan took pride in his beauty and position. Esau failed to reach out for what he did not yet have, the spiritual blessing imparted. The younger son reached out undeserving but empowered by God's grace, to grasp hold of God's heel and be saved.

Be like Jacob, who 'grabbed hold' of the birthright of faith as a child of Abraham.

Readings: Genesis 25:19 – 28:9, Romans 9, Malachi 1

6th Day of the 8th Month
Bul – also called Heshvan, usually falling in October/November
The Patriarchs
God's Covenant with Jacob
Torah Portion 'Vayetzei' – Genesis 28:10 – 32:3

..."I am the LORD God of Abraham your father and the God of Isaac; the land on which you lie I will give to you and your descendants. Also your descendants shall be as the dust of the earth; you shall spread abroad to the west and the east, to the north and the south; and in you and in your seed all the families of the earth shall be blessed...."
Genesis 28:13, 14

Jacob was sleeping out in the open air about to flee the land of Canaan. Suddenly, in a dream, he saw a ladder ascending to heaven, and angels of God ascending and descending upon the ladder. At the top of the ladder stood the LORD who spoke the above words, re-affirming God's covenant that He had given to Abraham (Genesis 12:1–3), Isaac (Genesis 26:1–5) and now made to him, Jacob (Genesis 28:13–15).

God's covenant promising the Land, a multitude of descendants, and the Seed (Messiah) through whom all the earth would be blessed, was given to the three generations – Abraham, Abraham's son Isaac and Isaac's son Jacob. Abraham was the father made righteous through faith, Isaac was the son born through the promise, and Jacob was the son chosen through Divine election. Each represents salvation through the Messiah, and through these three, God's covenant was to be fulfilled. They would receive the Land now called Israel, a multitude of descendants, now called the Jews, and the Messiah through whom all the nations would be blessed. Yeshua would become that Messiah, the 'ladder' to heaven. (John 1:51) And as Jacob served at great cost, tending sheep to receive the woman he loved, so Yeshua, the Good Shepherd would lay down His life to receive His Bride. (Hosea 12:12)

Thank God for this 'Everlasting Covenant' through which you can receive God's blessing.

Readings: Genesis 28:10 – 32:3, John 1:43–51, Hosea 12:12, Luke 24:46, 47

7th Day of the 8th Month
Bul – also called Heshvan, usually falling in October/November
The Patriarchs
Jacob is named Israel
Torah Portion 'VaYishlach' – Genesis 32:4 – 36:43

And He said, "Your name shall no longer be called Jacob, but Israel;
for you have struggled with God and with men, and have prevailed."

Genesis 32:28

Jacob had been in exile in the land of his father-in-law, but the time came
for him to return to the 'Promised Land'. He had been blessed with
the multiplication of wealth and family 'outside' the Land, but needed
to return to live in the Land of the covenant. And so he took his two
wives, their two maids, and all the children. His return to the Land
was part of God's covenant with him when he dreamt of the ladder at
Bethel. (Genesis 28:15)

Jacob was fearful as he returned. His brother Esau might have still
wanted to kill him for stealing his birthright from him, and he might
have had to contend for the Land, so he prepared a generous present
of flocks to 'appease' his brother. In the event (after wrestling with the
Angel), his brother received him peacefully, and opted to depart to
another country, Edom, since the land of Canaan (now Israel) was not
big enough for them both. (Genesis 36) The Land itself bore the legal
signs of God's covenant. Abraham had built altars on the mountains,
and dug wells. Isaac had re-opened Abraham's wells and dug more. And
Jacob had erected a pillar at Bethel. Now, at Peniel, Jacob met the 'Angel'
of God – who appeared as a man – Yeshua. There the Angel of God
wrestled all night with Jacob. When Jacob prevailed the Angel changed
Jacob's name to Israel – which means 'He will rule as God'. Yeshua is
the one who rules as God, and He conferred this name on Jacob, who
had prevailed to receive His blessing.

How is Israel 'wrestling' in the Land today to receive God's covenant blessings?

Readings: Genesis 32:4 – 36:43, Hosea 11:7 – 12:12, Obadiah 1:1–21

8th Day of the 8th Month
Bul – also called Heshvan, usually falling in October/November
The Patriarchs
God Breaking Through
Torah Portion 'Vayeshev' – Genesis 37:1 – 40:23

Then it happened, as he drew back his hand, that his brother came out unexpectedly; and she said, "How did you break through? This breach be upon you!" Therefore his name was called Perez. *Genesis 38:29*

This story about the birth of Perez, ancestor of Yeshua, (whose name was recorded in Matthew's and Luke's genealogies), occurs once the story of Joseph had begun. Joseph had been sold into slavery in Egypt by his brothers, who in their jealousy had actually wanted to kill him. Joseph is a picture of Yeshua. The devil wanted to destroy him and have him dead.

Judah, brother of Joseph and father of Perez, was destined by God to carry the seed of Abraham down his line to the birth of the Messiah after many generations, only he did not yet know this. Judah's firstborn son died without an heir. The firstborn male was very important. Yeshua would be a firstborn male, because he was to become the 'new Adam', the firstborn male of the human race. The firstborn male 'belonged' to God. (Exodus 13) Judah was chosen by God's 'divine election' to carry Abraham's seed to the Messiah through his blood line. He should have ensured that his firstborn son had an heir after his death by giving his other son to the widow. When this failed, the widow Tamar took measures to give birth to her dead husband's heir by disguising herself as a prostitute and receiving Judah's seed. Tamar carried twins. Zerah started to be born – could have been the firstborn – but then Perez burst out before him. The blame/responsibility was on Perez for breaking through and becoming the firstborn. He became the ancestor of the Messiah.

Meditate on the fact that God has 'broken through' into the human race, and your life.

Readings: Genesis 37:1 – 40:23, Matthew 1:3, Luke 3:33, Micah 2:12, 13.

HESHVAN

9th Day of the 8th Month
Bul – also called Heshvan, usually falling in October/November
The Patriarchs
Joseph in Egypt
Torah Portion 'MiKetz' – Genesis 41:1 – 44:17

Then Pharoah said to Joseph, "Inasmuch as God has shown you all this, there is no one as discerning and wise as you. You shall be over my house, and all my people shall be ruled according to your word; only in regard to the throne will I be greater than you." *Genesis 41:39, 40*

Here the relationship between Pharoah and Joseph is a picture of the relationship between God the Father and Yeshua, God the Son. Joseph worked in Pharoah's Palace, but despite being blameless and resisting temptation, he was imprisoned through false accusation. Whilst in prison he was able to interpret the dreams of the baker, and the butler. This is a picture for us of Yeshua coming to earth and opening up to us the mystery of the bread and the wine. Later, Joseph successfully interpreted Pharoah's dreams, and was made Prime Minister because of his wisdom. Pharoah 'took his signet ring off and put it on Joseph's hand' .... 'and he had him ride in the second chariot which he had; and they cried out before him, "Bow the knee!" So he set him over all the land of Egypt.' (Genesis 41:42, 43)

This foreshadows Yeshua, who was falsely accused and killed, but is now risen from the dead, having conquered death and hell, to become King over God's kingdom. God the Father has 'highly exalted Yeshua and given Him the name which is above every name, that at the name of Jesus every knee should bow, of those in heaven, and of those on earth, and of those under the earth, and that every tongue should confess that Jesus Christ is Lord, to the glory of God the Father.' (Philippians 2:9–11) The Egyptians bowed before Joseph, and so did Joseph's brothers when they came to him for bread, that they might live.

Draw near to Yeshua, bowing before Him as King to worship Him and feed on His bread.

Readings: Genesis 41:1 – 44:17, Ephesians 1:13–23, Philippians 2:1–11, Isaiah 45:23–25

10th Day of the 8th Month
Bul – also called Heshvan, usually falling in October/November
The Patriarchs
Jacob in Egypt
Torah Portion 'VaYigash' – Genesis 44:18 – 47:27

Then they (Joseph's brothers) went up out of Egypt, and came to
the land of Canaan to Jacob their father. And they told him, saying,
"Joseph is still alive, and he is governor over all the land of Egypt."
Genesis 45:25, 26

Joseph tested his brothers when they went down to him in Egypt to
see if their hearts had changed, demanding that his younger brother
Benjamin also come down to him in Egypt. In fear for Benjamin's safety,
Judah showed true brokenness for what they had done to Joseph. The
brothers' shame for how they had treated him many years earlier touched
Joseph's heart. Casting out the Gentiles from the room, Joseph revealed
his identity to his brothers, and they experienced his grace and kindness.
Similarly, one day all of Yeshua's Jewish 'brothers' will see who He really
is and experience the unmerited favour of God.

When Jacob, Joseph's father, received the news that his son was actually
alive his 'heart stood still, because he did not believe them.' (Genesis
45:26) When he revived he decided to go down to Egypt, and God
reassured him in a vision of the night, saying, '...do not fear to go down
to Egypt, for I will make of you a great nation there. I will go down
with you to Egypt, and I will also surely bring you up again; and Joseph
will put his hand on your eyes.' (Genesis 46:4) When he arrived, he
had an emotional reunion with his son whom he had long thought was
dead. Joseph was alive! When Jacob willingly obeyed God's command
to go to Egypt, he found Joseph. A 'move' to Egypt could have looked
like a step backwards but actually his obedience brought him into the
place where he would meet Joseph.

*Consider how obedience to go where God directs will always lead us closer
to Yeshua.*

Readings: Genesis 44:18 – 47:27, Luke 15:13–24

HESHVAN

11th Day of the 8th Month
Bul – also called Heshvan, usually falling in October/November
The Patriarchs
The Twelve Tribes of Israel
Torah Portion 'Vayechi' – Genesis 47:28 – 50:26

Then Israel stretched out his right hand and laid it on Ephraim's head, who was the younger, and his left hand on Manasseh's head, guiding his hands knowingly, for Manasseh was the firstborn. *Genesis 48:14*

Hebrews 11:22 says that 'By faith Jacob, when he was dying, blessed each of the sons of Joseph, and worshiped, leaning on the top of his staff.' It took faith for Jacob to defer from convention and bless the younger son of Joseph above the elder, and to bless the sons as his very own. Jacob said to Joseph, 'now your two sons, Ephraim and Manasseh, who were born to you in the land of Egypt before I came to you in Egypt, are mine.' (Genesis 48:5)

Ephraim and Manasseh joined Jacob's sons in giving their names to two of the tribes of Israel. The name Ephraim means 'double fruit, fruitfulness'. Joseph, in a sense, was made doubly fruitful among the tribes, having his name carried on, not by his one single name, but the two tribes of his sons in his place. Joseph became 'two tribes'. This is a picture for us of the inheritance of Yeshua being two fold – Jewish believers and Gentile believers. Joseph's two sons had a Gentile mother. The 'younger' entrant to God's blessings – the Gentiles – receive the unexpected honour of being called to become the 'larger part' of Yeshua's Bride, called forth as a mighty multitude out of many nations. (Genesis 48:19) The Apostle Peter would receive the revelation that the Gospel is for the Gentiles as well as the Jews. (Acts 10:34–38) God's kingdom would bear fruit in all the earth. Jacob blessed all the tribes, and prophesied that the tribe of Judah would bring forth the Messiah. (Genesis 49:10)

Read Deuteronomy 33:13–17 and consider God's call to Israel and the Bride to be fruitful.

Readings: Genesis 47:28 – 50:26, Deuteronomy 33:13–17, Acts 10:34–38, Mark 4:26

12th Day of the 8th Month
Bul – also called Heshvan, usually falling in October/November
The Formation of Israel
The Burning Bush
Torah Portion 'Shemot' – Exodus 1:1 – 6:1

And God said to Moses, "I AM WHO I AM". And He said, "Thus shall you say to the children of Israel, "I AM has sent me to you."
Exodus 3:14

Today as we begin the book of Exodus we shift from the formation of God's 'family' in Genesis, to the formation of His nation in Exodus. Just as God revealed Himself to the 'Patriarchs', promising the Seed of Messiah to come from them, God now reveals Himself to the nation of Israel that has emerged from the sons of God's covenant with Abraham, Isaac and Jacob.

God's instrument in the birth of Israel as a nation is Moses. Pharoah's daughter rescued him, 'drawing him out' of the bulrushes where he had been hidden. The name Moses means 'draw out'. God had called Moses to 'draw out' the Israelites from among the Egyptians to make them into a separate nation, called apart, separate and holy to God.

It was while Moses was tending sheep at Mount Horeb that God spoke to him from the burning bush, revealing Himself as the God of Abraham, Isaac and Jacob. God had heard the cry of the Israelites because of their Egyptian taskmasters. He would deliver them and bring them up to a good land, a land flowing with milk and honey. Moses asked God His name, and He replied saying, 'I AM WHO I AM'. He was to tell the children of Israel that 'I AM' had sent him. The starting place for a nation or individual to find their identity is to know who GOD IS. God will 'draw us out' into our identity and destiny as we 'know Him'.

It is not by introspection that you 'find yourself' but in looking up into the eyes of Yeshua.

Readings: Exodus 1:1 – 6:1, Luke 20:34–38, Acts 7:1–37

13th Day of the 8th Month
Bul – also called Heshvan, usually falling in October/November
The Formation of Israel
God's Promise of Redemption
Torah Portion 'Va'eira' – Exodus 6:2 – 9:35

Therefore say to the children of Israel: 'I am the LORD; I will bring you out from under the burdens of the Egyptians, I will rescue you from their bondage, and I will redeem you with an outstretched arm and with great judgements. I will take you as My people, and I will be your God.' *Exodus 6:6, 7*

God had promised to deliver Israel from the hand of the Egyptians. Moses went to Pharoah demanding that he set the Israelites free, but Pharoah would not let the Israelites go. He just made them work harder. This is a picture of our bondage and slavery to sin, and works without grace. They hold on tight and won't let us go. So God promised Moses something even more powerful. He would not just deliver Israel, He would redeem them. It was not enough for them to be free. Something more was needed. They needed redeeming.

Redemption involves the payment of a price. Pharoah thought that the Israelites belonged to him. They lived in his land and they served him. This is a picture of Satan claiming ownership of people because of their sin – and everyone has sinned. But God owned us first. He is our Creator. Redemption is when the original owner pays a price to receive back what was originally his. It was not possible for the Israelites to be delivered from Egypt without a ransom price being paid. God promised that when He redeemed the Israelites out of Egypt they would be truly His. They would be His people and He would be their God. The Egyptians had to pay the price for their idolatry – the plagues. But when we have the blood of Yeshua, which He paid to redeem us, on our life, then we belong to Him.

Thank God that through the blood covenant of Yeshua, you can be delivered and redeemed.

Readings: Exodus 6:2 – 9:35, Genesis 15:12–14, Romans 6, John 8:34–36

14th Day of the 8th Month
Bul – also called Heshvan, usually falling in October/November
The Formation of Israel
Redemption of the Firstborn
Torah Portion 'Bo' – Exodus 10:1 – 13:16

And all the firstborn of man among your sons you shall redeem.

Exodus 13:13

All of the firstborn had to be consecrated to God, and the firstborn son held a special position in the family. He would receive double the inheritance of the other brothers, and he had a position of privilege and special responsibility over his siblings. The firstborn represented having special favour and calling with God. Firstborn sons actually 'belonged to God'. In Numbers 3 we see how under the Law of Moses, parents had to pay redemption money to the priest of the temple to 'redeem' their son to 'be' their own son. Otherwise he would legally be God's son and would have to leave his family to go and serve God.

God called Israel his firstborn. (Exodus 4:22, 23) They belonged to Him. Yeshua is also called the 'firstborn' – the 'firstborn' of all creation and the 'firstborn' from among the dead – the first fruits of the resurrection. (Colossians 1:15–20) Now believers in Yeshua are the 'firstborn' of God. (Hebrews 12:23) As a child of God you have the status of the firstborn. We are the firstborn who have been redeemed by the blood of the Lamb Yeshua.

In Egypt, God sent ten plagues to demonstrate His ownership of Israel, His firstborn, to Pharoah. The Egyptians worshiped false gods and God directly challenged belief in their power through the ten plagues. The final plague, the death of the firstborn was God's final confrontation. The firstborn of every creature belongs to God. Only those redeemed by the blood of the Lamb on the night of Passover could survive God's claim of ownership.

Consider what it means for you, that you have been bought at a price, and are a firstborn son.

Readings: Exodus 10:1 – 13:16, Romans 8:28–39, Revelation 14:1–5

15th Day of the 8th Month
Bul – also called Heshvan, usually falling in October/November
The Formation of Israel
Israel Crossed the Red Sea
Torah Portion 'Beshalach' – Exodus 13:17 – 17:16

Then Moses and the children of Israel sang this song to the LORD, and spoke, saying: "I will sing to the LORD, for He has triumphed gloriously! The horse and its rider he has thrown into the sea!"

Exodus 15:1

After the Passover redemption of Israel, when the Angel of Death 'passed over' the firstborn Israelites who had the blood of the lamb on their doorposts, Pharoah let Israel go. When by faith, you receive the redeeming and cleansing blood of Yeshua on your life, Satan has to release his hold on you. You are free to rise up by faith, and enter your new life as a redeemed child of God. With repentance and confession, and faith and trust in your having received the righteousness of Yeshua, sinful patterns will release their grip, and your life will change. We are all called through faith in our redemption through the blood of the lamb, to 'forsake Egypt'. (Hebrews 11:27) We are not to stay living 'in Egypt' (our old life and sins).

Pharoah pursued the Israelites as they followed the pillar of cloud by day and fire by night. The pillar represents the leading of the Holy Spirit. Now the Holy Spirit enables us to 'cross over' into our new life. It was the power of God which parted the Red Sea and enabled the Israelites to cross over as though crossing on dry land. But when the Egyptians pursued in their chariots through the Red Sea, it closed in and drowned them. Similarly Satan's power was totally defeated at the cross. He has no right to touch you unless you let him. (Psalm 91) Redemption through the blood of the Lamb is as final and complete as crossing the Red Sea. Revelation 15:3, 4 has the victory song of Moses and the Lamb sung in Heaven.

By faith, like Moses, pass through the 'Red Sea' on dry land, to get free from your sins.

Readings: Exodus 13:17 –17:16, Hebrews 11:24–29, Psalms 136:1–15, Revelation 15

16th Day of the 8th Month
Bul – also called Heshvan, usually falling in October/November
The Formation of Israel
Israel Pledged to Keep the Law
Torah Portion 'Jethro' – Exodus 18:1 – 20:23

Both you and these people who are with you will surely wear yourselves out. For this thing is too much for you; you are not able to perform it by yourself. *Exodus 18:18*

Now the Israelites are journeying through the wilderness and they bring their disputes to Moses for him to judge. Moses' father-in-law Jethro, observed that the burden of the work was heavy for Moses and told him that he was trying to do too much. He suggested that others come alongside him to bear the burden with him, by judging the disputes and allowing Moses to concentrate on relating to God. This is a picture for us of the burden of works. They are too much for us. We need someone to come alongside us and bear the yoke. That person is Yeshua, who will deal with the difficulties in our lives for us if we will concentrate on our relationship of faith and trust in Him.

Immediately after this the Israelites came and camped at Mount Sinai. There Moses received God's call on Israel to be His holy nation, His special treasure, and to obey His voice. They readily agreed and said that they would. They accepted the Law, believing that they would be able to keep it perfectly. Up until this point Israel had received redemption from slavery, deliverance from Egypt, healing at Elim, and provision of Manna, all purely as gifts of God's grace. Now they claimed they would be able to obey all that God said. They did not yet know the weakness of their own sinful flesh. On Mount Sinai God gave them the Law, beginning with the Ten Commandments. Immediately, even before Moses descended the Mountain and God's presence, their sinful hearts were revealed. They fell into idolatry.

Deep down, do you believe you can keep the Law, or that you need God's help and grace?

Readings: Exodus 18:1 – 20:23, Exodus 32, Luke 18:8–27, Hebrews 12:18–29

HESHVAN

17th Day of the 8th Month
Bul – also called Heshvan, usually falling in October/November
The Formation of Israel
The Blood of the Covenant
Torah Portion 'Mishpatim' – Exodus 21:1 – 24:18

And Moses took the blood, sprinkled it on the people, and said, "This is the blood of the covenant which the LORD has made with you according to all these words." *Exodus 24:8*

The Law that God gave to Moses and the newly formed nation of Israel, was the solid foundation and basis of a just society. If they were to be God's special treasure and holy nation, they would have to keep His commandments. These involved right relationships based on justice, fairness, honesty and kindness. There was to be no murder, oppression or cruelty. A high value was attached to the life of every human being from the smallest to the greatest, and the right treatment of animals and property mattered too. Where there was any loss, damage or injury, recompense and restitution were to be paid, a life for a life. They were to be God's holy kingdom on earth. There was to be no compromise with the pagans.

The new nation of Israel would possess the land little by little, driving out their enemies under the guidance of the Angel of God, the LORD Himself. But this would only happen if they would put God first by faithfully keeping the feasts of the Lord, and dedicating the firstfruits of all the harvests, including their firstborn, to God. The people agreed to keep all these laws and conditions. And so the twelve tribes of Israel entered into covenant with God. They received the book of the Law, and Moses sprinkled the people with the blood from the offerings, which testified to the death of the giver of the covenant, Yeshua. (Hebrews 9:16–22) Moses and the 70 elders, the government of Israel, ate and drank in God's presence, in His kingdom, and seeing into heaven, saw the God of Israel.

The blood of Yeshua sprinkled on your life, means that you may 'eat' in His kingdom.

Readings: Exodus 21:1 – 24:18, Matthew 6:10, 11, Luke 22:14–30, Hebrews 9:16–28

18th Day of the 8th Month
Bul – also called Heshvan, usually falling in October/November
The Tabernacle
God's Instructions for the Tabernacle
Torah Portion 'Terumah' – Exodus 25:1 – 27:19

And let them make Me a sanctuary, that I may dwell among them.
Exodus 25:8

God wanted to dwell among His holy nation and to have a relationship with them. So He gave precise instructions for the construction of the tabernacle where He would meet with them at the 'Ark of the Covenant'. The Ark was covered with fine gold to represent God's righteousness. God's precise instructions demonstrate that we need to come to God through the way He prescribes for our salvation. But there was also room for the artistic creativity of the craftsman. This symbolises our own part in drawing near to God. We have an offering to bring. The people brought their gold, silver, bronze, their linens, fabrics, animal skins, oils, incense and precious stones for the construction of the tabernacle. God wants to receive our talents and gifts, and the loving service of every part of our lives.

The Ark of the Covenant contained the tablets of the Law, and was covered by the Mercy Seat. There the atoning blood would be sprinkled. God is looking for a Bride who comes to Him through His covenant of mercy and grace, through His blood which was shed for the forgiveness of our transgression of the Law. In the Holy Place outside the veil is the showbread, representing the body of Yeshua among us. We feed on Yeshua and enter through the 'veil' of His body to meet with Him. (Luke 23:45) The golden lampstand represents the Holy Spirit, and the coverings of the tent represent our being covered and hidden in Yeshua's righteousness. The screen has five pillars representing grace and the bronze altar and laver are where we are washed in the blood of Yeshua and His Word.

Enter into God's gates with thanksgiving and His courts with praise. (Psalm 100:4)

Readings: Exodus 25:1 – 27:19, Hebrews 9 – 10:22, Psalm 27:4, 5, Psalm 15

19th Day of the 8th Month
Bul – also called Heshvan, usually falling in October/November
The Tabernacle
The Priesthood
Torah Portion 'Tetzaveh' – Exodus 27:20 – 30:10

And you shall command the children of Israel that they bring you pure oil of pressed olives for the light, to cause the lamp to burn continually. In the tabernacle of meeting, outside the veil which is before the Testimony, Aaron and his sons shall tend it from evening until morning before the LORD. *Exodus 27:20, 21*

Aaron, the High Priest, and his sons, the priests, had the responsibility of keeping a perpetual light burning next to the veil of the tabernacle, which represented the body of Yeshua. The light never went out and so it represented Yeshua, the eternal light of the world.

Aaron and his sons were to offer up a continual burnt offering on the altar in front of the door of the tabernacle, of lambs, grain, oil and wine. (Exodus 29:42) The lambs spoke of the redeeming sacrifice of Yeshua, offered once for all, upon the cross, and whose one perfect sacrifice remains effective in Heaven throughout all eternity. The grain offerings spoke of His moral perfection, the oil and wine spoke of the life and blood of Yeshua. The burnt rams spoke of Yeshua our substitute, like the ram that was burned in place of Isaac on the mountain. (Genesis 22:13, 14) The bulls spoke of Yeshua's offering to take away our sin.

The High Priest wore special garments, and had 'Holiness to the Lord' written across His forehead. His blue robe spoke to us of the heavens, of Yeshua in Heaven, and the white linen garments spoke of Yeshua's perfection and righteousness. He bore on his shoulders and across his heart, the names of the tribes of Israel, as precious jewels bound up in gold, just as now Yeshua bears up our names before the Father, as He intercedes for us in Heaven.

Meditate on Yeshua, your continual sacrifice and High Priest in heaven, interceding for you.

Readings: Exodus 27:20 – 30:10, Hebrews 7:23–28, Romans 8:34, Hebrews 4:14–16

20th Day of the 8th Month
Bul – also called Heshvan, usually falling in October/November
The Tabernacle
God is a Jealous God
Torah Portion 'Ki Tissa' – Exodus 30:11 – 34:35

For you shall worship no other god, for the LORD whose name is Jealous, is a jealous God. *Exodus 34:14*

The children of Israel were not to forget their covenant with God, which was like a marriage covenant with God. They were not to be 'adulterous' and go after foreign religions and gods, and so provoke God's holy wrath. God is a consuming fire. He is a jealous God burning with godly jealousy for the love of His Bride. (Deuteronomy 4:24) Every individual matters, and our love for Him and for each other, matters. Each man of Israel belonged to God. They were counted by census, and each had to give a half shekel ransom for himself to the Lord. This would 'cover' them and make atonement for them when they stepped outside God's ownership of their life. Similarly through His grace we are Sons of God, His Bride.

Aaron the High Priest, and his sons, were to be anointed with special anointing oil, which was to be made with the quality sweet-smelling spices of myrrh, cinnamon, sweet-smelling cane and cassia. This was to be used to consecrate the tabernacle, its furniture, Aaron and his sons. It set them apart as Holy for His service. A special blend of incense was also placed before the Ark of the Covenant. These fragrances were to be unique and for this special purpose. They were not to be copied or put onto the flesh of ordinary people. Israel was to be His special possession, bearing His fragrance. So when the people committed idolatry, 3000 people died at the hands of the Levites. But God met with Moses, and promised that His presence would go with Him and He would give Him rest. (Exodus 33:14)

Thank God for the sweet fragrance of the Holy Spirit on your life, dedicated to Him.

Readings: Exodus 30:11 – 34, 35, Psalm 133, Song of Songs 4:10–16, Ephesians 5:1–21

21st Day of the 8th Month
Bul – also called Heshvan, usually falling in October/November
The Tabernacle
The Work and Construction
Torah Portion 'Vayachei' – Exodus 35:1 – 38:20

All who are gifted artisans among you shall come and make all that the LORD has commanded.... Exodus 35:10

Moses spoke to the children of Israel and gave them God's instructions concerning the work of the tabernacle. The people whose hearts were stirred by God, and whose spirit was willing, brought the raw materials for the construction of the tabernacle. (Exodus 35:21) He places His will and desires into our hearts, so that even sacrificial giving becomes a joyful sacrifice and privilege. God loves a cheerful giver. (2 Corinthians 9:7)

Those who were gifted artisans were called upon to use their natural gifting in the service of God. Today God continues to use us, His body, by anointing our natural gifts for His glory in His kingdom. Two of the tabernacle craftsmen are given particular mention in Exodus. God had filled Bezalel of the tribe of Judah with 'the Spirit of God, in wisdom and understanding, in knowledge and all manner of workmanship, to design artistic works, to work in gold and silver and bronze, in cutting jewels for setting, in carving wood, and to work in all manner of artistic workmanship.' (Exodus 35:31–33) The name Bezalel means 'In the Shadow of God'. Creation is a shadow of heavenly reality and all godly human creativity is a shadow of the creativity of God. The items that Bezalel created were shadows of the beautiful things in heaven. The whole design of the tabernacle was a copy and shadow of heavenly things. (Hebrews 8:5) The other craftsman mentioned was Aholiab whose name means 'Tent of Father'. He skilfully wove and sewed 'God's Tent'.

How can you use your gifts anointed by God to bring Him glory and reflect Heaven on earth?

Readings: Exodus 35:1 – 38:20, Hebrews 8:5, Acts 9:36–43

22nd Day of the 8th Month
Bul – also called Heshvan, usually falling in October/November
The Tabernacle
The Coverings
Torah Portion 'Pekudei' – Exodus 38:21 – 40:28

And he spread out the tent over the tabernacle and put the covering of the tent on top of it, as the LORD had commanded Moses.

Exodus 40:19

Moses raised up the tabernacle on the first day of the first month. The sockets of the sanctuary, the foundation on which it stood were made of silver. Silver represents redemption – it was the half-shekel silver coin which was used to redeem the men of Israel. The foundation of our relationship and reconciliation with God is our redemption through the blood of Yeshua. He alone is our secure foundation. (1 Corinthians 3:11)

The walls of the tabernacle were interconnecting wooden boards overlaid with gold. These represent believers, the wood representing our humanity, the gold representing the righteousness of Yeshua. They are held together by a pole which passes through each board, like the cross, the love of God uniting our hearts. The glory and splendour of the gold is hidden from view by the tent coverings. (Exodus 26) The curtains of woven linen, made of blue, purple and scarlet thread, remind us of the divinity and humanity of our Lord. The blue represents the heavens and divinity, the red, human blood. When mixed together, red and blue produce purple. The purple represents the Messiah, King Yeshua – God and Man. The covering of goats' hair as a tent, reminds us of the sin offering. Goat-hair is well known for enabling ventilation and being water resistant. The covering of rams' skins dyed red, speaks of the blood of our substitute, Yeshua, and the badgers' skins speak of our being hidden in the humility of Messiah. Finally, the tabernacle is covered with the cloud of God's presence.

Meditate on how these coverings protect your life, and attract the presence of the Lord.

Readings: Exodus 38:21 – 40:28, Song of Songs 3:9–11, John 19:1–14, Isaiah 61:10, 11

HESHVAN

23rd Day of the 8th Month
Bul – also called Heshvan, usually falling in October/November
Israel, Set Apart and Holy
The Blood Sacrifices
Torah Portion 'Vayikra' – Leviticus 1:1 – 6:7

Speak to the children of Israel, and say to them: 'When any one of you brings an offering to the LORD, you shall bring your offering of the livestock....' *Leviticus 1:2*

God is holy, and in order to relate to Him, His people needed to be made holy. So when they broke God's laws, or became defiled in some way they needed to be cleansed and restored back to God through sacrifices, offerings and washings. These sacrifices were not like the pagan sacrifices which are offered to placate or appease the 'gods'. They were an act of worship offered up to the one true God according to His pattern so that they do not represent man's offering to God, but God's offering to man to remove the barrier of sin.

Blood contains the 'life', and it was poured out from the animal in place of the life of the sinner, representing Yeshua's blood poured out, to save the lives of sinners from being condemned to hell. The Israelites placed their hand on the forehead of their animal being sacrificed to identify with it, the life of the animal being given instead of their own. Now we must identify with the sacrifice of Yeshua through repentance and faith. Yeshua is our 'burnt offering'. The whole animal was burnt, representing the complete giving of Yeshua in death on the cross. The smoke ascended up to God in heaven. Yeshua's sacrifice satisfied God's holy wrath against sin. The grain offerings represented the moral perfection of His life lived, crushed like grain ground finely in the millstone, baked in an oven (hidden suffering), in a pan (open suffering), and in a covered pan (general suffering), free from 'fermenting sin', preserved with the salt of the covenant, infused with the fragrance and oil of the Holy Spirit.

Meditate on Yeshua your 'burnt offering' and your 'grain offering', given for you.

Readings: Leviticus 1:1 – 6:7, 17:11, Isaiah 43:21–44:23, Hebrews 10

24th Day of the 8th Month
Bul – also called Heshvan, usually falling in October/November
Israel, Set Apart and Holy
The Sin, Trespass and Peace Offerings
Torah Portion 'Tzav' – Leviticus 6:8 – 8:36

Speak to Aaron and to his sons, saying, 'This is the law of the sin offering. In the place where the burnt offering is killed, the sin offering shall be killed before the LORD. It is most holy.' *Leviticus 6:25*

In addition to the burnt offerings and grain offerings, were the sin, trespass and peace offerings. The sin offering was offered in the same place as the burnt offering, but instead of being completely consumed by the fire on the altar it was to be cooked and eaten by the priests, and the blood sprinkled at the veil and at the altar to cleanse the sinner. It covered every aspect of human sin – sin committed intentionally and sin committed unintentionally. The sin offering represents the blood of Yeshua, shed to take away and atone for our sins. It is the blood which is the focus of this sacrifice, not the burning of the whole body. The blood of Yeshua washes away our sins. Only His blood can take away our sins forever.

Like the sin offering, the trespass offering was eaten by the priests, foreshadowing our 'eating' of the unleavened bread, the body of Yeshua. The ram speaks of Yeshua being our substitute. Every aspect of the life of Yeshua fulfilled God's holy Law, and became the substitute for our failure and lack in keeping God's law. The sinner also had to make restitution and reparation to the people they had sinned against, as do we.

The peace offering speaks of Yeshua's peace with the Father being conferred on us through His sacrifice. Through His blood we receive with thanksgiving, God's life in us.

Meditate on all these benefits which are yours since you believed on Yeshua's sacrifice.

Readings: Leviticus 6:8 – 8:36, Colossians 1:19–23, 2:11–15, 3:12–17

25th Day of the 8th Month
Bul – also called Heshvan, usually falling in October/November
Israel, Set Apart and Holy
Holiness
Torah Portion 'Sh'mini' – Leviticus 9:1 – 11:47

It shall be a statute forever throughout your generations, that you may distinguish between holy and unholy, and between unclean and clean.... *Leviticus 10:9, 10*

The Israelites offered their sacrifices to God, and Moses and Aaron went into the tabernacle of meeting and came out and blessed the people. 'Then the glory of the LORD appeared to all the people, and fire came out from before the LORD and consumed the burnt offering and the fat on the altar. When all the people saw it, they shouted and fell on their faces.' (Leviticus 9:23, 24) God revealed His glory to them.

Moses and Aaron had done what God had spoken, and God received it supernaturally by sending fire from heaven to consume the burnt offering. It was the sacrifice ordained by God, and it was burned by God's fire. It was holy, coming from God and going to God. The people simply obeyed. This is a picture for us of God meeting with us. It is His holiness, His fire, His sacrifice, that is acceptable to Him. We learn to walk in His holiness, close to Him.

Nadab and Abihu did not understand this. They took fire and offered incense to God which God had not commanded. To God this was profane. All holiness is received from Him. We cannot cleanse ourselves without Him. God's holy fire came down and consumed them and they died. The Lord said, 'By those who come near Me I must be regarded as holy; and before all the people I must be glorified.' (Leviticus 10:3) We receive His holiness by walking humbly in the fear of God, repenting of sin, walking in forgiveness, and obeying His voice. God even told the Israelites which creatures they could eat. Even that mattered.

What does God perceive as holy? How must we relate to God in His holiness?

Readings: Leviticus 9:1 – 11:47, 1 Samuel 15:1–23, 1 Kings 18:36–39, Hebrews 12:28, 29

26th Day of the 8th Month
Bul – also called Heshvan, usually falling in October/November
Israel, Set Apart and Holy
Diagnosis of Leprosy
Torah Portion 'Tazria' – Leviticus 12:1 – 13:59

Now the leper on whom the sore is, his clothes shall be torn and his head bare; and he shall cover his moustache, and cry, 'Unclean! Unclean!' *Leviticus 13:45*

When a leper was diagnosed, he had to tear his clothes and bare his head because he was 'unclean' before God and man. He was expressing his grief and despair at his condition, and ensuring that others did not touch him and so become infected and unclean. In contrast the priests were kept ritually clean. They were never permitted to tear their clothes or bare their heads in the service of the tabernacle. (Exodus 39:23, Leviticus 10:6) They were to deliver people from their ritual impurities. It was only when Yeshua claimed before the High Priest, to be the Son of God, that a Priest tore his clothes. (Matthew 26:65) The High Priest had made himself unclean by accusing Yeshua of blasphemy. At that moment the old order of the priesthood ended. It was no longer holy. It was stricken by God with spiritual leprosy.

The disease of leprosy is symbolic of sin. The word for leprosy, 'tsara', means to be scourged and stricken. King Uzziah was stricken on his forehead for presuming to act like a priest. (2 Chronicles 26) And Miriam was stricken with leprosy for speaking against Moses. (Numbers 12:10) The actual disease of leprosy leads to the eventual decay and rotting of the flesh, causing terrible deformity, pain and finally death. This is a picture of what sin does to us if we do not repent. When allowed free reign, it takes us down a path of spiritual decay, to death and hell. Highly infectious, it begins small, but grows to eventually consume the whole person. Only Yeshua can make us clean again by forgiving our sin and healing our disease.

Consider the seriousness of sin, and thank Yeshua for being your High Priest to cleanse you.

Readings: Leviticus 12:1 – 13:59, 2 Chronicles 26, Hebrews 5:1–11, 2 Corinthians 7:1

27th Day of the 8th Month
Bul – also called Heshvan, usually falling in October/November
Israel, Set Apart and Holy
Cleansing from Leprosy
Torah Portion 'Metzora' – Leviticus 14:1 – 15:33

The rest of the oil that is in the priest's hand he shall put on the head of him who is to be cleansed. So the priest shall make atonement for him before the LORD. *Leviticus 14:18*

When a person was struck down with leprosy, they were put outside the camp to avoid contaminating others. They were never permitted back in the camp or the city unless the priest had declared them healed, and he had ritually cleansed them. In the Scriptures the only people who were actually healed and cleansed of leprosy were healed miraculously by God. Healing comes through the atonement. Yeshua's death on the cross outside the city wall has purchased healing for all who have been 'cast outside the city wall' by their sin and sickness. At Golgotha, the city wall stood tall between Yeshua and God's holy temple. Yeshua's death on the cross not only atoned for our sins but it healed our diseases. Everyone who came to Yeshua was healed, including the lepers. And He sent His disciples out to heal the sick, cleanse the lepers, raise the dead and cast out demons. (Matthew 10:8)

The priest went to the healed person with two birds, wood, scarlet thread and hyssop. The word 'hyssop' comes from the meaning 'be gone'. The priest killed one bird over running water, then dipped his finger in the blood and sprinkled it on the healed person seven times. The second bird was released to fly away free. The blood of Yeshua shed at the cross, has released us from sickness and makes it flee. When Naaman came to Elisha to be healed of leprosy, Elisha told him to go to the River Jordan to immerse himself seven times (which is like the seven sprinklings of blood). (2 Kings 5) The priest anointed the person with oil.

By faith receive 'seven sprinklings' (a complete cleansing process) in His blood. (Isaiah 53:5)

Readings: Leviticus 14:1 – 15:33, 2 Kings 5, Psalm 51, John 19:28–34, Hebrews 9:19–22

28th Day of the 8th Month
Bul – also called Heshvan, usually falling in October/November
Israel, Set Apart and Holy
The Power of the Blood
Torah Portion 'Acharei Mot' – Leviticus 16:1 – 18:30

'And whatever man of the house of Israel, or of the strangers who dwell among you, who eats any blood, I will set My face against that person who eats blood, and will cut him off from among his people. For the life of the flesh is in the blood, and I have given it to you upon the altar to make atonement for your souls; for it is the blood that makes atonement for the soul.' *Leviticus 17:10, 11*

God gave Aaron, the High Priest very specific instructions about entering the tabernacle. He could only enter in through the veil of the tabernacle to the Most Holy Place once a year, on the Day of Atonement, Yom Kippur. And even then he could not enter without the blood from the sacrifices. It was the blood he carried that gave him safe entry to God's presence. Without the blood, he would have been struck dead by the holiness of God.

The blood is powerful because it keeps the flesh alive, it contains life, and God sees and hears it in a way that we do not. (Genesis 4:10) The Israelites were not permitted to eat any blood. If blood is ingested, those cells and DNA enter your body and integrate with your own. Blood is therefore not to be eaten on purpose, especially for 'spiritual reasons' such as demonic rituals. Yeshua makes atonement for our sins. We want to put our faith in the power of His life, permeating and entering every cell of our body and sustaining us, not in the blood of an animal. The blood of Yeshua has the spiritual power to cleanse and heal every cell of our body. The blood of Yeshua is powerful to dispel darkness and evil. His blood enables us to enter God's presence behind the veil. It cleanses us from all sin.

Meditate on the power of the blood of Yeshua in your life. (Luke 22:17–20)

Readings: Leviticus 16:1 – 18:30, Acts 15:19, 20, Mark 14:24, Revelation 1:5

HESHVAN

29th Day of the 8th Month
Bul – also called Heshvan, usually falling in October/November
Israel, Set Apart and Holy
A Holy Nation
Torah Portion 'Kedoshim' – Leviticus 19:1 – 20:27

And you shall be holy to Me, for I the LORD am holy, and have separated you from the peoples, that you should be Mine.

Leviticus 20:26

God called the Israelites to be a holy nation, holy because He is holy. Israel is called to be His people on earth, reflecting His nature to the world, being His people, a living example to the whole earth of what it means to live under God's holy government and laws, a light to the Gentile nations. Israel is called to be free from idol worship and to keep God's Sabbaths. Israel's relationships are to be ordered by God's standards of love, with reverence for parents and the elderly. There is not to be any compromise with foreign religions or the occult. There is to be no immorality, fornication, adultery or child sacrifice. Even the fruit of the trees was not to be eaten until after the fourth year of it coming under the ownership of the Israelites. In that way they did not eat the fruit of other religions. Everything was to be dedicated to God, pure, holy and without mixture, even the seeds and fabrics. They were to only eat the animals that God declared clean.

Now under the New Covenant, you are part of a holy nation, '... you are a chosen generation, a royal priesthood, a holy nation, His own special people, that you may proclaim the praises of Him who called you out of darkness into His marvellous light, who once were not a people but are now the people of God, who had not obtained mercy but now have obtained mercy.' (1 Peter 2:9, 10) All believers in Yeshua, whether Jewish or Gentile, are called by His mercy to live righteously as part of God's 'holy nation', with Him as our King.

Why is it God's mercy which qualifies you to be part of God's 'holy nation'?

Readings: Leviticus 19:1 – 20:27, John 11:49–52, 1 Peter 2:9

30th Day of the 8th Month
Bul – also called Heshvan, usually falling in October/November
Israel, Set Apart and Holy
A Holy Calendar
Torah Portion 'Emor' – Leviticus 21:1 – 24:23

You shall not profane my holy name, but I will be hallowed among the children of Israel, I am the LORD who sanctifies you, who brought you out of the land of Egypt, to be your God: I am the LORD.

Leviticus 22:32

The Lord now revealed Himself to the children of Israel as the God who sanctified them. The word 'sanctify' is from the root 'kadash', which means to make a proclamation of being set apart completely for the Lord. The holiness of the 'sanctified one' is evident to all, as God prepares and keeps him set apart and separate from those who serve other gods. Israel was set apart to be God's own holy nation, living His way, according to His laws, and keeping His feasts. Those who cursed or blasphemed God were to be cast out of the camp.

The priests were not to profane God's name by doing anything that the pagans do, like shaving the top of their heads and the edges of their beards. They were to keep God's feasts, not pagan ones. The word 'moedim' – 'appointed times', contains the word 'ed' which means 'witness'. The 'feasts' would testify to God's revelation of Himself to His people. He is the one who provides the harvests in their season. They do not need any pagan fertility rituals to guarantee the maturing of their harvests. In Galatians, the Apostle Paul warned the new Gentile Christians against returning to their old feasts and seasons, (which were pagan and held them in bondage). (Galatians 4:8–12) He desired that they became like him, not held in bondage by anything. (Galatians 4:12) When he could, Paul kept the biblical feasts. (Acts 18:21, 20:16) It appears from Ezekiel 45 the feasts will continue in the millennium.

What does it mean for you to be 'set apart' in God's holy nation, in regard to the calendar?

Readings: Leviticus 21:1 – 24:23, Hosea 2, Ezekiel 44:23, 24, 45:16–25, 2 Corinthians 6

1st Day of the 9th Month
Kislev, usually falling in November/December
Israel, Set Apart and Holy
The Jubilee Redemption
Torah Portion 'B'har' – Leviticus 25:1 – 26:2

The land shall not be sold permanently, for the land is Mine, for you are strangers and sojourners with Me. And in the land of your possession you shall grant redemption of the land. *Leviticus 25:23, 24*

Today is the New Moon. It was in this month that Jehoakim burned Jeremiah's scroll (Jeremiah 36), and in this month Nehemiah received the news that the walls of Jerusalem were still broken down and the gates burned with fire, and the Jews in the Land were in distress and reproach. (Nehemiah 1:1) At the end of the month is the 'Feast of Dedication'. In today's reading the children of Israel were to remember that the Land belongs to God and that they are sojourners passing through on their way to the heavenly Jerusalem. The Rechabites of Jeremiah 35:7 dwelt in tents to stand prophetically for this truth. Israelites were to respect the land and give it a year of rest every seventh year, and every 50th year they were to keep the Year of Jubilee. In the 50th year, land and possessions returned to their original owners, so they could return to the land allotted to their tribe, as their inheritance.

The Jubilee was necessary, because, over time there was a 'falling away' and 'back-sliding' away from God. Israel would need to be redeemed and restored back to God. (Isaiah 49) When Yeshua returns, the whole earth will be restored back to God. The Scriptures prophesy the redemption of Israel on the 'third day'. (Hosea 6:2, Luke 24:21) This final restoration will come in the millennium, under the reign of Yeshua, when the Land will be re-allotted to the tribes of Israel, and each will receive their inheritance. (Ezekiel 47, 48)

Meditate on God's faithfulness to redeem what has been lost, and bring restoration to you.

Readings: Leviticus 25:1 – 26:2, Isaiah 49, Ezekiel 47, 48

2nd Day of the 9th Month
Kislev, usually falling in November/December
Israel, Set Apart and Holy
Dwell in the Land
Torah Portion 'B'chukotai' – Leviticus 26:3 – 27:34

Yet for all that, when they are in the land of their enemies, I will not cast them away, nor shall I abhor them, to utterly destroy them and break My Covenant with them; for I am the LORD their God.

Leviticus 26:44

God has promised to bless His people when they are obedient. He said to them, "I will walk among you and be your God, and you shall be My people." (Leviticus 26:12) God is not a remote and distant King. The children of Israel would prosper when they obeyed Him, because God Himself would be able to walk among them. But if they disobeyed, God could not walk among them, and that would open the door for their enemies to come in. Yet God always showed His mercy. If they confessed their sins and those of their forefathers, He would restore them, and even if they were cast out into the nations because of their disobedience – which they were – He would never utterly destroy them, for the sake of His covenants with Abraham, Isaac and Jacob. (Leviticus 26:40–45)

Israel's ability to live in the Land with God's presence among them depended on their keeping the Law of Moses. For seventy years they were out of the Land, in exile in Babylon, so that the Land could make up the 70 years of Sabbatical rest that the Israelites failed to give it. (Leviticus 26:33–35) And the Land lay empty after they rejected their Messiah so that God could bring the Gentiles into the kingdom of God. (Romans 11:12, 15) Now, our ability to live in God's kingdom depends on our receiving God's New Covenant forgiveness of sins, and walking with God through the power of the Holy Spirit, obeying His voice.

Meditate on God's grace which will restore Israel and preserve you in His kingdom.

Readings: Leviticus 26:3 – 27:34, Jeremiah 16, 31, 1 Corinthians 6:9–11

3rd Day of the 9th Month
Kislev, usually falling in November/December
Israel in the Wilderness
The Levites
Torah Portion 'B'Midbar' – Numbers 1:1 – 4:20

Therefore the Levites shall be mine, because all the firstborn are Mine. On the day that I struck all the firstborn in the land of Egypt, I sanctified to Myself all the firstborn in Israel, both man and beast. They shall be Mine: I am the LORD. *Numbers 3:12, 13*

Now we come to the Torah portions from the book of Numbers which in Hebrew is called 'B'Midbar', meaning 'In the Wilderness'. This book records Israel's wanderings in the wilderness from Sinai to Kadesh, then round and round the wilderness back to Kadesh, where they had set out approximately 40 years earlier, then finally up towards Canaan, to the place where they would enter the Promised Land. The Israelites were hindered from entering the Promised Land by their sins, and these have been recorded as an example for us, especially in these last days, so that we do not fall into the same errors. (1 Corinthians 10:1–11) They would need Joshua (a picture of Yeshua) to actually take them into the Land. The book begins with the raising up and organisation of the tribes of Israel in the wilderness. The tabernacle with the cloud of God's presence was at the centre of the camp, with the tribes arranged around it in their allotted spaces. The camps are described as armies, and they had a total of 603,550 men of fighting age. This is a picture of the kingdom of God, where we are members of His spiritual army. (Ephesians 6:12) The tribe of Levi was different from the 'armies'. These men were set apart to serve the priests in the work of the tabernacle. They took the place of the 'firstborn' of all the tribes who would otherwise have had to serve God in the tabernacle. They released the firstborn of the tribes to fight.

Consider what the tribes/armies and the Levites represent now, and what your part is.

Readings: Numbers 1:1 – 4:20, 8, Ephesians 2:10, 6:10–20, 1 Corinthians 12:4–31

4th Day of the 9th Month
Kislev, usually falling in November/December
Israel in the Wilderness
The Nazirites
Torah Portion 'Nasso' – Numbers 4:21 – 7:89

> When either a man or woman consecrates an offering to take the vow of a Nazirite, to separate himself to the LORD, he shall separate himself from wine and similar drink.... *Numbers 6:2*

The children of Israel were to keep themselves holy before God by keeping God's Law. But God gave individuals the possibility of dedicating themselves to Him in a special way for a season by taking a Nazirite vow. This involved avoiding wine and strong drink and not partaking of any fruit of the vine, and not cutting their hair. Hair, interestingly, is seen as a sign of our position before God even in the New Testament (1 Corinthians 11:14, 15), and God knows about every hair on our head. (Luke 21:18, Matthew 10:30) He knows every smallest detail of our life, and everything that concerns us. The Nazirite lets God control his hair! He avoids pollution of the flesh and has a special relationship with God.

In the Scriptures, there were three men who were Nazirites, but without taking a vow. They were set apart to God from birth. These three were Samson, a Judge of Israel, Samuel, a Prophet of Israel, and John the Baptist, the forerunner of the Messiah. Each was born to parents who were barren, so their birth was miraculous and foretold to the parents. Each had a special anointing of the presence and power of God on their life. These three foreshadowed in their birth, the unique and miraculous virgin birth of the Messiah Yeshua.

Now, through Yeshua, we too have been predestined and set apart to the Lord. (Ephesians 1:3–12, Romans 8:29, 30) He calls us all to conceive in our barren hearts a unique and intimate relationship with Him, to know Him and be known by Him, abiding in the vine.

When Yeshua enters your heart he purifies it. You are set apart, predestined, to know God.

Readings: Numbers 4:21 – 7:89, Judges 13:2–25, 16:17, 1 Samuel 1:11, 18, Luke 1:13–17

KISLEV

5th Day of the 9th Month
Kislev, usually falling in November/December
Israel in the Wilderness
The Cloud
Torah Portion 'B'ha'alotcha' – Numbers 8:1 – 12:16

Whenever the cloud was taken up from above the tabernacle, after that the children of Israel would journey; and in the place where the cloud settled, there the children of Israel would pitch their tents. At the command of the LORD the children of Israel would journey, and at the command of the LORD they would camp. *Numbers 9:17, 18*

The picture of Israel moving on whenever the cloud of God's presence moved, and stopping wherever it stopped, is a picture for us of following the leading and guidance of the Holy Spirit. Yeshua said that He is the Way, the Truth and the Life. (John 14:6) The Father draws us to Himself. The cloud of God's presence led the Israelites out of Egypt.

Two silver trumpets were fashioned to call the congregation to meet before God at the tabernacle, to 'sound the advance' of the camps, or to sound an alarm in war. (Numbers 10:1–10) When the cloud moved, the allotted families carried the tabernacle, and the family of the Kohathites bore the holy things of the tabernacle on their shoulders following the Ark of the Covenant, and each tribe followed their standard. Moses invited his Midianite father-in-law to accompany them on the journey but he declined. (Numbers 10:29, 30) God calls us to invite others to come with us on the journey to the Promised Land. The journey the Lord led them on was not comfortable. The people complained, and yielded to the intense craving of the flesh, demanding meat. God consumed those on the edge of the camp with fire, and a plague consumed those who yielded to craving. This is a warning for us, not to complain about the path God leads us on, nor yield to the cravings of the flesh. (1 Corinthians 10:1–13)

Ask the Lord to help you recognise the 'cloud' of God, and the 'trumpets' blown by His men.

Readings: Numbers 8:1 – 12:16, 1 Corinthians 10:1–13, John 14, Song of Songs 1:4

6th Day of the 9th Month
Kislev, usually falling in November/December
Israel in the Wilderness
The Fruit of the Land
Torah Portion 'Shlach L'cha' – Numbers 13:1 – 15:41

Then they (the 12 spies) came to the Valley of Eshcol, and there cut down a branch with one cluster of grapes; they carried it between two of them on a pole. They also brought some of the pomegranates and figs. *Numbers 13:23*

Moses sent 12 spies from their camp into the Promised Land to see what the land was like. They came back from 'Nahal Eshcol'– (translated 'River of taking inheritance of the Bunch {or Cluster} of fruit') actually bearing an 'eshcol' – a bunch or cluster of grapes, pomegranates and figs. These three fruits represent God's inheritance of the Church, the Bride and Israel. The 12 spies returned to Moses but all except Joshua and Caleb gave a bad report, saying that it would be too difficult for Israel to take the Land because of the giants.

This unbelief was actually a rejection of God. (Numbers 14:11) Unbelief is a failure to trust in the faithfulness of God. God wants us to obey Him with total confidence – trusting that if we do what He tells us to, He will work things out for us. (Psalm 37, Proverbs 3:5) As a punishment for their unbelief, they were to stay in the wilderness one year for every day they spied the Land – making 40 years, and all of that generation would die before they could enter the Land, apart from Joshua (symbolising Yeshua) and Caleb (symbolising believers).

In Luke 21:29–36 Yeshua spoke about the final 'generation' of the nation of Israel which will be in the Promised Land when Yeshua returns. He wants us all to be full of anticipation and belief that Yeshua is going to return, to be watching the 'fig tree' of Israel, and praying to escape the things that will come to pass. We must believe God's Word.

Read Hebrews 3. What attitude is He seeking from us in the end-times? (Hebrews 3:6)

Readings: Numbers 13:1 – 15:41, Joshua 1:1–11, Psalm 37, Hebrews 3

KISLEV

7th Day of the 9th Month
Kislev, usually falling in November/December
Israel in the Wilderness
The Rebellion of Korah
Torah Portion 'Korach' – Numbers 16:1 – 18:32

Do this: Take censers, Korah and all your company; put fire in them and put incense in them before the LORD tomorrow, and it shall be that the man whom the LORD chooses is the holy one. *Numbers 16:6*

Korah challenged the leadership of Moses. He said that Moses had wrongly exalted himself above the assembly of the LORD because all the members of the congregation were holy. (Numbers 16:3) This was not what God had taught. God had appointed certain people to certain tasks. So Moses instructed Korah and all his company to bring censers filled with burning incense. This job would normally have been done by the priests. So they brought the censers to burn incense to God. Moses said that if the earth opened its mouth and swallowed them up, then the people were to understand that those men had rejected the Lord.

And that is exactly what happened. The earth swallowed Korah, and the men with him, his family and possessions and they went down into the earth to hell. Fire came down from heaven and consumed the two hundred and fifty who were burning incense. God confirmed His choice of Moses, and He confirmed His choice of Aaron for the priesthood, through the blossoming and fruiting of the almond rod, a symbol of resurrection.

Jude exhorted us to contend for the faith because certain people had entered the Church and people were perishing in the rebellion of Korah. (Jude 11) They had rebelled against God's chosen way of receiving salvation, His chosen Messiah, His commandments, His chosen nation Israel, and His chosen order in the Church, and created their own doctrines.

Consider the need for the reverent fear of God, and reverence and respect for authority today.

Readings: Numbers 16:1 – 18:32, Jude, Romans 13:1–7, 1 Samuel 12:14, 26:11

8th Day of the 9th Month
Kislev, usually falling in November/December
Israel in the Wilderness
The Ashes of the Red Heifer
Torah Portion 'Chukat' – Numbers 19:1 – 22:1

Speak to the children of Israel, that they may bring you a red heifer without blemish, in which there is no defect and on which a yoke has never come. *Numbers 19:2*

The ashes of the red heifer were to be used for the purification from sin. The red heifer without blemish was extremely rare. Tradition says that even Solomon could not find one. God had given them an ordinance that it was almost impossible to keep! The Hebrew word for 'red' – 'adom' is linked to the Hebrew for 'man' – 'adam'. The red heifer represents the unique and perfect man who has never 'carried the yoke' of slavery to sin, that is Yeshua.

The holy water, made clean and powerful with the ashes of the red heifer had the power, just in its sprinkled drops, to cleanse the unclean person who had been contaminated by death. Everyone has been touched by death in his own fallen nature. John 13 shows us Yeshua as the one who must wash us clean from the defilement of sin. He told Peter, "If I do not wash you, you have no part with Me." (John 13:8) This is the language of covenant. To enter the New Covenant, we must be washed by Yeshua. Once we have been washed free of our sins, we only need Yeshua to wash our feet each time we become defiled by our own sin or the sin of others. He keeps us clean and dries us with His forgiveness. Now because He has forgiven us we must wash each other's feet, forgiving their sins too, not holding grudges.

Water was provided from the rock in the wilderness, representing Yeshua, and when the people sinned and were bitten by serpents, they had to 'look at' the serpent on the pole to be healed. It is simply by 'looking to' Yeshua on the cross that we receive life. (Isaiah 45:22)

What defiles you? (Matthew 15:18–20) Are you watching over your heart to keep it pure?

Readings: Numbers 19:1 – 22:1, John 3:10–21, John 13, Hebrews 9:13, 14

KISLEV

9th Day of the 9th Month
Kislev, usually falling in November/December
Israel in the Wilderness
The Four Oracles of Balaam
Torah Portion 'Balak' – Numbers 22:2 – 25:9

I see Him, but not now; I behold Him, but not near; A Star shall
come out of Jacob; A sceptre shall rise out of Israel, And batter the
brow of Moab, and destroy all the sons of tumult. *Numbers 24:17*

Balaam, the Gentile 'Seer' set out to curse Israel in direct disobedience
to God's command not to. He was lured on by the promise of honour
from Balak, King of Moab, enemy of Israel. But Balaam's donkey would
not take him. When Balaam beat his donkey, it actually spoke! Then
Balaam was able to see the Angel of the Lord blocking his path. If God
could speak through a donkey, he could speak through Balaam, a man
who was more rebellious than his donkey. He was saved by his donkey
which stood between himself and the Angel with drawn sword. It would
be a donkey that would carry Yeshua into Jerusalem.

So Balaam went to the tops of four mountains and pronounced the
four prophetic oracles of God over the children of Israel encamped down
on the plains below. In the first oracle he said that God has blessed Israel
so he could not curse them. They are a nation 'dwelling alone' – 'not
reckoning itself among the nations'. (Numbers 23:8, 9) In the second
oracle he said that there is no sorcery or divination against Israel. God
is with them making them holy. (Numbers 23:23) In the third oracle
God said that He will exalt the king of Israel and his kingdom (Numbers
24:7), and in the fourth oracle He prophesied that 'A Star shall come
out of Jacob, A sceptre shall rise out of Israel.' (Numbers 24:17) The
loveliness of Israel and her Messiah will be exalted in the earth, despite
resistance from the nations.

Be reassured that Yeshua will return and 'destroy the sons of tumult.'
(Numbers 24:17)

Readings: Numbers 22:2 – 25:9, Genesis 49:8–12, Matthew 2:6, Micah
5:2, Revelation 22:16

10th Day of the 9th Month
Kislev, usually falling in November/December
Israel in the Wilderness
A Man to Shepherd Israel
Torah Portion 'Pinchas' – Numbers 25:10 – 30:1

"Let the LORD, the God of the spirits of all flesh, set a man over the congregation, who may go out before them and go in before them, who may lead them out and bring them in, that the congregation of the LORD may not be like sheep which have no shepherd."

Numbers 27:16, 17

Moses was soon to die. The people would soon enter the Promised Land because the unbelieving generation had all died, and only Joshua and Caleb, the believing spies who had brought the good report, remained, as God had promised, to enter the Promised Land. (Numbers 14:8) Moses was not able to enter the Land because he had rebelled against God's command to hallow Him at the waters of Meribah. (Numbers 20:7–13)

Knowing that he was soon to die, Moses interceded for God to give the children of Israel a leader, a 'shepherd'. God answered saying that Joshua, the son of Nun, 'a man in whom is the Spirit', was to become the new leader of Israel. (Numbers 27:18) But He had a greater Shepherd, Yeshua, who would lay down His life for the sheep. (John 10:11) Israel was to offer morning and evening sacrifices and offerings, one lamb every morning and evening. When Yeshua was nailed to the cross it was the hour of the morning sacrifice (9 am), and the hour that He died was the time of the evening sacrifice (3 pm). The Shepherd became the sacrifice to save Israel, like the shepherd who gives everything to care for his flock day and night. Yeshua had compassion on Israel, saying they were like sheep without a shepherd. (Mark 6:34) The shepherd king, David, foreshadowed the prophesied Messiah. (Ezekiel 34:23) Yeshua was sent to the lost sheep of Israel. (Matthew 15:24)

Meditate on Yeshua, your Good Shepherd, who will lead you into the Promised Land.

Readings: Numbers 25:10 – 30:1, Ezekiel 34, John 10:1–17, Psalm 23

11th Day of the 9th Month
Kislev, usually falling in November/December
Israel in the Wilderness
Pressing On
Torah Portion 'Matot' – Numbers 30:1 – 32:42

"Shall your brethren go to war while you sit here? Now why will you discourage the heart of the children of Israel from going over into the land which the LORD has given them?..." *Numbers 32:6, 7*

Before Moses could be taken up to heaven and the Israelites could cross into the Land, two situations needed to be resolved. The first was the fact that at Peor, the Israelites had partied and joined in the pagan feasts of the Midianites, causing them to fall into idolatry and immorality. (Numbers 25) The Israelites needed to be purified and separated from the pagans, in order to return to the true worship of God, and cross over into victory. If they had not done something drastic they would have slipped into foreign religions, and been lost forever. Gideon would later have to fight the Midianites in the Land. (Judges 7)

The other situation was the desire of the tribes of Reuben and Gad to settle in the Land where they were, before they even crossed over the Jordan River into the Promised Land. Moses conceded that they could make camps there for the women and children, but the men needed to go over with the other tribes to possess the Land. Otherwise they would be no better than the ten unbelieving spies who had discouraged the children of Israel from believing that they could possess the land of Canaan.

The Israelites had to fight their enemies, to overcome the opposition, to press into the Land. They could not be passive. They had to rise up, fight and overcome, which was exactly what they did. Because of this they were able to cross over into the Promised Land.

Ask God to show you what is holding you back from pressing into your inheritance.

Readings: Numbers 30:1 – 32:42, Judges 7, 8, Philippians 3:12 – 16, Hebrews 12:1–5

12th Day of the 9th Month
Kislev, usually falling in November/December
Israel in the Wilderness
An Inheritance
Torah Portion 'Masei' – Numbers 33:1 – 36:13

Then the LORD spoke to Moses, saying, "Command the children of Israel, and say to them, 'When you come into the land of Canaan, this is the land that shall fall to you as an inheritance – the land of Canaan and its boundaries....'" *Numbers 34:1, 2*

Before the Israelites crossed over into the land of Canaan to possess the Land that God had promised their forefather Abraham (Genesis 12:7), Moses wrote down a record of their wilderness journey, their starts and their stops, and the instructions for entering the new Land. They were to possess the Land as families and tribes, settling in the areas of land allotted to their particular tribe. The Levites would not possess land like the rest of the tribes, but would have cities to dwell in and common land for their herds and flocks. The borders of the Land were clearly delineated by God and there would be cities of refuge where accidental manslayers could be protected from the avengers of blood. (Numbers 35:11, 12, Joshua 20)

It was important for the inheritance of land to stay within the tribe. When a daughter was the inheritor, because she had no brothers, she had to marry within her tribe so that her husband could not take the family property off to another tribe. We have an inheritance through faith in Yeshua, our Bridegroom. The devil wants to rob and steal our inheritance and God's own inheritance of Israel. Caleb, the faith-filled spy, drove the giants out of the land God had given him. (Joshua 15:14) Caleb's daughter received land but she asked her father for more, another field, extra blessing, not only the upper springs, but the lower springs too. (Joshua 15:19) The meek shall inherit the earth. (Matthew 5:5, Psalm 37:11)

As a child of God, your inheritance is salvation, healing, peace, joy, provision, destiny, fruit....

Readings: Numbers 33:1 – 36:13, Joshua 14, 15, 1 Peter 1:3–5, Galatians 3:18, Psalm 37

13th Day of the 9th Month
Kislev, usually falling in November/December
Enter the Land
Defeat the Giants
Torah Portion 'Dvarim' – Deuteronomy 1:1 – 3:22

From Aroer, which is on the bank of the River Arnon, and from the city that is in the ravine, as far as Gilead, there was not one city too strong for us; the LORD our God delivered all to us. *Deuteronomy 2:36*

We now begin Deuteronomy, the fifth and final book of the five books of Moses. Its Hebrew name 'Dvarim' – 'Words', reminds us that these are the 'words' which Moses spoke at the end of his life, at the end of his own earthly journey, to prepare Israel for the next phase of their journey – entering the Land. The first chapters are Moses' recollections of their wilderness journey. They contain accounts of past failures and victories. It had taken the Israelites forty years to make an eleven-day journey, because of their unbelief and complaining. The time finally came when they had sat long enough at the mountain, and it was time to move on towards the Promised Land. They had encountered many enemies and learned many lessons. But they had seen the faithfulness of God, who delivered all their enemies into their hands, and gave them mighty victories, and great quantities of loot!

For us, we are reminded that God has prepared a Promised Land for us – a place of spiritual victory, holiness, and the blessings of eternal life – both in this world and in the world to come. But we are often like the Israelites, and we can sit for years at the mountain of unbelief in the wilderness, stuck in old recurring thought patterns, behaviours and defeat, without actually pressing in to receive the life Yeshua died to give us. If we will just believe His promises, obey God and step out in faith, He will deal with our enemies and bless us.

Which 'spiritual' enemies has God defeated so that you can enter the blessings of eternal life?

Readings: Deuteronomy 1:1 – 3:22, 1 Samuel 17, Psalm 135:10–12, Romans 8:37–39

14th Day of the 9th Month
Kislev, usually falling in November/December
Enter the Land
Love the LORD your God
Torah Portion 'V'Et'chanan' – Deuteronomy 3:23 – 7:11

"Hear, O Israel: The LORD our God, the LORD is one! You shall love the LORD your God with all your heart, with all your soul, and with all your strength." *Deuteronomy 6:4, 5*

Now in these final writings of Moses, he reminds Israel of their special calling. They are God's 'special treasure', chosen to know God as no other nation has known him. They are to keep the Ten Commandments of the covenant, written by God on tablets of stone, and they are to teach them to their children. God is jealous for their love and obedient worship.

God spoke to His people, 'Sh'ma Israel' – 'Hear O Israel, God is One.' He is not a multiplicity of idols like the pagans had. (Deuteronomy 6:4, 5) The word 'One', 'echad', can translate with all these meanings – 'united, first, alike, alone, altogether a piece, only, other, some, together'. 'One' contains within it the possibility of the Father, Son and Holy Spirit, three together as one entity, not three Gods, but One. Three persons in One, God is love.

Each person was to love the Lord with all their own 'trinity' of nature, with every part of their being. A lawyer once asked Yeshua which was the greatest commandment and He quoted this commandment from Deuteronomy 6:4, 5, and added, 'love your neighbour as yourself. On these hang all the law and the prophets.' (Matthew 22:37–40). Israel failed with this, as we all do. But Yeshua, in His grace, came and demonstrated perfect love for us. The new commandment He gave His disciples was to love one another 'as He has loved us'. (John 13:34, 35) We are only able to truly love God and our neighbour because He has shown us how, He has loved us. (1 John 4:19) We love with the love He has given us.

Think of the futility of trying to give love without having first received the love of God.

Readings: Deuteronomy 3:23 – 7:11, Matthew 22:34–40, Mark 12:28–34, 1 John 4:19–21

15th Day of the 9th Month
Kislev, usually falling in November/December
Enter the Land
Know Your Frailty
Torah Portion 'Ekev' – Deuteronomy 7:12 – 11:25

So He humbled you, allowed you to hunger, and fed you with manna which you did not know nor did your fathers know, that He might make you know that man shall not live by bread alone; but man lives by every word that proceeds from the mouth of the LORD.

Deuteronomy 8:3

Moses reflected on the lessons Israel had gone through in the wilderness, and which had enabled them to recognise their own weakness and frailty. They had only survived the wrath of God against their sin because of the intercession of Moses. They had had to eat manna from heaven to survive. They were unable to provide for themselves. The devil tested Yeshua with this same test of self-preservation, and attempt at independence from the Father. But He resisted with the words of Deuteronomy 8:3 (Matthew 4:4), saying that man does not live just on bread, but on every word that proceeds from God. We need God's Word for every aspect of our lives. Without Him we have nothing of eternal value. Nothing will last, apart from what comes from Him and through Him.

Israel had to realise that they were nothing without God. They were only blessed because of God's covenant with Abraham, Isaac, and Jacob, not because of anything special in themselves. They would need God to help them possess the Promised Land – 'little by little', lest the wild beasts become too numerous for them. They would need God to deliver their enemies over to them for them to destroy. (Deuteronomy 7:22, 23) Their part was to stop being rebellious and stiff-necked, and obey God's commandments, and depend on Him.

Meditate on the goodness of God which enables you to trust and obey Him with all your life.

Readings: Deuteronomy 7:12 – 11:25, Matthew 4:1–11, Matthew 6:25–34

16th Day of the 9th Month
Kislev, usually falling in November/December
Enter the Land
The Place that God Chooses
Torah Portion 'R'eh' – Deuteronomy 11:26 – 16:17

But you shall seek the place where the LORD your God chooses, out of all your tribes, to put His name for His dwelling place; and there you shall go. *Deuteronomy 12:5*

The Israelites would soon enter the Promised Land to live as free citizens with their own portions of land. They would no longer dwell in tents or eat manna. They would all have permanent dwellings, and land where they could grow food. God would abide in their midst. He would choose the place where He would put His name, the place where His glory would dwell in the midst of the tribes. (Deuteronomy 12:5–14) During the time of the Judges that place was Shiloh (Jeremiah 7:12), then from 3000 BC, Jerusalem, on Mount Moriah.

In the Land there would be a mountain of blessing, for their obedience to God – Mount Gerizim – and a mountain of cursing, if they forsook God – Mount Ebal. (Deuteronomy 11:26–32) Between these two mountains stood Shechem, which means, 'between the shoulders, the place of burdens'. God chose another mountain, Mount Moriah, to be the place where Yeshua would bear the burden of our sin upon Himself, and take our curse, and through His obedience bring us into His blessing. Mount Moriah was the place where Isaac carried the wood upon his shoulders and God provided the Lamb for the sacrifice. (Genesis 22:2) The temple was built in the land of Moriah, and there Yeshua died and rose again.

Now Yeshua calls us to rest and abide in Him. (John 15:7) God promised the tribe of Benjamin, 'The beloved of the LORD shall dwell in safety by Him, who shelters him all the day long, and he shall dwell between His shoulders.' (Deuteronomy 33:12)

Yeshua now places His name on your heart. He chooses to dwell there. Abide in Him.

Readings: Deuteronomy 11:26 – 16:17, John 15:7–17, Galatians 3:10–14, Psalm 91

17th Day of the 9th Month
Kislev, usually falling in November/December
Enter the Land
A Prophet Like Moses
Torah Portion 'Shoftim' – Deuteronomy 16:18 – 21:9

"The LORD your God will raise up for you a Prophet like me from your midst, from your brethren. Him you shall hear...." *Deuteronomy 18:15*

God told the Israelites through Moses that when they have settled in the Land and want to have a king to govern them, then they are only to appoint a king that He chooses. (Deuteronomy 17:15) The people also needed to understand that the priests were chosen by God, chosen from all the tribes to stand and minister in the tabernacle in the name of the Lord. (Deuteronomy 18:5) The Lord prepared the Israelites for the day when a Prophet would be raised up from their midst, who would speak the words of God as Moses had done. When this Prophet came, they were to 'hear Him'. To 'hear' means more than listen. It means to heed and obey. It means to reverence Him as God. Yeshua would come as God's 'Chosen' Prophet (like Moses), Priest (like Melchizedek) and King (like David).

Yeshua would be the ultimate Prophet, because He has the authority of God. Even the scribes in the temple noticed this. (Matthew 7:29) His words are the word of God since He is the Word of God. Many of the people instinctively called Yeshua 'a Prophet'.

Yeshua ascended a mountain with Peter, John and James. There He was transfigured in heavenly glory and talked with Moses and Elijah. Peter was talking, but a cloud overshadowed them, and a voice came out of the cloud saying, "This is My beloved Son. Hear Him!" (Luke 9:35) The Father affirmed Yeshua in the presence of Moses, as the one whose words must be heard. (Deuteronomy 18:15). Even Moses was to 'hear' Him.

Of all the voices which speak daily into your life, it is Yeshua's voice that you must 'hear'.

Readings: Deuteronomy 16:18 – 21:9, Luke 9:28–36, Acts 7:35–39, Hebrews 3:7, 15, 4:7

18th Day of the 9th Month
Kislev, usually falling in November/December
Enter the Land
Hung on a Tree
Torah Portion 'Ki Tetse' – Deuteronomy 21:10 – 25:19

If a man has committed a sin deserving of death, and he is put to death, and you hang him on a tree, his body shall not remain overnight on the tree, but you shall surely bury him that day, so that you do not defile the land which the LORD your God is giving you as an inheritance; for he who is hanged is accursed of God.

Deuteronomy 21:22, 23

The Law of Moses stated that the body of a man hung (executed) on a tree could not remain on the tree over night, because a man hung on a tree is 'accursed of God'. His body would defile the land. Sin and death defile. When Yeshua was crucified He died on a tree. John 19:31 states that Yeshua died just before the Sabbath on the Preparation Day and they checked that He was dead, hastily taking His body down from the cross for burial. They considered the body 'cursed'. It was cursed, not with any sin from Him (for He had committed no sin), but with our sin. (Isaiah 53)

Every time Israel broke the Law they brought the curse for breaking the Law on themselves and obscured from themselves the blessings of Abraham. When Yeshua died on the cross He took the curse for our sins onto Himself in exchange for His righteousness which He now gives to us. Now we can all enter into the blessings of Abraham, Jew and Gentile. God 'made Him who knew no sin to be made sin for us, that we might become the righteousness of God in Him.' (2 Corinthians 5:21) 'Christ has redeemed us from the curse of the Law, having become a curse for us (for it is written, "Cursed is everyone who hangs on a tree") that the blessing of Abraham might come upon the Gentiles in Christ Jesus, that we might receive the promise of the Spirit through faith.' (Galatians 3:13)

Yeshua took your curses upon Himself so that you can receive the blessings of Abraham.

Readings: Deuteronomy 21:10 – 25:19, 2 Corinthians 5:12–21, Galatians 2:19 – 3:29

19th Day of the 9th Month
Kislev, usually falling in November/December
Enter the Land
The Stones of the Law
Torah Portion 'Ki Tavo' – Deuteronomy 26:1 – 29:8

And it shall be, on the day when you cross over the Jordan to the land which the LORD your God is giving you, that you shall set up for yourselves large stones, and whitewash them with lime. You shall write on them all the words of this law.... *Deuteronomy 27:2, 3*

Israel was to enter the Promised Land and take possession of it, immediately establishing it upon the 'Covenant of the Law of Moses'. A physical monument was to be erected as soon as they crossed over, which would demonstrate to heaven and earth, that the people had submitted themselves to keep God's Law. At that stage their wellbeing, and their right to live in the Land, would depend on their obedience to those laws.

Israel was to set up large, whitewashed stones, with the words of the Law written on them. The tribes were to pronounce the blessings for keeping the Law from Mount Gerizim, and pronounce the curses for breaking the Law on Mount Ebal. The Law is unyielding, uncompromising, and has very clear practical, physical consequences. There is a penalty for sin. There is a Heaven and a Hell. The fact there were stones reminds us of the stones of the covenant God gave to Moses. Trying to keep the Law, or rebelling, made their hearts stony. (Ezekiel 36:26) When you try to 'earn' God's favour through works, you become a hypocrite – like the whitewashed tombs described by Yeshua, nice on the outside but inside full of dead men's bones, as you try to whitewash over your failures. (Matthew 23:27) But alongside the stones was an altar, also made of stones, which reminds us of God's provision of the perfect sacrifice to remove our stoniness. The New Covenant gives us a new heart of flesh.

Let humility, repentance, forgiveness and God's love soften any stoniness in your heart.

Readings: Deuteronomy 26:1 – 29:9, Matthew 23, Ezekiel 11:19, Ezekiel 36:23–38

20th Day of the 9th Month
Kislev, usually falling in November/December
Enter the Land
Choose Life
Torah Portion 'Nitsavim' – Deuteronomy 29:9 – 30:20

I call heaven and earth as witnesses today against you, that I have set before you life and death, blessing and cursing; therefore choose life, that both you and your descendants may live.... *Deuteronomy 30:19*

Moses exhorted the children of Israel to make a choice. There are two ways to live life, one leads to blessing and life, the other to cursing and death. The new generation of the children of Israel could not depend on the choices their parents and forefathers had made. That day they were to make a choice for themselves to enter into God's covenant, to obey and appropriate for themselves God's blessings. Otherwise they would suffer terrible curses of destruction, as Sodom and Gomorrah, Admah and Zeboiim had. (Deuteronomy 29:23, 24) The curses came into effect. The land lay barren and desolate for centuries, until the late 19th Century and early 20th Century, when the Jews started to return, as God had spoken.

God's Land would prosper under His rule. But it would wither and die when He was not exalted as King. In Deuteronomy 30 we have the promise of the return of the Jews from the nations to which they have been scattered, and the blessings of obedience which will spill over and be fulfilled in their entirety in the millennial reign of Yeshua as King, when the remnant will have been saved. Yeshua said that the way to destruction is wide, but the gate is narrow and the way difficult which leads to life, and few find it. (Matthew 7:13, 14) It takes humility to submit to His grace, to redeem and sanctify your life. He is your life and length of days. Everything in your life that is a blessing has come from Him.

Are you making choices which are choices for life and blessing?

Readings: Deuteronomy 29:10 – 30:20, Jeremiah 31:38–40, Matthew 7:13–29, James 4:7–10

21st Day of the 9th Month
Kislev, usually falling in November/December
Enter the Land
Be Strong and of Good Courage
Torah Portion 'Va Yelech' – Deuteronomy 31:1–30

"...And the LORD, He is the One who goes before you. He will be with you, He will not leave you nor forsake you; do not fear nor be dismayed." *Deuteronomy 31:8*

Moses was 120 years old and God revealed to him that he would not lead the Israelites into the Promised Land. God Himself would lead them and cross over the Jordan River before them. And Joshua would cross over before them. God would defeat their enemies for them. Therefore they were to be strong and of good courage, not afraid, because God promised to go with them, to never leave them nor forsake them. This is the Lord's promise to each one of us. Every time we cross over to take new 'ground' from the enemy – in our steps of obedience to the Father, in our wholeness, in our relationships, in our outreach to the lost and hurting, and finally in the day of our death when we cross over into the greater life of eternity, in all those situations, God will be with us going ahead of us and showing Himself strong for us, because we have submitted to Him as our Lord. (Joshua 1:1–9)

God also revealed to Moses that the children of Israel would, in the future, go astray after idols. He knew that fallen human nature, left on its own, is not able to live in obedience to God's Law. So God instructed Moses to teach them a song which would be passed on from generation to generation, to pass on the truth that God had revealed to their forefathers, but which was in danger of being forgotten. In this way, the revelation of Himself would be passed on, even when the people were straying and in rebellion. And the Book of the Law, written by Moses was to be testimony to His revealed truth and to their rebellion against God.

Meditate on Deuteronomy 31:8. Take strength and courage from the Holy Spirit.

Readings: Deuteronomy 31:1–30, Joshua 1, Isaiah 35:3, Isaiah 43:18, 19

22nd Day of the 9th Month
Kislev, usually falling in November/December
Enter the Land
The Song of Moses
Torah Portion 'Ha'azinu' – Deuteronomy 32:1–52

Rejoice, O Gentiles, with His people; For He will avenge the blood of His servants, And render vengeance to His adversaries; He will provide atonement for His land and His people. *Deuteronomy 32:43*

The Song of Moses distils the words of the Lord, like rain and dew to heaven and earth. (Deuteronomy 32:2) God is revealed as the Rock which journeyed with Israel in the wilderness. His work is perfect, His ways are justice. The descendants of Jacob are His inheritance whom He instructed in the wilderness. He kept Israel as the Apple of His Eye, (Deuteronomy 32:10), watching over her just as a mother eagle coaxes her young to fly.

But Israel forsook God their Creator and sacrificed to foreign gods. They provoked Him to jealousy by sacrificing to demons, and they forgot the Rock of their salvation. But as they had provoked God to jealousy, so God would provoke them to jealousy by 'those who are not a nation'. (Deuteronomy 32:21) The Gentiles in the kingdom are to provoke Jews to jealousy! (Romans 11:11) The false 'rock' of false gods proved to be no refuge to His people. God will execute His vengeance. He kills and He makes alive, He wounds and He heals. (Deuteronomy 32:39, Hosea 6:1–3) Whilst a day of judgement is coming for all of God's enemies, the song ends with a prophecy and encouragement for His Bride in days to come. It exhorts the Gentiles to rejoice with His people – this is the One New Man, Jew and Gentile worshipping together. (Deuteronomy 32:43, Ephesians 2:15) Yeshua will return and avenge the blood of His servants, and save Israel, His Land and His people. (Zechariah 14:3)

Yeshua is the rock for Jewish and Gentile believers. He exhorts us to rejoice together.

Readings: Deuteronomy 32:1 – 52, Ephesians 2, Romans 10:12 – 11:12, Zechariah 14:16–19

23rd Day of the 9th Month
Kislev, usually falling in November/December
Enter the Land
Blessings on the Children of Israel
Torah Portion 'Ve'zot HaBracha' – Deuteronomy 33:1 – 34:12

Of Benjamin he said: "The beloved of the LORD shall dwell in safety by Him, who shelters him all the day long; And he shall dwell between His shoulders." *Deuteronomy 33:12*

In this final Torah Portion, Moses blesses the tribes of Israel, like Jacob did before him, when he blessed his sons and their descendants before his death. (Genesis 49) Before Moses died he also pronounced blessings on the tribes. In the blessings of Moses, the Messiah is pictured in the blessing to Joseph, and the Jews who receive salvation through faith in God's grace are pictured as the sons of Benjamin. The rest of the blessings on the tribes are pictures of the tribes of Israel dwelling in the Land. They are pictured in the introduction as saints who sit down at the feet of the Lord and receive His words. They are God's people who receive the heritage of Israel and the manifestation of the kingdom of God, with God as King.

The picture of Benjamin, dwelling between the shoulders of the Lord, is one of total security. The word translated 'safety' is the Modern Hebrew word for 'security'. It pictures a time when Israel will dwell, nestled in the Land, safe and secure. This will be completely fulfilled in the millennium when Yeshua has returned. It is a comforting reassurance for all God's people, Jewish and Gentile, who will abide under the Kingship of the returned Messiah and for all the redeemed who find their safety from the powers of darkness in the tender care of Yeshua. Joseph is pictured as the one who was 'separate from his brothers', as Yeshua was separated from His Jewish brothers, so that the gospel could go out into all the earth.

You, the beloved of the Lord, are to dwell in security between His shoulders, all day long.

Readings: Deuteronomy 33:1 – 34:12, Luke 10:38–42, John 13:23, Zechariah 14:11

24th Day of the 9th Month
Kislev, usually falling in November/December
Eve of the Feast of Dedication – 'Hanukah' Eve
The Prophecy of Haggai

...from the twenty-fourth day of the ninth month, from the day that the foundation of the LORD's temple was laid – consider it. Is the seed still in the barn? As yet the vine, the fig tree, the pomegranate, and the olive tree have not yielded fruit. But from this day I will bless you.

Haggai 2:18, 19

This evening begins 'Hanukah' – the eight-day 'Feast of Dedication', mentioned briefly in John 10:22. This feast recalls the eight days of the dedication of the new altar at the Second Temple, recorded in the apocryphal book, Maccabees. (1 Maccabees 4:59) The old altar was desecrated by the Syrian, Antiochus IV Epiphanes, on 25th Kislev 167 BC, when he set up the 'abomination of desolation', and sacrificed pigs to Zeus. (1 Maccabees 1:54–59)

Approximately 250 years earlier, Haggai prophesied, on this day, concerning cleanliness and desecration. (Haggai 2:10–14) He asked whether holy things can make unclean things clean. The Jewish people knew that it is uncleanness which defiles by contact, whereas simple contact cannot make clean. A sacrifice is needed. So it was with the temple. They had started to rebuild the temple after returning from exile, but their hearts were not in it and they had not completed it. The temple was not easily made holy. God required the dedication of their hearts. That was what would make the temple and their worship holy.

On this day, the foundation of the temple had been laid. As yet there was no spiritual fruit – no vine, fig, pomegranate or olive fruit. And yet, from this day, God promised blessing. He encouraged Zerubbabel, Governor of Judah, and promised that He would shake the Gentile nations and destroy the strength of the Gentile kingdoms. He had chosen him.

What foundation stones of faith have you laid? God encourages you with His blessing.

Readings: Daniel 8:9–12, Haggai 1 – 2, Ezra 3, Zechariah 13

25th Day of the 9th Month
Kislev, usually falling in
November/December
**The Feast of Dedication –
'Hanukah' Day 1
The Dedication of the Altar**

Now the leaders offered the dedication offering for the altar when it was anointed; so the leaders offered their offering before the altar. For the LORD said to Moses, "They shall offer their offering, one leader each day, for the dedication of the altar." *Numbers 7:10, 11*

On this day, in 164 BC, the Jews returned to the temple (1 Maccabees 4:52–59), removed the 'abomination of desolation' and all the pagan idol worship, and rededicated the altar and sanctuary to God. The word for 'dedication' is 'hanukah' from the Hebrew word 'hen' meaning 'grace', and the word 'hanak' which means to educate or train. You could say that 'dedication' is connected with education or training in grace. God is dedicated to us through grace, and we are educated and trained in grace as we dedicate ourselves to Him.

The first time the word 'hanukah' occurs in Scripture is Numbers 7:10, 11 when Moses consecrated the tabernacle. Moses anointed the altar and dedicated it to God. The leaders of the tribes presented their offerings before the altar. Over the next twelve days each leader dedicated the same offering for the dedication of the altar – costly gifts of silver, gold, and the sacrificial animals which were burned upon the altar.

In Matthew 23:19 we learn that the altar 'sanctifies' the gifts. Anything we offer to God is made holy by His sacrifice for us. 'Educated in grace' we boldly approach Him, offering our lives, knowing that apart from Him our gifts are worthless. The silver represents redemption, the gold represents righteousness. We can only dedicate ourselves to Him because He gave Himself for us. In Revelation, He hears the cry from the martyrs 'under the altar'. (Revelation 6:9–11) Their blood has been poured out in dedication to God at His altar.

Dedicate the 'altar' of your heart to the Lord, in the knowledge of His sacrifice for you.

Readings: Numbers 7, Matthew 5:21–26, Matthew 23:16–22, Revelation 6:9–11

26th Day of the 9th Month
Kislev, usually falling in November/December
The Feast of Dedication –'Hanukah' Day 2
Yeshua walked in the Temple

Now it was the Feast of Dedication in Jerusalem, and it was winter.
And Jesus walked in the temple, in Solomon's porch. *John 10:22, 23*

The Apostle John mentioned that Yeshua walked in the temple during
the 'Feast of Dedication' and it was winter. (John 10:22) The winter
symbolises a time of spiritual deadness. This would explain the silence
of Scripture about the time of the Maccabees. The 'abomination of
desolation' had desecrated the temple, and the nation was culturally and
spiritually under the influence of Hellenism. Many Jews had a form of
religion but had synchronised it with the Greek culture which they had
willingly assimilated. They had become 'humanistic', and only a remnant
of Jews was concerned to stay faithful to God. The Jewish family, the
Maccabees, led the fight to reclaim the unique destiny of the Jews, and
to rebuild the altar. They had success and experienced miracles, but
there was not the anointing or prophetic word previously experienced.
The Messiah had not yet come.

Years later when Yeshua did come, He walked in the temple during this
feast, in Solomon's Porch. King Solomon's temple had been the height
and peak of Israel's splendour and glory. It had symbolised the reign
of the kingdom of God under a time of peace and prosperity. When
Solomon dedicated his temple he had prayed and 'fire came down from
heaven and consumed the burnt offering and the sacrifices; and the glory
of the LORD filled the temple.' (2 Chronicles 7:1) But Solomon fell
into apostasy with foreign wives, and the glory departed. The kingdom
was torn apart. Many years later Yeshua came and walked in Solomon's
porch. His feet walked where His glory had once been. Yeshua, the
holy temple of God, the perfect sacrifice, will dwell again in Zion, and
His light will shine for all eternity.

There is hope, even in the winter deadness, if you walk with the King.

Readings: 2 Chronicles 7, 9:3–4, 1 Kings 8 – 11, Luke 11:31, Revelation
21:22 – 22:5

27th Day of the 9th Month
Kislev, usually falling in November/December
The Feast of Dedication – 'Hanukah' Day 3
Yeshua, the Door of the Sheep

Then Jesus said to them again, "Most assuredly, I say to you, I am the door of the sheep." *John 10:7*

That Yeshua walked in the temple at the 'Feast of Dedication' is significant. This comes right in the middle of His teaching about the Good Shepherd. The dedication of the altar to God is a picture of Yeshua's own dedication to lay down his life for his flock, Israel. (Ezekiel 34:23, 24) He is like the shepherds who would lie down all night at the entrance to the sheepfold to defend and protect their sheep from wolves and predators. As He walked in the temple, the people would look on Him and have to decide who He was, whether He was their Good Shepherd or not. Many people believed in Him, but others, particularly the religious Pharisees, were in spiritual blindness. They could not 'see' who He was.

Yeshua walked in Solomon's porch. The porch is where the door is. Yeshua had been teaching the people, saying that He is the door of the sheep. He is their legitimate Shepherd who lays down His life for them. Many had come in the past, and many would come in the future, claiming to be the Messiah of Israel. A false shepherd will have power over a future rebuilt temple, and an 'abomination of desolation' will be raised up. (Daniel 9:26, 27, Matthew 24:15) But after great tribulation, Yeshua will return. He will be present at the gate of His glorious temple. (Ezekiel 43:1–9, 44:1–3) His temple will be holy; nothing will desecrate it. No evil can enter in to the glorious and manifest presence of God.

Yeshua, the true Messiah of Israel is recognised by His sheep. They will not follow a stranger, a false teacher or a false messiah. Yeshua alone is the holy sacrifice and the dedicated altar, His glory is at the gate, and only through Him can we enter eternal life.

Pray for blindness to fall from many eyes, so they may enter through Yeshua, the door.

Readings: John 9 – 10:23, Ezekiel 34, 43:1 – 44:5, Romans 11:25

28th Day of the 9th Month
Kislev, usually falling in November/December
The Feast of Dedication – 'Hanukah' Day 4
Told Plainly

Then the Jews surrounded Him and said to Him, "How long do You keep us in doubt? If you are the Christ, tell us plainly." *John 10:24*

As Yeshua walked in Solomon's Porch the religious Jews surrounded Him demanding to know if He is the Christ, the Messiah. Yeshua replied that He had already told them, but they did not believe. His works bore witness to Him being the Messiah. He had revealed Himself to be the Good Shepherd of the sheep who gives eternal life to those who hear His voice and follow Him. His 'I am ...' statements also declared His divinity, since the words 'I am' are part of the holy name of God revealed to Moses at the burning bush. (Exodus 3:14)

Then Yeshua told them plainly, 'I and My Father are one.' He was telling them that He was God, one with the Father. They could not accept that a human being, despite the testimony of His works, could be God. And so they concluded that He was blaspheming and the punishment of the Law for blasphemy was stoning to death. So they took up stones to kill Him, saying 'because You, being a Man, make Yourself God.' (John 10:33)

Yeshua quoted Psalm 82 about the mighty men being called 'gods'. Many exalt themselves, and demons demand worship. False pagan gods are promoted, as Zeus was at the desecration of the temple altar by Antiochus Epiphanes, and men call themselves gods. But they all fall before God. He is the judge of the earth and He will inherit all the nations. His works show that The Father is in Him and He is in the Father. Yeshua is the Divine Man, God as Man, He is the Son of God. The unbelieving religious men tried to seize Him but He escaped from their hand. The altar was dedicated to Him. He would choose when to die.

Many religions are content to make Jesus a 'god', but only His sheep worship Him as 'God'.

Readings: John 10:22–39, Psalm 82, Psalm 110, Matthew 27:50–54

29th Day of the 9th Month
Kislev, usually falling in November/December
The Feast of Dedication – 'Hanukah' Day 5
Yeshua beyond the Jordan

And He went away again beyond the Jordan to the place where John was baptizing at first, and there He stayed. *John 10:40*

The religious Jews at the temple rejected Yeshua as Messiah, and so He departed from them. He went away across the Jordan River, retreating to a safe place, where John had spoken many times about Him, while he was baptising. In that simple place many believed Him to be the Messiah, the Son of God. They had seen and believed in the works that He did. This was in direct contrast to the Jews in Jerusalem, who were bound into the religious establishment of the temple, and so had more difficulty believing in Yeshua.

Many of the rulers failed to recognise God among them, because they believed themselves to be righteous. They 'had religion'. Yeshua said of Himself, "He who believes in Me is not condemned; but he who does not believe is condemned already, because he has not believed in the name of the only begotten Son of God. And this is the condemnation, that the light has come into the world, and men loved darkness rather than light, because their deeds were evil. For everyone practicing evil hates the light...." (John 3:18–20)

The time had come for people to follow the Shepherd, not the temple. True worship would come from the altar of the hearts of those who believed in Him, who heard His voice and followed Him, who would die to self and exalt God. Many came to Yeshua across the Jordan, away from the unbelievers in the temple. Sometimes our 'institutions' actually hold us back from following God. God is not asking us to keep an institution alive, or to fulfil the will of a man. He is looking for people who will follow Him across the Jordan.

Determine to be a 'sheep following your Shepherd', not a member of a religious institution.

Readings: John 10:40–42, John 3, John 12:35–50

30th Day of the 9th Month
Kislev, usually falling in November/December
The Feast of Dedication – 'Hanukah' Day 6
Dedicated for a Purpose

...being High Priest that year he prophesied that Jesus would die for the nation, and not for that nation only, but also that He would gather together in one the children who were scattered abroad. John 11:51, 52

Caiaphas, who was the High Priest, prophesied concerning Yeshua, the Messiah in their midst, saying that it was expedient for one man to die for the people so that the nation of Israel should not perish. From that point on it was no longer safe for Yeshua to walk openly among the religious Jews because they wanted to kill him. So he stayed in Ephraim, near the wilderness, with His disciples. He was like a sacrificial lamb waiting to be sacrificed.

The temple and the priesthood had been rebuilt and preserved throughout the centuries so that in the fullness of time the Lamb of God could be slain upon Mount Moriah. The temple had been re-dedicated to God for one purpose alone, that which was spoken prophetically through the lips of the High Priest. The temple and the priests were needed, so that Yeshua, the Passover Lamb, could be slain according to God's Law. Without the dedicated temple, the Passover sacrifices, and the priests serving God, the full meaning of the Old Covenant pictures, types and shadows, would not have been fulfilled.

The death of Yeshua was for the salvation of Israel, the very nation whose existence, history and destiny had been based upon God's story of redemption, not of them only, but of the Gentiles too. The Lamb of God had to be slain according to the Law of God. The re-dedication of the temple prepared the way for a High Priest to prophesy accurately the necessary death of Yeshua, not for Israel only, but for the sins of the whole world.

Through the Holy Spirit, you will fulfil your destiny as you dedicate your life to obey God.

Readings: John 11:45–57, Acts 3, Acts 5:12–42

TEVET

1st Day of the 10th Month
Tevet, usually falling in December/January
The Feast of Dedication – 'Hanukah' Day 7
Cast out Paganism

And Ezra the priest, with certain heads of the fathers' households, were set apart by the fathers' households, each of them by name; and they sat down on the first day of the tenth month to examine the matter.

Ezra 10:16

We now enter the tenth month of the year, and come together to worship the Lord with joy at the beginning of a new month. As we draw near the end of the 'Feast of Dedication', it is fitting to notice this reference to the first day of the tenth month. We are back in the time of Ezra the Priest who returned with the exiles from Babylon to Jerusalem. Ezra sought the Lord with prayer and fasting, confessing the sins of His people to God. (Ezra 9) God had shown them great grace by allowing a remnant to return to Jerusalem and repair and rebuild the temple and wall, despite the fact that they had forsaken His commandments. While the people wept before God confessing their sins, Shechaniah the son of Jehiel, went and spoke to Ezra, saying that they had trespassed against God by taking pagan wives. (Ezra 10:1, 2) So Ezra fasted and prayed, and on the first day of the tenth month the heads of the families sat down to examine the matter, and they began to question the men who had taken pagan wives. It took them three months to complete, but the men gave their promise to separate from their pagan wives. They needed to re-dedicate themselves to the God of Israel.

The people of Judah could no longer tolerate the mixing of paganism with the biblical faith. They needed to purify themselves for Messiah to be born from among them. They had to be properly dedicated and set apart in preparation for Him. Now, in these days, Yeshua is calling His Bride to be divorced from the false doctrine and practices which have their roots in paganism, and which have infiltrated many churches, in preparation for His return.

Ask God whether anything you do has pagan origins, and resolve to separate from it.

Readings: Ezra 9, 10, 2 Corinthians 6:11–18

2nd Day of the 10th Month
Tevet, usually falling in December/January
The Feast of Dedication – 'Hanukah' Day 8
An Undefiled Temple

And He said to me, "Son of man, this is the place of My throne and the place of the soles of My feet, where I will dwell in the midst of the children of Israel forever. No more shall the house of Israel defile My holy name...." *Ezekiel 43:7*

In the time of the Babylonian captivity, the Holy Spirit exalted Ezekiel – the 'prophet and priest', and gave him a vision of the future temple, where the glory of the Lord had returned. The glory of the Lord had been grieved away from the previous defiled temple of Ezekiel 8, where occultism, paganism, idolatry and abominable practices took place. (Ezekiel 11:23) The image of jealousy stood in the entrance of the defiled temple. This may be the future 'abomination of desolation' which will stand in a temple built in the end times, as well as a symbol of the worship by men of a false 'messiah'. (Ezekiel 8:5)

The glorious temple of Ezekiel 40 – 48 appears to be connected to the Old Jerusalem and yet is also connected to the New Jerusalem. This could be the temple in the millennial reign when Yeshua has returned, as well as a picture of God dwelling in the 'temple of our hearts'. God tells us to not defile ourselves because we are now His holy temple. (1 Corinthians 3:16, 17) In Ezekiel 47 a river flows from the temple out to the east. At first the water is ankle deep, then it is knee deep, then waist deep, then so deep that you have to swim. When its waters reach the Dead Sea they heal the water, removing the salt and making it fresh again so that fish can live in it. Along the banks of the river grow trees which bear fruit every month and the leaves are for healing medicine. We can begin to experience this river now in our hearts through the Holy Spirit flowing through us in increasing measure, bringing life. In the New Jerusalem the Lamb of God will be the Temple. (Revelation 21:22, 23)

What grieves the Holy Spirit away from your heart? Ask Him to cleanse and fill you afresh.

Readings: Ezekiel 8, Ezekiel 11:13–23, Ezekiel 44 – 48, Ephesians 4:20 – 5:16

3rd Day of the 10th Month
Tevet, usually falling in December/January
A Prepared Bride
Grace and Favour

So Esther was taken to King Ahasuerus, into his royal palace, in the tenth month, which is the month of Tevet, in the seventh year of his reign. The king loved Esther more than all the other women, and she obtained grace and favour in his sight more than all the virgins; so he set the royal crown upon her head.... *Esther 2:16, 17*

We are now in the month when Esther was taken into the palace of the king and obtained His grace and favour, so that He chose her to be his new wife. The king reigned over all the Medes and Persians, and Esther was the orphan daughter of Jewish exiles to Babylon. Nobody in the palace knew that she was of Jewish descent, but God had brought her into the palace of this mighty king for a purpose. She was to be instrumental in rescuing the Jewish people from annihilation by the wicked Haman, who incited hatred against the Jews.

Esther spent a whole year in the palace being beautified, before she went in to meet the king. For six months she was prepared with oil of myrrh, and for six months with perfumes and preparations for beautifying women, and she obtained favour with her custodian in her place of preparation. She was given seven maidservants, and was moved to the best house of the women. This is a picture of Yeshua's Bride being shown God's favour, and prepared for intimacy with Him, so she can fulfil her calling in the end times, as she intercedes before the King of kings. Yeshua's 'Bride', comprising male and female, is set apart in a place of preparation, quietly aware of the Jewish roots of the faith whilst among Gentiles. Esther had seven maidservants, who remind us of the Holy Spirit who prepares us to meet the Lord. She experiences the favour of the king, because of God's covenant with the Jews, and she has an important task – to stand for the protection of God's covenant people.

Receive God grace and favour to you while you are being 'prepared' to meet the Bridegroom.

Readings: Esther 2, Ruth 2:13, 1 Samuel 2:26, Luke 1:30, Luke 2:52, Acts 7:44–46

4th Day of the 10th Month
Tevet, usually falling in December/January
A Prepared Bride
Loves Much

"Therefore I say to you, her sins, which are many, are forgiven, for she loved much. But to whom little is forgiven, the same loves little."

Luke 7:47

Yeshua was speaking here of the woman who anointed Him with oil, and washed his feet with her tears, and wiped them with her hair. Her great love for the Lord is a picture for us of the Bride of Yeshua – the believers who love Him greatly because they know that they have been forgiven a great deal. She knew fully that she was a sinner, and that she didn't deserve to receive God's grace. She knew that God loved her, despite the fact that she had broken God's commandments, and so she loved Him greatly. A forgiven heart loves much.

In contrast, the self-righteous are not aware that they are sinners and in desperate need of God's grace. Unaware of the greatness of God's love and mercy, they are unable to love God much. It is not how much we sinned that matters, but it is how much we know that we have been forgiven. The sign of having been forgiven is the ability to love God and our neighbour. We can only love God because He first loved us. (1 John 4:19) The Father loves us so much, that through believing in Yeshua, we are called 'children of God'. (1 John 3:1) Everyone who is forgiven through repentance and faith in God, no longer finds the command to love God and their neighbour burdensome because He puts His love in their hearts.

Jude 21 exhorts us to keep ourselves in the love of God, 'looking for the mercy of our Lord Jesus Christ unto eternal life.' We are to guard our hearts diligently, not allowing any root of bitterness to grow up, but quickly forgive others as God has forgiven us. The walls in our hearts come down, as we forgive others, and let His healing love and unity flow.

Ask God to reveal where you have unforgiveness in your heart, and forgive with God's love.

Readings: Luke 7:36–50, 1 John 2:3 – 5:5, 1 Corinthians 13, Revelation 2:4, 5

5th Day of the 10th Month
Tevet, usually falling in December/January
A Prepared Bride
Responds to the Lord

'....I am my beloved's, And his desire is toward me.' 'Come, my beloved, Let us go forth to the field....' *Song of Songs 7:10, 11*

The Song of Songs is a poetic picture of the Lord's invitation to each one of us to 'come away' and to develop an intimate relationship with Him, so that we grow to maturity in belonging to God, and being available to Him, knowing how much He loves us. We will come to the place where we forget about our own needs, and are willing to go with Him out into the fields to look at the state of the vineyard (the Church) and the pomegranates (the Bride). Though the imagery of the Bride is feminine, this invitation is for men and women.

We begin by praying for the Lord to draw us to Himself. (Song of Songs 1:4) He sees our desire to focus on Him even though we haven't succeeded in the past, and He says to us, 'you have dove's eyes' (which are single focussed, looking to Him). He reassures us of His love for us. (1:15) He sees our potential. He joyfully comes to us, partially revealing Himself to us as though through a lattice. (2:9) He calls to us to rise up and come away with Him. The expression of the love described, is a 'shadow' of spiritual intimacy with God.

In the time of darkness, the bride searches for her lover and finds Him. (3:1–4) Seeing His Kingly splendour, she loves Him. She sees the beauty of the Lord and He reveals to her how beautiful He finds her, and how much delight she brings Him. But then He wants to draw near and receive her love at a time inconvenient to her. When she fails to respond she loses His presence. He withdraws and she has to go and seek for Him. Finally she finds Him and learns to have an intimate relationship with Him. She learns to love Him and be loved.

What stage in this story of the Bride's maturing love do you think you have reached?

Readings: Song of Songs 1 – 8, Zephaniah 3:17

5/1/18

27/12/14
17/12/15

6th Day of the 10th Month
Tevet, usually falling in December/January
A Prepared Bride
Faith in the Covenant

For God so loved the world that He gave His only begotten Son, that whoever believes in Him should not perish but have everlasting life. *John 3:16*

The Lord is looking for a Bride who has faith in Him and in His covenant. She believes in the power of His blood – shed for her upon the cross for the forgiveness of her sins, and for her redemption from the curse. These believers come to Him humbly, like little children, not trying to depend on their own righteousness to find favour with God, but knowing that they don't deserve anything because of their own works or righteousness. The Bride simply receives, like a little child who knows that their Father loves them and wants to bestow His goodness. They are confident in, and trust in, the love of their Heavenly Father.

Yeshua said, "Assuredly, I say to you, unless you are converted and become as little children, you will by no means enter the kingdom of heaven. Therefore whoever humbles himself as this little child is the greatest in the kingdom of heaven...." (Matthew 18:3, 4) Childlike faith trusts in the perfect power of the blood of Yeshua. With this type of faith you will trust what God, your loving heavenly Father, says in His Word more than you'll trust what you perceive with your five senses. With faith you will obtain the blessing of God. He has called us to believe with faith for our salvation (Romans 1:16, 3:26), for our righteousness (Romans 10:10, 11), and for the fulfilment of all of His promises, including our healing – physical, emotional and spiritual. (Hebrews 11:33–35) Faith is able to suffer for Yeshua, believing in the eternal reward. Unbelief restricts God's work in our lives (Matthew 13:58), but faith pleases God, and He will reward it. (Hebrews 11:6)

How much are you trusting and believing in the New Covenant power of Yeshua's blood?

Readings: John 3:5–21, Mark 11:22–24, Romans 10, Hebrews 11

7th Day of the 10th Month
Tevet, usually falling in December/January
A Prepared Bride
A Worship Warrior

Let the high praises of God be in their mouth, and a two-edged sword in their hand.... *Psalm 149:6*

As well as the feminine image of the 'Bride' of Yeshua, we have the masculine image of the warrior. The Bride of Yeshua is like a soldier in the spirit. Ephesians 6 describes believers dressed in the whole 'armour of God' so that they can stand against the 'wiles of the devil'. (Ephesians 6:11) Equipped with the full armour of God's righteousness, salvation, faith, the preparation of the gospel of peace, the Holy Spirit and the Word of God, the Bride is to pray in the Spirit and make supplication for all the 'saints'. The Bride exercises spiritual victory over the enemy of our souls, to set captives free and enlarge the kingdom of God.

Faith in God, and the truth of His Word, is a shield to protect the Bride from the doubts and fears which assault her. And the Word of God is the Sword of the Spirit, with which we discern what is happening in our souls, and exercise authority in prayer, speaking out the Scriptures with our mouths, and believing God's truth with our hearts. Psalm 149 shows the saints of God wielding a two-edged sword in their hand, this time with the praises of God in their mouth. These saints are joyful. They dance before the Lord, sing praises to Him and worship Him with musical instruments. 'For the LORD takes pleasure in His people; He will beautify the humble with salvation.' (Psalm 149:4)

These saints experience the glory of God and sing joyfully on their beds, in the private place, not just the assembly. Their voices exalt God with praise, so His power is released in the spirit like a two-edged sword, causing shifts in the realm of the spirit which will even influence nations, bring justice and the vengeance of God, and bind up the works of darkness.

Develop a habit of singing and dancing in praise to God. Let new songs rise from your heart.

Readings: Ephesians 6:10–18, Psalm 149, Psalm 33:3, Hebrews 13:15

8th Day of the 10th Month
Tevet, usually falling in December/January
A Prepared Bride
Clothed in Fine Linen

"....Let us be glad and rejoice and give Him glory, for the marriage of the Lamb has come, and His wife has made herself ready." And to her it was granted to be arrayed in fine linen, clean and bright, for the fine linen is the righteous acts of the saints. *Revelation 19:7, 8*

Here the 'betrothed' has become the 'wife' of the Lamb. She is given white linen to wear, clean and bright, like the raiment of the armies of heaven in Revelation 19:14 and like the angels of Revelation 15:6. Her heavenly clothing is totally pure and bright. In Exodus 39:27 and Leviticus 16:4 the High Priest's pure linen garments foreshadow Yeshua our High Priest who confers on us His holiness. We also clothe ourselves in humility. (1 Peter 5:5)

In Matthew 22:1–14 Yeshua told a parable where a king invited guests to a wedding. Because many who were invited refused to go, he invited others in from the highways. But one guest was found to not have a wedding garment. This one was taken away to outer darkness, signifying hell. Yeshua then said, "many are called but few are chosen". (Matthew 22:14) This phrase also comes in Matthew 20:16. Few are found to be truly righteous.

We must be made righteous by the blood of Yeshua, but we must also walk in the righteousness conferred on us through grace. The fine linen is the righteous acts of the saints. We are to be clothed with heavenly life. (2 Corinthians 5:2–5) The lawless will not be part of Yeshua's Bride. (Revelation 21:8) His Bride must live clothed in His righteousness and do His works of righteousness, believing in Him, otherwise we may find ourselves shut out of the wedding feast, and told that we did not know Him. (Matthew 25:10–13) Yeshua's Bride must keep her 'lamp' filled with the Holy Spirit and live as His pure Bride. (James 2:17)

Do you believe that Yeshua has truly clothed you in His righteousness? Now live in it.

Readings: Revelation 19:6–16, Matthew 22:1–14, Matthew 25:1–13, James 2:18–26

✓ 6|1|17

9th Day of the 10th Month
Tevet, usually falling in December/January
A Prepared Bride
Loves His Appearing

Finally, there is laid up for me the crown of righteousness, which the Lord, the righteous Judge, will give to me on that Day, and not to me only but also to all who have loved His appearing. *2 Timothy 4:8*

The Apostle Paul was confident that the Lord had the crown of righteousness stored up for him on the Day of Yeshua's appearing. He was confident that He had fought the good fight, finished the race, and kept the faith. (2 Timothy 4:7) He had poured out his life in faithful service to God, preaching the Word in season and out of season.

Matthew 24 and 25 are the chapters where Yeshua teaches us how to be prepared for His return, so that it will not be a day of grief for us, but a good day, because we will be ready to meet Him. Matthew 24 teaches us that His return will come suddenly. Many will be like servants whose master has been absent for a long time, and so they have 'slackened' their behaviour, and mistreated their fellow servants. These might find themselves going to hell.

Matthew 25 gives the parable of the ten virgins, which is a solemn warning for us to keep being filled with the Holy Spirit, and stay close to the Lord. In the parable of the talents, the faithful servant is rewarded by His master for using his talents, but the unprofitable servant, who hides his talent in the ground is cast into outer darkness where there is weeping and gnashing of teeth. There is also the parable of the sheep and the goats. Those who have shown compassion in practical works of loving kindness, such as feeding the poor, visiting the sick, and caring for Yeshua's 'brethren' (Matthew 25:37–40, Galatians 6:9, 10), will be received into eternal life. But those who did not will be cast into eternal punishment.

Are these things part of your walk with God? Is there more you can do? Ask for God's help.

Readings: 2 Timothy 4:1–8, Matthew 24:36–51, Matthew 25, Philippians 2:12, John 15:6

10th Day of the 10th Month
Tevet, usually falling in December/January
The Fast of the 10th Month
The Siege of Jerusalem

> Now it came to pass in the ninth year of his reign, in the tenth month, on the tenth day of the month that Nebuchadnezzar king of Babylon and all his army came against Jerusalem and encamped against it; and they built a siege wall against it all around. *2 Kings 25:1, 2*

On this day, King Nebuchadnezzar of Babylon and his army began the siege of Jerusalem, which would end in the city's destruction, and the captives being taken off into exile in 586 BC. It is one of the fast days mentioned in Zechariah 8:19. Nebuchadnezzar's armies encamped around Jerusalem, building a siege wall so that the people were trapped inside the city, unable to escape and with no access to food. The siege is thought to have lasted either eighteen months or three years. While the siege lasted, the people inside the city suffered terrible starvation, and they were even driven to cannibalism just as Deuteronomy 28:52–57 had prophesied in the curses for disobedience.

Ezekiel received a word from the Lord on this day. The Lord said to him, "Son of man, write down the name of the day, this very day – the king of Babylon started his siege against Jerusalem this very day. And utter a parable to the rebellious house..." (Ezekiel 24:1–14) Jerusalem was like a bronze pot of boiling meat. As the water boiled, the scum rose to the surface. Normally a cook would scoop the scum off the surface of the water to remove the impurities. But when God 'boiled' Jerusalem by having it besieged by enemies to remove the 'scum' of sin from the people, the scum was not removed as it should have been. They did not repent. So He had to 'empty' the cooking pot, and actually melt it to destroy the scum. He had to take extreme measures, destroying Jerusalem itself (which is represented by the cooking pot). Only then could the impurity be destroyed and Jerusalem restored.

How has the Lord 'laid siege' to you in order to remove your sin?

Readings: Deuteronomy 28:52–57, Ezekiel 24:1–14, 2 Kings 24, Galatians 2:20, 2 Peter 3:9

11th Day of the 10th Month
Tevet, usually falling in December/January
Laying Siege
Live by the Spirit

"Son of man, behold, I take away from you the desire of your eyes with one stroke; yet you shall neither mourn nor weep, nor shall your tears run down...." *Ezekiel 24:16*

After Ezekiel received the parable of the boiling pot, his wife died, just as God had told him she would. The next morning – on this day, he arose without mourning or sorrow – as a sign to the people that God was going to destroy His delight – the temple. Ezekiel's wife was his joy and glory, but she was snatched away from him. God's delight and joy was His temple in Jerusalem, but He was willing to have it destroyed for the sake of His holy name, and His holiness among the people. He could not let the sin and defilement remain unchecked. He had to show the people that He was LORD. His action would cause them to know that.

The destruction of the temple is like death. Yeshua prophesied His death and resurrection saying, "Destroy this temple, and in three days I will raise it up." (John 2:19) God loved the temple, but He couldn't mourn its destruction. The Father loved His Son but He had to let Him die. Similarly the temple represents our lives, our hearts. We have to pass through a type of death, death to our 'flesh' life and rise to new life in the Spirit. (Romans 6:5–11) We have to be ruthless in dealing with our flesh. It is only through faith and the Holy Spirit that our 'sinful flesh' can 'die'. God wants to remove the impurities, the 'scum' that is the sins from our lives. This can only happen with the 'melting' of the whole pot. (Ezekiel 24:11) When we surrender our whole lives to Yeshua, daily yielding to Him, we learn to put to death the old works of the flesh, and live through the power of the Holy Spirit. We must be like Paul, who said, 'I have been crucified with Christ.' (Galatians 2:20)

Die to your own efforts to overcome sin, and yield to God, letting Him reign over you.

Readings: Ezekiel 24:15–27, Romans 6, 1 Peter 2:9–25

12th Day of the 10th Month
Tevet, usually falling in December/January
Laying Siege
God's Kingdom Siege

"You also, son of man, take a clay tablet and lay it before you, and portray on it a city, Jerusalem. Lay siege against it, build a siege wall against it, and heap up a mound against it; set camps against it also, and place battering rams against it all around...." *Ezekiel 4:1, 2*

Before the siege of Jerusalem ever took place, God gave Israel and Judah a graphic picture of what was to happen. At God's command the Prophet Ezekiel enacted the siege which would occur – using a map of Jerusalem and visual aids. God also had him lie down on his left side for three hundred and ninety days, to represent the three hundred and ninety years that the House of Israel would bear its iniquity, and he had to lie on his right side for forty days, to represent the forty years that the House of Judah would bear her iniquity. Israel would bear her iniquity nearly ten times longer than the southern kingdom of Judah, but that time would come to an end. Ezekiel also had to eat defiled 'Gentile' style bread of mixed grains to prophecy the dispersion of His people amidst many cultures and people groups. He had to cut his hair and divide it up to depict the different destinies of God's people in Israel and dispersed among the nations.

The Prophet Micah also prophesied before the Babylonian Exile, and like Ezekiel, his prophecies merged into prophecies of a future siege, exile and return. In 70 AD Jerusalem would experience another siege and a greater exile, into all nations even to the ends of the earth. But the final culmination is in a world-wide re-gathering into God's 'Messianic kingdom' of the future millennium. (Micah 4) In Micah 5:2 the Messiah comes forth out of Bethlehem, and is finally seen as the ruler of the whole earth. Israel gives birth, after much travail, to the King and the kingdom. (Micah 5:3, Revelation 12:1, 2, Isaiah 54:1)

God is not only laying siege to your life, but to Israel, for the fulfilment of the kingdom.

Readings: Ezekiel 4, 5, Isaiah 54, Micah 4, 5, Revelation 12

TEVET

13th Day of the 10th Month
Tevet, usually falling in December/January
Laying Siege
A Way of Escape

> But when you see Jerusalem surrounded by armies, then know that its desolation is near. Then let those who are in Judea flee to the mountains, let those who are in the midst of her depart, and let not those who are in the country enter her. *Luke 21:20, 21*

Yeshua prophesied the siege of Jerusalem which was to culminate in the destruction of Jerusalem. He warned His followers that when they saw Jerusalem surrounded by armies they must escape. The Early Church knew this prophecy so they took heed. When they saw that Jerusalem was surrounded by armies, but they were still able to escape, they took their opportunity. Vespasian had left his armies in Judah to go to Rome and become Roman Emperor, leaving his son Titus to march up from Egypt, to lay siege to Jerusalem.

Josephus Flavius, the Jewish Historian, described the siege of Jerusalem in his book 'The Jewish War'. Titus surrounded Jerusalem with a siege wall that was five miles long, blocking all the exits, so that all the Jews who remained in the city had to either surrender or starve. In AD 70, Jerusalem and its temple were finally destroyed. Most Jews either died in the siege and final overthrow of Jerusalem, or were taken captive into slavery by the Romans.

Yeshua's followers escaped because they knew and heeded His Words. Now Yeshua commands us to watch and pray in these last days, so that we might be counted worthy to escape all the things that are to come to pass, and to 'stand before the Son of Man'. (Luke 21:36) There will be signs in the heavens and terrible things happening on the earth. But we are to watch, and pray. We must not be weighed down with the cares of this world. God knows how much we can bear, and provides the way of escape. (1 Corinthians 10:13)

When you feel under siege, listen for God's word of instruction and obey it.

Readings: Luke 21:5–36, Genesis 19, 1 Corinthians 10:12, 13, 1 Thessalonians 4:15–5:24

14th Day of the 10th Month
Tevet, usually falling in December/January
Laying Siege
A Kingdom Which Cannot Be Shaken

Therefore, since we are receiving a kingdom which cannot be shaken, let us have grace, by which we may serve God acceptably with reverence and godly fear. *Hebrews 12:28*

In these last days God is once again 'laying siege' to the earth and to all the nations. He is shaking them so that He can bring forth from them an unshakable kingdom. He is shaking Israel to bring her to salvation, He is shaking the nations to bring them to salvation, and He is calling His Bride to stand firm, and to serve God in reverence and godly fear.

The Lord spoke through the Prophet Haggai, '"Once more (it is a little while) I will shake heaven and earth, the sea and dry land; and I will shake all nations, and they shall come to the Desire of All nations, and I will fill this temple with glory," says the LORD of hosts.' (Haggai 2:6, 7) Israel is being shaken by enemies who pressure her and seek to destroy her. But we know that in the end God will save the remnant which escapes. (Isaiah 4) All the nations are coming under God's shakings, to bring them to God, and so that they will recognise that the only lasting unshakable kingdom belongs to God. Nations are being shaken by failing economies, natural disasters, earthquakes, wars and freak weather conditions. They are shaken when evil is exposed. They are shaken by God when they touch the 'apple of God's eye' – Israel. In the last days, even the heavens and the earth will be shaken, so that that which cannot be shaken will come forth. He will preserve His own as He lays siege to the earth. And all Israel will be saved. (Romans 11:26) We are not to ignore the voice of God in His shakings, but receive His grace, through which we may serve God acceptably with reverence and godly fear. (Hebrews 12:23–29)

Receive God's grace to serve Him acceptably in the midst of shakings.

Readings: Hebrews 12, Joel 3, Isaiah 13, Isaiah 2

TEVET

15th Day of the 10th Month
Tevet, usually falling in December/January
Prepare the Way
John the Baptiser

This is he of whom it is written: 'Behold, I send My messenger before Your face, Who will prepare Your way before You.' *Luke 7:27*

For the rest of this month and the whole of next month our readings will be based upon the life and teachings of Yeshua in the gospels, most particularly with regards to the kingdom of God. We begin with the preparation for Yeshua's ministry on earth.

Just months before Yeshua was born, his cousin, John the Baptiser, was born to prepare the way for Messiah to appear in Israel. John's leap in the womb must have been a welcome sign for Yeshua's mother Mary, and for his mother Elizabeth. (Luke 1:41) His name, 'John', means 'God's favour'. John the Baptiser fulfilled Malachi 3:1, "Behold, I send My messenger, And he will prepare the way before Me...." When people questioned who John the Baptiser was, he denied that he was Elijah prophesied in Malachi 4:5, 6 who will come before the great and dreadful day of the LORD. Instead he quoted Isaiah 40:3 which says, 'The voice of one crying in the wilderness: "Prepare the way of the LORD; Make straight in the desert a highway for our God...."' (John 1:23)

Before John's birth, an angel told John's father that his child would turn the hearts of many of the children of Israel back to their God. He would go 'in the spirit and power of Elijah, to turn the hearts of the fathers to the children, and the disobedient to the wisdom of the just, to make ready a people prepared for the Lord.' (Luke 1:16, 17) Like Elijah, John the Baptiser turned people from their disobedience. He showed them where they had broken God's Law. He led them into repentance and showed them their need to return to God.

How does God prepare hearts to receive Yeshua? What is your part?

Readings: Luke 1, John 1:6–35, Matthew 11:1–19, 14:1–13, Revelation 11:3, 20:4

✓ 13/1/17.

Mon 6th

16th Day of the 10th Month
Tevet, usually falling in December/January
Prepare the Way
A Virgin Conceives

Then the angel said to her (Mary), "Do not be afraid, Mary, for you have found favour with God. And behold, you will conceive in your womb and bring forth a Son, and shall call His name JESUS."

Luke 1:30, 31

A young virgin named Mary was in her home town of Nazareth, when an angel appeared to her, and told her that she had found favour with God. She would conceive in her womb and bring forth a child. But this would not be the child of Joseph her betrothed. This would be the Son of God. His name would be 'Yeshua', which means 'Salvation'.

Mary asked the angel how this could happen since she was a virgin, and the angel answered her saying that the Holy Spirit would come upon her and the power of the Most High God would overshadow her. (Luke 1:26–38) The child would be conceived without a human father. The Holy Spirit had overshadowed the waters at creation, and the heavens and the earth were created. (Genesis 1:2) Now the Holy Spirit would overshadow the womb of a young Jewish girl, and she would conceive the Son of God.

In Genesis 1:2, God told Adam and Eve, that a woman would bear a child who would crush Satan under His feet. This child would not be born from the male seed of Adam. He would not be contaminated by Adam's sin of disobeying God, which had been passed to all of Adam's descendants – that is the entire human race. When Yeshua was born, He was the Son of God, born with a sinless soul. Only the blood of a sinless man could atone for the sins of the whole human race. Now, when we are born of God through the Holy Spirit, our spirit is washed free from the sin of Adam, and we become a new creation, a child of God.

Consider the power of the new birth, and what it means to be 'born of God'. (1 John 3:9)

Readings: Luke 1:26–56, John 3:1–21, 1 John 3:7–12, 1 John 5:5–8, 2 Corinthians 5:17–19

TEVET

17th Day of the 10th Month
Tevet, usually falling in December/January
Prepare the Way
Signs of the Messiah

Then Simeon blessed them, and said to Mary His mother, "Behold, this Child is destined for the fall and rising of many in Israel, and for a sign which will be spoken against (yes, a sword will pierce through your own soul also), that the thoughts of many hearts may be revealed." *Luke 2:34*

God's prophetic word and signs were present before and at the birth of Yeshua. John the Baptist leapt in Elizabeth's womb for joy (Luke 1:44), and Mary prophesied with joy saying, "My soul magnifies the Lord, and my spirit has rejoiced in God my Saviour..." (Luke 1:46, 47) She knew that the child in her womb was her 'Saviour' –'Yeshua'. (Matthew 1:21) Mary acknowledged that she was God's humble maidservant, and that she needed a saviour.

Mary gave birth to Yeshua in Bethlehem, the City of King David, in fulfilment of Micah 5:2. He was laid in an animal feeding trough because there was no room for them in the inn. In Genesis 33:17 the shepherd, Jacob, had named his livestock dwellings 'Succoth'. This is the word 'booth' used for the 'Feast of Succot' – 'Tabernacles'. Yeshua came to dwell or 'tabernacle' among us. An angel appeared to the shepherds who were watching their flocks in the fields, and told them that the sign that the Messiah had been born, was that they would find Him lying in a manger in Bethlehem. The shepherds went in haste and found it all as the angel had told them. They saw the 'Lamb of God' in the manger. He would be the Good Shepherd, the Shepherd of Israel. After eight days, Yeshua was circumcised according to God's command to Abraham, and dedicated in the temple according to the Law of Moses. In the temple, Simeon and Anna both discerned that the newborn baby was the Messiah.

What hints of Passover and Tabernacles do you find in the birth narrative of Yeshua?

Readings: Luke 2:1–39, Exodus 12:3–11, Genesis 33:16–20, Deuteronomy 16:14

18th Day of the 10th Month
Tevet, usually falling in December/January
Prepare the Way
Yeshua Aged Twelve

And the Child grew and became strong in spirit, filled with wisdom; and the grace of God was upon Him. *Luke 2:40*

It was the love of the Father which enabled Yeshua to grow strong in His Spirit. It was the voice of the Father that taught and instructed Him. The grace of God the Father was upon His life. He had an earthly father, Joseph, but He intimately knew His Heavenly Father. He was one with the Father. (John 10:30)

Each of us is on a journey to know our Heavenly Father, separate from our earthly father. We usually start by thinking God must be like our earthly father. Then we learn that our Heavenly Father is perfect, and is the Father of our earthly father too. He holds you and your earthly father in His hand. He heals any wounds to make you strong in spirit.

Yeshua went up to Jerusalem every year, with His parents, for the 'Feast of Passover'. When He was twelve He lingered behind in the temple, and it took his parents three whole days to find Him. He stayed behind because that was what His Heavenly Father asked Him to do, to do His business. He was obedient to His Heavenly Father and to his earthly father.

Yeshua assumed the posture of the teacher by sitting amidst the teachers. Teaching comes from a place of rest and authority. Jewish teachers pose questions to make people think and lead them to truth. Yeshua's question, 'Did you not know that I must be about My Father's business?' was an answer that people did not understand. He was implying an intimate relationship with the Father, alluding to Psalm 2:7 and Psalm 89:26, 27. He was telling them His identity, affirmed by the Father as the Son of God, God incarnate.

Your identity is secure in relation to Heavenly Father, in the Son and through the Holy Spirit.

Readings: Luke 2:41–52, Psalm 89:19–37, Psalm 2, John 10:25–39. John 14:6–21

16/1/17   26/12/18

19th Day of the 10th Month
Tevet, usually falling in December/January
Prepare the Way
The Baptism of Yeshua

And John bore witness, saying, "I saw the Spirit descending from heaven like a dove, and He remained upon Him." *John 1:32*

John the Baptiser baptised in the wilderness in fulfilment of Isaiah 40:3–5. The wilderness is the place of preparation and testing. It is where Israel was prepared and tested before entering the Promised Land, and it is the place Yeshua went to be prepared in baptism for His ministry before passing through the 'waters' of temptation.

John's baptism was a baptism of repentance. The people repented of their sins and had them washed away in preparation for receiving Yeshua's ministry to them. Yeshua did not need to be baptised because He had never sinned (1 Peter 2:22), but He said that He needed to be baptised to "fulfil righteousness". (Matthew 3:15) He was to be perfect in every way, keeping every requirement of the Law and every requirement of God towards man, so that He could become the perfect, sinless sacrifice in our place, lacking nothing.

When we are baptised, our immersion in water symbolises our death and burial to our old life, and we identify with the death and resurrection of Yeshua, being 'baptised' and born into new life in Him. When Yeshua was baptised, He identified with us, and was baptised into our humanity. At that moment the 'Trinity' of God was witnessed. The voice of the Father affirmed Him, speaking from heaven saying, "This is My beloved Son, in whom I am well pleased." (Matthew 3:17). And the Holy Spirit alighted on Him in the form of a dove. At His baptism Yeshua received the anointing of the Holy Spirit for ministry, fulfilling Daniel 9:24. Yeshua would baptise people to new life in the Holy Spirit. (John 1:33)

What does it really mean to be baptised into Yeshua?

Readings: John 1:26–36, Matthew 3, Mark 1:1–11, Romans 6:3–11, Colossians 2:11–15

20th Day of the 10th Month
Tevet, usually falling in December/January
Prepare the Way
The Temptations of Yeshua

Then Jesus was led up by the Spirit into the wilderness to be tempted by the devil. *Matthew 4:1*

Yeshua entered the wilderness to pass through temptations from the devil. After fasting for forty days, the hunger pangs signalled the onset of starvation. Weakness normally exposes our sinful flesh. It is our fleshly desires which cause us to sin (James 1:13, 14), and we are tempted in the main areas of lust and pride. (1 John 2:16) But when Yeshua experienced extreme physical weakness no sin was found in His flesh. He endured our weaknesses to the limits of human experience and testing, yet never sinned. (Hebrews 2:18, 4:15) Now He has become our strength, our Bread of Life, on whom we feed.

Satan came to Yeshua with the temptation to turn stones to bread. Yeshua who is the Word of God, and the Living Bread, replied with Scripture, the 'Sword of the Spirit', quoting Deuteronomy 8:3. Satan also tempted Him by quoting Psalm 91 and suggesting He force God to prove His promised protection, by throwing Himself off the pinnacle of the temple. Psalm 91 does promise God's protection, but on a condition – abiding under the Shadow of His wings – staying close to Him. The devil was suggesting you could test God's promise of protection even in a place of disobedience to God. But that is not so. We are not to test Him with our disobedience. Yeshua replied from Deuteronomy 6:16. The devil also tempted Yeshua to rule the earth – but with an authority given by Satan. Yeshua's kingdom however was to be received through the path of death and resurrection. He would only worship the Father, and would not bow the knee to Satan. (Deuteronomy 10:20) Satan tried to deceive by misusing the Word, and trying to make Him perceive situations wrongly. But Yeshua, the Word, knew the whole Word and Counsel of God. The Truth resisted the lies.

Ask God to help you to discern deception, and to resist the lies of the devil with God's Word.

Readings: Matthew 4:1–11, Ephesians 6:10–18, 1 Corinthians 10:1–13, Hebrews 5:12–14

TEVET

21st Day of the 10th Month
Tevet, usually falling in December/January
Prepare the Way
The Disciples Follow Yeshua

Again, the next day, John stood with two of his disciples. And looking at Jesus as He walked, he said, "Behold the Lamb of God!" The two disciples heard him speak, and they followed Jesus. *John 1:35–37*

Two of John the Baptiser's disciples were the first to become Yeshua's disciples. Groups of disciples (followers) would travel the Land with the Jewish Rabbis (Teachers), so that they could learn not only from the 'public' teachings of their masters, but also from their more intimate, informal life, words and teaching.

Andrew and his work companion, John, son of Zebedee, had left their job of fishing on the Lake in Galilee, to go south to the Jordan River, and become disciples of John the Baptiser. They were standing near John when Yeshua walked past, and he told them to look at Yeshua and 'behold' – the 'Lamb of God!' Andrew and John looked and took notice. They already knew from John that the Messiah was coming soon. They had repented of their sins and been baptised. They were ready to leave everything and follow Him. So they approached Yeshua and asked Him where He was staying. They wanted to spend some time with Him. They stayed all day with Yeshua. Then Andrew went and found his brother Simon Peter, and told him that they had found the Messiah. Andrew the fisherman was the first person to bring someone to Yeshua! And Simon Peter was another fisherman.

Yeshua called these two pairs of brothers – Andrew and Simon Peter, James and John – to leave their fishing nets and follow Him. Now He would equip them to launch out into deep and unknown waters, and let down their nets – not for fish, but for men. (Matthew 4:19)

What does it mean to become a disciple of Yeshua today?

Readings: John 1:35–51, Matthew 4:18–22, Mark 1:19–20, Mark 8:34–38

22nd Day of the 10th Month
Tevet, usually falling in December/January
The Beatitudes
Blessed are the Poor in Spirit

Blessed are the poor in spirit, for theirs is the kingdom of heaven.

Matthew 5:3

Yeshua called His first disciples to leave everything, and follow Him and preach the gospel of the kingdom in the hills and villages of Galilee. He quickly became known in the whole region, in Jerusalem and beyond, and multitudes came to Him to be healed of their sicknesses and diseases. Great crowds were drawn because of the miracles, but only His disciples followed Him up the difficult mountain path, to let Him sit and teach them how their lives must change. The Lord leads us to His holy mountain.

The first heart attitude that matters to Yeshua is humility. The poor in spirit are 'blessed' or 'happy'. These ones draw His attention, even amongst the crowd. Yeshua is looking for our recognition of our own state of wretchedness without Him – our own inability to do anything, or be anything, or have any righteousness that is worthy of God, apart from Him, and what He gives us. It is an attitude of contrition, repentance and absolute dependency on God – for righteousness, for salvation and for everything.

It is on hearing the Word of God, and receiving conviction from the Holy Spirit, that we realise what sinners we really are. We discover that we have fallen short of the mark. (Romans 3:23) We know that we have broken God's Laws, and need His grace and forgiveness. In Luke 18:9–14 it was the repentant Publican, not the self-righteous Pharisee who went away 'right with God'. The religious man didn't even know that he was a sinner. He was proud, and thought he was alright with God because of what he did. But it is the 'poor in spirit' who receive the kingdom of heaven. This is the way to enter salvation.

Do you guard your heart against pride, and pursue true humility – total dependence on God?

Readings: Matthew 5:1–3, Psalm 34:18, Luke 18:9–14, 2 Corinthians 8:9, 1 Peter 5:5–7

23rd Day of the 10th Month
Tevet, usually falling in December/January
The Beatitudes
Blessed Are Those Who Mourn

Blessed are those who mourn, for they shall be comforted.

Matthew 5:4

Those who mourn are the happy ones – because they receive the comfort of God. Yeshua is our example. We have two examples in Scripture of Yeshua weeping. Once was with grief at the death of Lazarus (John 11:35), and the other was over Jerusalem when He looked out over the city before His death, knowing that the people would reject His loving embrace. (Luke 19:41) Yeshua's heart was soft, and touched with compassion by human pain, sin and death. His tears demonstrated His love. (John 11:36)

Once we have entered the kingdom of God, He works to soften our hearts, to sensitise us to the evil of our own sin, the sin of others, and to the suffering in the world. What didn't bother us, before we entered the kingdom, now bothers us. We mourn when we sin and fail God. We mourn when we see the sin of others. Peter wept when he betrayed Yeshua. (Luke 22:62) But Yeshua kept His Word, and comforted him after His resurrection.

We are comforted by bringing the pain of our sins, failures, mistakes and human frailties to God, to be cleansed by the blood of Yeshua. When we approach Yeshua with mourning, we quickly receive the joy and comfort of His grace, in the realisation that God does not perceive us as sinners or failures, but as His beloved sons and daughters, covered in His righteousness. He washes away our grief with His loving comfort and His perspective of love and forgiveness towards us. He binds up the broken-hearted (Luke 4:18, Isaiah 61:1–3), and heals our wounds as we forgive others and receive His forgiveness. He comforts us, so that forgiven by God we can bring comfort to others.

Bring your pains and burdens to Yeshua and with Him, forgive and be forgiven.

Readings: Psalm 51, Isaiah 53, Isaiah 61:2, 3, John 11:1–44, 2 Corinthians 1:3–5

24th Day of the 10th Month
Tevet, usually falling in December/January
The Beatitudes
Blessed Are the Meek

Blessed are the meek for they shall inherit the earth. *Matthew 5:5*

Meekness is made possible in the soul that has been healed by God. It is made possible in the person secure in their identity in Messiah and their value to God. Meekness is not weakness, but strength constrained. The meek do not become aggressive, defensive, pushy, self-assertive or enter fights and quarrels to maintain or gain position. Instead they humbly submit to others, are willing to yield and take the lower place if necessary, lose position if necessary or be overlooked. In contrast pride would lead us to seek the higher place, recognition, and praise to make ourselves feel better.

Our call as believers is to the lowest place. Yeshua at the Last Passover Supper, took up the bowl and towel, and took the position of the servant, to wash the disciples' feet. Then He said, "If I then, your Lord and Teacher, have washed your feet, you also ought to wash one another's feet. For I have given you an example, that you should do as I have done to you." (John 13:14, 15) The principal way we wash each others' feet is by forgiving them when they sin against us. The meek do not easily take offence or get touchy, but submit to God as their vindicator. They trust God to keep them in the position that He has chosen for them. They trust God for their needs and well-being. They do not have to be in control.

When Moses' authority was challenged by Korah, he prostrated himself before God and received his instructions from God. God acted and kept Moses in the position of authority that He had given him. Moses was the meekest man on earth. (Numbers 12:3) God will vindicate the meek. They will inherit the earth! Yeshua will inherit the earth!

Ask God to help you develop more meekness in your life.

Readings: Psalm 37, Matthew 8:5–13, John 13, Philippians 2:1–24, Philippians 4:4–20

25th Day of the 10th Month
Tevet, usually falling in December/January
The Beatitudes
Blessed Are Those Who Hunger and Thirst for Righteousness

Blessed are those who hunger and thirst for righteousness, for they shall be filled. *Matthew 5:6*

People hunger and thirst for many things in life, such as love, success, health and prosperity. But none of these things on their own create the ultimate happiness that our souls crave. Deep in our hearts, what we really need and long for, is a deep and intimate relationship with our Heavenly Father, who alone can love and affirm us as we truly need to be loved and affirmed. He alone can heal our wounds and take away our pain. What we most need is for our Father God to forgive us our sins and accept us as 'righteous' (right with Him). Only Yeshua can give that to us. We are truly blessed when we direct our deep heartache aright to God, rather than turning it towards lesser pleasures and joys.

1 Corinthians 1:30 tells us that Yeshua is 'righteousness' personified. 'But of Him you are in Christ Jesus, who became for us wisdom from God – and righteousness and sanctification and redemption...' We are blessed when we hunger and thirst to receive undeserved grace through Yeshua and to know Him. Isaiah 55:1, 2, prophesies the invitation of God to receive the grace of God, saying, "Ho! Everyone who thirsts, come to the waters; and you who have no money, come, buy and eat. Yes, come, buy wine and milk without money and without price. Why do you spend money for what is not bread, and your wages for what does not satisfy? Listen carefully to Me, and eat what is good, and let your soul delight itself in abundance..." Yeshua met a woman at a well who had had many husbands. He told her "Whoever drinks of this water will thirst again, but whoever drinks of the water that I shall give him will never thirst. But the water that I shall give him will become in him a fountain of water springing up into everlasting life." (John 4:13, 14)

Which well are you drinking out of? Are you directing your longings to God?

Readings: Isaiah 55, Psalm 42:2, John 4, Isaiah 12:3, John 7:37, 38, Matthew 6:24–34

26th Day of the 10th Month
Tevet, usually falling in December/January
The Beatitudes
Blessed Are the Merciful

Blessed are the merciful, for they shall obtain mercy. *Matthew 5:7*

Mercy cannot exist without justice. Justice is the judgement between right and wrong, and between good and evil. Justice upholds God's moral law. Mercy recognises where God's justice and His Laws have been broken and where wrong has been done, but nonetheless chooses to withhold the deserved judgement. Mercy is an undeserved, generous and costly gift, given by the one who has suffered wrong, to the one who has sinned against them. To give mercy, is to give grace; undeserved goodness, a generous and costly gift. But God promises to reward the one who gives the costly gift of mercy. He promises that the merciful shall obtain mercy. This is the most precious gift, because we all need to receive mercy, from God and from others.

In our world many people are quick to judge and criticise. But Yeshua taught "Judge not, that you be not judged. For with what judgement you judge, you will be judged; and with the measure you use, it will be measured back to you." (Matthew 7:1, 2) When God forgave us our sins He showed us mercy and grace. Yeshua taught "For if you forgive men their trespasses, your heavenly Father will also forgive you. But if you do not forgive men their trespasses, neither will your Father forgive your trespasses." (Matthew 6:14, 15) We are to humbly give others the mercy we ourselves would want to receive.

Those who have truly humbled themselves and known God's grace, demonstrated in the first four beatitudes, have been equipped by God to exercise the virtue and gift of mercy, to demonstrate God's love and His immense, undeserved grace to unworthy sinners.

Are you quick to judge or quick to show mercy? Is your heart merciful?

Readings: Micah 6:8, 2 Samuel 22:26, James 2:13, Matthew 18:22–35, Luke 6:32–42

27th Day of the 10th Month
Tevet, usually falling in December/January
The Beatitudes
Blessed Are the Pure in Heart

Blessed are the pure in heart, for they shall see God. *Matthew 5:8*

John wrote in 1 John 3:2, 3, "Beloved, now we are children of God; and it has not yet been revealed what we shall be, but we know that when He is revealed we shall be like Him, for we shall see Him as He is. And everyone who has this hope in Him purifies himself, just as He is pure." King David prayed for God to create in him a clean heart. (Psalm 51:10) We must guard our hearts and keep them pure, because it is with our hearts that we discern God.

A pure heart is undefiled by sin and unforgiveness. It is the blood of Yeshua which purifies our hearts. 1 John 1:7 says, "if we walk in the light as He is in the light, we have fellowship with one another, and the blood of Jesus Christ His Son cleanses us from all sin." Unforgiveness in our hearts is like a wall which separates us from true heart-fellowship with the one we have not forgiven, and also from God. A root of bitterness in our hearts will defile. (Hebrews 12:15) In the Law there was to be no mixture of seeds or fabrics. The High Priest had to be dressed in pure linen to be able to enter the Holy of Holies of the tabernacle. Similarly our hearts are to be without the 'mixture' of deceit, gossip, hatred, sinful emotions, unforgiveness and sin, if we are to enter into 'His Holy Presence'.

The eyes of Yeshua are like a flame of fire. (Revelation 1:14) We cannot look into the face of God and be unchanged. When Moses spoke with God face-to-face, his own face shone with light. (Exodus 34:35) There is no darkness in God. He will reveal Himself to the pure in heart, and they will be able to discern the face of God and behold His expression, His words, His smile, and His love towards them in this world, and in the world to come.

Ask God to reveal any obstacle in your heart that prevents you seeing God's face.

Readings: 2 Corinthians 3:18, Psalm 51:10, 11, Psalm 24, Psalm 119:9–16, Titus 1:15, 2:14

28th Day of the 10th Month
Tevet, usually falling in December/January
The Beatitudes
Blessed Are the Peacemakers

Blessed are the peacemakers, for they shall be called sons of God.

Matthew 5:9

When a disciple of Yeshua has been beholding His face, he will become like His master. Yeshua was the ultimate peacemaker. He walked in humility, taking our sins upon Himself, to reconcile man to God. He broke down the dividing wall of hostility, not only between male and female, but also between Jew and Gentile. Followers of Yeshua who have beheld the glory of God with an unveiled face will be changed to take on the family likeness and be changed from one degree of glory to another. (2 Corinthians 3:18) They will walk in His love, peace and 'shalom', bearing the character of the Father, as sons of God.

Shalom means not only an absence of hostility, but a presence of wholeness. To feed the hungry or give hospitality to a stranger brings that person peace. To believe the best of others and refrain from spreading gossip brings peace. Praying for, and healing the sick, brings peace and wholeness. Sometimes just keeping your mouth shut can bring peace!

The humble man or woman of God will seek peace and pursue it (1 Peter 3:11), living as peaceably as possible with everyone, so much as it depends on them. (Romans 12:18) We must work hard to keep our relationships full of peace and love, not stirring up strife or hurting people, but overcoming evil with good. Paul wrote, "Beloved, do not avenge yourselves, but rather give place to wrath; for it is written "Vengeance is Mine, I will repay," says the Lord. Therefore "If your enemy is hungry, feed him; If he is thirsty, give him a drink; for in so doing you will heap coals of fire on his head." (Romans 12:19, 20) Yeshua bought us peace with God at a great price. We can pay the price to make peace with others.

How can you bring more peace into your relationships? Who can you bring peace to today?

Readings: Romans 12, Psalm 34:14, Genesis 13, 1 Thessalonians 5:11–28

29th Day of the 10th Month
Tevet, usually falling in December/January
The Beatitudes
Blessed Are Those Who Are Persecuted for Righteousness' Sake

Blessed are those who are persecuted for righteousness' sake, for theirs is the kingdom of heaven. Blessed are you when they revile and persecute you, and say all kinds of evil against you falsely for My sake. Rejoice and be exceedingly glad, for great is your reward in heaven, for so they persecuted the prophets who were before you.
Matthew 5:10, 11

The first and the last beatitudes both have the blessing of receiving the kingdom of heaven. This final beatitude includes a reward in heaven. Being persecuted for righteousness' sake is the culmination of all the other beatitudes. If we cultivate all the previous qualities in our lives, we will be noticed in the world for our difference, and like the prophets who challenged unrighteousness, we too will be persecuted.

The Apostle Paul wrote to Timothy "...Yes, and all who desire to live godly in Christ Jesus will suffer persecution..." (2 Timothy 3:12) Whether it is minor persecution such as rejection of friendship, or major persecution such as prison or martyrdom, the Bible clearly tells us that we will suffer persecution if we live a godly life in Yeshua. We may not even be openly preaching the gospel. Just our presence and life-style will provoke a reaction. To those who are perishing, our presence is like the fragrance of death. (2 Corinthians 2:16)

If people persecuted Yeshua, they will persecute us too. (John 15:19, 20) We do not belong to this world, but to heaven, and we serve a heavenly King. God chose us out of the world to be citizens of His kingdom, but we are meant to shine His light and truth out into the world. We are not to be sorrowful when we are persecuted for standing for righteousness, but we are to rejoice because we know that we have a great reward in heaven.

How do you react when people oppose you because of your faith? Do you rejoice?

Readings: John 15:18–27, Isaiah 53:3, Acts 9:1–16, 26:12–18, 2 Timothy 2:1–13

1st Day of the 11th Month
Shvat, usually falling in January/February
Receive the Kingdom of God
The Eleventh Hour

Now it came to pass in the fortieth year, in the eleventh month, on the first day of the month, that Moses spoke to the children of Israel according to all that the LORD had given him as commandments to them.... *Deuteronomy 1:3*

We now enter the eleventh month of the Biblical Calendar year. Today, on this new moon and first day of the month we dedicate ourselves afresh to God. On this day, Moses spoke to the children of Israel the words of the book of Deuteronomy, to prepare them to possess the Land. Soon they would cross over the Jordan River and enter the Promised Land. Moses reminded the people that it is only eleven days journey from Horeb, (where he had received the Law), to Kadesh Barnea. At Kadesh Barnea they could have crossed over into the Promised Land, (on the twelfth day), but because of unbelief they spent many more years camping in the desert. Eleven days' journey expanded into forty years of testing and refining, but now their wilderness time was coming to an end. This was like the 'eleventh hour' for Moses and the children of Israel. If the twelfth hour represents the final time of completion, then the eleventh hour is the time that God speaks to us, to rise and follow Him.

Yeshua told a parable about the kingdom of heaven. In the parable a landowner hired workers – some early in the morning, some later in the day, and some at the eleventh hour, just before the end of the day. By God's grace, the 'eleventh hour' recruits received the same pay as those who started work early in the day. (Matthew 20:1–16) We are now in the eleventh hour. The Lord blows His trumpet to call us to come away with Him, to rise up out of the wilderness, to worship Him, and be filled with His Spirit, to bring in the harvest.

Will you respond to God's call to rise up, and follow Him to be an 'eleventh hour' harvester?
Readings: Deuteronomy 1:1–8, Matthew 20:1–16, John 4:34–38

SHVAT

2nd Day of the 11th Month
Shvat, usually falling in January/February
Receive the Kingdom of God
Yeshua Calls for Disciples

Then He said to them, "The harvest truly is great, but the labourers are few; therefore pray the Lord of the harvest to send out labourers into His harvest." *Luke 10:2*

At the beginning of His ministry, Yeshua appointed twelve men to be His disciples and close companions. This group, which included fishermen, a tax collector, and a zealot, accompanied Him as He preached and 'brought the glad tidings of the kingdom of God' to all the towns and cities. (Luke 8:1) Peter, James and John had the closest relationships with Him, and certain women – Mary, called Magdalene, Joanna, the wife of Chuza, Susanna, and many others provided for Yeshua 'from their substance'. (Luke 8:2, 3)

He also appointed seventy and sent them out 'two by two', as He had already sent out the 'twelve' (Matthew 10:1–23, Mark 6:7–13, Luke 9:1–6), to go 'before His face into every city and place where He Himself was about to go.' (Luke 10:1) He sent them to preach the kingdom of God, to cast out demons, and to heal the sick. He told them that the harvest is great but that the labourers are few, so they were to pray to the Lord of the harvest to send out labourers into His harvest. They were not to carry money, possessions, spare clothing or shoes, but they were to heal the sick saying to them, 'The kingdom of God has come near to you.' (Luke 10:8) They were to stay where the people received them, and be provided for by them, but if they were not received, they were to depart that city and wipe off its dust from their feet. They were to be wise as serpents and harmless as doves. (Matthew 10:16) It takes wisdom to turn souls to God. (Daniel 12:3) They were sent out like 'lambs among wolves'. (Luke 10:3) Yeshua calls us to preach repentance and the remission of sins in His name, to all nations (Luke 24:47), baptising them and making disciples in His name. (Matthew 28:19)

What are you to do to bring God's kingdom to people and make disciples in all nations?

Readings: Mark 3:13–19, Matthew 10, Luke 10:1–24, Matthew 28:19–20, 2 Timothy 4:2

3rd Day of the 11th Month
Shvat, usually falling in January/February
Learn to Pray
Our Father in Heaven

Therefore do not be like them (the heathen). For your Father knows the things you have need of before you ask Him. In this manner, therefore, pray: Our Father in heaven.... *Matthew 6:8, 9*

To survive as a lamb among wolves we need to pray. The disciples saw Yeshua spending many hours in prayer – usually in solitude during the night. They knew that His relationship with the Father was central to His life so they asked Him how they should pray. (Luke 11:1) Many people love to pray, including heathens, but none prays like Yeshua.

The first thing Yeshua taught them was how not to pray. They must not be like the hypocrites (the religiously pious Pharisees), or the heathens. Hypocrites are more concerned with being seen and admired by people, than with obtaining praise from God. (Matthew 6:1–6) Hypocrites already have their reward from the people who admire them. So the first thing to learn is to pray in secret. Also they were not to pray like the heathen. (Matthew 6:7) The heathen repeat phrases over and over, like an incantation which draws demonic spirits to them. It is possible to pray habitual prayers without thinking about what you are saying, or directing your prayers properly to Father God. This is not right. God gave us a 'pattern' for relationship with our Father, not a 'mantra' to recite.

Yeshua taught us to remember to whom we are praying. We are praying to our loving, generous Father – God in Heaven! He cares for us, and knows us and our needs intimately. Our prayers come to the Father through Yeshua the Son, in the power of the Holy Spirit. We speak to our Father who loves us, hears us, and knows our needs before we ask.

Take time to remember the goodness and kindness of the Father before you approach Him.

Readings: Matthew 6:1–9, Luke 11:1–13, Romans 8:14–16, Mark 11:24, Matthew 7:7–11

SHVAT

4th Day of the 11th Month
Shvat, usually falling in January/February
Learn to Pray
Hallowed Be Thy Name

Hallowed be your name. *Matthew 6:9*

We begin our prayer time by remembering that we are speaking to our loving Heavenly Father, not performing a religious duty. Now we pray for God's name to be held in reverent respect. He is our Heavenly Father, but He is also the King of the Universe, the Creator of heaven and earth, the King of kings, the eternal God and we reverence Him.

We pray for God's name and holy nature to be held in reverent respect. Many people blaspheme and denigrate God's Holy name, but we are to honour the holiness of His name. God has many names in Scripture to describe His attributes. He is Emmanuel (God with us), He is the Lord of Hosts, He is the Lord our Healer, He is the Lord Almighty, He is the Lord who sees and provides, He is the Lord our Righteousness, He is the Lord our Peace, He is the Lord our Shepherd, He is God all-Powerful and all-Sufficient, He is the Lord who is there. He is holy, He is mighty, His name is wonderful, He is worthy of praise! Revelation 15:3, 4 contains a praise song sung by the angels in Heaven: "Great and marvellous are Your works, Lord God Almighty! Just and true are Your ways, O King of the saints! Who shall not fear You, O Lord, and glorify Your name? For You alone are holy. For all nations shall come and worship before You, for Your judgements have been manifested."

We can sing out our worship, praise, and thanksgiving to God. We can play a musical instrument to Him to bring Him pleasure. The Lord is enthroned on our praises. (Psalm 22:3) As we exalt Him, so His presence is increased in our lives. Praise prepares us to share our hearts with Him. It shows that we put His pleasure before our own needs and desires.

Enter His gates with thanksgiving, and into His courts with praise. (Psalm 100:4)

Readings: Psalm 100, Ephesians 5:17–20, Psalm 145

5th Day of the 11th Month
Shvat, usually falling in January/February
Learn to Pray
Thy Kingdom Come

Your kingdom come. Your will be done on earth as it is in heaven.
Matthew 6:10

Having praised God and entered into His presence, we are ready to bring Him our intercessions. The first intercession is to take up the burden of God's own heart – that His kingdom come. Yeshua preached the 'kingdom of God'. When a person receives salvation through Yeshua, they enter the kingdom of God. That means they come under the kingship and reign of God in their lives, and are no longer ruled by the power of darkness. (Ephesians 2:1–10) When we believe and trust in Yeshua for our salvation, we are transferred from the kingdom of darkness to the kingdom of God's Son. The kingdom has already come to the extent that He rules and reigns in our hearts. But His kingdom has still not come in many lives. The whole earth is waiting to come back under the rule and reign of Yeshua. Praying for His kingdom to come, means to pray for souls to be saved and submit to Yeshua as their King, and for Him to return to earth as King, and bring the whole world under His reign.

We are called to pray for souls to be saved, and to pray for God's rule and reign in their lives to increase, once they have been saved. In heaven, everything is perfect and in subjection to the King. All our healing, joy and provision are already provided and exist now in Heaven. We are to pray in faith for what God has already obtained for us in heaven to come down to earth, where we can receive His Holy Spirit and His miraculous provision, blessings, love, peace, good relationships, holiness, help, the intervention of angels, and freedom. We can pray for any situation on the earth! We never pray for bad things to happen. We pray for things on earth to line up with heaven, not hell, on earth. We are to come to God with childlike faith and receive good things from heaven.

Ask God to lead you in your intercession, and show you what He wants you to pray for.

Readings: 1 Timothy 2:1–7, Ephesians 6:18, Ephesians 2:1–10, Colossians 1:9–14

6th Day of the 11th Month
Shvat, usually falling in January/February
Learn to Pray
Give Us This Day Our Daily Bread

Give us this day our daily bread. *Matthew 6:11*

After praying for the expansion of God's kingdom on the earth, and in the lives and situations we know of, we can pray for our own needs. This order should reflect our whole lives – God first, then others, then ourselves. We are to recognise our dependency on our Heavenly Father, and ask Him to supply our needs – even if we have a job and provision, and feel well provided for. These things come from God, and every breath comes from Him.

When Israel was in the wilderness, God provided them with manna from heaven each day. They could not collect more than a day's supply or it would go rotten (except for Shabbat). Similarly we are not to be anxious about tomorrow. Yeshua's teaching in Matthew 6:25–34 ends with the exhortation to seek His kingdom and righteousness first above all the things that we need, and they will be given to us. Therefore we are not to worry about tomorrow, "for tomorrow will worry about its own things. Sufficient for the day is its own trouble." (Matthew 6:33, 34) Yeshua is our bread that we need above all else to stay alive. (John 6) He never forgets about us.

God wants us to ask Him specifically and directly for the things we need. The reason that sometimes we don't have some things is that we simply haven't asked Him! And sometimes we do not receive because we asked out of covetousness, or for our own pleasures. (James 4:2, 3) We are to ask with faith believing that we receive. (Mark 11:24) Yeshua told a parable about asking persistently for what we need. All who ask, He said, receive, because God is a good Father who gives good gifts to His children. (Luke 11:1–13)

Do you have any needs that you have not brought before your Heavenly Father?

Readings: Matthew 6:24–34, Luke 11:1–13, Mark 11:20–24

7th Day of the 11th Month
Shvat, usually falling in January/February
Learn to Pray
And Forgive Us Our Debts

And forgive us our debts, as we forgive our debtors. *Matthew 6:12*

We have great need of God's help, not only for our physical needs, but also for our spiritual, emotional and mental well-being. The next part of our praying brings us to our deepest heart need – a right standing and relationship with God and man. Unbelievers praying this prayer can come to salvation and the forgiveness of their sins. For believers who have already had their sins washed away by the blood of Yeshua, this is about daily trusting in Yeshua for our forgiveness so that we are not weighed down by our failings.

When we become conscious of a sin we are to confess it to God (1 John 1:9), and if it is something causing us bondage, we can also confess it to another believer who can pray with us to be set free. (James 5:16) We need to receive forgiveness consciously, so that we do not become self-condemning or hardened to sin. When we 'confess' to God, we give it to Him. This requires faith and trust, that He has taken it and paid the price for our forgiveness, in His death on the cross. We are to forgive ourselves, surrendering our sin to Yeshua, receiving His forgiveness and cleansing through His sinless blood.

The answer to this prayer though, does have one condition – that we forgive others their sins. Just as we want to be accepted and loved by God before we are perfect, so we must forgive and accept others their shortcomings, failures, sins and weaknesses. And when others have sinned against us, we must release forgiveness to them and let go of the offence. Yeshua paid for their sin on the cross too. It is powerful to pray for God to forgive them, like Stephen did (Acts 7:60), and like Yeshua prayed on the cross. (Luke 23:34)

Do you consciously give and receive forgiveness or do you get offended and guilty?

Readings: Matthew 6:12–15, Matthew 18, Luke 23:33, 34, Mark 11:25, 26

27/1/15

8th Day of the 11th Month
Shvat, usually falling in January/February
Learn to Pray
And Do Not Lead Us into Temptation

And do not lead us into temptation, but deliver us from the evil one.

Matthew 6:13

Having prayed to receive God's forgiveness and pronounced to Him our forgiveness of those who have sinned against us, God can heal the wounds of our soul. The prayer to not be led into temptation but delivered from the evil one, reminds us to pray for protection from such wounding, and stumbling into sin in the first place. Many bad situations that we experience result from our own lack of wisdom and flesh, from the weaknesses and sins of others or from a direct attack by the evil one. Very often it takes time and energy to bring peace and healing where there has been sin, strife, wounding, and robbery. It is much better to pray for God to help us avoid falling into the traps of the enemy in the first place.

The Greek word 'peirazo' (temptation) comes from the word 'to test', meaning a putting to proof by experiment. It is good to pray that God will lead us on a path free from the traps and snares of life – such as wrong and unhealthy relationships, being in the wrong place at the wrong time, and temptations of the flesh. Our prayer is that God will clearly lead and guide us along a good and safe path of protection, where we will be able to avoid the temptations and snares of the devil. We can pray the protection of Psalm 91 over our lives.

The Apostle Paul experienced one particular test which he described as a thorn in the flesh. God did not actually take that one away, but He said, "My grace is sufficient for you, for My strength is made perfect in weakness." (2 Corinthians 12:9) When Paul knew his own weakness, then he was strong. We too are strongest when we remember that actually we are weak, and need to pray for God's help, protection and strength to stand firm in Him.

Do you seek God's wisdom, protection and deliverance from temptations and wrong paths?

Readings: James 1:13–15, 1 Corinthians 10:12, 13, Proverbs 4, 5

9th Day of the 11th Month
Shvat, usually falling in January/February
Learn to Pray
For Yours Is the Kingdom

For Yours is the kingdom and the power and the glory forever. Amen
Matthew 6:13

Having prayed to be led along a good path free from temptation and to be delivered from all evil, we return to praise, and remember that God is all-victorious, all-powerful, the one who has conquered evil. He is the King of kings, and the kingdom of God belongs to Him. The final word – 'Amen', is a Hebrew word that has no adequate English translation. It means something like – 'This is a firm, trustworthy, true saying and prayer, and we believe it, and we can safely and confidently trust and be assured that it will come to pass.'

When we have been in prayer, sometimes travailing in our soul to bring to birth answers through the Holy Spirit interceding within us (Romans 8:26), it is good to return to the place of praise. This is like a balance to our soul. It brings us back into seeing God's heavenly perspective. Intercession can be an energetic spiritual exercise, but after sharing the pains of God's heart, or praying with compassion into heavy situations, it is good to remember that the joy of the Lord is our strength. (Nehemiah 8:10) Prayer and worship, especially with the gift of unknown tongues, breaks oppressions, brings release, joy and supernatural intervention.

The final word – 'Amen' – is usually said corporately. This reminds us that the first word that Yeshua used in this prayer is 'Our'. Corporate prayer is especially powerful. Yeshua said, "Again, I say to you that if two of you agree on earth concerning anything that they ask, it will be done for them by My Father in heaven. For where two or three are gathered together in My name, I am there in the midst of them." (Matthew 18:19, 20)

Consider the fact that when you pray as Yeshua instructed, the King of Heaven is with you.

Readings: Matthew 18:18–20, Romans 8 18–39, Acts 10:1–4

10th Day of the 11th Month
Shvat, usually falling in January/February
Build the Kingdom
The Branch

There shall come forth a Rod from the stem of Jesse, And a Branch shall grow out of his roots. *Isaiah 11:1*

When Yeshua came at His first coming, He fulfilled Isaiah 11:1, 2. Subsequent verses speak of His second coming as King. The Messiah is described as the Rod from the 'stem' of Jesse. The word translated 'stem' is 'geza' meaning to cut down trees, the trunk or stump of a tree (as felled or as planted), a stem or stock. The 'Branch' – in Hebrew 'netzer', is Yeshua. He would be like a new shoot springing up from the roots and stump of a cut down tree. The olive trees of Israel, for example, are very difficult to kill. These hardy little trees can be chopped down but still live. Their roots remain alive and new branches spring up from the stump. In Isaiah 11:1 the Messiah springs forth from the cut-down 'stump' of the dynasty of David, son of Jesse. (Ruth 4:22, Matthew 1:6) When Saul failed as king, David, the youngest son of Jesse was anointed by the prophet Samuel to become the new king of Israel. The new king would be a prophetic picture of the Messiah whose kingdom will not fail. God said to Samuel, "I am sending you to Jesse the Bethlehemite. For I have provided Myself a king among his sons." (1 Samuel 16:1) God provided King David, who received the covenant that God would bring forth the Messiah from his descendants. (2 Samuel 7:8–16) This was fulfilled in Luke 1:30–33 when the Angel announced Messiah's birth to Mary.

The 'tree' of the Davidic dynasty was 'cut down' to a mere tree stump by the Babylonian exile, but Yeshua came forth from His ancestry, His roots, to be Israel's Messiah.

Ask God to show you what He wants to sprout forth out of any barren 'stump' in your life.

Readings: Isaiah 11:1, 2, 1 Samuel 16, 2 Samuel 7, Luke 1:26–37

11th Day of the 11th Month
Shvat, usually falling in January/February
Build the Kingdom
The Spirit of the Lord

The Spirit of the LORD shall rest upon Him, The Spirit of wisdom and understanding, The Spirit of counsel and might, The Spirit of knowledge and of the fear of the LORD. *Isaiah 11:2*

Yeshua, the 'Branch' of Isaiah 11:1 was born in Bethlehem, 'the City of David', which is where Jesse, father of David, had lived. (1 Samuel 16:1) Yeshua was the 'branch' of new kingdom life from the tree-'stump' of the family of David. The kingdom of God is attached at its roots to the Jewish kingdom. At the time of Yeshua's birth, the direct descendants of King David, knew the prophecy concerning Bethlehem (Micah5:2), and expected the Messiah to be born from among them. They no longer lived in Bethlehem, a small city just south of Jerusalem. Many lived up in the north of Israel in the region called Galilee, in the town of 'Natzerat' (Nazareth) in Galilee. Mary and Joseph were Nazarenes.

The Hebrew word for 'branch' is 'netzer'. Yeshua is the 'Netzer', the branch from the stump of Jesse, who grew up in the town of 'Natzerat' (Nazareth). Nathanael commented, 'Can anything good come out of Nazareth?'(John 1:46) Perhaps people mocked the people of Nazareth for their expectation that the 'Netzer' would come forth from them.

The 'Branch' came forth from the living roots of the Davidic dynasty, and His life now flows through believers, through the Holy Spirit. The Hebrew name for 'Christians' is 'Notzrim' – 'Branches'. This reminds us of the seven-branched menorah of Zechariah 4, where the oil of the Holy Spirit flows through seven pipes, and the two olive trees and the two branches drip with oil. The life of the seven-fold Spirit of the LORD (Isaiah 11:2) is available to flow into you and bring new life in every area, or 'branch' of your life.

Consider how Pentecost (Acts 2) brings life and new branches to the old stump and roots.

Reading: Isaiah 11: 1, 2, Zechariah 4, John 1:40–51, John 15:5, Acts 2, Romans 9:13–24

SHVAT

12th Day of the 11th Month
Shvat, usually falling in January/February
Build the Kingdom
Gifts of Grace

For as we have many members in one body, but all the members do not have the same function, so we, being many, are one body in Christ, and individually members of one another. *Romans 12:4, 5*

The kingdom is now in our hearts through the Holy Spirit. It is no longer ruled by earthly 'kings' in Israel but by the heavenly King of Israel. Until Yeshua returns to rule and reign on earth and establish His kingdom, the life of God flows through our hearts to build His kingdom and bring heaven to earth in hearts and lives. He is establishing His will through every submitted life within His Bride. The Apostle Paul said that in Yeshua, we are all now members of one body, having different functions according to the gift of God's grace given to us, to edify and build each other up, and to bring souls into His kingdom.

In Romans 12:6–8 we read of gifts which are bound up with our personality and natural tendency. There are those who prophecy, in accordance with their level of faith, there are those who minister and serve using His ministering gift, there are teachers who teach, exhorters who exhort, givers who are to give with liberality, leaders who are to lead with diligence, and there are those who show mercy and are to do so with cheerfulness.

These gifts are not the usual 'job titles' that we see used in churches. Rather they are like hidden treasures hidden in different people. We are to recognise these treasures and honour them and receive from them. A teacher, for example, may not teach each week in a pulpit, but may teach others in everyday contexts such as conversations over dinner. A leader may not lead the church, but might, for example, organise a local project in the community.

Read Romans 12:6–8 and ask God to show you where these gifts are in the people you know.

Readings: Romans 12:1–13, 1 Peter 2:17, Romans 15, 16, 1 Corinthians 16, Colossians 4

13th Day of the 11th Month
Shvat, usually falling in January/February
Build the Kingdom
Spiritual Gifts

But the manifestation of the Spirit is given to each one for the profit of all.... *1 Corinthians 12:7*

The Holy Spirit works through every member of the body of Messiah through the manifestation of spiritual gifts – such as giving a word of wisdom, prophecy or knowledge, to build up and help someone in their walk of faith. Anyone who is filled with the Holy Spirit can exercise spiritual gifts for the edification of the whole body of Messiah. (Romans 15:2) We are to build each other up, not tear each other down. We must always be very careful when we use spiritual gifts that that is what we do, encouraging and blessing, not criticising or discouraging, or giving false words. The most important thing is love. (1 Corinthians 13)

1 Corinthians 12:8–11 has a list of spiritual gifts which are not so tied in with our personality as the Romans 12 gifts, but come from the Holy Spirit abiding in us, for the occasion when they are needed. Certain individuals may operate in certain gifts more than others, and we can ask God for the specific gifts. Paul exhorted the Corinthians to pursue spiritual gifts, especially prophecy. (1 Corinthians 14:1) The gifts are: the word of wisdom – spoken into a situation, the word of knowledge – which knows something by direct revelation from God rather than by natural knowledge, the gift of faith – which brings answers to prayer, the gift of healings, the gift of working miracles, the gift of prophecy, the gift of discerning spirits, the gift of tongues, and the gift of interpreting tongues. (1 Corinthians 12:8–10)

The Holy Spirit distributes the gifts individually as He wills. (1 Corinthians 12:11) We are to exercise the gifts not only in church services, but also in everyday life, prayer and relationships, so that God can build His kingdom, edify the body, and reach out to the lost.

Ask God to train you little by little in using spiritual gifts to build up the body of Messiah.

Readings: 1 Corinthians 12:1–11, 1 Corinthians 13, Isaiah 28:9–13

14th Day of the 11th Month
Shvat, usually falling in January/February
Build the Kingdom
The Body of Messiah

Now you are the body of Christ, and members individually. And God has appointed these in the church: first apostles, second prophets, third teachers, after that miracles, then gifts of healings, helps, administrations, varieties of tongues. *1 Corinthians 12:27, 28*

1 Corinthians 14:12–26 describes the Body of 'Christ' – 'Messiah'. Just as a body has many different parts which have different functions, so the Body of Messiah on the earth is made up of lots of different individuals and groupings which have different gifts, emphases, callings and characteristics. That is how it is meant to be. We are also different nationalities, and some are Jewish believers in Yeshua while others are Gentile believers in Yeshua. We have different jobs and situations in life. But we all receive the same Holy Spirit who knits us together as one, as brothers and sisters in Messiah's Body, who makes us all one.

The Apostle Paul foresaw the temptation of certain members to reject or demean others different from themselves. He told us we are not to do that. We mustn't look on others and say we don't need them. We must honour and receive them all, and recognise that we need them, and their differences from ourselves. They bring something to the body that we don't have. Just as with our physical body we give more modesty and honour to certain parts of our body, so we must do with the spiritual body of Messiah, by caring for the weak, being compassionate to the suffering, giving attention to those who need attention and help.

God has created order within the Body. First are the apostles, second the prophets, third the teachers. After that come people with gifts of miracles, healings, helps, administrations and varieties of tongues. The most important thing to remember is love.

Consider the different expressions of the Body of Messiah that you know of.

Readings: 1 Corinthians 12:12–31, Matthew 10:40–42, 1 Corinthians 15:9–11

15th Day of the 11th Month
Shvat, usually falling in January/February
Build the Kingdom
Spiritual Gifts in Church Meetings

Even so you, since you are zealous for spiritual gifts, let it be for the edification of the church that you seek to excel. *1 Corinthians 14:12*

God has given us the gift of speaking in other tongues. The words bubble up from our spirits in a 'prayer language' which is powerful because the Holy Spirit can speak and pray through us in words beyond our understanding to accomplish exactly what He wants to in the realm of the Spirit. Our spirit is strengthened and edified, and God's supernatural activity increases, as He answers and responds to these powerful prayers.

The Apostle Paul clearly prayed in tongues a great deal, because he confidently said, "I thank my God I speak with tongues more than you all." (1 Corinthians 14:18) However, Paul's greatest concern was for the edification of all the believers, and for any unbelievers who might come into a church meeting, that they might be saved. It is very obvious from this chapter that the spiritual gifts were used by all members of the congregation during church meetings. This is God's pattern for us today. Church should be a place where we can use and receive from the operation of spiritual gifts through all believers, not just leaders.

In a church meeting that is open to outsiders it is usually good to concentrate on using the gifts which people can understand – such as prophecy, or tongues with an interpretation. Then people will hear God's voice speaking directly to them, and if unbelievers are in attendance God may reveal the hidden issues of their heart, so that they may come to salvation. In Acts 2 foreigners heard and believed through the supernatural gift of languages. There is no hard and fast rule about tongues, except to be orderly and governed by love.

Do you use the gift of tongues (especially in your own prayers), and other gifts at church?

Readings: 1 Corinthians 14, 1 Corinthians 13:1, Acts 2:1–18

SHVAT

16th Day of the 11th Month
Shvat, usually falling in January/February
Build the Kingdom
Come to Maturity

And He Himself gave some to be apostles, some prophets, some evangelists, and some pastors and teachers, for the equipping of the saints for the work of ministry, for the edifying of the body of Christ, till we all come to the unity of the faith and of the knowledge of the Son of God, to a perfect man, to the measure of the stature of the fullness of Christ.... *Ephesians 4:11–13*

Here, the Apostle Paul gives what are called the 'five-fold ministries'. These are apostles, prophets, evangelists, pastors and teachers. In 1 Corinthians 12:28 Paul listed apostles, prophets and teachers but left out the pastors and evangelists. In many churches one or more of the ministries gets left out or we wrongly expect one man to embody them all.

The Apostle is first in both lists. The Apostle is often an itinerant person who is sent to churches or ministries with a position of authority and oversight. They have attained high levels in spiritual gifting, maturity and experience, and are sent by God for the covering and protection of churches and ministries. Prophets bring the direct word of God to churches and ministries. Evangelists evangelise, pastors take care of pastoral concerns in the flock, and teachers teach. These can all happen inside or outside the recognised church 'structures'.

The 'five-fold ministries' should equip and edify individuals, in the body, to grow to maturity and minister to others, and not keep them in the place of merely receiving. Every member of the body should be growing 'into ministry'. We are not to get saved and remain spiritual babes. The five-fold ministries should constantly equip and 'build up' people into wholeness and maturity, into people who can serve others, in the full stature of Christ.

Is Ephesians 4:11–16 happening in your life? Are you more mature now than a year ago?

Readings: Ephesians 4, 1 Corinthians 3:3–13, Hebrews 5:12, 12:11, Luke 6:40, 1 John 2:5

17th Day of the 11th Month
Shvat, usually falling in January/February
Parables of the Kingdom
The Parable of the Sower and the Seed

...Jesus went out of the house and sat by the sea. And great multitudes were gathered together to Him, so that He got into a boat and sat, and the whole multitude stood on the shore. Then He spoke many things to them in parables, saying: "Behold, a sower went out to sow...."

Matthew 13:1–3

Yeshua lodged in Peter's house in Capernaum, in Hebrew 'Cfar Nahum' –'Village of Comfort'. This was on the northern shore of the Sea of Galilee, the great lake in the north of Israel. Yeshua went out of the house and sat on the pebbly shore of the lake. To the east and west, hills and fields dropped down to the lake, shimmering hazy blue into the distance. A crowd followed him onto the shore so he got into a boat and sat to teach the people gathered at the water's edge. He spoke to them of the kingdom of God – the kingdom of Heaven, beyond the shore of the 'Village of Comfort'. Would a harvest come forth from these hearts?

"Behold, a sower went out to sow..." (Matthew 13:2) The people listened to Yeshua sat in the boat... The seed is the Word of God. The Word is the gospel of the kingdom, of Yeshua, the Son of God Himself. He is the Word. (John 1:1) He had come for a harvest, heaven in hearts, hearts in heaven. The seed he sowed fell on different types of ground. Some hearts were like the well-trodden paths that bordered the fields. The soil was so hard the seed couldn't sink in and it was snatched away by birds (the devil). Other seed fell in stony places. These responded immediately but having no root they withered away in the hot sun. Obstacles prevented the Word going deep. Other seed fell among the thorns of the cares of the world, and deceitfulness of riches, which sprang up and choked them. Other seed fell on good soil which received and understood, bearing fruit up to a hundred times over.

Meditate on Hosea 10:12. "Break up your fallow ground, for it is time to seek the LORD..."

Readings: Matthew 4:12–17, Matthew 13: 1–23, Hosea 10:11–13, Hosea 6:3

SHVAT

18th Day of the 11th Month
Shvat, usually falling in January/February
Parables of the Kingdom
The Wheat and the Tares

Let both grow together until the harvest, and at the time of harvest I will say to the reapers, "First gather together the tares and bind them in bundles to burn them, but gather the wheat into my barn."

Matthew 13:30

Yeshua told the parable of the wheat and the tares to speak about the growth of the church in the world after His return to heaven. At the end of the age the angels will gather the wheat into the barn. They will harvest souls, bringing those made righteous by God into His kingdom and the New Jerusalem.

However, Yeshua warned us that something sinister would happen. Surreptitiously and unnoticed, whilst the wheat grows, an enemy would sow tares among the wheat. This bad seed would grow up together with the wheat. The tares represent the infiltrators sown by the devil in the church. The church will always contain a mixture – of those who are truly born of God, those who appear to definitely not be, and those of whom it is hard to say whether or not they really belong to the Lord. Only God knows hearts. When the multitude had gone after Yeshua's teaching, and the disciples were back with Him in the house, He explained to them that at the end of the age, the angels will gather up out of His kingdom and cast into hell "all things that offend, and those who practise lawlessness." (Matthew 13:41)

The owner of the fields will not allow his servants to uproot the tares before harvest time because it is easy to make a mistake and pull up the good wheat too. Whilst it is right to guard doctrine, discerning good fruit from bad to keep from error, we are not to judge our brothers and sisters. God is the perfect judge who will judge rightly at the end of the age.

Instead of judging others we are to judge ourselves, to avoid offences and lawlessness.

Readings: Matthew 13:24–30, 37–43, Matthew 7:1–5, Matthew 7:15–25, Isaiah 11:1–5

19th Day of the 11th Month
Shvat, usually falling in January/February
Parables of the Kingdom
The Mustard Seed

"The kingdom of heaven is like a mustard seed, which a man took and sowed in his field, which indeed is the least of all the seeds; but when it is grown it is greater than the herbs and becomes a tree, so that the birds of the air come and nest in its branches." *Matthew 13:31*

In this parable, Yeshua was still teaching from the boat to the people on the shore of Galilee. The lowly mustard seed is Yeshua Himself. He became the least of all, bearing our sin and shame, He took the lowest place. Despised and rejected, mocked and scorned on a cross, between two thieves, He identified with the lowest of the low. Yeshua, the mustard seed, died on the cross and was laid in a tomb like a seed that is buried in the ground.

When He rose from the dead He opened a new chapter of history. A tree sprang up from the ground, and the kingdom of God began like a little sapling, with just three thousand Jews baptised in the Holy Spirit in Jerusalem. Lives were changed and the gospel spread out among the Gentiles too, then out into the earth, like a mighty tree. As it became bigger, the kingdom, which is in men's hearts, began to embrace outward forms which are like birds nesting in the tree. Early on, for example the Roman Empire became 'Christianised' and synchronised paganism with Christian belief, to nest itself in the tree. Eastern Christianity, Western Christianity, denominations and institutions, have all nested themselves in the tree. Some of these 'birds and their nests' are good – bringing the preaching of the gospel and charitable work, education, health care, and even the reformation of whole societies. But bad 'predatory type' birds have also nested themselves in the tree. Crusades, wars, inquisitions, superstitions, abuse, exploitation, anti-Semitism, and secret societies, for example, have all placed themselves under the umbrella of Christianity. God's kingdom however, is in hearts.

Have you ever confused the mustard tree (God's kingdom) with the birds which nest in it?

Readings: Matthew 13:31, 32, John 18:36, 1 Corinthians 6:9, 10, Luke 17:20, 21

SHVAT

20th Day of the 11th Month
Shvat, usually falling in January/February
Parables of the Kingdom
The Leaven

Another parable He spoke to them: "The kingdom of heaven is like leaven, which a woman took and hid in three measures of meal till it was all leavened." *Matthew 13:33*

This parable is about a woman quietly doing her work at home. She secretly places leaven in her flour, which does its job, spreading through all the flour to make it rise into a good loaf of bread or a cake. The point of this parable is that there is a principle of growth and spreading in the kingdom which happens quietly, thoroughly, and in a hidden way.

The kingdom spreads secretly, not just in our own hearts, to affect the whole of our life and personality, but it also spreads out into other hearts as we share the gospel and others also receive Yeshua in their hearts. Usually, when we read the Bible speaking of leaven, we think of 1 Corinthians 5:7, which instructs us to purge out the 'leaven' of sin, to become like unleavened bread without sin. We are accustomed to thinking of leaven as representing sin, or the puffing up of pride, which permeates the whole of humanity. We keep the 'Feast of Unleavened Bread' with the unleavened bread of sincerity and truth. (1 Corinthians 5:8)

It is true that unchecked sin in hearts will grow. But when we receive Yeshua in our hearts, He removes the old leaven, the power of sin from our hearts. Now, with Him in our hearts, there is a new, good leaven at work, a spreading of the power of righteousness, peace and joy through our soul, as we are transformed by the renewal of our minds in accordance to the Word of God. (Romans 12:2) It happens quietly in the secret place, as we spend time with Yeshua in the Word of God. It is not proclaimed on the television news or the front of newspapers. It is in your 'home' alone with Yeshua that you are changed. (Matthew 13:36)

Are you developing your 'hidden' relationship with God in the secret place?

Readings: Matthew 13:33–36, Matthew 6:1–6, 16–18, Genesis 18:6

21st Day of the 11th Month
Shvat, usually falling in January/February
Parables of the Kingdom
Treasure Hidden in a Field

"Again, the kingdom of heaven is like treasure hidden in a field, which a man found and hid; and for joy over it he goes and sells all that he has and buys that field." *Matthew 13:44*

We come now to the fifth of Yeshua's parables about the kingdom. He told this after He had come ashore from the lake and dismissed the crowd. He had gone back into the house, where only a few would have been able to gather, and His disciples came to Him and asked Him to explain to them the meaning of the parables. The vast majority of the people would have returned to their homes not really understanding the meaning of His stories. His teaching did not impart head information. Instead it was intended to provoke a heart response in each individual. They could choose to seek out the man Yeshua, and pursue Him into the house to understand the parable, or they could return to life as normal. Clearly the majority went back to where they came from, and let Yeshua slip away, back into the house.

But, to His disciples who had left their nets to follow Him, Yeshua taught them not only the meaning of the parable of the tares, but He gave them more parables. He told them that the kingdom of heaven is like treasure hidden in a field. A man found the treasure and was so delighted with it that he sold all he had to buy the field. Clearly the man who found this exquisite treasure could not just claim it as his own because he found it. He had to actually buy the field so that he could rightfully and legally claim ownership of the treasure that was hidden in the field. In order to do this he had to first go and sell all his previous possessions. Similarly, when we hear Yeshua, we can delight in His teachings, but we cannot receive His grace cheaply. We must pursue Him and leave our old life behind. To rightfully and lawfully receive the treasure of Yeshua, we must lay down our whole life to have Him.

You can also read the parable the other way round and see how Yeshua gave His all for you.

Readings: Matthew 13:44, Matthew 10:38, 16:24–27, 2 Corinthians 8:9, Isaiah 45:3

SHVAT

22nd Day of the 11th Month
Shvat, usually falling in January/February
Parables of the Kingdom
The Pearl of Great Price

"Again, the kingdom of heaven is like a merchant seeking beautiful pearls, who, when he had found one pearl of great price, went and sold all that he had and bought it." *Matthew 13:45, 46*

Pearls in Scripture have a holy, heavenly quality. In Matthew 7:6 Yeshua said, "Do not give what is holy to the dogs; nor cast your pearls before swine, lest they trample them under their feet, and turn and tear you in pieces." Pearls represent a treasure beyond this present world. In Revelation 21:21 each gate of heaven is made of a single great pearl.

Yeshua compared the kingdom of heaven to a merchant, seeking beautiful pearls. Many people are seeking for something beyond this world, for a hope of eternity, a touch of heaven. They look at the beauty of nature, majestic church buildings, beautiful art and music and they pursue various religious and mystical experiences in the hope of finding some connection with the beauty of God. Something in man reaches out for and recognises the beauty of heaven reflected on earth below, and reaches out to touch it.

However all these things, however beautiful they seem, are totally inferior to the greatest pearl of all, which is Yeshua. He is the most costly and expensive pearl of all. To have Yeshua exceeds all other religious or mystical experiences. Once you find the real Lord and see the beauty of the Son of God, all those other beautiful things fade in comparison, and nothing else satisfies, apart from knowing Him. In the parable the merchant went and sold everything he had to buy the pearl of great price. So too, we will trade in everything we have, to buy the pearl of great price, which is to know Yeshua, the doorway to heaven. With the Song of Songs we say, "Yes, he is altogether lovely." (Song of Songs 5:16)

What is your heavenly treasure?

Readings: Matthew 13:45, 46, Mark 1:16–20, 10:28, Luke 19:1–10, John 12:1–8, 1 Peter 1:8

23rd Day of the 11th Month
Shvat, usually falling in January/February
Parables of the Kingdom
The Dragnet

"Again, the kingdom of heaven is like a dragnet that was cast into the sea and gathered some of every kind, which, when it was full, they drew to shore, and they sat down and gathered the good into vessels, but threw the bad away..." *Matthew 13:47, 48*

This parable draws Yeshua's teaching on the kingdom of heaven in Matthew 13 to a close. He likens the kingdom of heaven to a dragnet cast into the sea and gathering fish. The disciples already understood that Yeshua had called them to become 'fishers of men'. (Matthew 4:19) As fishermen they had different types of nets for catching different types of fish. They could let down a net on the water and let it sink over a shoal, then gather it in, or they could take a pair of nets which they left out in the water to trap the fish inside, before they gathered them in. Different types of fish would be caught in different types and sizes of net. But the dragnet was different. This was cast into the sea and dragged through the water to gather every fish that came in its wake whatever type it was. None escaped.

This is a picture of the judgement of souls at the end of the age. The time of 'fishing' for souls will be over. Every type of 'fish' will be harvested at the judgement. All will be gathered in by the angels, and sorted into the good fish and bad fish. The shore, where the people had stood listening to Yeshua as he taught them from the boat, would in the parable become the place of 'judgement' where the angels would sort all the fish. At the judgement the condition of hearts will be revealed; like soil and its harvest, those who possess the true treasure will be saved, the tares of the field will be harvested and destroyed, and the different types of fish revealed. None will escape. People will either be saved unto eternal life, or cast into the furnace, where there will be wailing and gnashing of teeth. (Matthew 13:50)

Consider the importance of fishing for souls before the fish are finally sorted and 'judged'.

Readings: Matthew 13:47–53, Matthew 4:17–22, 2 Peter 2, 3

SHVAT

24th Day of the 11th Month
Shvat, usually falling in January/February
Signs of the Kingdom
Turning Water into Wine

And truly Jesus did many other signs in the presence of His disciples, which are not written in this book; but these are written that you may believe that Jesus is the Christ, the Son of God, and that believing you may have life in His name. *John 20:30, 31*

The Apostle John said that he wrote the accounts of Yeshua, so that those of us who have come after He appeared in the flesh, may believe that He indeed is the Messiah, the Son of God, and that by believing, we may have life in His name – in the fullness of who He is.

The first 'sign' of the identity of Yeshua came at the wedding at Cana in Galilee where He turned water into wine. This "manifested His glory, and His disciples believed in Him." (John 2:11) The first two chapters of John's Gospel begin with accounts of three consecutive days. (John 1:35, 43, 2:1) This miracle happened on the third day. The third day represents the resurrection, but also occurs in Hosea 6:2 where Hosea prophecies, "After two days He will revive us; on the third day He will raise us up, that we may live in His sight."

At the wedding of Cana, the wine ran out. Israel began with wine – a marriage to God on Mount Sinai. But the wine ran out. Israel broke the covenant. But Yeshua turned the water, contained in six large vessels, and used for ritual purification, to new wine. It was even better than the first wine. His wine purifies us from the inside out, more effective than any purification ritual. Yeshua said, "I am the true vine." (John 15:1) Yeshua gives the wine of the kingdom of God through the New Covenant in His blood, and the new wine of His grace. On the third day, in the 'marriage in heaven', and in the millennium, the Bride will drink of the seventh vessel, the best wine: the joy of living with the Bridegroom in God's kingdom.

Ask Yeshua which 'water' in your life He wants to make into 'wine'.

Readings: John 2:1–11, John 1:3, 14–18, Hosea 6:1–3, John 15:1–8

25th Day of the 11th Month
Shvat, usually falling in January/February
Signs of the Kingdom
The Healing of the Nobleman's Son

So Jesus came again to Cana of Galilee where He had made the water wine. And there was a certain nobleman whose son was sick at Capernaum. *John 4:46*

This nobleman, who lived in Capernaum, had a son who was sick and about to die. He was desperate for a miracle. He had heard about how Yeshua turned water into wine at Cana, and now he heard that Yeshua was back at Cana. So the nobleman went up to Cana to fetch the miracle worker, so that He could visit Capernaum to perform a miracle on his son. Perhaps then his son would live.

When the nobleman implored Yeshua to come to Capernaum and heal his son, Yeshua gave a surprising reply. He said, "Unless you people see signs and wonders, you will by no means believe." (John 4:48) They wanted the miracles, and for them the miracles proved there was something special about Yeshua, and that He was some type of miracle worker. Yeshua's reply and delay frustrated the nobleman, because He appeared not to understand that his son was about to die and how desperate the situation was.

But it wasn't Yeshua who didn't grasp the situation. It was the nobleman. He hadn't grasped that the man he was talking to was the giver of life itself. He gives life and takes it, and He can raise the dead. He didn't need to make the long walk to Capernaum. The boy's life came from Him in the first place. He is the way, the truth and the life! (John 14:6) He simply said, "Go your way, your son lives." (John 4:50) The man believed and went, and at that same hour the fever departed from his son and he didn't die. He lived! Not only that, but he and the whole of his household believed in Yeshua, the giver of life. They all lived!

It is not a miracle you need, but Yeshua! He is the way, truth and life who gives all you need.

Readings: John 4:46–54, John 14:5, 6, John 1:4, Revelation 21:6, 22:12–17

SHVAT

26th Day of the 11th Month
Shvat, usually falling in January/February
Signs of the Kingdom
Healing at the Pool of Bethesda

Now a certain man was there who had an infirmity thirty-eight years.
When Jesus saw him lying there, and knew that he already had been
in that condition a long time, He said to him, "Do you want to be
made well?" *John 5:5, 6*

The next sign took place at the Pool of Bethesda, which means in Hebrew
'House of Kindness,' situated near the temple in Jerusalem. The pool
had five porches which symbolise God's grace. It was a Jewish feast,
and Yeshua went to this pool located by the Sheep Gate. Yeshua called
Himself the 'Sheep Gate' or 'The Door of the Sheep.' (John 10:7) He
saw there a number of sick people lying beside the pool, waiting for the
supernatural activity to stir the waters to bring healing. The first who
got into the pool would be healed.

Standing there Yeshua noticed a man who had been sick for a very
long time – thirty-eight years. Yeshua asked him, "Do you want to be
made well?" The man was unable to answer a direct yes or no. He was
at the healing pool in the vague hope of getting healed, but in reality
his hope had dissipated a long time ago. He was unable to get healed
because others would always get in the pool before him when the waters
were stirred up for healing. The religious system had not shown him
kindness. No one had helped him get in the pool at the right time. His
sickness had been caused by his sin so he probably felt unworthy. He
explained his situation to Yeshua with no expectancy of any change. He
was sick with hopelessness, despair, loneliness, guilt, and infirmity. He
was a lost sheep. But the Good Shepherd had come to Him to show him
mercy in his utter helplessness. He told him to get up. He obeyed and
immediately was made well. Yeshua told him to sin no more.

*Thank the Father for His grace, mercy, and kindness which makes us
completely well.*

Readings: John 5:1–15, 24, John 10:1–18, Psalm 23

27th Day of the 11th Month
Shvat, usually falling in January/February
Signs of the Kingdom
The Feeding of the Five Thousand

Then those men, when they had seen the sign that Jesus did, said, "This is truly the Prophet who is to come into the world." *John 6:14*

The feeding of the five thousand was a watershed for people unsure about whom they believed Yeshua to be. Many of those who partook of the miraculous bread that day on a grassy place in Galilee perceived that Yeshua was the Prophet who had been prophesied by Moses in Deuteronomy 18:15. They knew this coming Prophet would be like Moses, so when He gave them heavenly bread, they remembered the manna in the wilderness. When Yeshua took five barley loaves and two small fish, and fed five thousand men, with twelve baskets of left-over fragments, they took this to be a sign of the Messiah.

Yeshua perceived they wanted to make Him king, so He departed from them, and later taught the people concerning the bread. He told them, "I am the Bread of Life". They needed to come to Him. (John 6:35) He had not come to give them mere physical bread, but spiritual bread, which imparts eternal life, His own life. He would have to give Himself and die for them, like bread that is eaten to give life. They could not understand this and 'From that time many of His disciples went back and walked with Him no more.' (John 6:66) He was not the type of earthly Messiah figure they were looking for. He had not come to defeat the Roman occupiers, but to give eternal life to souls. Yeshua asked the twelve disciples if they wanted to turn back too, but Peter answered, "Lord, to whom shall we go? You have the words of eternal life. Also we have come to believe and know that You are the Christ, the Son of the living God." (John 6:68, 69) However Yeshua knew that Judas would betray Him to death. Following Yeshua would cost everything, but be the path to life.

Meditate on John 6:63, 'It is the Spirit who gives life; the flesh profits nothing....'

Readings: John 6, John 1:14, John 12:20–28, Deuteronomy 8:3

SHVAT

28th Day of the 11th Month
Shvat, usually falling in January/February
Signs of the Kingdom
Walking on the Water

So when they had rowed about three or four miles, they saw Jesus walking on the sea and drawing near the boat; and they were afraid.

John 6:19

This was a time of great danger. The multitude had eaten the miraculous and heavenly bread that Yeshua had given them, but now the disciples were in great danger of perceiving Him to be an earthly type of king or Messiah, not a heavenly one. Mark tells us that the disciples had not understood about the bread, and their hearts were hardened. (Mark 6:52) This situation, where they could have tried to make him into an earthly king, reminds us of the temptations of Yeshua in the wilderness, when He resisted the temptation to create bread out of stones, or to test God, or worship Satan for earthly advantage.

So Yeshua made the disciples get into the boat and go towards Capernaum and Bethsaida. (Mark 6:45–52) They departed from the crowds. Yeshua also escaped the crowds, going to the mountain to pray in solitude to His Father in Heaven. During the night however, a great wind blew up against the disciples, making it hard for them to progress with their oars, and the waves had become very dangerous with the strong wind.

Yeshua went to them, walking on the water. They were afraid, thinking He was a ghost. He said to them, "It is I; do not be afraid." Then they willingly received Him into the boat, and immediately the boat was at the land where they were going. (John 6:20, 21) He demonstrated to them that He was God. These few disciples in a little rowing boat saw His mighty power demonstrated, as King of heaven and earth. He didn't need to be 'made' a king. He was Almighty God, King of kings! Even the wind, waves and time obeyed Him!

Whenever you are in a storm, receive Yeshua the King into your 'boat', and trust in Him.

Readings: John 6:15–21, Matthew 14:13–33, Mark 6:30–56

29th Day of the 11th Month
Shvat, usually falling in January/February
Signs of the Kingdom
The Healing of the Man Born Blind

And Jesus said, "For judgement I have come into this world, that those who do not see may see, and that those who see may be made blind."
John 9:39

Yeshua saw a blind man, and His disciples asked if the man or his parents had sinned for him to be born blind. Unlike the man at the pool of Betheseda, this man's infirmity had not been caused by any obvious or specific sin. But he was still blind, and he still needed Yeshua the light of the world to heal his blindness. Before this encounter, Yeshua had said to a woman caught in adultery, "I am the light of the world. He who follows Me shall not walk in darkness, but have the light of life." (John 8:12) The Pharisees had to acknowledge that they were not without sin. Sin brings darkness and 'blindness'. Yeshua gives light so that we can see the truth about God and ourselves, receive mercy, and follow Him.

Yeshua made clay with mud and saliva and anointed the man's eyes, and sent him to the pool named 'Sent' – (Siloam). This pool of water could have been so named because the water was 'sent' from the Gihon Spring outside the city wall into the city, through Hezekiah's water tunnel. The pool of Siloam is situated at the base of Mount Zion. When the man washed in the pool at the lowest place, he walked back up the mountain seeing. He had gone where Yeshua sent him and washed off the dirt from his eyes. Once He had washed He could receive the revelation of Yeshua. When we receive the new birth and have our sins washed away by the blood of Yeshua, we receive spiritual revelation and understanding which it was impossible to receive before. Spiritual truth is a mystery to those who have not had their sins washed away. They cannot understand it. It is only by being washed in the blood of Yeshua, and cleansed from our sins, that we are able to truly perceive the light of the world.

In the end-times the blindness will be removed from the eyes of the Jewish nation to 'see'.

Readings: John 8:12–9:41, 2 Corinthians 3:1–4:6, Romans 11:25–27, Zechariah 12:10

SHVAT

30th Day of the 11th Month
Shvat, usually falling in January/February
Signs of the Kingdom
The Raising of Lazarus

Jesus said to her, "I am the resurrection and the life. He who believes in Me, though he may die, he shall live. And whoever lives and believes in Me shall never die." *John 11:25, 26*

We have seen so far in the signs of the kingdom, different aspects of the divinity of Yeshua. Now, in this seventh sign recounted by John, showing the works of Yeshua, He brings a dead man, Lazarus, back to life. He does this so that the onlookers will believe ᵗhat the Father had sent Him. (John 11:42) In this sign, Yeshua showed us that He is the one who has power over the ultimate and final enemy, death. He is the resurrection and the life. Even if we die, we live on in the world beyond, and on Resurrection Day He will bring us into resurrected life. Whoever believes in Yeshua shall never 'die'. The sting and fear of death is taken away. Though this mortal body may stop breathing, the soul and spirit will never die. It will simply pass into a greater and better life through Yeshua. Through Him we can escape an eternity in the fires of hell, to live with Him forever.

Lazarus, the man Yeshua raised back to life, was a friend of His. The sisters of Lazarus had sent Yeshua the message, "Lord, behold, he whom You love is sick." (John 11:3) He was expected to know who this meant, and that they were sure He would do something! When Yeshua came in His own perfect timing to the now grieving sisters, He demonstrated His love by weeping with them. But He also groaned in His Spirit. He did not grieve like they did. He was roused to bring the power of heaven against the power of death, to overcome it. His motivation was love. He didn't even require them to have faith. He simply looked to heaven, thanked the Father, knowing that He heard Him, and cried with a loud voice "Lazarus come forth!" Lazarus, who had been dead four days, came back to life.

Give thanks for the hope of resurrection. Pray for Israel's physical and spiritual resurrection.

Readings: John 11, 2 Corinthians 4:7–18, Ezekiel 37:1–14, 1 Corinthians 15

1st Day of the 12th Month in a Leap Year
Adar 1, usually falling in February/March
The Leap Month
Going Deeper

For though by this time you ought to be teachers, you need someone
to teach you again the first principles of the oracles of God....
Hebrews 5:12

Today we enter a new month. If this year is a leap year, then this is the
correct day on the Lunar Calendar. If however this year is not a leap year
on the Jewish Lunar Calendar, you may want to skip to the beginning
of the 12th month (Adar 2) so you can read about 'Purim' on the actual
days it occurs. You will need to check on the calendar for this year to
see if it has Adar 1 and Adar 2. If it does, that would signify that this
is a leap year and you need to read this leap month now. If however it
has just one Adar month, then this is not a leap year and you will need
to go straight to the readings for the 12th month (Adar).

The reason for having the leap month is that the Jewish Lunar
Calendar year contains fewer days than the Roman solar calendar year,
(approximately 354 days compared with 364 or 365 days). The leap
month occurs seven times in every nineteen years and is now worked out
according to arithmetical calculations. This enables the Lunar Calendar
to stay correlated with the correct seasons of the year. Otherwise Passover,
which is meant to be kept in the spring at the time of the barley harvest,
would move further and further into the year. In ancient times the leap
month was utilised when the barley crop was deemed to need another
month to ripen before harvesting at Passover.

If we are God's harvest field, we could suppose that the leap month
is a time for us to have some extra 'ripening' or maturing. This is like
Hebrews 5:12, which speaks of the need to learn again the first principles
of the oracles of God. We will look deeper into the cross.

*Deeper understanding and receiving from the cross is the key to your spiritual
maturity.*

Readings: Hebrews 5:12 – 14, 1 Corinthians 1–3

ADAR 1

2nd Day of the 12th Month in a Leap Year
Adar 1, usually falling in February/March
Psalm 22
Forsaken by God

My God, My God, why have You forsaken Me? *Psalm 22:1*

To go deeper into the meaning of the cross we will look in detail over the whole of this month at the prophetic scriptures of Psalm 22 and then Isaiah 53. Psalm 22 begins with the words 'My God, My God, why have You forsaken Me?' (Psalm 22:1) Yeshua actually quoted these words while He was hanging on the cross. (Matthew 27:46, Mark 15:34) This is one of the seven utterances of Yeshua from the cross and all seven of His utterances from the cross can be related to Psalm 22 in some way. The gospel writers quote this verse in Aramaic, which is closely related to the Hebrew of Psalm 22:1 'Eli, Eli, lama azavthani?' (Psalm 22:1) We have all experienced alienation from the Father in our own hearts because of our sin, but when Yeshua hung suffering on the cross, He experienced separation from His Father in Heaven more extremely than anyone else, and for the first time ever. Up until that point He always had intimate fellowship with the Father, continually experiencing His abiding presence in His life, so that He never did or said anything which He did not see the Father doing or saying. The Father and the Son were One. (John 10:30) On the cross God Himself was torn apart and separated. (Mark 15:38) The Father became inaccessible to the Son when He who knew no sin was made sin for us. (2 Corinthians 5:21) Sin could not enter the holy Godhead. He had to be separated from the Father in death. Adam and Eve, when they first sinned, had to be cast out from the Garden of Eden. Their intimate fellowship with God was broken and death entered the world. On the cross, Yeshua bore our separation from the Father, so that we can be reconciled to God and have fellowship with the Father through the Holy Spirit. (2 Corinthians 5:18–21)

Leave your sin at the cross, in Yeshua, and, forgiven, receive fellowship with the Father.

Readings: Psalm 22:1, 2, Genesis 2, 3, Mark.15:33–39, 2 Corinthians 5:17–21, Romans 5:1, 2

3rd Day of the 12th Month in a Leap Year
Adar 1, usually falling in February/March
Psalm 22
Despised and Ridiculed

All those who see Me ridicule Me; They shoot out the lip, they shake the head, saying, "He trusted in the LORD, let Him rescue Him; Let Him deliver Him, since He delights in Him!" Psalm 22:7, 8

In Psalm 22:3 we are reminded that God is holy, and is enthroned in the praises of Israel. The fathers of Israel, despite their many failings were heard by God when they cried out to Him. God delivered them from their troubles when He heard their cries. And yet Yeshua did not experience deliverance from the cross. He had to pass through the dark suffering alone and without the comfort of the Father.

In the eyes of men, Yeshua became as nothing, of no more worth than a worm. He became a 'reproach of men, and despised by the people.' (Psalm 22:6) Yeshua experienced the entirety of our rejection by His fellow men. The Jewish nation, the whole human race, represented by the Romans, and God the Father, rejected Him. None could deliver Him, not even His mother. In Psalm 22:8, those ridiculing say, "He trusted in the LORD, let Him rescue Him; Let Him deliver Him, since He delights in Him!" We see these words fulfilled at the base of the cross, where the chief priests, scribes and elders mocked Him, saying, "He saved others; Himself He cannot save. If He is the King of Israel let Him now come down from the cross, and we will believe Him. He trusted in God, let Him deliver Him now if He will have Him; for He said, 'I am the Son of God.'" Even the robbers who were crucified with Him reviled Him with the same thing. (Matthew 27:41–44) At His trial He was mocked and spat upon. He took our rejection so that we can experience self-worth and acceptance with God.

Yeshua bore your rejection so that your security and safety can be in God. (Psalm 31:19, 20)

Readings: Psalm 22:3–8, Matthew 27:27–54, Mark 15:29–32, Luke 23:35, Ephesians 1:3–6

ADAR 1

4th Day of the 12th Month in a Leap Year
Adar 1, usually falling in February/March
Psalm 22
His Mother

But You are He who took Me out of the womb, You made Me trust while on My mother's breasts. *Psalm 22:9*

Your Bible should have the words You, He, Me and My in Psalm 22 beginning with capital letters. The use of the capital letter shows that these are the words of Yeshua to His Father and also about Himself. They are not merely the words of King David who wrote the Psalm. They were divinely inspired to express the words of God Himself.

Yeshua had a human mother, and He came forth from her womb in the normal manner, and was nurtured at her breasts. He acknowledged that His relationship with His mother from His birth was a vital part of His emotional well-being. It was those weeks and months as a small infant at the breast that He learnt to trust. This is true for all of us. We all came into the world totally dependent on our mother for our life. Her life sustained and kept us. Babies who do not have that nurturing either die or they grow up with severe emotional problems. It is the love, life, and joy of the mother that give the child its sense of well-being and ability to cope with life. The ability to trust comes from that first experience of trusting.

Yeshua, whilst nailed to the cross looked down at His mother and at the disciple John, and said to her, "Woman, behold your son!" and to John, "Behold your mother!" (John 19:26, 27) From that hour the disciple took Yeshua's mother to his own home. Yeshua provided for His mother in her time of vulnerability and need, by giving her a new son. He understands the pain of loss and separation between parent and child. At the cross He provides for any lack and heals our pain, nurturing and filling our hearts with His love.

Ask God to help you forgive your parents, to receive His healing love, and to love them.

Readings: Psalm 22:9, Exodus 20:12, Luke 2, Matthew 10:37, Matthew 12:46–50

5th Day of the 12th Month in a Leap Year
Adar 1, usually falling in February/March
Psalm 22
Trusting God

> I was cast upon You from birth, from My mother's womb You have been My God. Be not far from Me, for trouble is near; for there is none to help. *Psalm 22:10, 11*

Yeshua received human nurture from His mother, but we see that, from the moment of birth, He actually depended on God. That too is true for all of us. Our human mother cares for us, but it is God who gives us life. From His birth however, Yeshua actually knew His Heavenly Father as God. As a human being Yeshua was unique, because He never rebelled or strayed from God. The rest of us learned that we have an independent 'will' by about the age of two. We quickly needed training in wisdom and behaviour. Without that discipline from our parents we would have learned no boundaries, and life would be chaotic, and we would become lawless and disobedient. As we grew older the evidence became apparent that we have indeed inherited sin from the parents of the human race, Adam and Eve, and we became responsible and accountable for breaking God's commandments.

It was not so with Yeshua. From His birth He submitted to the Father as His Lord. It was in His nature before He could even understand, since He was one with the Father. He was God manifest as a human being, even as a baby. He never knew what it was like to not have the Father near. That is, until He took our sin upon Himself in the Garden of Gethsemane, and went to the cross bearing our transgression before God. At the cross He was alone and without help. He remembered the help of the Father that He no longer experienced. It was by faith that He trusted at the cross, to pass through death on our behalf to conquer it. Yeshua cried out with a loud voice, and quoting Psalm 31:5 said, "Father, 'into Your hands I commit My spirit.' Having said this, He breathed His last." (Luke 23:46)

Yeshua committed His spirit to God in death so we can commit our spirit to God in life.

Readings: Psalm 22:10–11, Psalm 31, Psalm 37:5–6, 39–40

6th Day of the 12th Month in a Leap Year
Adar 1, usually falling in February/March
Psalm 22
Father Forgive Them

Many bulls have surrounded Me; strong bulls of Bashan have encircled
Me, they gape at Me with their mouths, like a raging and roaring lion.

Psalm 22:12, 13

While Yeshua hung on the cross, the people surrounded Him below.
They are described graphically in Psalm 22 as being like strong bulls of
Bashan encircling Him, gaping at Him with their mouths, like a raging
and roaring lion.

Those people who surrounded Yeshua in His final hours, and who
watched Him as He suffered in agony on the cross, are likened to strong
animals. They are senseless and without reasoning. The bulls of Bashan
remind us of the king and people of Bashan who opposed Moses in the
wilderness. (Numbers 21:33–35) They didn't know why they did what
they did. The Israelites had not done anything against them. Their
hatred wasn't rational. Before Yeshua, the people became like dumb and
senseless animals driven by base instincts. They were driven by irrational
and demonically-inspired hatred against God.

Luke 23:34 tells us that Yeshua, when He was crucified at Calvary
said, "Father, forgive them, for they do not know what they do." He
asked His Father to forgive them. That was what He had come to do.
Human beings need to be rescued from their hatred and rebellion against
the Father. None of us truly understands the horror of our sin. We do
not even know or understand ourselves. Just as lions are not taught to
rage and roar, they simply do so because that is their nature, so it is in
the nature of mankind to oppose God and live independent of Him.
But Yeshua, whose nature is love, loved His enemies to the end, giving
mercy in place of cruel injustice, giving undeserved forgiveness and
unconditional love.

Meditate on Yeshua's example of loving His enemies, even on the cross.

Readings: Psalm 22:12–13, Numbers 21:33–35, Acts 7:51–60, Romans
5:6–11

7th Day of the 12th Month in a Leap Year
Adar 1, usually falling in February/March
Psalm 22
Thirsty

I am poured out like water, and all My bones are out of joint; My heart is like wax; it has melted within Me. *Psalm 22:14, 15*

We come now to the extraordinary verses of biblical prophecy which describe in detail what Yeshua was to experience when He was crucified on the cross. These words were written centuries before the Roman method of execution, crucifixion, had ever even been conceived of. A man from South Africa, Dr James van Zijl, made a study of the physical experience of crucifixion from his point of view as a medical doctor. He came to the conclusion that Psalm 22:14–18 accurately describes the experience of crucifixion.

When He was crucified, Yeshua would have suffered extreme thirst and dehydration. We know this not only from medical science, but from the words of Yeshua on the cross when He said, "I thirst!" (John 19:28) The one through whom living water flows (John 4:14, 7:37, 38), was poured out like water physically, mentally and spiritually in our place, so that He can fill us with His Spirit. He became our drink offering. Drink offerings were offered with the sacrifices and offerings of the Old Covenant. He was 'poured out' to the Father.

Yeshua's shoulders would have been dislocated on the cross and his bones pulled out of joint. His heart became like melted wax. Acute heart failure would have caused water to accumulate around His heart (like melted wax). This was released when the soldiers pierced His side. The tight chest muscles restricted His breathing, causing a shortage of oxygen, profuse perspiration, muscle cramps, and weakness, and His tongue would have clung to his jaws as described in verse 15. Yeshua became thirsty that we may drink of His life.

Thank Yeshua for pouring Himself as the drink offering so that you can receive living water.

Readings: Psalm 22:14, 15, John 19:28–30, John 4:7–34, 7:37–41

8th Day of the 12th Month in a Leap Year
Adar 1, usually falling in February/March
Psalm 22
Pierced

For dogs have surrounded Me; the congregation of the wicked has enclosed Me, they pierced My hands and My feet; I can count all My bones. They look and stare at Me, they divide My garments among them, and for My clothing they cast lots. *Psalm 22:16–18*

King David wrote these prophetic words about 1000 years before the crucifixion took place on Mount Moriah. And over 800 years before he wrote, Abraham obeyed God by taking his son Isaac to the very same Mount Moriah to offer a sacrifice. When Isaac carried the wood, he foreshadowed Yeshua carrying the cross. The Father does not require human sacrifice. A ram, caught by its horns in a thicket, sufficed for Abraham. God Himself would provide the Lamb, not bound and laid on an altar, but nailed to a cross. (Genesis 22:8–14)

Crucifixion nails discovered by archaeologists are four-sided, approximately fifteen centimetres in length, with a sharp point at the end which was hammered through the wrists, tearing apart the bones. The large median nerve pulled across the edge of the nail would cause the most extreme pain ever, cramping the thumbs and causing the imbedding of the thumb nails deep into the palm of the hands. A longer nail would have been driven through the feet, one on top of the other, piercing through the small bones, the knees in a bent position. It was only by placing His full weight on the feet, and straightening the knees, that the chest muscles could slacken to release air from the lungs to allow for a breath to be snatched quickly before replacing the weight on the dislocated shoulders. In these contorted positions and pain, He could feel and count all His bones, made visible as He hung naked upon the cross, His clothing having been given away by lots. (John 19:23–24)

Thank the Father for providing the Lamb of God to suffer and pass through death for you.

Readings: Psalm 22:16–21, Genesis 22:1–14, John 19:23–24, Revelation 1:7

9th Day of the 12th Month in a Leap Year
Adar 1, usually falling in February/March
Psalm 22
God's Answer

Save Me from the lion's mouth and from the horns of the wild oxen! You have answered Me. *Psalm 22:21*

Yeshua was not delivered from suffering and death on the cross, because that was the very purpose for which He came into the world. But the Father did deliver Him from the grip of death, to raise Him up in His resurrection body, never to die again. The grip of death is described as the power of the dog, the lion's mouth, and the horns of wild oxen. Normally people do not escape these. Once you are trapped and caught by them there is no way out. But the Father heard Yeshua's cry, and on the third day brought Him back from the grip of death. He answered Him and raised Him back to resurrection life.

God has answered the cry of every human being who is held by the grip of the fear of death. As the first fruits of the resurrection, we have the hope of the resurrection from the dead; and before the resurrection, if He has not returned before we die, we will have life with Him in Heaven. The Apostle Paul wrote, 'So when this corruptible has put on incorruption, and this mortal has put on immortality, then shall be brought to pass the saying that is written: "Death is swallowed up in victory." "O Death, where is your sting? O Hades, where is your victory?" The sting of death is sin, and the strength of sin is the law. But thanks be to God, who gives us the victory through our Lord Jesus Christ.' (1 Corinthians 15:54–57) The fear of death holds people in bondage. Hebrews 2:14–15 says that He shared our flesh and blood, that 'through death He might destroy him who had the power of death, that is, the devil, and release those who through fear of death were all their lifetime subject to bondage.'

If you have any fear of death, ask the Lord to remove it through faith in the risen Lord.

Readings: Psalm 22:21, 24, Psalm 23:4, Hebrews 1, 2, 1 Corinthians 15:50–58

10th Day of the 12th Month in a Leap Year
Adar 1, usually falling in February/March
Psalm 22
His Brethren

I will declare Your name to My brethren; in the midst of the assembly I will praise You. *Psalm 22:22*

Psalm 22:22–28 describes the kingdom benefits won by Yeshua on the cross. The first is us! We are called His brethren. We know He is calling us His brethren in this verse because it is stated as such in Hebrews 2:12. Yeshua is described as the captain of our salvation, made perfect through sufferings and bringing many sons to glory. Those sons are the redeemed, all those who are saved through faith in His perfect sacrifice upon the cross to take away our sins. He makes Himself equal with us. We are told that those who are sanctified (us), and the one who sanctifies, (Yeshua), are all 'of one' and for that reason He is not ashamed to call them brethren, quoting Psalm 22:22.

Yeshua is the Son of God, but we who are being transformed and conformed in His perfect image are now called sons of God. We have been adopted by the Father into His family as sons. Galatians 4:5 says those who were under the law are redeemed that we may obtain adoptions as sons. Ephesians 1:5, 6 says that we have been predestined to be adopted as sons 'by Jesus Christ to Himself, according to the good pleasure of His will, to the praise of the glory of His grace, by which He made us accepted in the Beloved.' This is who we are. We are not to think of ourselves as 'worms' and 'miserable sinners'. We are the redeemed, clothed in the righteousness of God, humbly adopted into His family as sons and daughters of God. We join the Son in the great assembly, honouring and praising the Father.

Yeshua will bring forth salvation and praise from every nation to bring worship to the Father. He is our satisfaction. We are to seek Him and praise Him, and live forever!

Thank the Father for adopting you as a son or daughter of God, and for what that means.

Readings: Psalm 22:22–28, Hebrews 2:10–18, Hebrews 10:12–14, Ephesians 1:3–6

11th Day of the 12th Month in a Leap Year
Adar 1, usually falling in February/March
Psalm 22
With Him in Paradise

All the prosperous of the earth shall eat and worship, all those who go down to the dust shall bow before Him. Psalm 22:29

This verse, as we approach the end of Psalm 22, gives us the hope of Heaven. The prosperous are those who have received God's grace. There is no one richer on the earth than someone who has received of the abundant grace of God and the love of the Father. With Him, we are richer than the richest multi-millionaire in the world, because we have heaven in our hearts. The saved will eat of the bread of the broken body of Yeshua, His life given for us. His life is our life, and sustained by Him we worship the Father. For the saved, their worship does not end when they die (go down to the dust), but continues in the world beyond, where they will bow before the Lord of Heaven and earth.

This brings us to another of the utterances of Yeshua from the cross. Yeshua was crucified between two thieves. They faced death, with the Messiah in between them. Luke, in his Gospel, calls them criminals. At first they both mocked and reviled Yeshua, but then their true hearts were revealed, and one of the criminals joined in the mockery of the soldiers, blaspheming and saying, "If You are the Christ, save Yourself and us." (Luke 23:39) His heart was hardened and he had lost the fear of the Lord. In his anger and bitterness he failed to recognise his true need. He thought he needed to be saved from the cross. He didn't realise he needed to have his soul saved. The other criminal however acknowledged his guilt before God and he recognised that, unlike him, Yeshua had done no wrong. So he said to Yeshua, "Lord, remember me when You come into Your kingdom." Yeshua responded, full of grace, "Assuredly, I say to you, today you will be with Me in Paradise." (Luke 23:43)

Meditate on the heart attitude which finds salvation, and the promise of Paradise.

Readings: Psalm 22:29, Matthew 27:38–44, Luke 23:32–43

ADAR 1

12th Day of the 12th Month in a Leap Year
Adar 1, usually falling in February/March
Psalm 22
It is Finished

A posterity shall serve Him, It will be recounted of the Lord to the next generation, They will come and declare His righteousness to a people who will be born, that He has done this. *Psalm 22:30, 31*

Psalm 22 ends with the affirmation that there would be a 'generation' – a great company of people stretching through the centuries to come, who would be redeemed through Yeshua, to serve Him. This 'generation' of believers would declare to those who come after them, the righteousness of Yeshua; that He made a complete and perfect work on the cross. His fame would be passed from generation to generation. What Yeshua accomplished on the cross would be passed from adult to child, until the end of the age.

This brings us to the final utterance of Yeshua on the cross. Yeshua, knowing that He had atoned for the sin of the world on the cross, and knowing 'that all things were now accomplished' (John 19:28) said, "I thirst!" There was a vessel of sour wine there so they filled a sponge with sour wine, put it on hyssop, and put it to His mouth. 'So when Jesus had received the sour wine, He said, "It is finished!" And bowing His head, He gave up His spirit.' (John 19:30)

The root of the Hebrew verb for 'finish, make perfect, perish, complete and end', is 'kalah'. This is the same as the Hebrew word for bride, 'kalah'. Normally, at a Jewish betrothal, the bride and bridegroom symbolically drink from a shared cup of wine. Yeshua took sour wine in sorrow, to finish, complete, and make perfect the payment for His Bride. When Yeshua cried "It is Finished!" sin and death were atoned for, and His Bride, purchased.

You are the posterity of Yeshua, paid for in full upon the cross. Worship and serve Him.

Readings: Psalm 22:30, 31, John 19:28–30, Exodus 12:21–27

13th Day of the 12th Month in a Leap Year
Adar 1, usually falling in February/March
Isaiah 53
God's Servant

Behold, My Servant shall deal prudently; He shall be exalted and extolled and be very high. *Isaiah 52:13*

Today we begin to look at another passage from the Old Testament which prophesies Yeshua and His suffering upon the cross. As in Psalm 22, your Bible should have capital letters on the words He, His and My and any other words that refer to God the Father or God the Son, Yeshua. The prophetic passage in Isaiah 53 actually begins towards the end of Isaiah 52 with the exhortation to 'look at' or 'behold' God's Servant. This Servant is Yeshua. It is written My Servant – with capital letters to show He is the Son of the Father, One God. The Son came to earth, leaving the glory of Heaven, to do the will of the Father.

We are to look and see the wisdom of the Son. In Proverbs 8, Yeshua is Wisdom personified. Though He humbles Himself to become a servant, we are told 'He shall be exalted and extolled and be very high.' (Isaiah 52:13) In Philippians 2:7–9 Yeshua, 'being in the form of God, made Himself of no reputation, taking the form of a bondservant', and 'coming in the likeness of men', and 'being found in appearance as a man, He humbled Himself and became obedient to the point of death, even the death of the cross. Therefore God also has highly exalted Him and given Him the name which is above every name...' Yeshua is the ultimate expression and example of humility. This is in contrast to the pride of Lucifer (Satan) who, though created by God, wanted to make Himself equal with God. Isaiah 14:11–15 describes his fall. Pride always comes before a fall. (Proverbs 16:18) Yeshua's humility defeated the pride of man, to redeem with His blood, people from all the earth.

Do you happily take the lowest place? Are you willing to be considered of no reputation?

Readings: Isaiah 52:13–15, Luke 22:24–27, Philippians 2:1–11, Isaiah 14:11–15

14th Day of the 12th Month in a Leap Month
Adar 1, usually falling in February/March
Isaiah 53
No Beauty to Desire

For He shall grow up before Him as a tender plant, And as a root out of dry ground. He has no form or comeliness; And when we see Him, There is no beauty that we should desire Him. *Isaiah 53:2*

Isaiah 53 begins with the question – 'Who has believed our report?' The question is – who can recognise the Son of God? 'To whom has the arm of the LORD been revealed?' (Isaiah 53:1) This prophecy shows that it would be easy for people to 'miss' the Messiah when they saw Him and not recognise who He was. He would not look as they expected their Messiah to look. When the people, who lived in Israel, saw Yeshua walking in their land, they saw the Jewish man Yeshua. They saw a young man, the son of a carpenter. They saw a man who grew up in Nazareth like a 'tender plant, and as a root out of dry ground.' (Isaiah 53:2) He was from that rather unusual, rejected group of people in Nazareth, and people wondered if anything good could come from among them. (John 1:46) He was born in a stable. He was the son of Mary and Joseph. He had brothers and sisters. He served His parents. He didn't grow up in a palace. He didn't wear fine clothes and a crown and sit on a throne. He didn't look like a king.

It was easy to miss the fact that this man was the Messiah, and not recognise Him. He walked the hills of Judea, Samaria and Galilee. He sat in boats with fishermen. He slept out rough on the Mount of Olives. Sometimes there was no water to wash in. His hair got matted, dusty and greasy. Walking all those miles He got sweaty and smelly in the soaring heat. The Messiah could not be physically recognised. He had to be spiritually revealed.

Yeshua took every aspect of your physical shame that you may share in His glory.

Readings: Isaiah 53:1, 2, Isaiah 61:3, Hebrews 12:1, 2

15th Day of the 12th Month in a Leap Year
Adar 1, usually falling in February/March
Isaiah 53
A Man of Sorrows

He is despised and rejected by men, A Man of sorrows and acquainted with grief. And we hid, as it were, our faces from Him; He was despised, and we did not esteem Him. *Isaiah 53:3*

Not only did most people, including the temple authorities fail to recognise their Messiah, but they also rejected Him. The King of glory came from the highest place in Heaven to walk on earth, and experience the derision and rejection of the people He created and loved. Yeshua, God incarnate as a Man, suffered many sorrows and was acquainted with grief. The Hebrew word for sorrows, 'makobot', also means 'afflictions, griefs, and pains'.

Yeshua experienced the different types of grief that we as human beings experience. When He heard that His cousin, John the Baptiser, was dead He obviously experienced grief and loss, because we are told that He departed by boat to a deserted place by Himself. (Matthew 14:13) He experienced heavy sorrow for others – weeping over Jerusalem (Luke 19:41), and weeping at the death of Lazarus. (John 11:35) He must have experienced the loss of His earthly father Joseph, since Joseph does not occur in the later stories of Yeshua. He experienced the grief of seeing the afflictions that people suffer as a consequence of sin and their rejection of Him. Another type of grief that He experienced was rejection. The Scribes and the Pharisees continually tried to accuse Him of breaking their laws, (meaning their own man-made laws), accusing Him of breaking the Sabbath, speaking with women and the outcasts of society, and accusing Him of blasphemy. The authorities at the temple, which He loved, rejected Him. In the Garden of Gethsemane His disciples failed to pray, but fell asleep as anguish and bitter sorrow fell upon Him. He was denied and was betrayed to death, imprisoned, mocked, scourged and crucified as a 'cursed outcast'. He suffered grief.

Yeshua took your rejection and grief so you may experience His esteem, comfort and joy.

Readings: Isaiah 53:3, Matthew 27:27–31, Psalm 94:19

ADAR 1

16th Day of the 12th Month in a Leap Year
Adar 1, usually falling in February/March
Isaiah 53
Our Griefs and Sorrows

Surely He has borne our griefs and carried our sorrows.... *Isaiah 53:4*

Yeshua bore our 'griefs' – which in this verse can also be translated 'sicknesses'. Sickness in our soul usually eventually manifests in sickness in our body. It is possible to have grief and sadness 'locked up' in our spirit from the past. Wounds and traumas from such things as abandonment, rejection, abuse, and betrayal, never disappear. They just sink into our subconscious to re-emerge as surprising reactions when our 'buttons are pushed', causing sudden outbursts of anger or tears, passivity and addictions, and disease.

This verse gives us hope. No-one can pass through life entirely escaping the pains and traumas of life, because we live in a fallen world with imperfect people. But we are told in the verse that He has 'borne' – that means –'lifted up from us' and 'carried away from us' all the consequences of our sin and the sin of other people. This is like the scapegoat, which, on the Day of Atonement, carried away the sins of Israel into the wilderness. (Leviticus 16:21, 22) Yeshua carries away our grief. When Yeshua died on the cross He took upon Himself all the pain that you have experienced or will ever experience. It came upon Him. In the wilderness, Aaron the High Priest laid his hand on the head of the goat to transfer the sins of Israel onto it, so that it could carry them away, never to be seen again. Similarly you are to make a transaction at the cross, giving Him your sin or pain, exchanging it with Him. When you repent of your sins, and forgive whoever has hurt you, and you receive His forgiveness, and forgive yourself, Yeshua not only takes away the sin and guilt, but He also takes away the pain and the wound. The sickness of soul and body will go. Then you will need to transform your thinking to see God as the good and loving Father that He truly is.

Ask Yeshua to show you what grief, pain and sickness He wants to lift off you today.

Readings: Leviticus 16:20–22, Numbers 21:4–9, Psalm 147:3, 103:1–5, Romans 12:1, 2

17th Day of the 12th Month in a Leap Year
Adar 1, usually falling in February/March
Isaiah 53
Misunderstood

Yet we esteemed Him stricken, smitten by God and afflicted.

Isaiah 53:4

When Yeshua became our scapegoat to bear away our griefs and sorrows, to heal all our wounds, we didn't understand what He was doing. Nobody who looked at Yeshua as He hung on the cross understood that He was taking away into Himself, all the guilt, sin, wounds, sickness, and diseases, of the whole of mankind, bearing it away as the perfect sacrifice. People thought that He was being stricken and afflicted by God. They thought it was some sort of divine retribution.

At His trial, scourging, and crucifixion, the crowd and onlookers, (which represents each one of us), thought He was suffering because of His own sins. They falsely accused him of blasphemy, or made the false accusation that He had been stirring up trouble, and that He planned to tear down the temple and rebuild it in three days. (Mark 14:57–59) They did not understand His true purpose. They did not understand that He was totally sinless and blameless. He was the perfect Lamb of God without spot or blemish.

Yeshua knew what it was to be completely misunderstood, falsely blamed and accused, assumed to be guilty of sin He had not committed. It was our sin that He, the innocent One took on our behalf, yet we did not understand. We thought He was crucified because of His own sins or weaknesses. The people did not understand who He was, or what He was doing, or why He was doing it. He took in our place all misunderstanding and false accusation. He knows and understands us completely. Now, when people judge us wrongly and misunderstand us, we know that He understands us and does not accuse us.

When people misjudge you and misunderstand you, take comfort that God delights in you.

Readings: Mark 14:55 – 15:14, Matthew 26:55–27:26, Job 42, Isaiah 61:7

18th Day of the 12th Month in a Leap Year
Adar 1, usually falling in February/March
Isaiah 53
Wounded

But He was wounded for our transgressions.... *Isaiah 53:5*

We have all transgressed God's commandments. We are all transgressors. None of us has perfectly kept all the 10 Commandments. Every one of us stands guilty before God of breaking His perfect laws. Romans 3:10–12 says, "There is none righteous, no, not one; there is none who understands; There is none who seeks after God. They have all turned aside; They have together become unprofitable; There is none who does good, no, not one." No matter how righteous we think we may be, before God, our righteousness is 'like filthy rags' (Isaiah 64:6), such is His extreme holiness. Every one of us deserves to go to hell.

Yeshua is the only Man who has never broken any of God's commandments. Innocent before the Father, He took upon Himself the guilt of our transgressions in our place. He stood before Pontius Pilate falsely accused of breaking the law. The crowd, given the choice between Barabbas the criminal, and Yeshua, chose to release Barabbas but have Yeshua sentenced to death. The innocent One was punished in place of the guilty. Roman soldiers whipped Yeshua, and His head was wounded by the crown of thorns. The thorns of the crown were probably those of a local bush, about 2.5 cm long, with barbs like fish hooks which became irreversibly embedded in the flesh. The whip with which He was scourged had a short wooden handle, and nine leather thongs, each with glass, bone, and stone embedded into it. These dug into the flesh with every stroke, cutting right to the bone, ripping out pieces of flesh. Yeshua received these wounds, because He had taken your transgressions on Himself, so that you can escape the torment and wounds of hell, and to give you in exchange, His undeserved grace, and the glories of heaven.

Thank Yeshua for taking the wounds that you deserve for breaking His commandments.

Readings: Isaiah 53:5, Luke 23:16–25, Isaiah 64:6, Jeremiah 31:16–20

19th Day of the 12th Month in a Leap Year
Adar 1, usually falling in February/March
Isaiah 53
Bruised

He was bruised for our iniquities.... *Isaiah 53:5*

Our iniquities are all our faults, defects, things we do wrong, our failings and shortcomings. Some of these we may have inherited from the sins of our fathers. They can be wrong mind-sets, attitudes of heart and inclinations, as well as obvious sin. Very often we are not aware of our own iniquities. They are more subtle than the obvious sins prohibited in the 10 Commandments. In Psalm 51, King David asked God to wash him clean from his iniquities and cleanse him from all his sins. (Psalm 51:1, 2)

Yeshua was bruised for our iniquities. Our iniquities merit our bruising. Very often we bruise and hurt others and ourselves by our iniquities. We are careless of people's feelings and treat people roughly, without the respect and care that they deserve. Isaiah prophesied that the Messiah would not break a bruised reed, and this is quoted in Matthew 12:20. God wants to give us His ability to be sensitive to the needs and feelings of others, not carelessly bruising the sensitive and tender ones, especially those closest to us.

Yeshua was bruised, not only from the wounds that He received, but from the cross that He carried. He had to bear its heavy weight across His shoulders. Yeshua took upon Himself all of our bruises – where we have been hurt by others, or where we deserve to be hurt back for the wounds we ourselves have inflicted on others. He took our emotional pains and lacks. He carried our heavy burdens, so that we may receive the tender mercy of God, who does not look on our faults, but sees goodness in us, and rejoices over each one of us, despite all of our shortcomings, because He was bruised for our iniquities in our place.

Ask God to help you always to show the same tender kindness to others as He does to you.

Readings: Psalm 51: 1, 2, Isaiah 42:1–9, Matthew 12:15–23

20th Day of the 12th Month in a Leap Year
Adar 1, usually falling in February/March
Isaiah 53
Chastised

The chastisement for our peace was upon Him.... *Isaiah 53:5*

Yeshua took our punishment, our chastisement upon Himself. He removes our guilt to give us peace with God, with ourselves and with our neighbour. Under the Law of Moses, peace offerings were offered by fire to the Lord. Leviticus 3 tells us that Aaron the Priest put his hand on the head of the animal that was offered, it was killed at the door of the tabernacle of Meeting, and the blood was sprinkled around the altar. God gives us peace – in our minds and in our hearts when He removes our guilt at the cross. The whole animal, including its entrails, was burnt. God is concerned about our innermost parts – where we usually carry our hidden tensions, guilt and anxieties, and where we have need for the peace of the Lord.

Yeshua, our peace offering, took our chastisement as He passed through the fires of God's holy wrath against sin. His blood was sprinkled in the most holy place in heaven, to bring us peace with God. It is His blood, which He sprinkles in Heaven, which has reconciled us with the Father. There is no longer any accusation against us. It has all been cancelled and erased. When nagging thoughts, fears and guilt recur, we are to point to the blood sprinkled on the Mercy Seat in Heaven, and silence our accuser. We have peace with God. Now we must find peace with ourselves, forgiving ourselves and our neighbour. We are to live in the conscious awareness of His smile of favour and grace, because He has heard our prayers of repentance, and He holds no guilt of sin against us.

Yeshua is our peace and He gave us His peace. He does not want us to punish ourselves. He wants us to let the past go, be free and walk in His deep and certain peace.

The peace offerings were offered with thanksgiving. Give thanks for your peace with God.

Readings: Leviticus 3, 7:11–18, Numbers 10:10, Acts 10:36, Revelation 1:4

21st Day of the 12th Month in a Leap Year
Adar 1, usually falling in February/March
Isaiah 53
His Stripes

And by His stripes we are healed. *Isaiah 53:5*

The sufferings and afflictions of Yeshua not only bought for us the salvation of our souls, but also the healing of our bodies. Just as the death of Yeshua on the cross, and His blood poured out for us, are effective through faith to cleanse us from all sin and redeem us back to God, so too, through faith in Him, His stripes, His wounds, are effective to heal and remove any physical disease or condition in our bodies, and restore us to perfect health.

The word 'stripes' in this verse, recalls for us the stripes that were made across Yeshua's back when He was scourged and whipped before being crucified. These stripes were prophesied, not only in this verse, but also in Isaiah 50:6 which says "I gave My back to those who struck Me, and My cheeks to those who plucked out the beard; I did not hide My face from shame and spitting." The stripes of Yeshua are also prophesied in Psalm 129:3, which says "...The plowers plowed on my back; they made their furrows long."

The scourging of Yeshua is recounted in Matthew 27:26, Mark 15:15 and John 19:1. According to Roman law no more than 40 lashes could be given but the Jews decided upon 39 lashes. These wounds were taken by the sinless Lamb of God, Yeshua, in exchange for your healing. Psalm 103 tells us that God forgives all your iniquities and heals all your diseases. The Apostle Peter wrote that Yeshua 'Himself bore our sins in His own body on the tree, that we, having died to sins, might live for righteousness – by whose stripes you were healed.' (1 Peter 2:24) This says that you 'were healed', not 'will be healed'. It is an accomplished fact. He has done it. Now you can receive it through faith.

Thank Yeshua for your healing provided through the stripes, the wounds on His body.

Readings: Isaiah 50:4–6, Psalm 129:1–4, Psalm 103:1–5, 1 Peter 2:18–25, James 5:14–18

ADAR 1

22nd Day of the 12th Month in a Leap Year
Adar 1, usually falling in February/March
Isaiah 53
Like Sheep

All we like sheep have gone astray; We have turned, every one, to his own way; And the LORD has laid on Him the iniquity of us all.

Isaiah 53:6

This verse is familiar to many of us from hearing it sung in Handel's "Messiah". We are likened to sheep which go astray and turn to their own way. For people familiar with the ways of sheep, this is easy to understand. Sheep on the whole, will not come happily trotting towards you if you call their name. They are nervous and timid creatures, and will quickly dart away when approached, not thinking or caring where they are going. They will wander off on whatever path they find in front of them. They find their way through fences, walls and hedges, stubbornly choosing their own foolish way, not considering the consequences or the dangers of that particular course of action. They get stuck, lost, and end up in desperate and dangerous situations, where they are totally dependent on their shepherd to rescue them. Even when their shepherd is trying to rescue them they will often try to escape his clutches.

This is a picture of us in our iniquity. We do not understand the forces of sin which drive us. Wounds and lies from the devil cause us not to trust and obey our good shepherd. Failing to believe that He is good and kind, we run away and choose our own path. We wilfully try to work out our own destiny, pursuing our own dreams and desires, away from our heavenly Father. We get ourselves stuck, in a dangerous place, far from the Father.

Yeshua the Good Shepherd lovingly pursued and rescued His sheep when He died on the cross, following us into our dark place of separation from the Father. He bore on Himself the iniquity of His sheep so that you can be restored safely back to fellowship with the Father.

Yield to the Father like a sheep caught up in the arms of the Good Shepherd. (1 Peter 2:25)

Readings: Psalm 23, John 10:11, Hebrews 13:20, 21, 1 Peter 2:25

23rd Day of the 12th Month in a Leap Year
Adar 1, usually falling in February/March
Isaiah 53
Oppressed and Afflicted

He was oppressed and He was afflicted, Yet He opened not His mouth.... *Isaiah 53:7*

Yeshua is not only the Good Shepherd of the Sheep, but He came to become one of us. He became as it were a 'sheep'. He is not only the 'Lamb of God' in the sacrificial death that He died, but in the life that He lived. He became 'a sheep', identifying with us in our human condition, and He suffered everything that we suffer. By the time He died on the cross, He had identified with all of our conditions. In the Garden of Gethsemane, in His scourging and on the cross, He physically took all of our oppressions and afflictions upon Himself. The powers of darkness, which come against human beings, came against Yeshua. Physically, emotionally, spiritually, He followed His sheep into the darkest places of isolation, depression, grief, shock, pain, trauma and oppression, from men, and demons, that any person has ever experienced. He has even experienced the feelings experienced by people in their last moments before being executed. His body was smashed, His soul was crushed, and yet in the midst of it all, He retained the strength and dignity of the sinless Lamb of God, the Son of God. He never opened His mouth in complaint, blasphemy, self-defence or any sinful utterance. He never sinned.

Now, we can ask Yeshua to show us our own hidden, concealed wounds and afflictions of our soul and memories, and ask Him to reveal how He is present with us in them. In our moment of affliction He was there. He did not leave us. We are healed when He shows us His presence with us in our afflictions, as the one who was afflicted with us, who understands, and now heals our wounds with His everlasting love.

Ask the Lord to reveal how He comes alongside you in your afflictions, to help and to heal.

Readings: Hebrews 4:14–16, Colossians 1:19–23, James 5:13, Psalm 34:19, 2 Corinthians 1:4

ADAR 1

24th Day of the 12th Month in a Leap Year
Adar 1, usually falling in February/March
Isaiah 53
A Lamb to the Slaughter

He was led as a lamb to the slaughter, And as a sheep before its shearers is silent, So He opened not His mouth. *Isaiah 53:7*

Yeshua, the Lamb of God went to His death like a lamb to the slaughter. Two lambs were slaughtered in the temple every day, one in the morning, one in the evening. (Exodus 29:38, 39) At Passover, seven lambs were slaughtered each day of the 'Feast of Unleavened Bread', to fulfil the requirement of the Law, and thousands more would have been slaughtered for all the Passover meals held in homes across Jerusalem. At the 'Feast of Tabernacles', fourteen lambs were sacrificed every day. Each year numerous lambs were herded into the temple to be slaughtered. Helpless and defenceless, each lamb succumbed to the sharp knife and its life slipped away. Each lamb foreshadowed the silence of Yeshua who went to the cross without recrimination, protest, self-defence or explanation. Like a sheep gripped between the knees of its shearer, He was silent. He yielded to the will of the Father.

Yeshua was put on trial by the religious authorities. The chief priests, elders and council, sought false testimonies against Yeshua to put Him to death. They struggled to find any, but finally two people came forward and said, "This fellow said, 'I am able to destroy the temple of God and to build it in three days.'" (Matthew 26:61) When the High Priest asked Yeshua for His answer He kept silent. When questioned further under oath, He openly declared Himself to be the Son of Man. Accused of blasphemy, He was spat upon, mocked, struck and beaten. The following morning He was delivered to Pilate, the Governor of Judea. When Pilate asked Him if He was the King of the Jews He said, "It is as you say." But while He was being accused by the chief priests and elders, He answered nothing. (Matthew 27:12)

When is it best to remain silent? Why did Yeshua hold His silence?

Readings: Zechariah 2:13, Proverbs 16, Proverbs 23:9, Proverbs 21:23

25th Day of the 12th Month in a Leap Year
Adar 1, usually falling in February/March
Isaiah 53
Imprisoned

He was taken from prison and from judgement, And who will declare His generation? For He was cut off from the land of the living; For the transgressions of My people He was stricken. *Isaiah 53:8*

The night before His death, the religious authorities imprisoned Yeshua. An ancient prison pit has been excavated on Mount Zion. Carved deep into the rock, there is total darkness and no means of escape. The King of Heaven experienced an actual dark prison, as well as the mental, spiritual and emotional pit, to purchase freedom for all souls imprisoned in darkness. He came, declaring from Isaiah 61:1, "The Spirit of the Lord GOD is upon Me, because the LORD has anointed Me to preach good tidings to the poor; He has sent Me to heal the broken hearted, to proclaim liberty to the captives, and the opening of the prison to those who are bound." Yeshua frees us from our own pit and prison with the key of the forgiveness of our sins, and our forgiveness of those who have sinned against us. Unforgiveness would hold us captive to past wrongs. Forgiveness releases us from the desire for vengeance, allowing God to be judge and vindicator. Then the light can come in.

Psalm 88 is a vivid description of a soul in torment and in prison. It describes a soul drawing near to death with no hope. It says, "You have laid me in the lowest pit, In darkness, in the depths. Your wrath lies heavy upon me, And You have afflicted me with all Your waves, You have put away my acquaintances far from me; You have made me an abomination to them; I am shut up, and I cannot get out; My eye wastes away because of affliction." (Psalm 88:6–9) Even His deep suffering came from the hand of the Father. It was His will to pass through such suffering to purchase our freedom.

Is your heart held captive and in bondage by any lust or unforgiveness? You have the key!

Readings: Psalm 88, Psalm 30, Acts 8:18–23, Ephesians 4:7–10, 20–32, 1 Peter 4:1–3

26th Day of the 12th Month in a Leap Year
Adar 1, usually falling in February/March
Isaiah 53
Grave of a Rich Man

And they made His grave with the wicked – but with the rich at His death, Because He had done no violence, Nor was any deceit in His mouth. *Isaiah 53:9*

Isaiah prophesied the manner of Yeshua's death and burial, saying that 'they made His grave with the wicked' and with the rich. Yeshua's body was laid in a tomb in the vicinity of the crucifixion site, where criminals were executed. His grave was 'with the wicked'. John wrote, 'Now in the place where He was crucified there was a garden, and in the garden a new tomb in which no one had yet been laid.' (John 19:41) The execution site at Golgotha, which is translated 'The Place of the Skull', was, unusually, right in the vicinity of a garden which contained a new, unused and therefore ritually clean tomb, hewn into the rock. (Luke 23:53) Cheap tombs were made from natural caves. Expensive tombs were hewn from the rock. The tomb was the tomb of a rich man, hewn out of rock, in a rich man's garden, fulfilling the prophecy that He would be buried with the rich.

Joseph of Arimathea, a secret disciple of Yeshua went, along with another secret disciple of Yeshua – Nicodemus, to seek permission from Pilate to take and bury the body of Yeshua. (John 19:38, 39) Nicodemus was a Pharisee and a secret believer, one of the Jewish authorities. (John 3:1, 7:50) Pilate granted these two noble and influential men permission to take the body of Yeshua, knowing that He was not a violent criminal or liar, and so His body did not deserve to be thrown into a public grave with the accursed bodies of crucified criminals. These two rich men also fulfilled Isaiah's prophecy, by giving Yeshua's body a burial 'fit for a king', similar to the burial of king Asa in 2 Chronicles 16:14, with linen strips and a hundred pounds of myrrh and aloes.

Thank the Father that in His burial, Yeshua identified with the high and the lowly.

Readings: Matthew 27:57–28:8, Mark 15:42–16:7, Luke 23:50–24:12, John 19:31–20:16

27th Day of the 12th Month in a Leap Year
Adar 1, usually falling in February/March
Isaiah 53
The Pleasure of the LORD

Yet it pleased the LORD to bruise Him; He has put Him to grief. When You make His soul an offering for sin, He shall see His seed, He shall prolong His days, And the pleasure of the LORD shall prosper in His hand. *Isaiah 53:10*

In this verse we see again the doctrine of the Trinity, One God, a unity of three Persons, three yet one, Father, Son and Holy Spirit. 'It pleased the LORD to bruise Him' speaks of the entire Godhead YHWH (Yahweh) – the 'I AM' – being pleased for the Son – (the 'Servant' mentioned in Isaiah 52:13) to be bruised. The crucifixion of Yeshua was not an accident, disaster, disappointment or failure. Rather it was God's purpose all along. Right from the beginning, God had prepared the Lamb of God, to take away the sins of the world. Before Adam and Eve sinned in the Garden of Eden, the Father had a sacrifice prepared for the eventuality that His children fell into sin. He had provided from within Himself, from the Godhead, to give His own Son. Yeshua fulfilled the Father's pleasure.

The death of Yeshua on the cross was not a calamity. It was a triumph! When Yeshua rose from the dead, suddenly the truth was evident! Yeshua prolonged His days for all of eternity! Sin, death and evil were defeated! Yeshua was not a pathetic victim. He was a mighty conqueror! He had obtained a victory which no other could obtain. This brought great pleasure and joy to the Father. Genesis 3:15 was fulfilled. The Messiah's heel had been bruised, but in that event He had bruised the head of the serpent forever. The prophecy 'I will put enmity between you and the woman, And between your seed and her Seed. He shall bruise your head and you shall bruise His heel' was fulfilled! He would receive His harvest.

Meditate on God's victory. What difference does that make to your suffering and failures?

Readings: Genesis 3:8–15, Colossians 2:11–15, Romans 8:18–39

ADAR 1

28th Day of the 12th Month in a Leap Year
Adar 1, usually falling in February/March
Isaiah 53
Many Justified

He shall see the labor of His soul, and be satisfied, By His knowledge My righteous Servant shall justify many, For He shall bear their iniquities. *Isaiah 53:11*

The Hebrew word for 'justify' – 'tsadaq' – means 'to make right, cleanse, clear self, do justice, and turn to righteousness'. In Job, the word is translated as 'vindication'. (Job 11:2, 13:18, 25:4, 32:2) It contains within it the idea of being declared and made righteous, cleared of any fault or sin, made right with God. The Son of God is the 'Tsadiq Avdi' – 'My Righteous Servant'. The meaning of this verse could be paraphrased something like this: 'Knowing fully what He was doing, God's righteous Servant will make many righteous with His righteousness.' 'All their lacks and shortfalls will be carried away by Him, like the 'scapegoat'.'

The transferral of the righteousness of Yeshua onto those who believe in Him is fully prophesied in these verses. In the sight of the Father, when we have allowed Yeshua to carry away our sins, God's work is complete in His eyes. He is satisfied, because when He looks at us, He no longer sees our sins. They have been carried away irretrievably. Now He sees the righteousness of Yeshua covering our whole lives. In the sight of the Father we are as righteous as Yeshua, because He has given us His righteousness. This means that God does not look at us with a critical gaze, finding fault with us. Instead He looks with total grace, and is delighted in us, seeing only the righteousness of Yeshua. For most of us, if someone took something that belonged to us and claimed it as their own, we would feel deprived. But Yeshua is not like that. He is satisfied. When He gives us His grace He is not depleted. He is filled up and satiated. We bring Him joy and satisfaction because that is why He came.

When you receive your righteousness by faith, you bring joy and satisfaction to the Lord.

Readings: Titus 3:4–7, Romans 3:19–28, Isaiah 61:10, Zechariah 3:4

29th Day of the 12th Month in a Leap Year
Adar 1, usually falling in February/March
Isaiah 53
Divide the Spoil

Therefore I will divide Him a portion with the great, And He shall divide the spoil with the strong, Because He poured out His soul unto death, and He was numbered with the transgressors, And He bore the sin of many, and made intercession for the transgressors.

Isaiah 53:12

Because Yeshua poured out His soul unto death, executed with the criminals, bearing all the sins of everyone, for we have all broken the Laws of God, the Father will divide the 'spoil/booty' – in Hebrew, 'shalal' – with Him. This word 'shalal' is first found in Genesis 49:27, in Jacob's prophetic blessing on the tribe of Benjamin. This tribe is described as a ravenous wolf which devours the prey and divides the spoil.

Satan's intent is to rob, steal, and destroy from each one of us. Satan holds multitudes of souls in captivity, in the kingdom of darkness, through his deceptions, and the powers and principalities that operate under his thrall. Yeshua defeated Satan when He died and rose again. Now Yeshua retrieves the 'spoil' of souls from the grip of the enemy. Yeshua explained how demons operate under a 'strong man' who needs binding before you can plunder 'his goods'. Yeshua said, "...if I cast out demons by the Spirit of God, surely the kingdom of God has come upon you. Or how can one enter a strong man's house and plunder his goods, unless he first binds the strong man? And then he will plunder his house...." (Matthew 12:28, 29) Yeshua defeated the powers of darkness to transfer millions of souls from the kingdom of Darkness to the kingdom of Light. The Father has shared this task with His sons and daughters who will implement His victory, become mighty and strong in the authority of God, and bring Him the spoil, bringing His salvation to many souls.

Ask the Father to show you your part in bringing 'souls' as spoil from the grip of the enemy.

Readings: John 12:30–33, Genesis 49:27, Exodus 15:9, Matthew 12:24–30, Zechariah 14:1–9

1st Day of the 12th Month (Adar)
or the 13th Month (Adar 2) in a Leap Year
Usually falling in February/March/April
Israel's Enemies
Haman's Lot

In the first month, which is the month of Nisan, in the twelfth year of King Ahasuerus, they cast Pur (that is, the lot), before Haman to determine the day and the month, until it fell on the twelfth month which is the month of Adar. *Esther 3:7*

On this, the first day of the month, we worship God for His faithfulness to all of His covenant promises, and thank Him for His perfect plan of redemption. Today we enter the twelfth month (thirteenth in a leap year) and turn especially to the book of Esther. This is the month when we look to God's final victory over anti-Semitism, and His mighty works to defeat His enemies and bring about the fullness and completion of the kingdom of God.

In the first month of the year, in the fifth century BC, Haman – a mighty man in the court of the King Ahasuerus, King of the Medes and Persians – sought to bring about the destruction of the Jews. He cast 'lots' – 'purim' – to determine the day on which he would see them destroyed. He hated the Jews because they followed the laws of God. (Esther 3:8) This shows that anti-Semitism is actually hatred of God, his Kingship, His kingdom laws, covenants and ordinances. Hatred towards Israel, Jews and true Christians has this same root.

On the thirteenth day of the first month, a decree was written by Haman's command to destroy the Jews. They were to be executed on the thirteenth day of the twelfth month. (Esther 3:12, 13) But the slaughter he planned for that day, never happened, because God intervened through His servants Mordecai and Esther, and through His miraculous power. The rise and fall of the wicked Haman is a picture for us of anti-Semitism and anti-Israelism in the last days, and is also a picture of the anti-Christ which will precede Yeshua's return.

Thank the Father that whatever evil arises, He is on the throne, and His kingdom will come.

Readings: Esther 3, Psalm 2, Psalm 68, Ezekiel 31:1, 10, 11. (Esther 1)

2nd Day of the 12th Month (Adar)
or the 13th Month (Adar 2) in a Leap Year
Usually falling in February/March/April
Israel's Enemies
The Amalek Spirit

Then he looked on Amalek, and he took up his oracle and said: "Amalek was first among the nations, but shall be last until he perishes." *Numbers 24:20*

These words were spoken by Balaam the Seer in his fourth prophetic oracle, after he had declared that the Messiah would come forth out of Jacob, out of Israel (Numbers 24:17), and have dominion over Moab and Edom. Amalek, descendant of Esau, became one of the mighty nations that lived in the south of Canaan – the Amalekites. These people put fear into ten of Israel's twelve spies. (Numbers 13:28, 29, 14:45) They ambushed Israel on their way out of Egypt and fought against Israel at Rephidim. Joshua and Israel prevailed against them when the hands of Moses were held aloft by Aaron and Hur. (Exodus 17:8–16) Later when the Amalekites opposed Israel, Samuel instructed Saul, King of Israel to destroy them all. (1 Samuel 15:2, 3) But Saul failed to kill them all, keeping alive their king, Agag. This man was an ancestor of the wicked Haman. (Esther 3:1) Saul lost the kingdom for this disobedience to God, and David eventually became king in his place. Samuel was angry that Saul had kept Agag alive, and killed the man himself, hacking his body into pieces before God. (1 Samuel 15:33) Saul later perished at Gilgal, where he was actually killed by an Amalekite. David became king and defended Israel against the Amalekites, raiding them, slaughtering them, and recovering his people who had been taken captive by them at Ziklag. (1 Samuel 27:8, 1 Samuel 30).

Amalek is the spirit which tries to thwart God's plan of redemption. Our prayers and worship enable Yeshua to drive back the forces of darkness which oppose His coming kingdom. The Amalek spirit possessed Haman to try to kill the Jews, but Yeshua reigns!

Read Exodus 17:8–16. Joshua is a picture of Yeshua. Lift up the arms of Israel in prayer.

Readings: Exodus 17:8–16, 1 Samuel 15, 2 Samuel 8:9–18, Psalm 110

3rd Day of the 12th Month (Adar)
or the 13th Month (Adar 2) in a Leap Year
Usually falling in February/March/April
Israel's Enemies
A Controversy with the Nations

A noise will come to the ends of the earth – for the LORD has a controversy with the nations; He will plead His case with all flesh....
Jeremiah 25:31

The Lord has a controversy with the nations because of their wickedness. They have opposed His people Israel. The Ammonites were judged by God for saying 'Aha!' against the sanctuary of God when it was profaned, and against the Land of Israel when it was desolate. The people of Ammon were judged for clapping their hands, stamping their feet, and rejoicing in heart with 'disdain for the Land of Israel'. The Moabites were judged for saying 'Look! The house of Judah is like all the nations'. (Ezekiel 25:6, 8) Today the nations want Israel to be like all the other nations, and ignore her unique calling which testifies to the existence of God. They do not acknowledge God's covenant with His people.

God judged the Edomites for taking vengeance against the house of Judah (the Jews). The Philistines also sinned against God for dealing vengefully. They 'took vengeance with a spiteful heart, to destroy because of the old hatred.' (Anti-Semitism) (Ezekiel 25:15) Tyre was likened to Satan himself (Ezekiel 28) and judged for saying against Jerusalem 'Aha! She is broken who was the gateway of the peoples; now she is turned over to me; I shall be filled; she is laid waste.' (Ezekiel 26:2) God was angry and judged them for preying on Israel's desolation. Mount Seir was judged for killing Israelites and wanting to possess the Land for itself. (Ezekiel 35:5, 10) The Lord hears the slanders and taunts against Israel. (Ezekiel 36:3, 15) He said, "Surely I have spoken in My burning jealousy against the rest of the nations and against all Edom, who gave My Land to themselves as a possession, with wholehearted joy and spiteful minds, in order to plunder its open country." (Ezekiel 36:5)

The nations are making the same mistakes today. Are you with God or with the nations?

Readings: Ezekiel 25, 35, 36, Joel 3, Ezra 6:15

4th Day of the 12th Month (Adar)
or the 13th Month (Adar 2) in a Leap Year
Usually falling in February/March/April
Israel's Enemies
David and Goliath

Then David said to the Philistine, "You come to me with a sword, with a spear, and with a javelin. But I come to you in the name of the LORD of hosts, the God of the armies of Israel, whom you have defied...."

1 Samuel 17:45

1 Samuel 17 tells the story of David's victory over the mighty Philistine, Goliath. The Philistines had been warring with the Israelites and contending with them for the Land. Joshua and Caleb had believed with faith that the mighty giants could be defeated. But when the Israelites were confronted with the challenge from Goliath, no one had the courage to fight him, except for the young man David, who had never fought in a battle before. David had courage because He knew His God. David's testimony was, "The LORD, who delivered me from the paw of the lion and from the paw of the bear, He will deliver me from the hand of this Philistine." (1 Samuel 17:37) David knew the love of God, his Heavenly Father.

Today Israel is like a young and small 'David' in the face of Goliath. The might of the nations is rising up like a mighty Goliath, challenging little Israel (David) for her right to live in the Land, mocking, taunting and slandering her. But God is able to bring deliverance in the midst of the battle. David put his faith in God who said to Goliath, "...the battle is the LORD's, and He will give you into our hands." (1 Samuel 17:47) Yeshua has defeated the greatest foe, death, at the cross. Whether our battles are physical, like Israel's battle for survival, or mental, or spiritual, we have in our hands, like David, the sling and five stones – five being the number of grace. We all depend on the simplicity of God's grace for God's victory in our lives, including Israel in her battle against Goliath. (1 Samuel 17:45)

Meditate on Romans 8:37: ".....we are more than conquerors through Him who loved us."

Readings: Judges 2:20 – 3:6, Judges 6:11–16, 1 Samuel 17

ADAR 2

5th Day of the 12th Month (Adar)
or the 13th Month (Adar 2) in a Leap Year
Usually falling in February/March/April
Israel's Enemies
Jehoshaphat Prevails

And he said, "Listen, all you of Judah and you inhabitants of Jerusalem, and you, King Jehoshaphat! Thus says the LORD to you: 'Do not be afraid nor dismayed because of this great multitude, for the battle is not yours, but God's....'" *2 Chronicles 20:15*

These words were prophesied by Jahaziel the Levite when the Spirit of the LORD came upon him. King Jehoshaphat had proclaimed a fast throughout all Judah, and he had sought God's help because of the Moabites, Ammonites, Syrians, and the great multitude from beyond the sea, which had come up against Judah and gathered at En Gedi. Jehoshaphat stood in the temple crying out to God, remembering that God would hear and save them if they called out to Him there in that special place of His presence where His name abides.

Jehoshaphat (whose name means 'Yahweh Judges'), had been careful to uphold justice, appointing many judges in the land of Judah. (2 Chronicles 19) Jahaziel told the Judeans not to be afraid because God was with them, and that He would fight for them. So Jehoshaphat bowed with his face to the ground, and all the people bowed and worshipped the Lord. 'Loud and high' praises were sung out to God by certain Levitical families. Then Jehoshaphat told the people to believe in the Lord and His prophets, so they would prosper, and He appointed singers to sing to the LORD, and praise the beauty of His holiness. The singers went out before the army, praising the Lord for His mercy, leading the people the way God had said they should go. As they sang and praised God, the Lord set ambushes against their enemies, and their enemies' armies destroyed each other so that Judah did not have to fight at all. God had conquered their enemies while His people worshipped and obeyed Him.

The nations are in the valley of Jehoshaphat. (Joel 3:2) Pray that Israel will worship God!

Readings: 2 Chronicles 19, 20, Psalm 149, Acts 16:19–40

6th Day of the 12th Month (Adar)
or the 13th Month (Adar 2) in a Leap Year
Usually falling in February/March/April
Israel's Enemies
A Confederacy

'They have said, "Come, and let us cut them off from being a nation, that the name of Israel may be remembered no more." For they have consulted together with one consent; They form a confederacy against You....' *Psalm 83:4, 5*

Psalm 83 prophetically describes a joining together of nations in craftiness and tumult to eradicate the nation of Israel. In so doing they come against Almighty God. These nations are the 'tents of Edom' (South East of the Dead Sea), the Ishmaelites (who wore crescent ornaments in Judges 8:21–26 and include the Midianites east of the Red Sea in Arabia), Moab and the Hagrites (east of the Dead Sea and Jordan River), Gebal (north of Tyre on the Mediterranean coast), Ammon (east of the Jordan River), Amalek (to the south of Israel), Philistia (containing Gaza on the Mediterranean Coast), Tyre (north of Israel on the Mediterranean coast) and Assyria (on the Tigris River, modern Iraq), which also helps the children of Lot – Moab and Ammon).

These peoples form a 'confederacy' – in Hebrew 'brit', which is a 'covenant' – to destroy Israel. Incidentally, the Palestinian National Covenant openly calls for the destruction of the Jewish State of Israel. Israel's cry is for God to deal with their enemies as He dealt with Midian. God had Sisera their captain killed by a Gentile woman with a tent peg, while he was sleeping (Judges 4:21), and Jabin the Canaanite king was killed by the Israelites near Jezreel. Gideon then killed the Princes of Midian – Oreb and Zeeb, Zebah and Zalmunna. (Judges 7:25, 8:21) They had wanted to take the Land of Israel for their own possession. Psalm 83 is a prayer for God to bring His 'storm' –to pursue Israel's enemies and confound them, so that they might come to know that the God of Israel is the one true God.

Pray for the people who are united against Israel to receive a revelation of the God of Israel.

Readings: Psalm 83, Judges 4 – 8, Obadiah 1:6–8, Job 37:9–13

ADAR 2

7th Day of the 12th Month (Adar)
or the 13th Month (Adar 2) in a Leap Year
Usually falling in February/March/April
Israel's Enemies
Edom

"And Edom shall be a possession, Seir also, his enemies, shall be a possession, While Israel does valiantly, Out of Jacob One shall have dominion, and destroy the remains of the city." *Numbers 24:18, 19*

The name 'Edom' means 'red' or 'rosy' in Hebrew. The Edomites are the descendants of Esau the elder son of Isaac, who forsook and sold his birthright for a meal of red lentil stew. Disinherited, Esau took his family to live in Edom, the land to the south-east of the Dead Sea. The rocky, mountainous landscape takes on a rosy red hue, especially in the evening sunlight. To the south is the Red Sea. The most famous stronghold of Edom was the famous city of Sela in Mount Seir, now known as Petra. This was probably the strong city of Psalm 108:10 since its terrain makes it virtually impenetrable to enemy forces. The Edomites have always been formidable enemies to Israel, though the Kings, Jehoshaphat and Amaziah, experienced victories against them. (2 Chronicles 20:10, 2 Chronicles 25:11, 12) Psalms 60 and Psalm 108 show King David's recognition that Israel could only be victorious over the Edomites through God's help. In the time of Yeshua, some Edomites lived in southern Judea and were called Idumaeans. (Mark 3:8)

Obadiah prophesied concerning Edom, and as in Psalm 83, he mentions the covenant, or confederacy. (Obadiah v7) God's contention against Edom concerns her deep hatred of Israel, and this prophecy is relevant to these end times. Her sins include violence (terrorism) against Israel, casting lots for Jerusalem – taking possession of her land, gloating and rejoicing in the day of Israel's calamity, and plundering and killing those who escape in the day of trouble. As they have done to Israel, so it will be done to them. (Obadiah v15)

Thank God for His sovereignty, His deliverance and that His kingdom will come.

Readings: Numbers 24:18, 19, Isaiah 34:5–17, Ezekiel 35, Obadiah

8th Day of the 12th Month (Adar)
or the 13th Month (Adar 2) in a Leap Year
Usually falling in February/March/April
Israel's Enemies
On the Mountains of Israel

...therefore thus says the Lord GOD: "Surely I have spoken in My burning jealousy against the rest of the nations and against all Edom, who gave My land to themselves as a possession, with wholehearted joy and spiteful minds, in order to plunder its open country."

Ezekiel 36:5

Ezekiel prophesied to the mountains of Israel, which were for a time, in the times of the kings, divided into two kingdoms. (1 Kings 11:26–39) The northern kingdom of Israel included the mountains of Samaria and Ephraim. The southern kingdom of Judah included the mountains of Jerusalem, and the mountains of Bethlehem and Hebron. These mountains form the core part of the ancient Land that God covenanted to the descendants of Abraham, Isaac and Jacob forever. Here, they built altars and dug wells (Genesis 12:7, 8, Genesis 13:14–17, Genesis 26:17–33, Genesis 35:6–15) and they purchased land. Abraham bought the Machpelah in Hebron (Genesis 50:13), and King David bought the threshing floor on Mount Moriah, where Solomon built the temple. (2 Samuel 24:18–25) Yeshua was born in Bethlehem in Judea, in the mountains which had been the southern kingdom of Judah.

Ezekiel's prophecy from the Lord, to the mountains of Israel, describes the time when the enemies of Israel say, 'Aha! The ancient heights have become our possession.' (Ezekiel 36:2) Ezekiel prophesies that God speaks with His burning jealousy against the people who take the mountains of ancient Israel away from the Jews, God's covenant people. He raises His hand in an oath that these nations, which surround, and come against God's Land and people, shall bear their own shame. But God will purify and bless Israel, giving them a new heart and a new spirit, and they'll be able to live in the Land, knowing that God is the LORD.

Read Ezekiel 36. How is this being fulfilled? How can Israel get a new heart and spirit?

Readings: Ezekiel 36, 2 Corinthians 5:17–21, Jeremiah 31:27–40

ADAR 2

9th Day of the 12th Month (Adar)
or the 13th Month (Adar 2) in a Leap Year
Usually falling in February/March/April
Israel's Enemies
God's Justice

"Rejoice, O Gentiles, with His people; For He will avenge the blood of His servants, And render vengeance to His adversaries; He will provide atonement for His land and His people." *Deuteronomy 32:43*

God is a God of justice. At Yeshua's first coming He atoned for our sins by becoming the perfect sacrifice to bring us peace with God. But His second coming will not be a day of peace, but the 'Day of His Vengeance', prophesied in Isaiah 59:18, Isaiah 61:2, and Isaiah 63:4. On that day, God will pour out His vengeance upon those who have martyred 'His servants' – the true Bridal Church. He will also bring justice for the Land of Israel and His people, the Jews, when He renders vengeance on His adversaries – on all those who oppose the Jews, and their possession of the Land of Israel.

Isaiah 63 prophesies the Day of the Vengeance of the Lord. On that day He will deal with Edom, trampling them in His fury. Yeshua will be seen in His glory. 'Who is this who comes from Edom, With dyed garments from Bozrah, This One who is glorious in His apparel, Travelling in the greatness of His strength? –"I who speak in righteousness, mighty to save."' (Isaiah 63:1) (Also see Isaiah 16:5) Yeshua's garments will have blood sprinkled on them – from the winepress of His wrath – reminding us of atonement. The blood is from the nations God has trampled and humbled to bring atonement – the payment for peace for His people. (Isaiah 63:2–6) Isaiah 59:17, 18 prophesies, "For He put on righteousness as a breastplate, And a helmet of salvation on His head; He put on the garments of vengeance for clothing, And was clad with zeal as a cloak. According to their deeds, accordingly He will repay, Fury to His adversaries, Recompense to His enemies..." Yeshua will enforce justice.

Consider how God feels about Israel, and His Bride, if He is going to avenge their enemies.

Readings: Isaiah 51:17–23, Isaiah 59, Isaiah 63, Nahum 1

10th Day of the 12th Month (Adar)
or the 13th Month (Adar 2) in a Leap Year
Usually falling in February/March/April
Israel's Enemies
Gog and Magog

"And it will come to pass at the same time, when Gog comes against the land of Israel," says the Lord GOD, "that My fury will show in My face. For in My jealousy and in the fire of My wrath I have spoken: 'Surely in that day there shall be a great earthquake in the land of Israel...'" *Ezekiel 38:18, 19*

In Ezekiel 37 we have the dry bones coming together, and rising to new life as a nation, and an exceedingly great army. The houses of Israel and Judah come together to form one new kingdom in the Land of Israel, and purified by God, they are ruled over by the Messiah, the Son of David, whom we know will be Yeshua at His second coming. Yeshua will shepherd God's people Israel, and He will make a covenant of peace with them, and the temple of God will be in their midst. The true Messiah will bring a true covenant of peace, not the false peace created by the counterfeit covenant of the anti-Christ. (Daniel 9:26b, 27)

It will be when Israel is at peace – living without walls, bars or gates, that Gog of the land of Magog, and other nations, will make an evil plan to plunder the land inhabited by God's people. When Israel is living in safety, this great company will come up against her from the nations. Some of the names of the invading nations go back to their earliest names found in Genesis 10 when they were named after the grandsons of Noah. Other names are familiar to us today. When these nations invade Israel, God will show the fire of His wrath, and there will be a great earthquake and war, and God will bring Gog into judgement with pestilence and bloodshed, flooding rain, great hailstones, fire and brimstone. This echoes the prophecy of Revelation 20:7–10 which shows how they will finally perish.

Consider: God will use His preservation of Israel to show the nations that He is the LORD.

Readings: Ezekiel 38, 39, Revelation 16:16 – 17:14, Revelation 20

ADAR 2

11th Day of the 12th Month (Adar)
or the 13th Month (Adar 2) in a Leap Year
Usually falling in February/March/April
Esther's Fast
For Such a Time as This

And Mordecai told them to answer Esther: "Do not think in your heart that you will escape in the king's palace any more than all the other Jews. For if you remain completely silent at this time, relief and deliverance will arise for the Jews from another place, but you and your father's house will perish. Yet who knows whether you have come to the kingdom for such a time as this?" *Esther 4:13, 14*

In the first month of the year, wicked Haman cast 'lots' – 'purim' – to determine the day and the month when he would destroy all the Jews who lived in the whole kingdom of Ahasuerus, (king of Persia, in the 5th Century BC). The lot fell on the 13th day of the 12th month. Haman is a picture of the devil, whose greatest scheme to destroy the Jews comes at the end of the age. In the third month however, God turned events on their head through the intervention of Mordecai, (a picture of Yeshua), and Esther, (a picture of the Bride, the Esther Church, which speaks out in defence of the Jews). It was in the third month, when the Church would be born, that Esther, who had become the wife and Queen of King Ahasuerus, learned of Haman's plot to destroy the Jews. Esther's older cousin, Mordecai the Jew, who brought up the orphan Esther, had a message conveyed to Esther in the palace, informing her of Haman's plan to eradicate the Jews. He urged her to intervene and not stay silent.

God wanted to use Esther to bring deliverance to the Jews. If she did nothing, she and her father's house would perish. God had ordained for her to come to the palace of the king for such a time as this – it would be her divine destiny to intervene on behalf of her people, the Jews. So she called for three days of prayer and fasting. Now is the time for the 'Esther Church' to follow Queen Esther's example, and seek God earnestly on behalf of the Jews.

Is God calling you to pray and take action for the deliverance of the Jews from their enemies?

Readings: Esther 1 – 4

12th Day of the 12th Month (Adar)
or the 13th Month (Adar 2) in a Leap Year
Usually falling in February/March/April
Esther's Fast
Who Will Be Worshipped?

Now Haman thought in his heart, "Whom would the king delight to honour more than me?" *Esther 6:6*

Haman is a picture of the devil. He had a position of power in the palace of the king and he even wore the king's signet ring. The king gave him freedom to do as he wished. This is a picture of Lucifer (Satan), who, Scripture tells us, made a sound with stringed instruments before he fell because of his pride. (Isaiah 14:11) It is commonly thought that he was the chief worshipper in heaven before he fell. Isaiah 14:12–15 says, "How you are fallen from heaven, O Lucifer, son of the morning! How you are cut down to the ground, you who weakened the nations! For you have said in your heart: 'I will ascend into heaven, I will exalt my throne above the stars of God; I will also sit on the mount of the congregation on the farthest sides of the north; I will ascend above the heights of the clouds, I will be like the Most High.' Yet you shall be brought down to Sheol, To the lowest depths of the Pit..."

Satan wants to be worshipped on the Temple Mount in Jerusalem, the place of God's throne where God's name dwells. This is clearly evident from these verses, and when we look at current events surrounding the Temple Mount, we might even suppose that an anti-Christ figure or the spirit of anti-Christ will seek 'worship' on the Temple Mount, possibly in a rebuilt temple. Already, many bow the knee to the false 'god' in that place. Satan wants to be worshipped as God, and usurp God's place of worship. The 'rise' in the fortunes of Haman in Esther 3, is a picture for us of the 'rise' of the anti-Christ. Mordecai, in contrast, is misunderstood, judged, and overlooked, as he sits at the city gate. Haman believed that when the king wanted to honour someone, it must be him. But no, the king honoured Mordecai.

When the Church fasts and prays, Satan loses honour, and Yeshua is glorified.

Readings: Esther 3, Esther 5:9 – 6:14, Isaiah 14:3–17

13th Day of the 12th Month (Adar)
or the 13th Month (Adar 2) in a Leap Year
Usually falling in February/March/April
Esther's Fast
The Third Day

Now in the twelfth month, that is, the month of Adar, on the thirteenth day, the time came for the king's command and his decree to be executed. On the day that the enemies of the Jews had hoped to overpower them, the opposite occurred, in that the Jews themselves overpowered those who hated them. *Esther 9:1*

Today we remember the third day of Esther's Fast, and the turning of events on this day, so that the Jews were able to defend themselves. Instead of being killed as Haman had decreed, the king issued a new decree through Mordecai, saying that the Jews could defend themselves. When 75,000 people attacked the Jews, they were able to overpower them.

The third day brings in God's kingdom. Jonah was vomited from the belly of the great fish on the third day. Yeshua rose on the third day. Hosea prophesied a 'revival' for the Jews 'on the third day'. (Hosea 6:2) Esther 5:1, 2 states, 'Now it happened on the third day that Esther put on her royal robes and stood in the inner court of the king's palace, across from the king's house, while the king sat on his royal throne in the royal house, facing the entrance of the house. So it was, when the king saw Queen Esther standing in the court, that she found favour in his sight, and the king held out to Esther the golden sceptre that was in his hand. Then Esther went near and touched the top of the sceptre.'

On the third day, Esther, who represents the Church of this generation which stands with Israel, found favour with the king. She approached him boldly, as we are to approach God's throne of grace. (Hebrews 4:16) The king gave her what she requested, and consequently, the evil of Haman was exposed, and he and his sons perished on the gallows.

What simple act is God asking you to do? What is your bold request to the Father?

Readings: Esther 5, 7, 8, 9:1–14, Psalm 23:5a, Hebrews 4:16

14th Day of the 12th Month (Adar)
or the 13th Month (Adar 2) in a Leap Year
Usually falling in February/March/April
Purim
Resting, Feasting and Gladness

And on the fourteenth day of the month they rested and made it a day of feasting and gladness. *Esther 9:17*

On this, the fourteenth day of the month, the Jews killed three hundred men at Shushan, but did not lay a hand on the plunder. Three hundred is the number of overcoming. Gideon's army consisted of 300 men (Judges 7:16) and the numbers 3, 30, 300 and 3000 occur in the story of Samson. (Judges 15) On this day, the Jews of Sushan 'overcame' their enemies. The rest of the Jews in the provinces had already overcome their enemies, on the thirteenth, so on this day, they were able to rest and rejoice, as Mordecai commanded them.

Mordecai, who was awarded a position of power and authority in the kingdom, wrote that the Jews should celebrate annually on the 14th and 15th of Adar, in remembrance of the days on which they had rest from their enemies and when their sorrow turned to joy. Unwalled towns celebrate Purim on the 14th, but walled cities celebrate on the 15th in remembrance of the walled city of Shushan. The fortified city of Shushan was the greatest stronghold, and so the battle took longer there than in the provinces.

The custom begun by Mordecai continues today. These two days are a Jewish holiday celebrated with feasting and joy, sending presents to one another, and giving gifts to the poor. These days are to be kept without fail until the end of the age, and they are called 'Purim' after the 'lots' that were cast by Haman. The victory over the unwalled cities and villages shows that the anti-Semitism was widespread across the land. 75,000 people came up against the Jews. But through the intervention of Esther and Mordecai, the Jews survived.

Israel has to defend herself against her enemies to survive. Pray for Israel's Defence Forces.

Readings: Esther 9:15–32, Judges 7, Judges 14 – 16

15th Day of the 12th Month (Adar)
or the 13th Month (Adar 2) in a Leap Year
Usually falling in February/March/April
Shushan Purim
Complete Rest

For Mordecai the Jew was second to King Ahasuerus, and was great among the Jews and well received by the multitude of his brethren, seeking the good of his people and speaking peace to all his countrymen. *Esther 10:3*

Today is Shushan Purim. King Ahasuerus ruled and reigned from Shushan (also called Susa), which was the Capital of Elam in Persia (modern day Iran). Shushan was a walled city – particularly strong in its resistance of, and hatred towards, the Jews. It took the Jews an extra day to defeat and overcome the 300 men who tried to kill them. But the Jews did overcome, and enjoyed feasting and rejoicing in Shushan. What is more, Mordecai, the Jew, rose to prominence in this city and nation which had hated the Jews with particular ferocity. Wicked Haman had lived in this city. But the stronghold came down. The spiritual stronghold of anti-Semitism fell. God loves His Esther Church and His brave Israel.

The final verse of the Book of Esther says that Mordecai the Jew was second to King Ahasuerus. This is a picture of the Father and the Son ruling and reigning in God's millennium kingdom on earth. Mordecai (a picture of Yeshua) was 'great among the Jews and well received by the multitude of his brethren.' The day will come when Yeshua will be great among the Jews and well received by them. Then it says that Mordecai sought 'the good of his people', and he spoke peace to all his countrymen. (Esther 10:3) When Yeshua rules and reigns in the midst of His people Israel, He will bring peace to earth and 'goodwill to all men'. (Luke 2:14) Jerusalem is a walled city, so Jerusalemites celebrate Purim today. Jerusalem will finally experience true peace and goodwill when Yeshua rules among His brethren, the Jews, who will listen to Him, and receive His lasting and eternal peace and joy.

Rejoice with Israel and Jerusalem that God's kingdom will come, Haman is a defeated foe!

Readings: Esther 10, Ezekiel 39 – 40:5, 43:1–9

16th Day of the 12th Month (Adar)
or the 13th Month (Adar 2) in a Leap Year
Usually falling in February/March/April
Ephraim and Judah
The Scattered Tribes

Say to them, 'Thus says the Lord GOD: "Surely I will take the stick
of Joseph, which is in the hand of Ephraim, and the tribes of Israel,
his companions; and I will join them with it, with the stick of Judah,
and make them one stick, and they will be one in My hand."'
Ezekiel 37:19

The Lord instructed the Prophet Ezekiel to take up two sticks and make
them look like one stick by the way he held them in his hand. This was a
prophetic picture of what the Lord is beginning to do in these last days,
and will complete supernaturally in the millennium reign of Messiah
Yeshua. He will gather together the scattered tribes of Israel (James 1:1),
bringing together again as one, the northern and southern kingdoms.
God will restore 'all things' (Mark 9:12), including the tribes of Israel,
and unite them under Yeshua.

The twelve tribes were divided into two kingdoms after the death of
Solomon, as a punishment for his idolatry. The northern kingdom of
Israel, which consisted of 10 tribes, came to be identified by the dominant
tribe of Ephraim (from which its first king, Jeroboam originated). (1
Kings 11:26, 31) The southern kingdom consisted of the two tribes of
Judah and Benjamin, plus the Levites in Jerusalem. The idolaters who
resided in the northern kingdom of Israel/Ephraim were taken captive
by the Assyrians in 722 BC (2 Kings 18:11) and never returned. The
southern kingdom, and all the faithful who resided in Jerusalem, became
identified by the dominant tribe of Judah, and named Jews. They were
taken captive to Babylon over 100 years after the exile of the northern
kingdom, and most returned from exile to Jerusalem, and were called
Jews, or Israel. Yeshua is Israel's Shepherd. He came to seek and save the
'lost' (Luke 19:10) and give them a new identity under the King of Israel.

*The Father Heart of God will restore what has been 'lost', both in Israel
and in your life.*

Readings: 1 Kings 11, 12, Ezekiel 37, Revelation 7:4–8

ADAR 2

17th Day of the 12th Month (Adar)
or the 13th Month (Adar 2) in a Leap Year
Usually falling in February/March/April
Ephraim and Judah
Made One

And it shall come to pass in the place where it was said to them, 'You are not My people,' There it shall be said to them, 'You are sons of the living God.' Then the children of Judah and the children of Israel shall be gathered together, and appoint for themselves one head; and they shall come up out of the land, for great will be the day of Jezreel!
Hosea 1:10b, 11

The book of Hosea describes the tribe of Ephraim as being like an idolatrous wife who is taken back by her husband to himself. At first it appears impossible. She has sinned greatly, worshipping foreign gods and committing abominable pagan practices. However Hosea 6:1–3 speaks about the 'third day', when Ephraim is revived and restored. In Hosea 14 the seemingly impossible happens: Ephraim is restored back to God. Revelation 7 speaks of the holy remnant in the end-times, formed from the tribes, but the tribe of Dan is replaced by the Levites, and idolatrous Ephraim with Joseph. Ezekiel 47:13 – 48:20, however, describes the Land of Israel in the millennium, divided into tribal territories and by this time the formerly idolatrous tribes of Dan and Ephraim are restored. The return of Israel prophesied in Isaiah 11:11, is from Assyria and Egypt, Pathros, Cush, Elam, Shinar, Hamath, the Islands of the sea, and of Judah, from the four corners of the earth. The tribes might well include the Gentile Bride, as part of the Commonwealth of Israel (Ephesians 2:12), possibly as the 'double fruitfulness' of Ephraim. (See 11th Day of the 8th Month) One of the 'scattered tribes' of the northern kingdom, Manasseh, has actually been found in north-east India. Between 2000 and 2011 AD, 1,700 people from the northern tribe of Manasseh returned to the Land of Israel. The miracle of restoration has begun.

Thank God that if He can receive back Ephraim, He can save and receive back any sinner.

Readings: Isaiah 11, Hosea 1, 2, 3, 6, 14, Jeremiah 31:9, 16–20, Luke 15:11–32

18th Day of the 12th Month (Adar)
or the 13th Month (Adar 2) in a Leap Year
Usually falling in February/March/April
Elijah the Prophet
The Coming of Elijah

> Behold, I will send you Elijah the prophet before the coming of the great and dreadful day of the LORD. *Malachi 4:5*

These are the final verses of the Prophets in the Scriptures. They prophesy that Elijah the prophet will come again, before the 'great and dreadful day of the Lord.' This prophecy meant that when Yeshua came at His first coming, the Jewish people were looking for the sign of the coming Messiah in the return of Elijah the Prophet. Elijah had lived in the time of Ahab, who was King of Israel 874–853 BC. People wondered if John the Baptiser was Elijah since he claimed to prepare the way for the Messiah. But John the Baptiser denied that he was Elijah. (John 1:21) Yeshua explained to His disciples that John the Baptiser had come in the 'spirit of Elijah'. He said of John; '...if you are willing to receive it, he is Elijah who is to come.' (Matthew 11:14) He was not 'Elijah' himself – this is not 'reincarnation'. He fulfilled the role that Elijah was prophesied to have in preparing the way for the Messiah.

Moses and Elijah appeared in glory with Yeshua on the mountain top at His 'transfiguration', when He was seen by Peter, James and John. (Matthew 17:4) Elijah had left this earth supernaturally, without dying and leaving behind his body. He was caught up to heaven, in his body, in a heavenly chariot. (2 Kings 2:11) This gave rise to the expectation that Elijah would re-appear in his physical body before the appearance of the Messiah. For this reason it is also said that Elijah could be one of the 'two witnesses', prophesied to come to Jerusalem in the last days before Messiah returns, which is possible. (Revelation 11:3–13) We can expect a similar 'preparation' for the second Coming of Messiah, as at His first.

How is the Holy Spirit preparing us for the return of Yeshua? (Revelation 21:2)

Readings: Malachi 4:5, 6, John 1, Matthew 17:1–13, Revelation 11:3–13

ADAR 2

19th Day of the 12th Month (Adar)
or the 13th Month (Adar 2) in a Leap Year
Usually falling in February/March/April
Elijah the Prophet
The Hearts of Fathers and Children

"... And he will turn the hearts of the fathers to the children, and the hearts of the children to their fathers, lest I come and strike the earth with a curse." *Malachi 4:6*

Elijah the Prophet, who will come before the great and dreadful day of the LORD, will turn the hearts of the fathers to the children, and the hearts of the children to their fathers, lest the Lord come and strike the earth with a curse.

This prophecy will be fulfilled before Yeshua returns at the great and dreadful day of the LORD. It had a partial fulfilment through John the Baptiser, but there is a further fulfilment yet to come. We can understand more of what the spirit of Elijah – seen in John the Baptiser – will be. The angel announced to Zecharias, before the birth of his son, that he would 'turn many of the children of Israel to the Lord their God.' He will also go before Him (the Messiah) in the spirit and power of Elijah, "...'to turn the hearts of the fathers to the children,' and the disobedient to the wisdom of the just, to make ready a people prepared for the Lord.'" (Luke 1:16, 17)

In the end-times, many of the children of Israel will similarly return to the Lord their God, and hearts of fathers will turn to their children and vice versa, and a 'remnant' will be prepared for the return of the Lord. The restoration of parent/child relationships is foundational. Societies break down, and fall under a curse, when there is fatherlessness, lawlessness and a departure from biblical values. The Lord said through Jeremiah, "Stand in the ways and see, and ask for the old paths, where the good way is, and walk in it; then you will find rest for your souls...." (Jeremiah 6:16) This is God's call to Israel and the Bride.

How can we, like John the Baptiser, remove stumbling blocks and return to the ancient paths?

Readings: Luke 1:13–17, Matthew 3:1–3, Luke 3:1–6

20th Day of the 12th Month (Adar)
or the 13th Month (Adar 2) in a Leap Year
Usually falling in February/March/April
Elijah the Prophet
Fathers

And He said to them, "Why did you seek Me? Did you not know that I must be about My Father's business?" But they did not understand the statement which He spoke to them. Then He went down with them and came to Nazareth, and was subject to them, but His mother kept all these things in her heart. And Jesus increased in wisdom and stature, and in favour with God and men. *Luke 2:49*

Yeshua is the ultimate example of a perfect relationship with His earthly father and His Heavenly Father, and He walked in the blessings of those right relationships. Yeshua submitted to His Heavenly Father first, and then to His earthly father. When He appeared to His parents to have done wrong, He hadn't actually done wrong, because He was obeying His Heavenly Father. His earthly father, Joseph, should have been sensitive to how God was leading his son. Fathers are meant to hear from God about their children, and encourage them in the path that God has prepared for them, affirming them, releasing them, preparing them for their destiny.

Yeshua's whole identity and destiny was bound up with the temple. Mary and Joseph knew the Scriptures, and went to the feasts, but they hadn't understood that they symbolised the destiny of their son. Now, at age twelve, that was the place He was meant to be. The whole temple symbolised Him and the work that He had come to do. The temple belonged to His Father. He was the Son of God. At age twelve, Yeshua made His identity known to the Jewish people, and to Mary and Joseph, and He revealed that He was, indeed, the Son of God. We too need our Heavenly Father to affirm us in our identity, as no earthly father is able to fully do.

Listen for the loving voice of your Heavenly Father, affirming your identity and destiny.

Readings: Luke 2:41–52, Matthew 3:16, 17, Matthew 7:11, John 14:8–21, Galatians 4:6, 7

21st Day of the 12th Month (Adar)
or the 13th Month (Adar 2) in a Leap Year
Usually falling in February/March/April
Elijah the Prophet
Spiritual Fathers

And it came to pass, as though it had been a trivial thing for him (King Ahab) to walk in the sins of Jeroboam the son of Nebat, that he took as wife Jezebel the daughter of Ethbaal, king of the Sidonians; and he went and served Baal and worshiped him. *1 Kings 16:31*

The Prophet Elijah ministered during the reign of King Ahab, king of the northern kingdom of Israel. King Ahab was a weak man, easily manipulated by his over-domineering and evil wife. We are told, 'there was no one like Ahab who sold himself to do wickedness in the sight of the LORD because Jezebel his wife stirred him up.' (1 Kings 21:25) Ahab was unable to stand strong in his identity against her influence. He allowed her to control him. He had not been strengthened by a godly father. Omri, his father, did evil things just like his ancestor Jeroboam had done. The sin of idolatry was passed down from generation to generation. Ahab was trying to be king without a true relationship with the heavenly King. But God sent Elijah, the Prophet who turned the hearts of the fathers to their sons and sons to their fathers. He brought Ahab to repentance. (1 Kings 22:27–29)

Elijah was strong to stand up to the idolatry, to the sin of the king, to Jezebel and to the prophets of Baal. The prophets called themselves 'sons of the prophets'. (2 Kings 2:3, 5) Elijah was like a father to Elisha. When Elijah was taken up into heaven Elisha cried out, "My father, my father, the chariot of Israel and its horsemen!" (2 Kings 2:12)

The Apostle Paul was a father to the younger men. His letter to Philemon shows his concern for his spiritual son Onesimus, and he also spoke to Timothy and Titus as sons. The Church and the world needs 'spiritual fathers and sons' like Elijah and Paul in the end-times.

Receive strength and authority from God your Father. Pray for Him to raise up 'fathers'.

Readings: Isaiah 63:15–19, 2 Kings 2, 1 Timothy 1:2, 18, 2 Timothy 1:2, Titus 1:4, Philemon

405

22nd Day of the 12th Month (Adar)
or the 13th Month (Adar 2) in a Leap Year
Usually falling in February/March/April
Elijah the Prophet
The Famine

And Elijah the Tishbite, of the inhabitants of Gilead, said to Ahab, "As the LORD God of Israel lives, before whom I stand, there shall not be dew nor rain these years, except at my word." *1 Kings 17:1*

King Ahab of the northern kingdom of Israel served the pagan god Baal, and worshipped him. We are told 'he set up an altar for Baal in the temple of Baal, which he had built in Samaria. And Ahab made a wooden image. Ahab did more to provoke the LORD God of Israel to anger than all the kings of Israel who were before him.' (1 Kings 16:32, 33) Therefore Elijah the prophet spoke the word of the Lord and stopped the rain. (1 Kings 17:1)

The word Baal is the Hebrew word for 'husband', and was at one time used to signify that the God of Israel was their Lord and Husband. But the word came to be used instead for the multitude of false gods, which the pagans attached to certain places, to be the owners or 'husbands' of the land. They worshipped Baal as the 'god' of weather, fertility and war. The Israelites, instead of obeying God's commandments, and receiving the consequent provision and protection of God Almighty, copied the pagans and put their trust in their worship of these pagan 'false gods' (demons). They set up fertility symbols, had a temple to worship Baal in Samaria, had temple prostitutes, they practiced child sacrifice, and committed perverse acts. (1 Kings 16) They thought that if they did these things, the 'gods' (demons) would give them rain to make their crops grow, and the blessing of fertile lands. Elijah had to 'shut up the heavens' from bringing rain on behalf of Almighty God, to free people from the delusion that their evil cults could provide them with rain, prosperity and blessing. So the streams dried up and the whole land suffered famine, and Elijah was fed supernaturally.

What type of suffering might you have to see, for false gods and idols to fall in your land?

Readings: Job 5:8–10, Amos 4:7, 1 Kings 16:23 – 17:16, Luke 4:23–27, James 5:17

ADAR 2

23rd Day of the 12th Month (Adar)
or the 13th Month (Adar 2) in a Leap Year
Usually falling in February/March/April
Elijah the Prophet
The Contest on Mount Carmel

And Elijah came to all the people, and said, "How long will you falter between two opinions? If the LORD is God, follow Him; but if Baal, follow him." But the people answered him not a word. *1 Kings 18:21*

Elijah challenged King Ahab, and the people of Israel, to a contest between Baal and 'Yahweh' the God of Israel, to prove to them which one was the true God. Elijah told them to gather the four hundred and fifty prophets of Baal, and the four hundred prophets of Asherah, (the female god) who ate at Jezebel's table, to assemble on Mount Carmel (in the north of Israel). Elijah also called for two bulls to be brought. The prophets of Baal were to take one of the bulls for themselves, cut it in pieces, lay it on wood and call on their god Baal to bring down fire to consume the sacrifice. Of course no fire came. So they leapt around the altar they had made, but still no fire came. Elijah mocked them in their foolishness.

Then Elijah prepared the altar of the Lord that was broken down, and he took twelve stones according to the twelve tribes of Israel, and he built an altar in the name of 'Yahweh', the Lord God of Israel. He made a trench around the altar, put wood on the altar, cut up the bull in pieces and laid it on the altar. Then he poured water on the sacrifice and the wood so that the water ran down and filled the trench. Then at the time of the 'evening sacrifice' at the temple in Jerusalem, Elijah called on the Lord God saying, "...Hear me, O LORD, hear me, that this people may know that You are the LORD God, and that You have turned their hearts back to You again." (1 Kings 18:37) Then the fire of the LORD fell and consumed everything including the water. When the people saw it they fell on their faces and they said, "The LORD (Yahweh), He is God! The LORD, He is God!" (1 Kings 18:39)

How is the LORD (Yahweh) proving that He is God in the end-times, so people get saved?

Readings: 1 Kings 18, Romans 11:25, 26, Revelation 8:1–5

24th Day of the 12th Month (Adar)
or the 13th Month (Adar 2) in a Leap Year
Usually falling in February/March/April
Elijah the Prophet
The Rain Comes

Then Elijah said to Ahab, "Go up, eat and drink; for there is the sound of abundance of rain." *1 Kings 18:41*

After Elijah proved 'Yahweh', the LORD, to be the one, true, living God, and all other 'gods' false, he went up to the top of Mount Carmel, bowed down on the ground, put his face between his knees, and charged his servant to look toward the sea for the approaching rain. Elijah interceded with fervent and persevering prayer. James wrote, 'Elijah was a man with a nature like ours, and he prayed earnestly that it would not rain; and it did not rain on the land for three years and six months. And he prayed again, and the heaven gave rain, and the earth produced its fruit.' (James 5:17, 18)

The coming of the rain represents the end of God's judgements, and the beginning of His blessing. The famine in the Land lasted three and a half years. (Luke 4:25) This is half of seven years which is half the length of the final seven years of Daniel's 'weeks/sevens'. (Daniel 9:27) It could be that the famine represents the desolation that will happen in either the first or second half of the Tribulation. The two witnesses will have power to 'shut up' the rain, so that no rain falls in the days of their prophecy. (Revelation 11:6)

When the LORD returns to reign in His kingdom, He will bless it with fruitfulness and spiritual blessings. At the seventh time of looking, Elijah's servant spotted a cloud, the size of a man's hand. So Elijah told Ahab to prepare his chariot and 'go down' before the rain would stop him. Then the clouds, wind and heavy rain came, and the hand of the LORD came upon Elijah, and he ran all the way to Jezreel.

Pray for lives which have been shaken, to experience the blessings of God's rain.

Readings: 1 Kings 18:41–46, Acts 14:14–17, Revelation 11:1–6, Zechariah 14:16–19

ADAR 2

25th Day of the 12th Month (Adar)
or the 13th Month (Adar 2) in a Leap Year
Usually falling in February/March/April
The Latter Rain
The Call to Repentance

Be glad then, you children of Zion, and rejoice in the LORD your God; for He has given you the former rain faithfully, and He will cause the rain to come down for you – the former rain, and the latter rain in the first month. *Joel 2:23*

To have a harvest you need rain to water the crops and make them grow. Rain in the Bible is a sign of God's blessing. (Psalm 72:5–7) In Israel the summer is totally dry. The first rain comes in the autumn, softening the ground for farmers to plough and sow the grain. These first showers are called the 'former rain', in Hebrew 'yoreh' or 'moreh'. They mark the onset of the rainy season. But sometimes the rain is slow in coming and farmers watch with anxiety as the water levels in reservoirs sink lower and lower. If winter passes and no rain has come to fill the aquifers and reservoirs, people really start praying for the 'latter rain' to come and soak the ground, so that the crops can start growing and produce a harvest.

The 'latter rain' – 'malqosh' – comes at the end of the rainy season, and brings on the crops. It is often torrential, accompanied by thunder storms. (Zechariah 10:1) The Prophet Joel says that it comes in the first month. In the book of Joel the harvest had failed in Zion. (Joel 1:12) The blessings of obedience had not come. Deuteronomy 11:13, 14 says, 'And it shall be that if you earnestly obey My commandments which I command you today, to love the LORD your God and serve Him with all your heart and with all your soul, then I will give you the rain for your land in its season, the early rain and the latter rain, that you may gather in your grain, your new wine, and your oil.' Disobedience meant God could not bless them. But God called the people to repentance, so that He could send the latter rain, in the first month, the month of Passover – symbolising the time of deliverance and forgiveness of sins.

Meditate on God's promise to bring the latter rain when we repent and seek God.

Readings: Joel 1, 2, Jeremiah 3:2–5, Jeremiah 5:24, 25

26th Day of the 12th Month (Adar)
or the 13th Month (Adar 2) in a Leap Year
Usually falling in February/March/April
The Latter Rain
He Will Come

Let us know, Let us pursue the knowledge of the LORD, His going forth is established as the morning; He will come to us like the rain, like the latter and former rain to the earth. *Hosea 6:3*

The coming of the rain is likened to the coming of the Messiah. Just as there are two times when the people of Israel look for and pray for rain – the time of the former rains and the time of the latter rains – so there are two comings of the Messiah. The prophet Joel even hinted at this by saying that the latter rain comes in the first month, (when we have Passover), which speaks of the deliverance of Israel, and of our souls. The harvest of 'grain, new wine and oil', began at Yeshua's first coming. At His second coming, He will come like the torrential latter rain – every eye will see Him and He will reign in power and glory over all the earth. Then He will receive another mighty harvest 'of grain, new wine and oil', of souls saved, holy and redeemed, throughout all the earth. (Joel 2:18, 19, 24)

Zechariah 10:1 exhorts us to ask the Lord for the latter rain. We are to pray for Him to come, in the presence and power of His Holy Spirit among us, even before He returns in glory. His presence among us is like rain, like the favour of the King. (Proverbs 16:15) We are also to pray for His return, saying, 'Your kingdom come, your will be done, on earth as it is in heaven.' (Matthew 6:10) We long for His presence among us even more than the Israelis long for the rains to come and soak the dry land parched by the summer sun. James wrote, 'See how the farmer waits for the precious fruit of the earth, waiting patiently for it until it receives the early and latter rain. You also be patient. Establish your hearts, for the coming of the Lord is at hand.' (James 5:7, 8)

Ask the Lord for the latter rain. (Joel 2:28–32)

Readings: Hosea 6:1–3, Zechariah 10, James 5:7, 8

ADAR 2

27th Day of the 12th Month (Adar)
or the 13th Month (Adar 2) in a Leap Year
Usually falling in February/March/April
The Latter Rain
The Fig Tree and the Vine

The fig tree and the vine yield their strength. *Joel 2:22*

When the former rain and the latter rain come upon the earth, the fig tree and the vine flourish and bring forth a harvest of fruit. The fig tree represents Israel, the vine represents the Church. The 'former rain' of the Holy Spirit, first poured out on the Church in Jerusalem at Shavuot (Joel 2:28, 29), gives strength to Jewish and Gentile believers in Messiah, anointing them, and empowering them to bear fruit, spiritual fruit and a harvest. They are the One New Man of Jews and Gentiles. (Ephesians 2:15) The Bride of Messiah drinks of the Holy Spirit to become strong and fruitful. Showers of refreshing bring new life.

The 'latter rain' of the following verses (Joel 2:30–32), brings forth the end-time harvest, and whoever calls on the name of the Lord, will be saved. 'For in Mount Zion and in Jerusalem there shall be deliverance, as the Lord has said, among the remnant whom the Lord calls.' (Joel 2:32) All the destruction and devastation that the locusts (Israel's enemies) will have brought to the Land will be restored. It will once again be fertile with grass growing for the beasts of the field. (Joel 2:25, 22) The Land will recover and so will the people. They will rejoice, because God will cause their vats of grain, wine, and new oil to be full again, and they will no longer be a reproach among the nations. (Joel 2:18, 19, 24)

The fig tree and vine will 'yield their strength'. The word 'strength' is the word 'valiant' used to describe Ruth and Boaz, and the Proverbs 31 woman. (Ruth 2:1, 3:11, Proverbs 31:10) Israel and the Church will be restored to God as a valiant and virtuous company, who will have stood strong against the forces of darkness, resisted, and overcome.

Pray for God to refresh, strengthen and encourage all believers who are suffering.

Readings: Joel 1:7, 10–12, Joel 2:14–32, Joel 3, Hebrews 13:3

28th Day of the 12th Month (Adar)
or the 13th Month (Adar 2) in a Leap Year
Usually falling in February/March/April
The Lion of God
The Lion of the Tribe of Judah

But one of the elders said to me, "Do not weep. Behold, the Lion of the tribe of Judah, the Root of David, has prevailed to open the scroll and to loose its seven seals." *Revelation 5:5*

The Apostle John saw into Heaven, and He saw Yeshua revealed in His glory. He saw the throne of God in Heaven, and the Father sitting on the throne, and in His hand He held a scroll. The scroll had writing on both sides of it, and it was sealed with seven seals. Then John saw a strong angel proclaiming with a loud voice, "'Who is worthy to open the scroll and to loose its seals?" And no one in heaven or on the earth or under the earth was able to open the scroll, or to look at it.' John wept much, because no one was found worthy to open and read the scroll, or to look at it. (Revelation 5:1–3)

One of the elders said to him, "Do not weep, Behold, the Lion of the tribe of Judah, the Root of David, has prevailed to open the scroll and to loose its seven seals." (Revelation 5:5) The word 'prevailed' is the Greek word 'nikao' which means 'to subdue, conquer, overcome, prevail and get the victory.' Yeshua, the Son of God is the only one who is worthy to be the King of all the earth. He is the 'Lion of the tribe of Judah'. Lions live in prides which remind us of tribes. Prides of lions, like tribes, are attached to territories, and each pride has a dominant male. Yeshua is the mighty leader, the Messiah who was prophesied to come forth from the tribe of Judah. Only He was able to overcome sin and conquer death for the human race. He alone was sinless. He alone was the perfect sacrifice to redeem and 'purchase back' the earth for His possession. Jacob had prophesied over Judah the coming of 'Shiloh' – the Messiah – saying, 'to Him shall be the obedience of the people.' (Genesis 49:10) The 'Lion of the tribe of Judah' has prevailed to reclaim the earth.

Worship the Lord with thanksgiving that He is worthy to rule and reign over all the earth.

Readings: Revelation 5, Genesis 49:9–12, Micah 5:2–5a

29th Day of the 12th Month (Adar),
or the 13th Month (Adar 2) in a Leap Year
Usually falling in February/March/April
The Lion of God
The Lion Roars

"The LORD roars from Zion, and utters His voice from Jerusalem; the pastures of the shepherds mourn, and the top of Carmel withers."

Amos 1:2

The prophet Amos spoke these words concerning God's judgements, which were pronounced on the ancient strongholds of the Middle East. In the end-times the same roar is going out from the 'Lion of the tribe of Judah'. His voice goes out from Jerusalem and 'the top of Carmel withers'. That is a powerful roar! Apparently sometimes the roar of a lion can be heard up to five miles away. In this prophecy the LORD roars from Jerusalem and His words of judgement will reverberate out to the surrounding peoples and nations, for their sins against God. Just the sound of His voice has this effect. His Word is powerful.

God's roar is going out across the nations. Amos 3:8 says, 'A lion has roared! Who will not fear? The Lord GOD has spoken! Who can but prophesy?' God's Word goes out and will go out in the end-times. His Words will be spoken out through His servants the prophets, to whom the Lord reveals His secret. (Amos 3:7) When the Lord has His controversy with the nations (Jeremiah 25:31), "The LORD will roar from on high, and utter His voice from His holy habitation; He will roar mightily against His fold. He will give a shout, as those who tread the grapes, against all the inhabitants of the earth." (Jeremiah 25:30) But His roar will cause Ephraim (Israel) to return to the Land. 'He will roar like a lion. When He roars, then His sons shall come trembling from the west...' (Hosea 11:10) And when God is judging the nations 'The LORD also will roar from Zion, and utter His voice from Jerusalem; the heavens and earth will shake; But the LORD will be a shelter for His people, and the strength of the children of Israel.' (Joel 3:16)

How is the roar of the 'Lion of the tribe of Judah' being heard in these days?

Readings: Hosea 11, Joel 3:12–21, Amos 3:1–8

30th Day of the 12th Month (Adar)
or the 13th Month (Adar 2) in a Leap Year
Usually falling in February/March/April
The Lion of God
The Lion is the Lamb

And I looked, and behold, in the midst of the throne and of the four living creatures, and in the midst of the elders, stood a Lamb as though it had been slain, having seven horns and seven eyes, which are the seven Spirits of God sent out into all the earth. Then He came and took the scroll out of the right hand of Him who sat on the throne.

Revelation 5:6

When the Apostle John saw into heaven, he learned that the 'Lion of the tribe of Judah' was the only one able to open the scroll and loose its seals. But when he looked he didn't see a lion, but a Lamb in the midst of the throne. The Lion was the Lamb, the Lamb of God who had been slain. Yeshua, glorified in heaven, still bears the wounds from the cross and the lashings of the whip. Those wounds remain for eternity, the source of His 'prevailing', His victory. He is the Lamb who was slain, the perfect sacrifice.

In John's vision, the Lamb took the scroll out of the right hand of Him who sat on the throne. '...The four living creatures and the twenty-four elders fell down before the Lamb, each having a harp, and golden bowls full of incense, which are the prayers of the saints. And they sang a new song, saying, "You are worthy to take the scroll, and to open its seals; For You were slain, and have redeemed us to God by Your blood out of every tribe and tongue and people and nation, and have made us kings and priests to our God; and we shall reign on the earth."' (Revelation 5:8–10)

The Biblical Year begins and ends with the Lamb of God. He is the Alpha and the Omega. In eternity, there will be no sun. The Lamb is the light. (Revelation 21:23) There will be no temple. The Lamb is its temple. (Revelation 21:22) He is coming quickly!

Worship the Lamb with the words of the songs in Revelation 5:12, 13

Readings: John 1:1–29, Revelation 21, 22